Essays in Economics:
Consumption and Econometrics

Essays in Economics

Volume 2: Consumption and Econometrics

James Tobin

Yale University

1975

North-Holland Publishing Company – Amsterdam · Oxford
American Elsevier Publishing Company, Inc. – New York

Library of Congress Catalog Card Number 70-183276
ISBN North-Holland 0 7204 3088 7
ISBN American Elsevier 0 444 10684 7

Publishers:
NORTH-HOLLAND PUBLISHING COMPANY – AMSTERDAM
NORTH-HOLLAND PUBLISHING COMPANY, LTD. – OXFORD

Sole distributors for the U.S.A. and Canada:
AMERICAN ELSEVIER PUBLISHING COMPANY, INC.
52 VANDERBILT AVENUE, NEW YORK, N.Y. 10017

PRINTED IN THE NETHERLANDS

PREFACE

This is the second of two volumes of essays in economic science published from 1940 to 1972. The first volume, published in 1972, contained twenty-four papers on macroeconomics. The first four chapters of this volume continue the macroeconomic theme; they concern the theory of the relationship between unemployment and inflation and the unpleasant dilemma their connection poses for policy. Part V, ten papers on the consumption function, is also related to macroeconomic theory. But these papers also relate to the theory of individual behavior, and a number of them report the results of empirical econometric research. These two interests carry over to Parts VI and VII. In Part VI consumer theory and statistical method are applied to the problem of rationing. The three papers of Part VII are attempts to develop and to apply econometric methods suitable for the empirical analysis of consumer behavior.

With minor exceptions, mostly editorial in nature, the papers in this volume are reprinted as they were originally published. Chapter 26, however, is a rewritten amalgam of material published originally in two separate comments on papers presented at conferences. Those comments would not be meaningful here, but the substance of the model I presented is quite relevant.

I am grateful to Walter Dolde, F. Trenery Dolbear, Jr., Harold Watts, and H.S. Houthakker for allowing me to include here papers I wrote in collaboration with them, and I am even more grateful for those collaborations. I also acknowledge with gratitude the permissions of the original publishers of these papers, listed elsewhere, to reprint them here. I also express my deep appreciation to Mrs. Laura Harrison, Koen Suryatmodjo, and Stephen Webb, who helped prepare these volumes for publication.

CONTENTS

PART IV

INFLATION AND UNEMPLOYMENT

CHAPTER 25

THE CRUEL DILEMMA

This year we in the U.S.A. are rediscovering that the terms of trade our economy offers us between inflation and unemployment are not to our liking. If we have as little as we would like of one, we have more than we want of the other. This is an unpleasant fact of life, not only here but in all non-communist industrial economies. It does no good to ignore it. Critics of federal economic policy want the government to check inflation by curtailing aggregate demand. They may be right. But many of them do not see, or do not say, that cutting demand will lower employment and production at the same time it slows the rise in prices. Other critics find the present rate of unemployment too high; they would expand demand in order to reduce it further. Many do not see, or do not say, that the same expansion of demand would raise both prices and the rate of increase of prices. Both 4 per cent per year inflation and 4 per cent unemployment are too high. But the fact is that the government commands no simple way to reduce one figure without raising the other.

Much discussion of current policy is based on an over-simple model which my generation of economists learned and taught – both perhaps too well – thirty and twenty years ago. The model did double duty, applying both to full-scale war mobilization and to large-scale unemployment. In this model, full employment and the productive capacity of the economy are well defined. If aggregate demand, in real terms, exceeds this capacity, there is "excess demand", or an "inflationary gap". Prices, if uncontrolled, will rise continuously – without inducing any gains in output – until events or policies lop off the excess demand.

Presented October 14, 1966 at the Conference on Pricing Theories, Practices and Policies, Wharton School, University of Pennsylvania and published in *Price Issues in Theory, Practice, and Policy*, Almarin Phillips (Ed.) (University of Pennsylvania Press, 1967).

Eliminating excess demand is economically painless, though it may be politically painful; it stops inflation without touching employment or output. On the other hand, if aggregate real demand is less than the economy's full employment capacity, there is insufficient demand, a "deflationary gap". However large or small the departure from full employment, so long as it stays the same, prices are stable. An increase in demand, moving the economy toward full employment, may mean a one-shot increase in the price level, necessary to induce employers to expand output and employment. But it does not set off a *continuing* inflation. We hear the echoes of this doctrine in diagnoses of the current situation as one of clearly excess demand.

The mid-fifties did not fall easily into either of these patterns. Prices rose rapidly in 1955–58 while unemployment was constant or rising. Yet it was hard to attribute the inflation to generalized excess demand, since unemployment hovered at 4 per cent plus, whereas it had been as low as 2.9 per cent in 1953. This popularized the concept of cost inflation, and the dichotomy of cost-push and demand-pull became commonplace. The "new inflation", as it was called, supposedly originated in the setting of higher wages by unions or higher mark-ups by managements.

Subsequent discussion has pretty much obliterated the notion of a simple well-defined full employment capacity, and therefore at the same time fuzzed up the distinction between the two kinds of inflation. We now think of a zone of unemployment rates, each one associated with a certain rate of continuing inflation – the less the unemployment the higher the rate of inflation. There is presumably some rate of unemployment at which prices would be stable. But higher demand can obtain more employment and output as well as inflation. Such inflation is neither demand-pull nor cost-push – or rather it is both. It could not happen without the pressure of higher demand, which gives individuals and groups more power to obtain increments in their rates of money income. Their use of this power may be called "cost-push", but its strength is not independent of the state of demand.

This approach, of course, is summarized in the Phillips curve, which relates the rate of increase of money wages – and thus indirectly the rate of increase of prices – inversely to the unemployment rate. We could redefine "demand-pull" to mean increases in the speed of inflation associated with demand-induced reductions in the rate of unemployment, and redefine "cost-push" to mean unfavorable upward shifts in the Phillips curve, so that we get faster inflation at any given rate of unemployment. But this greatly alters the significance of the terms and of the dichotomy between them. Better to abandon them.

The Phillips curve approach forces us to confront squarely the fact that our goals for prices and employment are not wholly reconcilable. That is, they are not wholly reconcilable by government management of aggregate demand through fiscal and monetary policies. The first question that arises, therefore, is how bad the situation is. What are the terms of trade in our economy between inflation and unemployment? I have no quantitative estimates and must confine myself to some general comments.

It is hard to answer this question by inferences from the data. We have not many relevant observations, and we know that observed movements of price level are influenced by lots of things besides the contemporaneous level of unemployment. A fundamental problem is that the economy has not settled down long enough at a steady unemployment rate to permit us to observe the corresponding permanent rate of inflation, if there is one. We should not forget one lesson of the first and simpler model – namely that movement toward fuller employment is likely to cause a once-for-all rise in the price level. To some unknown extent recent rises in prices are from this source – in the early sixties the price level was not high enough to induce full employment output even with stable labor costs. Bowen and Berry (*Review of Economics and Statistics*, May 1963) estimate that a one percentage point per year decrease in unemployment causes an increase of 0.81 in the percentage annual rate of wage inflation.

Moreover, it is plausible that larger increases, both in money wages and in mark-ups, are required to effect a given increase in the rate of utilization of the economy's capital and labor resources when the shift occurs quickly than when it occurs slowly. If so, some of the recent and current speed of inflation is attributable to the surge of the economy last winter. But we do not know how much of the current rate of inflation to attribute to these sources and how much to regard as a permanent by-product of 4 per cent unemployment.

Nor do we know the answer to the even more basic question whether continuation of 4 per cent unemployment would, so long as it generates any inflation, generate an accelerating inflation. This would be the orthodox prediction: Wages and other incomes rise because people want real gains, and the bargaining power of individuals and groups depends on the real situation. If they find that they are cheated by price increases they will simply escalate their money claims accordingly. On this view the Phillips curve would blow up if growth at a steady utilization rate were maintained. Only cyclical interruptions in the learning process have saved us from accelerating inflation. On this interpretation, the only true equilibrium full employment is the degree of unemployment that corresponds to zero inflation – any higher rate of utilization can be called excess demand. This is a dismal conclusion if true, because it appears to take a socially explosive rate of unemployment – more than 6 per cent in the U.S.A. – to keep the price level stable.

The Phillips curve idea is in a sense a reincarnation in dynamic guise of the original Keynesian idea of irrational "money illusion" in the supply of labor. The Phillips curve says that increases in money wages – and more generally, other money incomes – are in some significant degree prized for themselves, even if they do not result in equivalent gains in real incomes. Empirical support for this view is found in statistical variants of the Phillips curve where the elasticity of money wage increase with respect to price increases is generally found to be smaller than one. A number of institutional reasons can be advanced to explain this phenomenon. (1) Annual money income gains are a symbol of continuing success and status for unions, individuals, managements. (2) Even in relatively weak sectors, reductions in money wages and prices are opposed by a host of psychological, legal, and institutional barriers. Minimum wage laws provide one floor. But even when they are inoperative, money wage rates and salaries are seldom reduced; such drastic action would be a real judgment of failure on the employee or the employer, or both. The same barriers do not apply to reductions in relative *real* wages and prices so long as they are accomplished by wage and price increases elsewhere. This means that the changes in wage and price structure needed to induce resource shifts impart an upward bias to the overall price level.

If we do not like the terms of trade our economy now offers us between inflation and unemployment, what can we do about it? There are two general strategies. One is to try to make the terms less severe. The other is to make them easier to live with, by reducing the social costs of inflation or unemployment or both. I will speak of these two strategies in turn.

The first is to try to shift the Phillips curve down – so that less inflation is associated with low unemployment. This strategy has both long-run and short-run aspects.

One fairly uncontroversial set of long-run measures concerns the improvement of the labor market and of labor mobility. The better the labor force is adapted in advance to geographical and industrial shifts in the composition of demand, the smaller the wage and price increases needed to accomplish such adaptations. In general, expansion of demand both reduces unemployment and increases unfilled vacancies. By manpower and labor market policies we need to reduce the number of unfilled vacancies associated with any given rate of unemployment.

A second and more controversial class of long-run measures are those directed to making labor and product markets more competitive. According to the orthodox diagnosis of the problem, this is the only fundamental solution. On that diagnosis, the problem is that high levels of demand enable the various groups in the economy to claim in total more output than is being produced. For example, strategically placed unions and industries become able, when demand is high, to improve their terms of trade against the rest of the economy. Other groups must either accept lower real incomes or unemployment or fight back in kind. If they will not accept lower real incomes, they give the inflationary spiral another twist. To the extent that this is a correct diagnosis of the problem, the only eventual solution is to eliminate these mutually inconsistent concentrations of power. We should not let a general tightening of markets to unemployment rates of 4 per cent or less provide any groups with the power to levy extortionate claims.

Of course it is easier to make this diagnosis than to prescribe a realistic remedy – realistic either economically or politically. I will not be foolhardy enough to invade the provinces of my colleagues who are expert on anti-trust and on labor legislation. I do observe that the bargaining powers of unions are in considerable degree granted to them by federal legislation. In return for these privileges, it seems to me, the public could require unions to be effectively open to new members and apprentices. It is especially important to eliminate racially discriminatory barriers to entry.

A third fundamental remedy is an increase in the capital–labor ratio. Observe that at present preferred industrial operating rates, around 92 per cent of capacity, are reached concurrently with 4 per cent unemployment. We would have more discipline of price increases if there were more excess capacity. Over the long run we could induce this result by mixtures of monetary and fiscal policy favorable to investment. Another way of making the same point is the following: The faster the growth of productivity, the less inflationary the course of prices. This often asserted proposition makes sense if the Phillips curve makes sense, but not necessarily otherwise. If money wages have a trend of their own, they will not automatically rise faster when the growth of productivity speeds up. We know, of course, that in the really long run we cannot make productivity grow faster than the natural rate of improvement of technology. But we can buy time in the intermediate long run by deepening and modernizing capital. More orthodox analysis would be that increases in (marginal) productivity mean equivalent increases in labor's bargaining power. They do nothing to resolve the fundamental excess of claims over resources.

These are long-run measures. In the short run we cannot improve the labor market, break up concentrations of economic power, or increase the ratio of capacity to labor force. That leaves us with incomes policy or guideposts, what Paul Samuelson described as "talking the Phillips curve down". In spite of my complicity in the origins of the guideposts, I did not intend to discuss or defend them here (unless a canvass of the obstacles to other approaches is a defense). But I will make the following point, because it is too little appreciated:

One principal purpose of guideposts is to guide the government. For a variety of reasons unconnected with macroeconomic policy the government is involved in the setting of certain prices and wages. In national emergency labor disputes, the government will not tolerate a stoppage and substitutes some other mechanism of settlement for industrial warfare to the bitter end. The guideposts set standards of public interest in the terms of the settlement. Too often previously the government – aided and abetted by the industrial relations fraternity and their mystique that the results of collective bargaining are always good because the process is good – was interested solely in the fact of a settlement, not in the content. Under the guideposts, the government seeks peace but not peace at any price level. Other ways in which the government is involved in wage and price decisions are: minimum wage legislation, management of stockpiles, pay scales of government employees, agricultural price supports, utility regulation, regulations regarding wages and prices in government contract work. Not all these policies follow the guideposts, but they should.

I have sketched various approaches to improving the trade-off of inflation for unemployment. The second strategy is to mitigate the social costs of falling short of one or both goals. On the side of unemployment, one obvious step is to extend the coverage of unemployment compensation and improve the size and duration of its benefits. Likewise, the costs of unemployment would be smaller if it were more evenly distributed and if long-term unemployment were diminished. We certainly need improvements in the employment service, the better to match the beneficiaries of unemployment insurance with available vacancies. But, many of the unemployed do not have previous work experience, and for many young people the important thing, individually and socially, is the work experience rather than the money. Moreover, there is no national recompense for the loss of output due to operating the economy at higher rather than lower rates of unemployment.

The ill effects of inflation could be mitigated in a number of ways: balance of payments troubles by flexibility of the exchange rate, internal inequities by making available purchasing-power bonds, variable annuities, and other enrichments of the menu of financial assets. Those who regard every inflation as symptomatic of a basic real disequilibrium, who therefore disbelieve in the Phillips curve except as a descriptive device of solely transient stability, will regard such measures as futile and perhaps dangerous. They do nothing to remove the real causes; they only accelerate the inevitable explosion. Those who believe in the Phillips curve world will acknowledge that measures to protect potential victims of inflation will sometimes lead to more inflation. But the process is not explosive, and once the sting is removed from inflation, there is nothing wrong with having more of it.

My only conclusion can be that we must take all three approaches at once. In the short run, the guideposts, battered as they are, are the only tool we have. I very much agree with Myron Joseph's suggestion that the wage–price canons for the year be divorced from the permanent and eternal guideposts, and also with his plea that labor and management representatives must participate in the formulation of the canons. The political and ideological climate may be more favorable for such cooperation now than it was in 1961–62. Certainly the Council of Economic Advisers cannot be in the business of judging every wage contract and price change, not to mention the surveillance of the invisible sins of omitted price cuts which are as damaging as visible price increases.

A series of short runs becomes a long run, and some day we have to start on the difficult structural reforms needed to dissolve the cruel unemployment–inflation dilemma or to make it less painful. Otherwise our position will always be as uncomfortable as in 1956 and again in 1966.

CHAPTER 26

PHILLIPS CURVE ALGEBRA

I have found a simple algebraic model a convenient framework of discussion of the issues raised by the Phillips curve. The model does not resolve any of the controversial questions of theory, econometrics, and policy. But it does illuminate the differences of assumption and empirical estimate on which the controversies turn.

Let $g_x(t)$ be the instantaneous proportionate rate of growth of any variable x at time t: $g_x(t) = [\dot{x}(t)]/[x(t)]$. Let $g_x^e(t)$ be the expected rate of change of x. Where it is clear that the variables are functions of time, the notation (t) will be dropped for simplicity. Let p be the price level, w the money wage rate, m the marginal productivity of labor, and u the unemployment rate. Then

$$g_w - g_p = g_m. \tag{1}$$

Rate of change of real wages equals rate of change of marginal productivity of labor.

$$g_w = \alpha g_p^e + \beta g_m + h(u), \tag{2}$$

where $0 \leq \alpha \leq 1$ and $h'(u) < 0$.

Rate of change of the money wage depends directly on expected rate of change of prices, directly on the rate of growth of labor's marginal productivity, inversely and non-linearly on unemployment. The function h is the short-run wage Phillips curve; it might include other aspects of the time series of u in addition to its contemporaneous value. The reason

Adapted from my Discussion of papers at a *Symposium on Inflation: Its Causes, Consequences and Control, January 31, 1968,* Stephen W. Rousseas (Ed.) (Kazanjian Foundation, 1968), pp. 48–54, and from my Comment, *Brookings Papers on Economic Activity* (1971 : 2), pp. 512–14.

for calling it the *short-run* Phillips curve is that the inflation expectation g_p^e is taken as constant. No feedback from current wages and prices on to such expectations is taken into account in $h(u)$.

There is also a short-run price Phillips curve, easily obtained from (2) by using (1):

$$g_p = \alpha g_p^e + (\beta - 1)g_m + h(u). \tag{3}$$

To obtain long-run Phillips curves it is necessary to specify the generation of expectations:

$$g_p^e = \int_{-\infty}^{t} \mu\, e^{-\mu(t-\tau)} g_p(\tau)\, d\tau. \tag{4}$$

Expected price change is a weighted average, with exponentially receding weights, of actual price changes current and past. From (4) can be derived an expression for the time derivative of g_p^e, the expected rate of inflation.

$$\dot{g}_p^e = \mu(g_p - g_p^e). \tag{5}$$

Expectations are adapted to actual experience at a speed of μ.

Combining (5) with (3) gives

$$\frac{1}{\mu}\dot{g}_p^e = h(u) - (1 - \beta)g_m - (1 - \alpha)g_p^e. \tag{6}$$

In equilibrium, with $\alpha < 1$, expected and actual price changes are constant and equal, and depend inversely on the unemployment rate.

$$g_p^* = g_p^{e*} = \frac{h(u) - g_m(1 - \beta)}{1 - \alpha}. \tag{7}$$

This is the long-run price Phillips curve, taking account of feedback; the relation of inflation to unemployment is $[h(u)]/(1 - \alpha)$ instead of $h(u)$. There is also a long-run wage Phillips curve:

$$g_w^* = \frac{h(u) + g_m(\beta - \alpha)}{1 - \alpha}. \tag{8}$$

Note that an increase in α will raise the long-run equilibrium rate of inflation. An improvement in the productivity trend g_m, often prescribed as a partial remedy for inflation, diminishes the equilibrium rate of inflation only if β is smaller than α. The parameter β measures the fraction of productivity improvements that are translated into *money* wage increases.

The dynamics expressed in (6) is that expected inflation will accelerate (decelerate) so long as it is below (above) its equilibrium value for the prevailing rate of unemployment:

$$\frac{1}{\mu}\dot{g}_p^e = (1 - \alpha)(g_p^* - g_p^e). \tag{9}$$

By using (5), the dynamics can be expressed in terms of the actual rate of inflation rather than the expected rate.

$$g_p = g_p^e + \frac{\dot{g}_p^e}{\mu} = g_p^* + \alpha(g_p^e - g_p^*). \tag{10}$$

Differentiating (10) with respect to time gives:

$$\frac{\dot{g}_p}{\mu} = \frac{(1 - \alpha)}{\mu}\dot{g}_p^* + \alpha\frac{\dot{g}_p^e}{\mu} = \frac{(1 - \alpha)}{\mu}\dot{g}_p^* + (1 - \alpha)(g_p^* - g_p). \tag{11}$$

When the determinants of equilibrium inflation, u and g_m, are stable, the speed at which actual inflation approaches equilibrium is the same as that at which expected inflation approaches equilibrium.

All these results apply for $\alpha < 1$. The situation is quite different if $\alpha = 1$. Equation (6) becomes:

$$\frac{1}{\mu}\dot{g}_p^e = h(u) - (1 - \beta)g_m. \tag{12}$$

Likewise, using (5) once again, we have:

$$\frac{1}{\mu}\dot{g}_p = h(u) - (1 - \beta)g_m + h'(u)\dot{u} - (1 - \beta)\dot{g}_m. \tag{13}$$

As before, the acceleration of actual inflation is the same as that of expected inflation, provided the underlying determinants, unemployment and productivity trend, are constant.

According to (12) and (13) there is a unique equilibrium rate of unemployment u^*, such that $h(u^*) = (1 - \beta)g_m$. This has come to be known as the natural rate. When u is equal to u^*, inflation will be neither accelerating or decelerating. It will be occurring at some constant rate.

That rate is indeterminate in this model. It is determined wholly outside the labor market. According to monetarists the decisive factor is the rate of growth of the quantity of money; more eclectic macroeconomists would list other influences on the rates of expansion of aggregate demand and supply. Believers in the natural rate theory are not logically compelled to be monetarists, nor do monetarists necessarily have to regard α as surely equal to 1.

Some of the structural remedies for the Phillips trade-off in case $\alpha < 1$ would also lower the natural rate of unemployment in case $\alpha = 1$. These include labor market reforms which would improve the short-run Phillips curve $h(u)$, increases in g_m provided $\beta < \alpha$, and reductions of β. The efficacy of these remedies does not depend on whether there is incomplete or complete feedback of experience into expectation in the long run.

Deviation of u to the low side of u^* will mean ever-accelerating inflation; to the high side, ever-accelerating deflation. If $\alpha = 1$ we cannot buy lower unemployment with creeping inflation. The creep will become a gallop. Only the unemployment rate u^* is consistent with steady inflation, and it is impartially consistent with steady inflation at any rate, including zero and below.

The usual test of the natural rate hypothesis is to estimate α directly in (2) and (3). Empirical estimates of α are significantly less than one in the overwhelming majority of cases. But in these regressions the variable g_p^e is not actually observed. Economists and econometricians have largely ignored such direct observations of price expectations as exist in favor of *a priori* assumption of an adaptive mechanism like (4) and (5). So some average of actual price changes, contemporary and past, is used as a proxy for g_p^e. The coefficient of the proxy is not a pure estimate of α, but an estimate of α compounded with the dependence of current expectation on the proxy. Failure of the coefficient to equal one does not prove that α is not equal to one. Maybe the expectations mechanism has been inadequately modeled, so that there is not in the sample time series a one-to-one feedback of experience into expectation, even though there could in reality be such a feedback if by macroeconomic policy u were held constant.

Another possible test arises from comparison of (11) and (13), or of their counterparts for $\dot{g}_w$. This test confronts directly the accelerationist hypothesis and depends on the measurement of the changes in rates of change. According to (11) $\dot{g}_p$ depends (i) on the determinants of g_p^*, namely u and g_m, (ii) on the changes in these determinants, $\dot{u}$ and $\dot{g}_m$, and (iii) and g_p itself, negatively. According to (13), $\dot{g}_p$ depends on the same variables listed in (i) and (ii), u and g_m and their time derivatives, but *not* on (iii) g_p itself. The natural rate hypothesis says that *ceteris paribus* the rate at which inflation is accelerating does not depend on the speed of inflation itself.

CHAPTER 27

THE WAGE–PRICE MECHANISM

In this summary paper, I shall try to view the Econometrics of Price Determination Conference – with particular reference to the problems of unemployment and inflation currently afflicting the U.S.A. and other industrial countries – from the perspective of a general economist interested in macroeconomics and in stabilization policy. Suppose that such an economist attended the Conference hoping to distill from the papers presented a simple working model of wage and price determination that summarized the conventional wisdom of the assembled experts. Recognizing that much of what he would hear and read would be empirical econometric results, the economist would want to observe both the theoretical models used by the investigators and the numerical results of their analyses. What would he write down, or tell his students, or report to his policy-making superiors on his return?

I think he would be able to place his findings in the framework developed from the following four equations:

Price Adjustment Equation

$$g_p - a_{12}g_u = -a_{13}\gamma + a_{14}g_p + f(u - u^e). \qquad (1)$$

Here p is the price level; w is the money wage rate; p is the rental cost of capital services; g_x denotes the geometric rate of growth of any variable x, $\Delta x/x$; γ is the trend rate of growth of productivity; u is the actual unemployment rate, and u^e its expected normal or average value; the α's are

Originally presented October 1970 as an Overview of the Federal Reserve/Social Science Research Council Conference on the Econometrics of Price Determination, and published in *The Econometrics of Price Determination Conference*, S. Weiner (Ed.) (Board of Governors, Federal Reserve System, 1973).

References in the text are to other papers of the Conference, published in the proceedings.

non-negative constants, and f is a function with $f(0) = 0$ and the sign of the derivative f' to be determined. The aggregate unemployment rate enters the relationship as a surrogate for the general pressure of demand on available resources. The equation applies to a self-contained closed economy, ignoring for simplicity and brevity the costs of materials imported from abroad or from other sectors – costs that naturally figure in the equations for industries and for open economies reported at the Conference. In this summary I shall also ignore short lags in the adjustment of prices to their determinants.

Wage Adjustment Equation

$$-a_{21}g_p^e + g_w = a_{23}\gamma + h(u, \dot{u}). \qquad (2)$$

Here g_p^e represents "expected" price inflation, and h is a function of both the unemployment rate and its rate of change with both partial derivatives negative.

Price Expectation Adjustment

$$g_p^e(t) = \sum_{i=1}^{\infty} \alpha_{3i}g_p(t - i), \qquad (3)$$

where $\sum_i \alpha_{3i} = 1$, $\alpha_{3i} \geqq 0$ all i.

Normal Utilization Adjustment

$$u^e(t) = \sum_{i=1}^{\infty} \alpha_{4i}u(t - i), \qquad (4)$$

where $\Sigma \alpha_{4i} = 1$, $\alpha_{4i} \geqq 0$ all i.

These four equations form a subsystem of a complete model. Given an initial price history, the subsystem is capable of determining prices, price expectations, and wages. Unemployment, past and present, and rental cost of capital can be taken as exogenous to the subsystem. In a complete system, of course, unemployment and the costs of capital are endogenous and are indeed structurally related to prices and price expectations through relationships other than those of the subsystem. But it is at least conceivable that these feedbacks are canceled by policy-makers with the wisdom and determination to achieve an unemployment series of their own choosing. Even if this were not so, the subsystem would be worth exploring for its own sake. That was the purpose of the Conference.

Combining Equations (1) and (2) gives the short-run Phillips curve for price inflation:

Short-run Phillips Curve for Price Inflation

$$g_p = \alpha_{12}\alpha_{21}g_p^e + (\alpha_{12}\alpha_{23} - \alpha_{13})\gamma \\ + \alpha_{14}g_p + f(u - u^e) + \alpha_{12}h(u, \dot{u}), \tag{5}$$

or

$$g_p - g_p^e = (\alpha_{12}\alpha_{21} - 1)g_p^e + (\alpha_{12}\alpha_{22} - \alpha_{13})\gamma \\ + \alpha_{14}g_p + f(u - u^e) + \alpha_{12}h(u, \dot{u}). \tag{6}$$

A long-run equilibrium solution of the subsystem, if one exists, would consist of those stationary values g_p^*, g_w^*, and g_p^{e*} corresponding to a stationary unemployment series u^* with capital cost constant ($g_p = 0$) or otherwise specified. We can then ask the "comparative statics" question how the equilibrium rates of price and wage change depend on the value of u^*. In such an equilibrium, $u^e = u^*, \dot{u} = 0$. Also, expected and actual inflation are the same, and their common value is:

Long-run Phillips Curve for Price Inflation

$$g_p^* = g_p^{e*} = \frac{(\alpha_{12}\alpha_{22} - \alpha_{13})\gamma + \alpha_{14}g_p + \alpha_{12}h(u, 0)}{1 - \alpha_{12}\alpha_{21}}. \tag{7}$$

From Equation (6) it is clear that such an equilibrium exists and is stable only if $\alpha_{12}\alpha_{21} < 1$. If $\alpha_{12}\alpha_{21} > 1$, any gap between actual and expected inflation, for constant u, will become larger rather than smaller. For example, a positive gap between actual and expected inflation will pull up the rate of expected inflation but will accelerate actual wage and price inflation even more.

If $\alpha_{12}\alpha_{21} = 1$, there is no equilibrium. The long-run Phillips curve is vertical. The value of u, call it u_n, that satisfies

$$(\alpha_{12}\alpha_{22} - \alpha_{13})\gamma + \alpha_{14}g_p + \alpha_{12}h(u_n, 0) = 0 \tag{8}$$

is the natural rate of unemployment. According to Equation (6), at u_n, $g_p = g_p^e$ and therefore g_p and g_p^e can be constant. However, this can be true at any rate of inflation or deflation. If u is steadily smaller than u_n, Equation (6) states that actual inflation, g_p, is always greater than expected inflation, g_p^e. The gap never diminishes; the speed of inflation is always increasing. Similarly, a steady rate of unemployment above the natural rate means ever-accelerating deflation.

One natural specification is that:

(a) $\alpha_{12} = \alpha_{13}$: Changes in money wages and in labor productivity have the same effect on prices; namely, the elasticity of output with respect to labor input.

(b) $\alpha_{14} = 1 - \alpha_{12}$: Changes in rental costs of capital services affect prices by the elasticity of output with respect to capital that under constant returns to scale is the complement of the labor elasticity, α_{12}.

(c) $g_p = g_p^*$: At given rates of interest and depreciation, rental costs move with capital goods prices and therefore with general prices in a one-sector model.

With these assumptions, Equation (7) simplifies to:

$$g_p^* = g_p^{e*} = \frac{(\alpha_{22} - 1)\gamma + h(u, 0)}{1 - \alpha_{21}}. \tag{9}$$

The crucial parameter, on which the existence of a long-run trade-off depends, is simply α_{21}. If $\alpha_{21} = 1$, the natural rate of unemployment is given by:

$$(\alpha_{22} - 1)\gamma + h(u_n, 0) = 0. \tag{10}$$

I turn now to what the Conference had to say about wage–price equations and their parameters.

1. Price Adjustment Equation

In a sense, structural Equation (1) was the major business of the Conference. Four papers (those by Hymans, Klein, de Menil and Enzler and Hirsch) describe the aggregate price equations of various econometric models of the U.S. economy; one paper (that by Bodkin) covers models of the Canadian economy; and one (by Ball and Duffy) tries a uniform price equation on 12 countries. In addition, two papers (those of Eckstein and Wyss, and Heien and Popkin) present disaggregated sectoral price equations. With the help of Professor Nordhaus' lucid and comprehensive introductory paper, the reader can place these contributions in the perspective of previous theoretical and empirical results. I cannot hope to do justice to this wealth of material. However, I will mention major items of consensus and controversy and then point out some implications for policy.

(1) The Conference papers give no reason to doubt that changes in input prices and productivity have a symmetrical effect on output prices. In terms of Equation (1), α_{12} and α_{13} are equal. This is taken for granted in a number of specifications where wage rates and productivity are combined into unit labor cost. (See the studies by Klein, Hirsch, and Hymans.) Ball and Duffy test the hypothesis and find no reason to reject it, especially when they distinguish permanent and transitory productivity movements.

(2) The evidence is that prices move with unit labor costs at standard rates of output and capacity utilization; that is, for $u = u^e$ in Equation (1). The parameter γ in Equation (1) represents the normal productivity trend rather than actual period-to-period productivity movement, which also reflects changes in employment and output during cyclical swings in demand and utilization. These cyclical cost movements are among the possible determinants of price summarized in the term $f(u - u^e)$, but these movements are not easy to disentangle from other cyclical influences.

In some econometric equations (in papers by de Menil and Enzler, Eckstein and Wyss, and Heien and Popkin), productivity change is simply represented by a trend and actual productivity is never explicitly introduced. In other equations (see Hymans, and Hirsch), the standard productivity trend is calculated from a weighted average of past productivity. Hirsch uses both actual and trend productivity and is led to assign major weight to the latter. Ball and Duffy rely on actual labor cost in the first instance and then find their Z variable, which allows for deviations of productivity from trend, to be a highly significant correction. Klein's Wharton Model now uses actual labor costs but is shifting to normal costs.

One asymmetry in the calculation of normal costs should be noted. In the calculation of the costs that move prices, the consensus is to smooth productivity changes but not to smooth wage rates. Current wage rates are taken as permanent and combined with trend productivity.

(3) The central estimate of α_{12} and α_{13} is one. That is, prices move in proportion to standard unit labor costs, whose rate of change is $g_w - \gamma$. This is specified in the most successful U.S. model equation, for the FR–MIT–Penn (FMP) Model (de Menil–Enzler), and in the OBE (Office of Business Economics) Model (Hirsch). In the DHL–III (Michigan) Model (Hymans) labor costs appear to be incompletely passed on, an apparent misspecification that was costly in the 1965–69 simulation contest.

Ball and Duffy (see their Table 1-C) obtain an unconstrained estimate virtually equal to one for the U.S.A. Their results for most other countries fall short of one, but this is to be expected for open economies. If Ball and Duffy used a trade matrix to close their 12-nation economy, it would be surprising if prices everywhere did not completely reflect international changes in wage costs. In their industry price equations Eckstein and Wyss find the coefficient on wages generally higher, and the coefficient on other input prices lower, than would be consistent with 100 per cent pass-through of costs. They attribute this fact to deficiencies in their input price indexes, so that wages act as a proxy for other costs.

(4) Even in a closed economy there are capital costs as well as labor costs. Nordhaus points out that in theory the long-run elasticity of price with respect to labor cost should not be unity but the elasticity of output with respect to labor, probably 0.65 to 0.75. In Equation (1) he would expect $\alpha_{12} + \alpha_{14}$ to equal one, although each of them is less than one. In view of his observation, how can the assumptions and findings described in the previous section be justified?

One approach, already outlined in the derivation of Equations (9) and (10), is that of de Menil and Enzler. The rental cost of capital, ρ, is $(r + \delta)q$, where r is the appropriate nominal interest rate, δ the depreciation rate, and q the price of capital goods. If r and δ are constant and q moves with labor costs $(g_w - \gamma)$, then α_{14} will be picked up in the coefficient of wage change and productivity trend. This is what would happen along a balanced growth path, with a constant capital/output ratio. To apply it to other situations, however, de Menil and Enzler must assume that in short-run pricing, firms ignore changes in capital costs.

Marshall tells us that in the short run, prices are related to marginal variable costs – a doctrine that we could amend in the spirit of modern price theory to refer to *standard* variable costs. If the quasi-rents earned in the short run diverge from long-run capital costs, there will be adjustments. But they will be long-run output adjustments by the slow processes of investment and disinvestment, rather than direct and immediate price adjustments. In the end Nordhaus' equilibrium conditions will hold, but it is neither necessary nor plausible to carry them in price adjustment equations.

According to Eckstein and Wyss, interest rates enter prices directly only in three pathologically concentrated industries. Heien and Popkin estimate what they call "neoclassical" price equations to compare with their "standard" equations. What they mean by neoclassical is that price always moves with long-run marginal cost, although it seems to me that neoclassical theory can perfectly well accommodate Marshallian price, output, and investment adjustments to disequilibrium. In any case their neoclassical equations yield mostly ones for wage rate elasticities and contain only a few significant coefficients for capital costs, mostly for regulated industries.

Price economics makes strange bedfellows, and the notion that interest rates are directly marked up in prices finds support both in literal adherents of neoclassical competitive theory and in Galbraithians who regard oligopoly as the predominant mode and large steel manufacturers as typical pricemakers. But the Conference provided little comfort for those who complain that restrictive monetary policy is directly inflationary.

(5) Equation (1) with $\alpha_{12} = \alpha_{13} = 1$ is consistent with the theory that as a strong first approximation prices are determined by variable costs. This is true in competitive industries where firms lack the power to do otherwise. In non-competitive industries prices appear to be a percentage mark-up over variable cost at normal operating rates. Indeed, prices are set primarily on this basis no matter how far or in which direction actual operating rates deviate from normal. The amount of the mark-up presumably maximizes profits at the expected average operating rate for which the capacity is designed.

Why are prices set for this level of demand even when actual demand is larger or smaller? The behavior evidently reflects monopolistic and oligopolistic calculations that long-run profits are not served by demand-related price adjustments. In an oligopoly, if a firm cuts prices to try to sustain sales in the face of declining demand, how do the rivals know that the firm is not cutting prices to capture a larger share of the market? The tacit collusion against price warfare on which oligopoly is based is a fragile structure. It can withstand price changes that are easily seen to be cost-related, but it may be destroyed by other price movements. Moreover, both monopoly and oligopoly covet long-term customer relationships that may be undermined by frequent demand-related price adjustments.

(6) The term $f(u - u^e)$ in Equation (1) allows for some competitive deviation from the standard pricing practice just described – that is, for some price adjustments up or down when demand and utilization are greater or smaller than "normal". If these adjustments are demand-related, f' will be negative. A modest effect of demand pressure is estimated in the aggregate price equations of the econometric models presented at the Conference. Demand pressure is variously represented – by capacity utilization, unfilled orders, percentage change in sales, or shipments. In the disaggregated price equations for 2-digit industries presented by Eckstein and Wyss, demand pressure is represented by capacity utilization and changes in shipments. Demand effects are significant in 11 of the 16 industries studied.

On the other hand, the variable $u - u^e$ is associated with variables that might work the opposite way. In many industries average productivity moves inversely with utilization, at least over a wide range. Basing mark-ups on actual unit labor costs rather than on unit labor costs at normal operating levels would contribute to a positive f'. This inverse relation of price to utilization would be even stronger if mark-ups were based on *full* costs per unit. The extreme is what Eckstein and Wyss call "profit-preserving pricing", or target-return pricing related to actual costs. Some of us would call it the "Blough effect" because of the steel companies' claim that prices must be raised at 60 per cent operating rates in order to restore normal profits. However, Eckstein and Wyss detected this behavior in only three of their cases. And in general inverse price-utilization relations seem to be weak or non-existent in the econometric results. To the extent that utilization rates affect percentage mark-ups, demand pressure variables dominate and mark-ups are wider the higher the rate of utilization.

The price equations of the Conference suggest a number of conclusions related to current controversies about inflation and inflation policy. Among the conclusions are:

(a) Price-setting behavior is consistent with the Phillips curve model. Some economists – namely Harrod and Keyserling – have alleged that inflation is inversely, rather than directly, related to utilization. They rely on the observation that average costs, variable and total, decline with utilization in many branches of industry. The evidence in the Conference papers is that this cost behavior, however prevalent it may be, is not reflected in pricing. Indeed the opposite is true: demand-induced mark-up behavior adds to the slope of the short-run Phillips curve (f' is negative).

(b) Price-setting behavior is neutral as far as the long-run trade-off between inflation and unemployment is concerned. This follows from the finding that α_{12} is one or the equivalent set of assumptions leading to Equation (9): wage changes are fully reflected in prices. Any trade-off that exists must therefore be due to an asymmetry: price changes are not fully reflected in wages, $\alpha_{21} < 1$. By the same token, the source of inflationary bias in the economy is the labor market rather than the product market. By inflationary bias I mean the fact that modern industrial economies regularly experience inflation even at high and socially unacceptable rates of unemployment and underutilization. This bias cannot be attributed to product pricing, which apparently passes on proportionately the changes in labor costs. In general, changes in labor costs are passed in both directions – down as well as up.

This conclusion is at odds with the belief widespread in the profession and among the public at large that industrial concentration – monopoly and oligopoly in product markets – is a major culprit. Non-competitive market structure may or may not be responsible for excessive mark-ups, but it evidently does not produce ever-increasing mark-ups. (Indeed, Hirsch detects a slight downward trend in mark-ups.) Nor does this market structure seem to contribute to a ratchet effect, with mark-ups rising in prosperous sectors and prosperous phases of the business cycle and failing to decline in depressed sectors and in recessions.

However, there may be a more subtle and indirect sense in which industrial concentration is responsible for inflationary bias. Perhaps the pricing behavior of a modern economy is the shelter for the wage behavior that appears to be the proximate source. If the competitive model found by Eckstein and Wyss in seven industries applied generally, prices would be so sensitive to demand that utilization would be quite stable. In that case, perhaps wages would be very flexible also. In agriculture, for example, wages are very largely the earnings of self-employed individuals and necessarily move with prices. The features of the labor market that contribute to asymmetry in the relation of money wages to labor demand – stickiness in the face of low demand, and responsiveness to high demand – may be the inevitable by-product of the market organization of modern industry. The papers of the Conference do not address such fundamental structural issues.

2. Wage Adjustment Equation

Phillips curves for wages of the general form of Equation (2) were presented for three econometric models: for the FMP Model by de Menil and Enzler, for the DHL–III Model by Hymans, and for the OBE Model by Hirsch. These wage equations did remarkably well in tracking recent wage experience through 1969. Their success was all the more remarkable because the simulations covered several quarters beyond the period of fit. It is doubtful that the model equations would do as well for 1970 and 1971 when they would translate the rise in unemployment rates into a moderation of wage inflation not yet observed.

The most important empirical finding is that α_{21}, the coefficient of feedback of price inflation on to wages, is significantly less than one. The estimate ranges from 0.42 in the DHL Model to 0.77 in the OBE Model. This implies that a long-run Phillips trade-off does exist. The asymptotic Phillips curve [Equation (7) or (9)] is much steeper than the short-run trade-off, but it is not vertical.

The model suggests that cycles in the rate of unemployment will produce clockwise hysteresis loops around the long-run Phillips curve. Thus, the decline in unemployment (1965–69) starting from a history of virtually stable prices and price expectations, produced its full quantum of inflation only with a lag. Likewise, the 1970–71 period of rising unemployment inherited inflationary expectations from the previous boom, so that inflation remains above its long-run values for the prevailing rates of unemployment. The prognosis is optimistic – the inflation will taper off even while the unemployment rate is once again declining. Indeed, the models imply a permanent rate of inflation of about 4 per cent at 4 per cent unemployment – no higher than actual inflation at higher unemployment rates in 1970. The simulations also suggest that nothing permanent, and little of a temporary nature, can be gained on the inflation front by slow rather than rapid restoration of full employment.

Before we take too much consolation or comfort from these conclusions, we must remember that the econometric estimates of the trade-off are more pessimistic than statistical Phillips curves estimated before 1966. The addition of 4 or 5 years of observation has raised the feedback coefficient by perhaps 0.20 and the long-run rate of inflation for 4 per cent unemployment by perhaps 0.02. We certainly cannot be confident that a conference 3 or 4 years from now will not record further pessimistic revisions in our estimates. The 1966–70 experience is historically unique. Perhaps our econometricians are right to regard the observations of this recent period as generated by the same structure as previous observations, with our estimates of the Phillips curve improved by data in a new range. It is also possible that the whole structure has changed adversely, and is still changing, and that the optimism of the current estimates is a misplaced residuum of observations from a more distant and benign past. It is too early to tell.

3. Natural Rate Hypothesis

An adherent of the "natural rate" hypothesis would challenge the "long-run" econometric trade-off curves on the ground that a feedback coefficient less than unity reflects irrational "money illusion" that cannot persist in the long run. Pragmatists could dodge the challenge by accepting the principle but arguing that a trade-off exists in as long a run as regularity of structure permits either econometric estimation or practical policy-making. From this standpoint, a more meaningful question is whether the estimated feedback would be greater if enough lagged price terms were used. The equations at hand might have used more, but they are not alone in their conclusion. As Nordhaus reports, virtually all empirical feedback estimates are less than one. This is true even when Equation (3) takes the form

$$\ddot{g}_p^e = \beta(g_p - g_p^e)$$

implying that g_p^e depends on all past values of g_p with exponentially diminishing weights.

A vertical long-run Phillips curve is built into the monetarist model of the Federal Reserve Bank of St. Louis, which is the basis for the Conference paper by Andersen and Carlson. The natural rate of unemployment is *assumed*, perhaps optimistically, to be 4 per cent. The wage–price block of the St. Louis Model diverges from the other models in taking price inflation and unemployment to be jointly dependent on aggregate demand variables – money GNP and the Okun gap between potential and actual real output. In the other models aggregate real demand determines unemployment, which can be taken as the semi-exogenous variable for the wage–price subsystem. [This is not quite true in the long run. The rate of productivity advance may depend upon the *composition* of output and therefore on the mixture of monetary and fiscal policy; Equation (7) or (9) says that the rate of inflation will depend on γ as well as on u^*. Hirsch reports such an effect in simulations of the OBE Model.]

The St. Louis procedure may be preferable to the usual practice. The two would be equivalent if Okun's law always held exactly, but it does not; conceivably the market pressures that move prices and wages are better related to the gap than to actual unemployment.

Although the Andersen–Carlson simulations are based on a "monetarist" model, the distinctive controversial feature of the model – the equation explaining money GNP by the money stock – need not engage us here. These inflation simulations can be interpreted as describing the consequences of alternative growth rates of money GNP, whether these would be generated by the money stock, as Andersen and Carlson believe, or in some other way. After all, one does not have to accept monetarist doctrine, in the sense that money is all that matters for the course of nominal GNP, in order to accept the natural rate hypothesis. (Nor do monetarists have to accept that hypothesis; some items of scripture are separable.)

The Andersen–Carlson simulations are instructive, especially for the natural rate exponents who today advocate deflationary aggregate demand policy. These exponents point out that the economy can return to its natural unemployment rate at any rate of inflation, and suggest, therefore, that we might as well take the extra time needed to make the permanent inflation rate close to zero. A policy of expanding nominal income at its long-run non-inflationary rate would, according to Andersen and Carlson, keep the economy above 6 per cent unemployment until 1976. In contrast, a policy ultimately consistent with 2.5 per cent inflation would never entail inflation above 6 per cent and would reduce unemployment to below 5 per cent in 1975. The contrast may not be a Phillips trade-off, but it is certainly a trade-off relevant for policy-makers.

Robert Lucas, in his outstanding theoretical presentation, provides through his original approach a different challenge to the significance of findings that the feedback coefficient is less than unity. He models a world in which econometricians would certainly find this result, but in which there nevertheless would be no durable trade-off on which policy-makers could rely. In the Lucas model individual firms and businessmen do not have complete information about the prices of the things they buy and sell. They decide on quantities on the basis of the best probabilistic price estimates they can make, conditional on the information they have available. Aggregate money demand is subject to random errors about its systematic predictable trend. When the error is positive, individuals underestimate the unknown prices of the things they buy and overproduce or oversupply labor in response to apparently favorable prices of what they sell. Underproduction and underemployment occur when the random error in aggregate money demand is negative. A history of deviations of this kind will provide the statistical appearance of a trade-off. But the appearance is deceptive. The deviations in aggregate demand that produce this appearance must necessarily be random surprises. If the government systematically steps up aggregate demand to obtain higher employment and production, its policy will be learned and absorbed into the procedures by which citizens estimate the prices they do not directly observe.

Interestingly enough, one of Lucas' precursors was J.M. Keynes:[1]

"For a time at least, rising prices may delude entrepreneurs into increasing employment beyond the level which maximizes their individual profits measured in terms of the product. For they are so accustomed to regard rising sale-proceeds in terms of money as a signal for expanding production, that they may continue to do so when this policy has in fact ceased to be to their best advantage; i.e., they may under-estimate their marginal user cost in the new price environment."

Lucas' paper provides a rigorous defense of the natural rate hypothesis, and the study's rigor and sophistication have the virtue of making clear exactly what the hypothesis requires. The structure of the economy, including the rules guiding fiscal and monetary policy, must be stable and must be understood by all participants. The participants not only must receive the correct information about the structure but also must use all of the data correctly in estimating prices and in making quantitative decisions. These participants must be better econometricians than any of us at the Conference. If they are, they will always be – except for the unavoidable mistakes due to purely random elements in the time sequence of aggregate money demand – at their utility- and profit-maximizing real positions. These positions are invariant to any *systematic* changes in the sequence of aggregate money demand, either in the level of such demand or in any of its time derivatives.

Once again, a pragmatist might conclude that he agrees with the natural rate hypothesis in principle but also believes that, in as long a run as can be of concern to policy-makers in an uncertain and changing world, a trade-off does exist for policy-makers as well as for statisticians.

4. Price Expectations

As the preceding review makes clear, expectations of inflation play a crucial role in the theory and estimation of trade-off equations. The almost invariable practice in estimation is to represent expectations of inflation by a weighted average of past actual rates of inflation. Our research is certainly vulnerable at this point. On the one hand, the lagged variables may show statistically significant effects for reasons quite remote from their putative influence on expectations. And on the other hand, they are almost surely inaccurate gauges of expectations. Consumers, workers, and businessmen may not be as good econometricians as Lucas would have them be, but they do read newspapers and they do know better than to base price expectations on simple extrapolation of price series alone.

Empirical data on price expectations do exist. These data, although perhaps incomplete, provide evidence, and it is no credit to econometric studies of the wage–price nexus that such information is ignored. George Katona and company have collected price expectation data from consumer surveys since 1946. They show that people learn from experience but do not follow any simple extrapolative model.

The long-term trend of expectations in the Michigan surveys is certainly one of increasing acceptance of creeping inflation. In 1949 only 8 per cent of respondents expected general price increases during the coming year. In 1969 this number was 75 per cent. The public, however, has been quite sensitive to economic and political events associated with inflation. The Korean War caused a large bulge – 77 per cent of those surveyed expected inflation at the beginning of 1951 and 53 per cent in 1952. In the recession that followed, consumers returned substantially to their pre-Korean War views. The military and economic escalation of the Vietnam War in 1966 produced another bulge. Subsequent expectations seemed to reflect promptly – and with more accuracy than actual price behavior – fluctuations in the economic situation and in government policy.

The extrapolation model, after all, does not really make sense. Price movements observed and experienced do not necessarily convey information on the basis of which a rational man should alter his view of the future. When a blight destroys half the mid-western corn crop and corn prices subsequently rise, the information conveyed is that blights raise prices. No trader or farmer under these circumstances would change his view of the future of corn prices, much less of their rate of change, unless he is led to reconsider his estimate of the likelihood of blights. The fear that the invasion of Korea in 1950 would lead to a full-scale war touched off a frenzy of speculative buying; no rational person would give the resulting inflation a positive weight in calculating the future. On the other hand, if recent experience leads the public, as well as professional economists, to conclude that the Phillips curve is worse than they thought, they are correct to build this information into their future calculations.

The St. Louis monetarist model includes a mechanism for generation of price expectations that is more sophisticated than other econometric work, at least any other work reported at the Conference. Anticipated price change depends not only on price history but also on past values of other macroeconomic variables, total spending, and unemployment. The idea is admirable, but its execution is puzzling. Why should an observed price increase when unemployment was 3 per cent receive twice as much weight in the formation of expectations as it would receive when unemployment was 6 per cent? Perhaps the price increase should if it were low relative to what might be considered normal at 3 per cent unemployment because then it conveys new information. The reverse would be true for a price increase of a magnitude that would be surprising at 6 per cent but that would be normal at 3 per cent unemployment.

5. Concluding Comments

The Conference was timely and constructive. The empirical work on wages and prices is impressive and promising. Our ignorance and uncertainty are still vast, but the Conference papers constitute a solid foundation on which to build future research. The generalist of my opening paragraph might well conclude and report that there is more reason to be optimistic about wage–price econometrics than about resolution of the inflation–unemployment dilemma.

Note

[1] J.M. Keynes, *The General Theory of Employment, Interest and Money* (New York: Harcourt, Brace and Co., 1936), p. 290.

CHAPTER 28

INFLATION AND UNEMPLOYMENT

The world economy today is vastly different from the 1930s, when Seymour Harris, the chairman of this meeting, infected me with his boundless enthusiasm for economics and his steadfast confidence in its capacity for good works. Economics is very different, too. Both the science and its subject have changed, and for the better, since World War II. But there are some notable constants. Unemployment and inflation still preoccupy and perplex economists, statesmen, journalists, housewives, and everyone else. The connection between them is the principal domestic economic burden of presidents and prime ministers, and the major area of controversy and ignorance in macroeconomics. I have chosen to review economic thought on this topic on this occasion, partly because of its inevitable timeliness, partly because of a personal interest reaching back to my first published work in 1941.

1. The Meanings of Full Employment

Today, as 30 and 40 years ago, economists debate how much unemployment is voluntary, how much involuntary; how much is a phenomenon of equilibrium, how much a symptom of disequilibrium; how much is compatible with competition, how much is to be blamed on monopolies, labor unions, and restrictive legislation; how much unemployment characterizes "full" employment.

Full employment – imagine macroeconomics deprived of the concept. But what is it? What is the proper employment goal of policies affecting

Presidential address delivered at the eighty-fourth meeting of the American Economic Association, New Orleans, Louisiana, December 28, 1971, reprinted from *American Economic Review* (March 1972), 1–18.

aggregate demand? Zero unemployment in the monthly labor force survey? That outcome is so inconceivable outside of Switzerland that it is useless as a guide to policy. Any other numerical candidate, yes even 4 per cent, is patently arbitrary without reference to basic criteria. Unemployment equal to vacancies? Measurement problems aside, this definition has the same straightforward appeal as zero unemployment, which it simply corrects for friction. [1]

A concept of full employment more congenial to economic theory is labor market equilibrium, a volume of employment which is simultaneously the amount employers want to offer and the amount workers want to accept at prevailing wage rates and prices. Forty years ago theorists with confidence in markets could believe that full employment is whatever volume of employment the economy is moving toward, and that its achievement requires of the government nothing more than neutrality, and nothing less.

After Keynes challenged the classical notion of labor market equilibrium and the complacent view of policy to which it led, full employment came to mean maximum aggregate supply, the point at which expansion of aggregate demand could not further increase employment and output.

Full employment was also regarded as the economy's inflation threshold. With a deflationary gap, demand less than full employment supply, prices would be declining or, at worst, constant. Expansion of aggregate demand short of full employment would cause at most a one-shot increase of prices. For continuing inflation, the textbooks told us, a necessary and sufficient condition was an inflationary gap, real aggregate demand in excess of feasible supply. The model was tailor-made for wartime inflation.

Postwar experience destroyed the identification of full employment with the economy's inflation threshold. The profession, the press, and the public discovered the "new inflation" of the 1950s, inflation without benefit of gap, labelled but scarcely illuminated by the term "cost-push". Subsequently the view of the world suggested by the Phillips curve merged demand-pull and cost-push inflation and blurred the distinction between them. This view contained no concept of full employment. In its place came the trade-off, along which society supposedly can choose the least undesirable feasible combination of the evils of unemployment and inflation.

Many economists deny the existence of a durable Phillips trade-off. Their numbers and influence are increasing. Some of them contend that there is only one rate of unemployment compatible with steady inflation, a "natural rate" consistent with any steady rate of change of prices, positive, zero, or negative. The natural rate is another full employment candidate, a policy target at least in the passive sense that monetary and fiscal policy-makers are advised to eschew any numerical unemployment goal and to let the economy gravitate to this equilibrium. So we have come full circle. Full employment is once again nothing but the equilibrium reached by labor markets unaided and undistorted by governmental fine tuning.

In discussing these issues, I shall make the following points. First, an observed amount of unemployment is not revealed to be voluntary simply by the fact that money wage rates are constant, or rising, or even accelerating. I shall recall and extend Keynes's definition of involuntary unemployment and his explanation why workers may accept price inflation as a method of reducing real wages while rejecting money wage cuts. The second point is related. Involuntary unemployment is a disequilibrium phenomenon; the behavior, the persistence, of excess supplies of labor depend on how and how fast markets adjust to shocks, and on how large and how frequent the shocks are. Higher prices or faster inflation can diminish involuntary, disequilibrium unemployment, even though voluntary, equilibrium labor supply is entirely free of money illusion.

Third, various criteria of full employment coincide in a theoretical full stationary equilibrium, but diverge in persistent disequilibrium. These are (1) the natural rate of unemployment, the rate compatible with zero or some other constant inflation rate, (2) zero involuntary unemployment, (3) the rate of unemployment needed for optimal job search and placement, and (4) unemployment equal to job vacancies. The first criterion dictates higher unemployment than any of the rest. Instead of commending the natural rate as a target of employment policy, the other three criteria suggest less unemployment and more inflation. Therefore, fourth, there are real gains from additional employment, which must be weighed in the social balance against the costs of inflation. I shall conclude with a few remarks on this choice, and on the possibilities of improving the terms of the trade-off.

2. Keynesian and Classical Interpretations of Unemployment

To begin with *The General Theory of Employment, Interest, and Money* is not just the ritual piety economists of my generation owe the book that shaped their minds. Keynes's (1936) treatment of labor market equilibrium and disequilibrium in his first chapter is remarkably relevant today.

Keynes attacked what he called the classical presumption that persistent unemployment is voluntary unemployment. The presumption he challenged is that in competitive labor markets actual employment and unemployment reveal workers' true preferences between work and alternative uses of time, the presumption that no one is fully or partially unemployed whose real wage per hour exceeds his marginal valuation of an hour of free time. Orthodox economists found the observed stickiness of money wages to be persuasive evidence that unemployment, even in the Great Depression, was voluntary. Keynes found decisive evidence against this inference in the willingness of workers to accept a larger volume of employment at a lower real wage resulting from an increase of prices.

Whenever unemployment could be reduced by expansion of aggregate demand, Keynes regarded it as involuntary. He expected expansion to raise prices and lower real wages, but this expectation is not crucial to his argument. Indeed, if it is possible to raise employment without reduction in the real wage, his case for calling the unemployment "involuntary" is strengthened.

But why is the money wage so stubborn if more labor is willingly available at the same or lower real wage? Consider first some answers Keynes did not give. He did not appeal to trade union monopolies or minimum wage laws. He was anxious, perhaps over-anxious, to meet his putative classical opponents on their home field, the competitive economy. He did not rely on any failure of workers to perceive what a rise in prices does to real wages. The unemployed take new jobs, the employed hold ones, with eyes open. Otherwise the new situation would be transient.

Instead, Keynes emphasized the institutional fact that wages are bargained and set in the monetary unit of account. Money wage rates are, to use an unKeynesian term, "administered prices". That is, they are not set and reset in daily auctions but posted and fixed for finite periods of time. This observation led Keynes to his central explanation: Workers, individually and in groups, are more concerned with relative than absolute real wages. They may withdraw labor if their wages fall relatively to wages elsewhere, even though they would not withdraw any if real wages fall uniformly everywhere. Labor markets are decentralized, and there is no way money wages can fall in any one market without impairing the relative status of the workers there. A general rise in prices is a neutral and universal method of reducing real wages, the only method in a decentralized and uncontrolled economy. Inflation would not be needed, we may infer, if by government compulsion, economy-wide bargaining, or social compact, all money wage rates could be scaled down together.

Keynes apparently meant that relative wages are the arguments in labor supply functions. But Alchian (pp. 27–52 in Phelps *et al.* (1970)) and other theorists of search activity have offered a somewhat different interpretation, namely that workers whose money wages are reduced will quit their jobs to seek employment in other markets where they think, perhaps mistakenly, that wages remain high.

Keynes's explanation of money wage stickiness is plausible and realistic. But two related analytical issues have obscured the message. Can there be involuntary unemployment in an equilibrium, a proper, full-fledged neoclassical equilibrium? Does the labor supply behavior described by Keynes betray "money illusion"? Keynes gave a loud "yes" in answer to the first question, and this seems at first glance to compel an affirmative answer to the second.

An economic theorist can, of course, commit no greater crime than to assume money illusion. Comparative statics is a non-historical exercise, in which different price levels are to be viewed as alternative rather than sequential. Compare two situations that differ only in the scale of exogenous monetary variables; imagine, for example, that all such magnitudes are ten times as high in one situation as in the other. All equilibrium prices, including money wage rates, should differ in the same proportion, while all real magnitudes, including employment, should be the same in the two equilibria. To assume instead that workers' supply decisions vary with the price level is to say that they would behave differently if the unit of account were, and always had been, dimes instead of dollars. Surely Keynes should not be interpreted to attribute to anyone money illusion in this sense. He was not talking about so strict and static an equilibrium.

Leijonhufvud's (1968) illuminating and perceptive interpretation of Keynes argues convincingly that, in chapter 1 as throughout the *General Theory*, what Keynes calls "equilibrium" should be viewed as persistent disequilibrium, and what appears to be comparative statics is really shrewd and incisive, if awkward, dynamic analysis. Involuntary unemployment means that labor markets are not in equilibrium. The resistance of money wage rates to excess supply is a feature of the adjustment process rather than a symptom of irrationality.

The other side of Keynes's story is that in depressions money wage deflation, even if it occurred more speedily, or especially if it occurred more speedily, would be at best a weak equilibrator and quite possibly a source of more unemployment rather than less. In contemporary language, the perverse case would arise if a high and ever-increasing real rate of return on money inhibited real demand faster than the rising purchasing power of monetary stocks stimulated demand. To pursue this Keynesian theme further here would be a digression.

What relevance has this excursion into depression economics for contemporary problems of unemployment and wage inflation? The issues are remarkably similar, even though events and Phillips have shifted attention from levels to time rates of change of wages and prices. Phillips curve doctrine [2] is in an important sense the postwar analogue of Keynesian wage and employment theory, while natural rate doctrine is the contemporary version of the classical position Keynes was opposing.

Phillips curve doctrine implies that lower unemployment can be purchased at the cost of faster inflation. Let us adapt Keynes's test for involuntary unemployment to the dynamic terms of contemporary discussion of inflation, wages, and unemployment. Suppose that the current rate of unemployment continues. Associated with it is a path of real wages, rising at the rate of productivity growth. Consider an alternative future, with unemployment at first declining to a rate one percentage point lower and then remaining constant at the lower rate. Associated with the lower unemployment alternative will be a second path of real wages. Eventually this real wage path will show, at least to first approximation, the same rate of increase as the first one, the rate of productivity growth. But the paths may differ because of the transitional effects of increasing the rate of employment. The growth of real wages will be retarded in the short run if additional employment lowers labor's marginal productivity. In any case, the test question is whether with full information about the two alternatives labor would accept the second one – whether, in other words, the additional employment would be willingly supplied along the second real wage path. If the answer is affirmative, then that one percentage point of unemployment is involuntary.

For Keynes's reasons, a negative answer cannot necessarily be inferred from failure of money wage rates to fall or even decelerate. Actual unemployment and the real wage path associated with it are not necessarily an equilibrium. Rigidities in the path of money wage rates can be explained by workers' preoccupation with relative wages and the absence of any central economy-wide mechanism for altering all money wages together.

According to the natural rate hypothesis, there is just one rate of unemployment compatible with steady wage and price inflation, and this is in the long run compatible with any constant rate of change of prices, positive, zero, or negative. Only at the natural rate of unemployment are workers content with current and prospective real wages, content to have their real wages rise at the rate of growth of productivity. Along the feasible path of real wages they would not wish to accept any larger volume of employment. Lower unemployment, therefore, can arise only from economy-wide excess demand for labor and must generate a gap between real wages desired and real wages earned. The gap evokes increases of money wages designed to raise real wages faster than productivity. But this intention is always frustrated, the gap is never closed, money wages and prices accelerate. By symmetrical argument, unemployment above the natural rate signifies excess supply in labor markets and ever-accelerating deflation. Older classical economists regarded constancy of money wage rates as indicative of full employment equilibrium, at which the allocation of time between work and other pursuits is revealed as voluntary and optimal. Their successors make the same claims for the natural rate of unemployment, except that in the equilibrium money wages are not necessarily constant but growing at the rate of productivity gain plus the experienced and expected rate of inflation of prices.

3. **Is Zero-inflation Unemployment Voluntary and Optimal?**

There are, then, two conflicting interpretations of the welfare value of employment in excess of the level consistent with price stability. One is that additional employment does not produce enough to compensate workers for the value of other uses of their time. The fact that it generates inflation is taken as prima facie evidence of a welfare loss. The alternative view, which I shall argue, is that the responses of money wages and prices to changes in aggregate demand reflect mechanics of adjustment, institutional constraints, and relative wage patterns and reveal nothing in particular about individual or social valuations of unemployed time *vis-à-vis* the wages of employment.

On this rostrum four years ago, Milton Friedman identified the non-inflationary natural rate of unemployment with "equilibrium in the structure of real wage rates" (p. 8). "The 'natural rate of unemployment'", he said, ". . . is the level that would be ground out by the Walrasian system of general equilibrium equations, provided that there is embedded in them the actual structural characteristics of the labor and commodity markets, including market imperfections, stochastic variability in demands and supplies, the costs of getting information about job vacancies and labor availabilities, the costs of mobility, and so on". Presumably this Walrasian equilibrium also has the usual optimal properties; at any rate, Friedman advised the monetary authorities not to seek to improve upon it. But in fact we know little about the existence of a Walrasian equilibrium that allows for all the imperfections and frictions that explain why the natural rate is bigger than zero, and even less about the optimality of such an equilibrium if it exists.

In the new microeconomics of labor markets and inflation, the principal activity whose marginal value sets the reservation price of employment is job search. It is not pure leisure, for in principle persons who choose that option are not reported as unemployed; however, there may be a leisure component in job seeking.

A crucial assumption of the theory is that search is significantly more efficient when the searcher is unemployed, but almost no evidence has been advanced on this point. Members of our own profession are adept at seeking and finding new jobs without first leaving their old ones or abandoning not-in-labor-force status. We do not know how many quits and new hires in manufacturing are similar transfers, but some of them must be; if all reported accessions were hires of unemployed workers, the mean duration of unemployment would be only about half what it is in fact. In surveys of job mobility among blue-collar workers in 1946–47 (see Lloyd Reynolds, pp. 214–15, and Herbert Parnes, pp. 158–59), 25 per cent of workers who quit had new jobs lined up in advance. Reynolds found that the main obstacle to mobility without unemployment was not lack of information or time, but simply "anti-pirating" collusion by employers.

A considerable amount of search activity by unemployed workers appears to be an unproductive consequence of dissatisfaction and frustration rather than a rational quest for improvement. This was the conclusion of Reynolds's survey twenty-five years ago (p. 215) and it has been re-emphasized for the contemporary scene by Robert Hall, and by Peter Doeringer and Michael Piore for what they term the "secondary labor force". Reynolds found that quitting a job to look for a new one while unemployed actually yielded a better job in only a third of the cases. Lining up a new job in advance was a more successful strategy: two-thirds of such changes turned out to be improvements. Today, according to the dual labor market hypothesis, the basic reason for frequent and long spells of unemployment in the secondary labor force is the shortage of good jobs.

In any event, the contention of some natural rate theorists is that employment beyond the natural rate takes time that would be better spent in search activity. Why do workers accept such employment? An answer to this question is a key element in a theory that generally presumes that actual behavior reveals true preferences. The answer given is that workers accept the additional employment only because they are victims of inflation illusion. One form of inflation illusion is over-estimation of the real wages of jobs they now hold, if they are employed, or of jobs they find, if they are unemployed and searching. If they did not under-estimate price inflation, employed workers would more often quit to search, and unemployed workers would search longer.

The force of this argument seems to me diluted by the fact that price inflation illusion affects equally both sides of the job seeker's equation. He over-estimates the real value of an immediate job, but he also over-estimates the real values of jobs he might wait for. It is in the spirit of this theorizing to assume that money interest rates respond to the same correct or incorrect inflationary expectations. As a first approximation, inflation illusion has no substitution effect on the margin between working and waiting.

It does have an income effect, causing workers to exaggerate their real wealth. In which direction the income effect would work is not transparent. Does greater wealth, or the illusion of greater wealth, make people more choosy about jobs, more inclined to quit and to wait? Or less choosy, more inclined to stay in the job they have or to take the first one that comes along? I should have thought more selective rather than less. But natural rate theory must take the opposite view if it is to explain why under-estimation of price inflation bamboozles workers into holding or taking jobs that they do not really want.

Another form of alleged inflation illusion refers to wages rather than prices. Workers are myopic and do not perceive that wages elsewhere are, or soon will be, rising as fast as the money wage of the job they now hold or have just found. Consequently they under-estimate the advantages of quitting and searching. This explanation is convincing only to the extent that the pay-off to search activity is determined by wage differentials. The pay-off also depends on the probabilities of getting jobs at quoted wages, therefore on the balance between vacancies and job seekers. Workers know that perfectly well. Quit rates are an index of voluntary search activity. They do not diminish when unemployment is low and wage rates are rapidly rising. They increase, quite understandably. This fact contradicts the inflation illusion story, both versions. I conclude that it is not possible to regard fluctuations of unemployment on either side of the zero-inflation rate as mainly voluntary, albeit mistaken, extensions and contractions of search activity.

The new microeconomics of job search (see Edmund Phelps *et al.*, is nevertheless a valuable contribution to understanding of frictional unemployment. It provides reasons why some unemployment is voluntary, and why some unemployment is socially efficient.

Does the market produce the *optimal* amount of search unemployment? Is the natural rate optimal? I do not believe the new microeconomics has yet answered these questions.

An omniscient and beneficent economic dictator would not place every new job seeker immediately in any job at hand. Such a policy would create many mismatches, sacrificing efficiency in production or necessitating costly job-to-job shifts later on. The hypothetical planner would prefer to keep a queue of workers unemployed, so that he would have a larger choice of jobs to which to assign them. But he would not make the queue too long, because workers in the queue are not producing anything.

Of course he could shorten the queue of unemployed if he could dispose of more jobs and lengthen the queue of vacancies. With enough jobs of various kinds, he would never lack a vacancy for which any worker who happens to come along has comparative advantage. But because of limited capital stocks and interdependence among skills, jobs cannot be indefinitely multiplied without lowering their marginal productivity. Our wise and benevolent planner would not place people in jobs yielding less than the marginal value of leisure. Given this constraint on the number of jobs, he would always have to keep some workers waiting, and some jobs vacant. But he certainly would be inefficient if he had fewer jobs, filled and vacant, than this constraint. This is the common sense of Beveridge's rule – that vacancies should not be less than unemployment.

Is the natural rate a market solution of the hypothetical planner's operations research problem? According to search theory, an unemployed worker considers the probabilities that he can get a better job by searching longer and balances the expected discounted value of waiting against the loss of earnings. The employed worker makes a similar calculation when he considers quitting, also taking into account the once-and-for-all costs of movement. These calculations are like those of the planner, but with an important difference. An individual does not internalize all the considerations the planner takes into account. The external effects are the familiar ones of congestion theory. A worker deciding to join a queue or to stay in one considers the probabilities of getting a job, but not the effects of his decision on the probabilities that others face. He lowers those probabilities for people in the queue he joins and raises them for persons waiting for the kind of job he vacates or turns down. Too many persons are unemployed waiting for good jobs, while less desirable ones go begging. However, external effects also occur in the decisions of employers whether to fill a vacancy with the applicant at hand or to wait for someone more qualified. It is not obvious, at least to me, whether the market is biased toward excessive or inadequate search. But it is doubtful that it produces the optimal amount.

Empirically, the proposition that in the U.S.A. the zero-inflation rate of unemployment reflects voluntary and efficient job-seeking activity strains credulity. If there were a natural rate of unemployment in the U.S.A., what would it be? It is hard to say because virtually all econometric Phillips curves allow for a whole menu of steady inflation rates. But estimates constrained to produce a vertical long-run Phillips curve suggest a natural rate between 5 and 6 per cent of the labor force. [3]

So let us consider some of the features of an overall unemployment rate of 5 to 6 per cent. First, about 40 per cent of accessions in manufacturing are rehires rather than new hires. Temporarily laid off by their employers, these workers had been awaiting recall and were scarcely engaged in voluntary search activity. Their unemployment is as much a deadweight loss as the disguised unemployment of redundant workers on payrolls. This number declines to 25–30 per cent when unemployment is 4 per cent or below. Likewise, a 5–6 per cent unemployment rate means that voluntary quits amount only to about a third of separations, layoffs to two-thirds. The proportions are reversed at low unemployment rates.

Second, the unemployment statistic is not an exhaustive count of those with time and incentive to search. An additional 3 per cent of the labor force are involuntarily confined to part-time work, and another $\frac{3}{4}$ of 1 per cent are out of the labor force because they "could not find job" or "think no work available" – discouraged by market conditions rather than personal incapacities.

Third, with unemployment of 5–6 per cent the number of reported vacancies is less than $\frac{1}{2}$ of 1 per cent. Vacancies appear to be understated relative to unemployment, but they rise to $1\frac{1}{2}$ per cent when the unemployment rate is below 4 per cent. At 5–6 per cent unemployment, the economy is clearly capable of generating many more jobs with marginal productivity high enough so that people prefer them to leisure. The capital stock is no limitation, since 5–6 per cent unemployment has been associated with more than 20 per cent excess capacity. Moreover, when more jobs are created by expansion of demand, with or without inflation, labor force participation increases; this would hardly occur if the additional jobs were low in quality and productivity. As the parable of the central employment planner indicates, there will be excessive waiting for jobs if the roster of jobs and the menu of vacancies are suboptimal.

In summary, labor markets characterized by 5–6 per cent unemployment do not display the symptoms one would expect if the unemployment were voluntary search activity. Even if it were voluntary, search activity on such a large scale would surely be socially wasteful. The only reason anyone might regard so high an unemployment rate as an equilibrium and social optimum is that lower rates cause accelerating inflation. But this is almost tautological. The inferences of equilibrium and optimality would be more convincing if they were corroborated by direct evidence.

4. Why is there Inflation without Aggregate Excess Demand?

Zero-inflation unemployment is not wholly voluntary, not optimal, I might even say not natural. In other words, the economy has an inflationary bias: When labor markets provide as many jobs as there are willing workers, there is inflation, perhaps accelerating inflation. Why?

The Phillips curve has been an empirical finding in search of a theory, like Pirandello characters in search of an author. One rationalization might be termed a theory of stochastic macroequilibrium: stochastic, because random intersectoral shocks keep individual labor markets in diverse states of disequilibrium; macroequilibrium, because the perpetual flux of particular markets produces fairly definite aggregate outcomes of unemployment and wages. Stimulated by Phillips's 1958 findings, Richard Lipsey proposed a model of this kind in 1960, and it has since been elaborated by Archibald (pp. 212–23) and Holt (pp. 53–123 and 224–56) in Phelps et al., and others. I propose now to sketch a theory in the same spirit.

It is an essential feature of the theory that economy-wide relations among employment, wages, and prices are aggregations of diverse outcomes in heterogeneous markets. The myth of macroeconomics is that relations among aggregates are enlarged analogues of relations among corresponding variables for individual households, firms, industries, markets. The myth is a harmless and useful simplification in many contexts, but sometimes it misses the essence of the phenomenon.

Unemployment is, in this model as in Keynes reinterpreted, a disequilibrium phenomenon. Money wages do not adjust rapidly enough to clear all labor markets every day. Excess supplies in labor markets take the form of unemployment, and excess demands the form of unfilled vacancies. At any moment, markets vary widely in excess demand or supply, and the economy as a whole shows both vacancies and unemployment.

The overall balance of vacancies and unemployment is determined by aggregate demand, and is therefore in principle subject to control by overall monetary and fiscal policy. Higher aggregate demand means fewer excess supply markets and more excess demand markets, accordingly less unemployment and more vacancies.

In any particular labor market, the rate of increase of money wages is the sum of two components, an equilibrium component and a disequilibrium component. The first is the rate at which the wage would increase were the market in equilibrium, with neither vacancies nor unemployment. The other component is a function of excess demand and supply – a monotonic function, positive for positive excess demand, zero for zero excess demand, non-positive for excess supply. I begin with the disequilibrium component.

Of course the disequilibrium components are relevant only if disequilibria persist. Why are they not eliminated by the very adjustments they set in motion? Workers will move from excess supply markets to excess demand markets, and from low wage to high wage markets. Unless they overshoot, these movements are equilibrating. The theory therefore requires that new disequilibria are always arising. Aggregate demand may be stable, but beneath its stability is never-ending flux: new products, new processes, new tastes and fashions, new developments of land and natural resources, obsolescent industries and declining areas.

The overlap of vacancies and unemployment – say, the sum of the two for any given difference between them – is a measure of the heterogeneity or dispersion of individual markets. The amount of dispersion depends directly on the size of those shocks of demand and technology that keep markets in perpetual disequilibrium, and inversely on the responsive mobility of labor. The one increases, the other diminishes the frictional component of unemployment, that is, the number of unfilled vacancies coexisting with any given unemployment rate.

A central assumption of the theory is that the functions relating wage change to excess demand or supply are non-linear, specifically that un-employment retards money wages less than vacancies accelerate them. Non-linearity in the response of wages to excess demand has several important implications. First, it helps to explain the characteristic observed curvature of the Phillips curve. Each successive increment of unemployment has less effect in reducing the rate of inflation. Linear wage response, on the other hand, would mean a linear Phillips relation.

Second, given the overall state of aggregate demand, economy-wide vacancies less unemployment, wage inflation will be greater the larger the variance among markets in excess demand and supply. As a number of recent empirical studies have confirmed (see George Perry and Charles Schultze), dispersion is inflationary. Of course, the rate of wage inflation will depend not only on the overall dispersion of excess demands and supplies across markets but also on the particular markets where the excess supplies and demands happen to fall. An unlucky random drawing might put the excess demands in highly responsive markets and the excess supplies in especially unresponsive ones.

Third, the non-linearity is an explanation of inflationary bias, in the following sense. Even when aggregate vacancies are at most equal to unemployment, the average disequilibrium component will be positive. Full employment in the sense of equality of vacancies and unemployment is not compatible with price stability. Zero inflation requires unemploy-ment in excess of vacancies.

Criteria that coincide in full long-run equilibrium – zero inflation and zero aggregate excess demand – diverge in stochastic macroequilibrium. Full long-run equilibrium in all markets would show no unemployment, no vacancies, no unanticipated inflation. But with unending sectoral flux, zero excess demand spells inflation and zero inflation spells net excess supply – unemployment in excess of vacancies. In these circumstances neither criterion can be justified simply because it is a property of full long-run equilibrium. Both criteria automatically allow for frictional unemployment incident to the required movements of workers between markets; the no-inflation criterion requires enough additional unemploy-ment to wipe out inflationary bias.

I now turn to the equilibrium component, the rate of wage increase in a market with neither excess demand nor excess supply. It is reasonable to suppose that the equilibrium component depends on the trend of wages of comparable labor elsewhere. A "competitive wage", one that reflects relevant trends fully, is what employers will offer if they wish to maintain their share of the volume of employment. This will happen where the rate of growth of marginal revenue product – the compound of productivity increase and price inflation – is the same as the trend in wages. But in some markets the equilibrium wage will be rising faster, and in others slower, than the economy-wide wage trend.

A "natural rate" result follows if actual wage increases feed fully into the equilibrium components of future wage increases. There will be acceleration whenever the non-linear disequilibrium effects are on average positive, and steady inflation, that is stochastically steady inflation, only at unemployment rates high enough to make the disequilibrium effects wash out. Phillips trade-offs exist in the short run, and the time it takes for them to evaporate depends on the lengths of the lags with which today's actual wage gains become tomorrow's standards.

A rather minor modification may preserve Phillips trade-offs in the long run. Suppose there is a floor on wage change in excess supply markets, independent of the amount of excess supply and of the past history of wages and prices. Suppose, for example, that wage change is never negative; it is either zero or what the response function says, whichever is algebraically larger. So long as there are markets where this floor is effective, there can be determinate rates of economy-wide wage inflation for various levels of aggregate demand. Markets at the floor do not increase their contributions to aggregate wage inflation when overall demand is raised. Nor is their contribution escalated to actual wage experience. But the frequency of such markets diminishes, it is true, both with overall demand and with inflation. The floor phenomenon can preserve a Phillips trade-off within limits, but one that becomes ever more fragile and vanishes as greater demand pressure removes markets from contact with the zero floor. The model implies a long-run Phillips curve that is very flat for high unemployment and becomes vertical at a critically low rate of unemployment.

These implications seem plausible and even realistic. It will be objected, however, that any permanent floor independent of general wage and price history and expectation must indicate money illusion. The answer is that the floor need not be permanent in any single market. It could give way to wage reduction when enough unemployment has persisted long enough. But with stochastic intersectoral shifts of demand, markets are always exchanging roles, and there can always be some markets, not always the same ones, at the floor.

This model avoids the empirically questionable implication of the usual natural rate hypothesis that unemployment rates only slightly higher than the critical rate will trigger ever-accelerating deflation. Phillips curves seem to be pretty flat at high rates of unemployment. During the great contraction of 1930–33, wage rates were slow to give way even in the face of massive unemployment and substantial deflation in consumer prices. Finally, in 1932 and 1933, money wage rates fell more sharply, in response to prolonged unemployment, lay-offs, shutdowns, and to threats and fears of more of the same.

I have gone through this example to make the point that irrationality, in the sense that meaningless differences in money values *permanently* affect individual behavior, is not logically necessary for the existence of a long-run Phillips trade-off. In full long-run equilibrium in all markets, employment and unemployment would be independent of the levels and rates of change of money wage rates and prices. But this is not an equilibrium that the system ever approaches. The economy is in perpetual sectoral disequilibrium even when it has settled into a stochastic macro-equilibrium.

I suppose that one might maintain that asymmetry in wage adjustment and temporary resistance to money wage decline reflect money illusion in some sense. Such an assertion would have to be based on an extension of the domain of well-defined rational behavior to cover responses to adjustment speeds, costs of information, costs of organizing and operating markets, and a host of other problems in dynamic theory. These theoretical extensions are in their infancy, although much work of interest and promise is being done. Meanwhile, I doubt that significant restrictions on disequilibrium adjustment mechanisms can be deduced from first principles.

Why are the wage and salary rates of employed workers so insensitive to the availability of potential replacements? One reason is that the employer makes some explicit or implicit commitments in putting a worker on the payroll in the first place. The employee expects that his wages and terms of employment will steadily improve, certainly never retrogress. He expects that the employer will pay him the rate prevailing for persons of comparable skill, occupation, experience, and seniority. He expects such commitments in return for his own investments in the job; arrangements for residence, transportation, and personal life involve set-up costs which will be wasted if the job turns sour. The market for labor services is not like a market for fresh produce where the entire current supply is auctioned daily. It is more like a rental housing market, in which most existing tenancies are the continuations of long-term relationships governed by contracts or less formal understandings.

Employers and workers alike regard the wages of comparable labor elsewhere as a standard, but what determines those reference wages? There is not even an auction where workers and employers unbound by existing relationships and commitments meet and determine a market-clearing wage. If such markets existed, they would provide competitively determined guides for negotiated and administered wages, just as stock exchange prices are reference points for stock transactions elsewhere. In labor markets the reverse is closer to the truth. Wage rates for existing employees set the standards for new employees, too.

The equilibrium components of wage increases, it has been argued, depend on past wage increases throughout the economy. In those theoretical and econometric models of inflation where labor markets are aggregated into a single market, this relationship is expressed as an autoregressive equation of fixed structure: current wage increase depends on past wage increases. The same description applies when past wage increases enter indirectly, mediated by price inflation and productivity change. The process of mutual interdependence of market wages is a good deal more complex and less mechanical than these aggregated models suggest.

Reference standards for wages differ from market to market. The equilibrium wage increase in each market will be some function of past wages in all markets, and perhaps of past prices, too. But the function need not be the same in every market. Wages of workers contiguous in geography, industry, and skill will be heavily weighted. Imagine a wage pattern matrix of coefficients describing the dependence of the percentage equilibrium wage increase in each market on the past increases in all other markets. The coefficients in each row are non-negative and sum to one, but their distribution across markets and time lags will differ from row to row.

Consider the properties of such a system in the absence of disequilibrium inputs. First, the system has the "natural rate" property that its steady state is indeterminate. Any rate of wage increase that has been occurring in all markets for a long enough time will continue. Second, from irregular initial conditions the system will move toward one of these steady states, but which one depends on the specifics of the wage pattern matrix and the initial conditions. Contrary to some pessimistic warnings there is no arithmetic compulsion that makes the whole system gravitate in the direction of its most inflationary sectors. The ultimate steady-state inflation will be at most that of the market with the highest initial inflation rate, and at least that of the market with the lowest initial inflation rate. It need not be equal to the average inflation rate at the beginning, but may be either greater or smaller. Third, the adjustment paths are likely to contain cyclical components, damped or at most of constant amplitude, and during adjustments both individual and average wage movements may diverge substantially in both directions from their ultimate steady-state value. Fourth, since wage decisions and negotiations occur infrequently, relative wage adjustments involve a lot of catching up and leap-frogging, and probably take a long time. I have sketched the formal properties of a disaggregated wage pattern system of this kind simply to stress again the vast simplification of the one-market myth.

A system in which only relative magnitudes matter has only a neutral equilibrium, from which it can be permanently displaced by random shocks. Even when a market is in equilibrium, it may outdo the recent wage increases in related markets. A shock of this kind, even though it is not repeated, raises permanently the steady-state inflation rate. This is true cost-push – inflation generated neither by previous inflation nor by current excess demand. Shocks, of course, may be negative as well as positive. For example, upward pushes arising from adjustments in relative wage *levels* will be reversed when those adjustments are completed.

To the extent that one man's reference wages are another man's wages, there is something arbitrary and conventional, indeterminate and unstable, in the process of wage setting. In the same current market circumstances, the reference pattern might be 8 per cent per year or 3 per cent per year or zero, depending on the historical prelude. Market conditions, unemployment and vacancies and their distributions, shape history and alter reference patterns. But accidental circumstances affecting strategic wage settlements also cast a long shadow.

Price inflation, as previously observed, is a neutral method of making arbitrary money wage paths conform to the realities of productivity growth, neutral in preserving the structure of relative wages. If expansion of aggregate demand brings both more inflation and more employment, there need be no mystery why unemployed workers accept the new jobs, or why employed workers do not vacate theirs. They need not be victims of ignorance or inflation illusion. They genuinely want more work at feasible real wages, and they also want to maintain the relative status they regard as proper and just.

Guideposts could be in principle the functional equivalent of inflation, a neutral method of reconciling wage and productivity paths. The trick is to find a formula for mutual deescalation which does not offend conceptions of relative equity. No one has devised a way of controlling average wage rates without intervening in the competitive struggle over relative wages. Inflation lets this struggle proceed and blindly, impartially, impersonally, and non-politically scales down all its outcomes. There are worse methods of resolving group rivalries and social conflict.

5. The Role of Monopoly Power

Probably the most popular explanation of the inflationary bias of the economy is concentration of economic power in large corporations and unions. These powerful monopolies and oligopolies, it is argued, are immune from competition in setting wages and prices. The unions raise wages above competitive rates, with little regard for the unemployed and under-employed workers knocking at the gates. Perhaps the unions are seeking a bigger share of the revenues of the monopolies and oligopolies with whom they bargain. But they do not really succeed in that objective, because the corporations simply pass the increased labor costs, along with mark-ups, on to their helpless customers. The remedy, it is argued, is either atomization of big business and big labor or strict public control of their prices and wages.

So simple a diagnosis is vitiated by confusion between levels and rates of change. Monopoly power is no doubt responsible for the relatively high prices and wages of some sectors. But can the exercise of monopoly power generate ever-rising prices and wages? Monopolists have no reason to hold reserves of unexploited power. But if they did, or if events awarded them new power, their exploitation of it would raise their real prices and wages only temporarily.

Particular episodes of inflation may be associated with accretions of monopoly power, or with changes in the strategies and preferences of those who possess it. Among the reasons that wages and prices rose in the face of mass unemployment after 1933 were NRA codes and other early New Deal measures to suppress competition, and the growth of trade union membership and power under the protection of new federal legislation. Recently we have witnessed substantial gains in the powers of organized public employees. Unions elsewhere may not have gained power, but some of them apparently have changed their objectives in favor of wages at the expense of employment.

One reason for the popularity of the monopoly power diagnosis of inflation is the identification of administered prices and wages with concentrations of economic power. When price and wage increases are the outcomes of visible negotiations and decisions, it seems obvious that identifiable firms and unions have the power to affect the course of inflation. But the fact that monopolies, oligopolies, and large unions have discretion does not mean it is invariably to their advantage to use it to raise prices and wages. Nor are administered prices and wages found only in high concentration sectors. Very few prices and wages in a modern economy, even in the more competitive sectors, are determined in Walrasian auction markets.

No doubt there has been a secular increase in the prevalence of administered wages and prices, connected with the relative decline of agriculture and other sectors of self-employment. This development probably has contributed to the inflationary bias of the economy, by enlarging the number of labor markets where the response of money wages to excess supply is slower than their response to excess demand. The decline of agriculture as a sector of flexible prices and wages and as an elastic source of industrial labor is probably an important reason why the Phillips trade-off problem is worse now than in the 1920s. Sluggishness of response to excess supply is a feature of administered prices, whatever the market structure, but it may be accentuated by concentration of power *per se*. For example, powerful unions, not actually forced by competition to moderate their wage demands, may for reasons of internal politics be slow to respond to unemployment in their ranks.

6. Some Reflections on Policy

If the makers of macroeconomic policy could be sure that the zero-inflation rate of unemployment is natural, voluntary, and optimal, their lives would be easy. Friedman told us that all macroeconomic policy needs to do, all it should try to do, is to make nominal national income grow steadily at the natural rate of growth of aggregate supply. This would sooner or later result in price stability. Steady price deflation would be even better, he said, because it would eliminate the socially wasteful incentive to economize money holdings. In either case, unemployment will converge to its natural rate, and wages and prices will settle into steady trends. Under this policy, whatever unemployment the market produces is the correct result. No trade-off, no choice, no agonizing decisions.

I have argued this evening that a substantial amount of the unemployment compatible with zero inflation is involuntary and non-optimal. This is, in my opinion, true whether or not the inflations associated with lower rates of unemployment are steady or ever-accelerating. Neither macroeconomic policy-makers, nor the elected officials and electorates to whom they are responsible, can avoid weighing the costs of unemployment against those of inflation. As Phelps has pointed out, this social choice has an intertemporal dimension. The social costs of involuntary unemployment are mostly obvious and immediate. The social costs of inflation come later.

What are they? Economists' answers have been remarkably vague, even though the prestige of the profession has reinforced the popular view that inflation leads ultimately to catastrophe. Here indeed is a case where abstract economic theory has a powerful hold on public opinion and policy. The prediction that at low unemployment rates inflation will accelerate toward ultimate disaster is a theoretical deduction with little empirical support. In fact the weight of econometric evidence has been against acceleration, let alone disaster. Yet the deduction has been convincing enough to persuade this country to give up billions of dollars of annual output and to impose sweeping legal controls on prices and wages. Seldom has a society made such large immediate and tangible sacrifices to avert an ill defined, uncertain, eventual evil.

According to economic theory, the ultimate social cost of anticipated inflation is the wasteful use of resources to economize holdings of currency and other non-interest-bearing means of payment. I suspect that intelligent laymen would be utterly astounded if they realized that *this* is the great evil economists are talking about. They have imagined a much more devastating cataclysm, with Vesuvius vengefully punishing the sinners below. Extra trips between savings banks and commercial banks? What an anticlimax!

With means of payment – currency plus demand deposits – equal currently to 20 per cent of GNP, an extra percentage point of anticipated inflation embodied in nominal interest rates produces in principle a social cost of $\frac{2}{10}$ of 1 per cent of GNP per year. This is an outside estimate. An unknown, but substantial, share of the stock of money belongs to holders who are not trying to economize cash balances and are not near any margin where they would be induced to spend resources for this purpose. These include hoarders of large-denomination currency, about one-third of the total currency in public hands, for reasons of privacy, tax evasion, or illegal activity. They include tradesmen and consumers whose working balances turn over too rapidly or are too small to justify any effort to invest them in interest-bearing assets. They include corporations who, once they have been induced to undertake the fixed costs of a sharp-pencil money management department, are already minimizing their cash holdings. They include businessmen who are in fact being paid interest on demand deposits, although it takes the form of preferential access to credit and other bank services. But, in case anyone still regards the waste of resources in unnecessary transactions between money and interest-bearing financial assets as one of the major economic problems of the day, there is a simple and straightforward remedy, the payment of interest on demand deposits and possibly, with ingenuity, on currency too.

The ultimate disaster of inflation would be the breakdown of the monetary payments system, necessitating a currency reform. Such episodes have almost invariably resulted from real economic catastrophes – wars, defeats, revolutions, reparations – not from the mechanisms of wage–price push with which we are concerned. Acceleration is a scare word, conveying the image of a rush into hyperinflation as relentlessly deterministic and monotonic as the motion of falling bodies. Realistic attention to the disaggregated and stochastic nature of wage and price movements suggests that they will show diverse and irregular fluctuations around trends that are difficult to discern and extrapolate. The central trends, history suggests, can accelerate for a long, long time without generating hyperinflations destructive of the payments mechanism.

Unanticipated inflation, it is contended, leads to mistaken estimates of relative prices and consequently to misallocations of resources. An example we have already discussed is the alleged misallocation of time by workers who over-estimate their real wages. The same error would lead to a general over-supply by sellers who contract for future deliveries without taking correct account of the increasing prices of the things they must buy in order to fulfill the contract. Unanticipated deflation would cause similar miscalculations and misallocations. Indeed, people can make these same mistakes about relative prices even when the price level is stable. The mistakes are more likely, or the more costly to avoid, the greater the inflationary trend. There are costs in setting and announcing new prices. In an inflationary environment price changes must be made more frequently – a new catalog twice a year instead of one, or some formula for automatic escalation of announced prices. Otherwise, with the interval between announcements unchanged, the average misalignment of relative prices will be larger the faster the inflation. The same problem would arise with rapid deflation.

Unanticipated inflation and deflation – and unanticipated changes in relative prices – are also sources of transfers of wealth. I will not review here the rich and growing empirical literature on this subject. Facile generalizations about the progressivity or equity of inflationary transfers are hazardous; certainly inflation does not merit the cliché that it is "the cruelest tax". Let us not forget that unemployment has distributional effects as well as deadweight losses.

Some moralists take the view that the government has promised to maintain the purchasing power of its currency, but this promise is their inference rather than any pledge written on dollar bills or in the Constitution. Some believe so strongly in this implicit contract that they are willing to suspend actual contracts in the name of anti-inflation.

I have long contended that the government should make low-interest bonds of guaranteed purchasing power available for savers and pension funds who wish to avoid the risks of unforeseen inflation. The common objection to escalated bonds is that they would diminish the built-in stability of the system. The stability in question refers to the effects on aggregate real demand, *ceteris paribus*, of a change in the price level. The Pigou effect tells us that government bondholders whose wealth is diminished by inflation will spend less. This brake on old-fashioned gap inflation will be thrown away if the bonds are escalated. These considerations are only remotely related to the mechanisms of wage and price inflation we have been discussing. In the 1970s we know that the government can, if it wishes, control aggregate demand – at any rate, its ability to do so is only trivially affected by the presence or absence of Pigou effects on part of the government debt.

In considering the intertemporal trade-off, we have no license to assume that the natural rate of unemployment is independent of the history of actual unemployment. Students of human capital have been arguing convincingly that earning capacity, indeed transferable earning capacity, depends on experience as well as formal education. Labor markets soggy enough to maintain price stability may increase the number of would-be workers who lack the experience to fit them for jobs that become vacant.

Macroeconomic policies, monetary and fiscal, are incapable of realizing society's unemployment and inflation goals simultaneously. This dismal fact has long stimulated a search for third instruments to do the job: guideposts and incomes policies, on the one hand, labor market and manpower policies, on the other. Ten to fifteen years ago great hopes were held for both. The Commission on Money and Credit in 1961 (pp. 39–40) hailed manpower policies as the new instrument that would overcome the unemployment–inflation dilemma. Such advice was taken seriously in Washington, and an unprecedented spurt in manpower programs took place in the 1960s. The Council of Economic Advisers set forth wage and price guideposts in 1961–62 in the hope of "talking down" the Phillips curve (pp. 185–90). It is discouraging to find that these efforts did not keep the problem of inflationary bias from becoming worse than ever.

So it is not with great confidence or optimism that one suggests measures to mitigate the trade-off. But some proposals follow naturally from the analysis, and some are desirable in themselves anyway.

First, guideposts do not wholly deserve the scorn that "toothless jawboning" often attracts. There is an arbitrary, imitative component in wage settlements, and maybe it can be influenced by national standards.

Second, it is important to create jobs for those unemployed and discouraged workers who have extremely low probability of meeting normal job specifications. Their unemployment does little to discipline wage increases, but reinforces their deprivation of human capital and their other disadvantages in job markets. The National Commission on Technology, Automation and Economic Progress pointed out in 1966 the need for public service jobs tailored to disadvantaged workers. They should not be "last resort" or make-work jobs, but regular permanent jobs capable of conveying useful experience and inducing reliable work habits. Assuming that the additional services produced by the employing institutions are of social utility, it may well be preferable to employ disadvantaged workers directly rather than to pump up aggregate demand until they reach the head of the queue.

Third, a number of measures could be taken to make markets more responsive to excess supplies. This is the kernel of truth in the market-power explanation of inflationary bias. In many cases, government regulations themselves support prices and wages against competition. Agricultural prices and construction wages are well-known examples. Some trade unions follow wage policies that take little or no account of the interests of less senior members and of potential members. Since unions operate with federal sanction and protection, perhaps some means can be found to insure that their memberships are open and that their policies are responsive to the unemployed as well as the employed.

As for macroeconomic policy, I have argued that it should aim for unemployment lower than the zero-inflation rate. How much lower? Low enough to equate unemployment and vacancies? We cannot say. In the nature of the case there is no simple formula – conceptual, much less statistical – for full employment. Society cannot escape very difficult political and intertemporal choices. We economists can illuminate these choices as we learn more about labor markets, mobility, and search, and more about the social and distributive costs of both unemployment and inflation. Thirty-five years after Keynes, welfare macroeconomics is still a relevant and challenging subject. I dare to believe it has a bright future.

References

Beveridge, W.H., *Full Employment in a Free Society* (New York 1945).

Doeringer, P. and Piore, M., *Internal Labor Markets and Manpower Analysis* (Lexington, Mass. 1971).

Friedman, M., "The Role of Monetary Policy," *Amer. Econ. Rev.*, 58 (Mar. 1968), 1-17.

Hall, R., "Why is the Unemployment Rate so High at Full Employment?," *Brookings Papers on Economic Activity*, 3 (1970), 369-402.

Keynes, J.M., *The General Theory of Employment, Interest, and Money* (New York 1936).

Leijonhufvud, A., *On Keynesian Economics and the Economics of Keynes* (New York 1968).

Lipsey, R.G., "The Relation Between Unemployment and the Rate of Change of Money Wage Rates in the United Kingdom, 1862-1957: A Further Analysis," *Economica*, 27 (Feb. 1960), 1-31.

Parnes, H.S., *Research on Labor Mobility*, Social Science Research Council, Bull. 65 (New York 1954).

Perry, G.L., "Changing Labor Markets and Inflation," *Brookings Papers on Economic Activity*, 3 (1970), 411-41.

Phelps, E.S., "Inflation and Optimal Unemployment Over Time," *Economica*, 34 (Aug. 1967), 254-81.

Phelps, E.S. *et al.*, *Micro-economic Foundations of Employment and Inflation Theory* (New York 1970).

Phillips, A.W., "The Relation Between Unemployment and the Rate of Change of Money Wage Rates in the United Kingdom, 1861-1957," *Economica*, 25 (Nov. 1958), 283-99.

Reynolds, L.G., *The Structure of Labor Markets* (New York 1951).

Schultze, C.L., "Has the Phillips Curve Shifted? Some Additional Evidence," *Brookings Papers on Economic Activity*, 2 (1971), 452-67.

Tobin, J., "A Note on the Money Wage Problem," *Quart. J. Econ.*, 55 (May 1941), 508-16.

Commission on Money and Credit, *Money and Credit: Their Influence on Jobs, Prices, and Growth* (Englewood Cliffs 1961).

Economic Report of the President 1962 (Washington 1962).

U.S. National Commission on Technology, Automation, and Economic Progress, *Technology and the American Economy* (Washington 1966).

Notes

[1] This concept is commonly attributed to W.H. Beveridge, but he was actually more ambitious and required a surplus of vacancies.

[2] Phillips himself is not a prophet of the doctrine associated with his curve. His 1958 article was probably the most influential macroeconomic paper of the last quarter century. But Phillips simply presented some striking empirical findings, which others have replicated many times for many economies. He is not responsible for the theories and policy conclusions his findings stimulated.

[3] See Lucas and Rapping, pp. 257-305, in Phelps *et al.* (1970).

PART V

THE CONSUMPTION FUNCTION

CHAPTER 29

THE CONSUMPTION FUNCTION

Economists have long been interested in the factors determining the proportions in which a society divides its income between consumption and saving. In the past thirty years theoretical and empirical investigation of these factors has been focused by the concept of the *consumption function*, a list of the variables that influence *consumption* together with the direction and magnitude of their effects. *Income* itself is, of course, high on any such list; and much of recent investigation has concerned the nature, reliability, and measurement of the dependence of consumption on income.

Since *saving* is by definition the difference, positive or negative, between *income* and *consumption*, whatever relationships are summarized in a consumption function can equally well be summarized in a saving function. It is a matter of indifference whether attention is directed to the determinants of consumption or to the determinants of saving; the results of one approach can always be translated into the other. For example, the proposition that U.S. households in the aggregate spend for consumption 93 per cent of their income after taxes can also be stated by saying that they save 7 per cent of the income at their disposition. In either form, incidentally, the statement is no better than a good first approximation.

1. Reasons for Interest in Consumption-saving Behavior

Why have economists been interested in the division of social income between consumption and saving? There are two main reasons. The first

Prepared for, and with minor condensation printed in, *International Encyclopedia of the Social Sciences*, Vol. III (1968), pp. 358-68.

is the importance of saving for accumulation of the wealth of nations and for growth in their capacity to produce goods and services. Broadly speaking, consumption uses productive resources in the present, while saving enlarges the resources available for production and consumption in the future, by increasing stocks of finished goods or materials, productive plant and equipment, and net claims on foreign countries.

In practice it is difficult to measure these concepts of social accounting – net national product or income, consumption, saving, and wealth – in ways that correspond to the fundamental distinction between provision for the present and provision for the future. Very likely saving, as measured in our national accounts, understates our society's provision for the future. One problem is to measure the value of the services rendered by existing stocks of producers' and consumers' durable goods, and to allow for their depreciation and obsolescence. This is difficult enough for business plant and equipment. Housing is the only consumers' durable asset for which such accounts are estimated; for other consumers' durable goods, consumption is simply equated to new purchases. And no attempt is made in U.S. national accounts to estimate the accumulation of real wealth by governments, even before allowance for depreciation.

An even greater practical and conceptual problem, which has attracted considerable research interest recently (see Schultz et al., 1962), is to identify and to measure the saving embodied in human beings in the form of increased education, new skills, and greater capacities. The national accounts do not now count any educational outlays as saving nor associate with them any increase in national wealth.

In spite of these and other difficulties, there can be no doubt of the importance for economic growth of the processes of individual and social decision which determine the share of saving, as conventionally measured, in net national product. This has been underscored in recent years by the shortages of capital confronting the less developed countries.

The second principal reason for concern with the consumption function is an outgrowth of the Great Depression of the 1930s, and of the revolutions in economic thought and policy to which it led. An economy will not produce at the rate which its manpower and capital resources permit unless total effective demand for goods and services suffices to purchase its capacity, or "full employment" output. If private consumption demand falls short of capacity output, the difference must be made up by non-consumption spending: private investment at home or abroad, and government expenditure. If these sources of demand do not absorb the saving which the economy would perform at full employment, then output, employment, and the use of industrial capacity will all fall short of their full employment levels. The national propensity to save will not be realized in additions to national wealth but wasted in unemployment and idle capacity.

The observation that saving is not always an unmixed blessing has a long history, associated with "under-consumption" explanations of the business cycle. But it received its most sophisticated, convincing, and influential expression in J.M. Keynes's *General Theory of Employment, Interest, and Money* (1936). Keynes emphasized that consumption is on the whole a predictable and reliable component of aggregate demand. He saw investment spending, in contrast, as inherently volatile and unstable. And in its periodic failure to use the potential saving of the economy he found the main reason for the repeated lapses of capitalist economies into recession and depression. He feared, further, a chronic tendency in wealthy countries for full employment saving to outrun investment, leading in the absence of corrective policies to chronic un-employment.

The same theoretical apparatus can be applied to the opposite problem, excess demand and inflation, even though this was not the economic disease originally at the center of Keynes's attention. Inflation occurs when non-consumption spending, by governments or private enterprises, more than fills the gap between full employment output and the consumption expenditure which it normally induces.

Keynes's theory was the major impetus to research on the consump-tion function in recent decades. This theoretical impetus was reinforced by the simultaneous development of national accounts providing the statistical raw material for empirical research on the subject. Note that the Keynesian motivation for understanding the social choice between consumption and saving does not require, to the same degree as the growth motivation first mentioned, close identification of consumption with the present and saving with the future. What is more important for Keynes's purpose is identification of consumption with the predictable, and investment with the volatile, elements of national expenditure.

2. Keynes's "Propensity to Consume"

Keynes's consumption function is a simple relationship between national consumption – and accordingly national saving – on the one hand, and national income on the other. He called this relationship "the propensity to consume" and derived certain conclusions as to its form from what he asserted to be a "psychological law", i.e., that the community will divide an increase in income in some regular proportion between an increase in consumption and an increase in saving. That is, both the "marginal propensity to consume" (*mpc*) and the "marginal propensity to save" (*mps*) are between zero and one. (By definition the two marginal propensities sum to one.) This is all his theory required, but Keynes went further and speculated that the "average propensity to consume" (*apc*), the share of national income consumed, would be found to decline with increases in total income. This decline could reflect either or both of the following: (a) the *mpc* falls with income; (b) a certain component of consumption expenditure is independent of income – this means that the *apc* will be lower for higher incomes even if the *mpc* is constant, as is illustrated in Figure 29.1. Evidently Keynes believed in both.

Figure 29.1 displays a Keynesian consumption function and in the lower panel the corresponding saving function. Along the horizontal axes is measured net national income (Y). The vertical axis represents consumption (C) in the upper panel and saving (S) in the lower. The 45° line from the origin in the upper panel is a reference line, showing how much consumption would be if it were always exactly equal to income. The other line, more gently sloped, is the consumption function. It says that below a break-even level of national income Y_0 the nation will wish to consume more than its income, drawing on past savings. Above Y_0, however, consumption falls short of income, by an increasing margin. The *mpc* is the slope of this line, *m*, positive but less than one. Given $1 increase in income, the community will increase its consumption by $ *m* and increase its saving, or diminish its dissaving, by $ (1 − *m*). In Figure 29.1 the *mpc* is constant; a diminishing *mpc* would be pictured by a consumption function curving away from the 45° reference line, and by an upward curving saving function. But even along the linear consumption function in Figure 29.1, the *apc* declines with income. Below

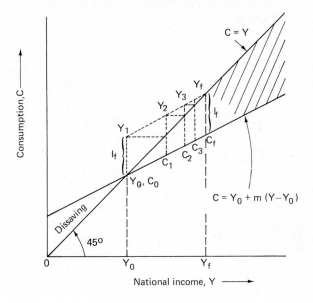

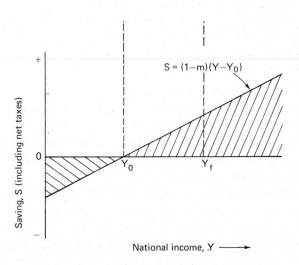

Fig. 29.1. The Keynesian consumption function.

Y_0 the ratio of consumption to income C/Y exceeds one; at Y_0 it is exactly one; above Y_0 it is below one.

3. The Multiplier

The use which Keynes made of the consumption function in explaining unemployment can also be indicated in Figure 29.1. Net national product or income Y is three things at once:

(a) The sum of the incomes earned for productive services (wages and salaries, interest, rents, profits), plus taxes paid by businesses prior to the payment or calculation of these factor incomes. (National accounting practice distinguishes *net national product* and *national income,* by deducting these "indirect business taxes" from *net national product* in order to arrive at *national income.* This means that *net national product* measures the market value of net output, at prices which include these taxes, while *national income* values production at prices corresponding to the income payments to productive factors. This distinction is not made in this essay; the two terms are used interchangeably to refer to the market value of net output).

(b) The total market value of goods and services produced.

(c) Total purchases of goods and services, the sum of consumption expenditure, private investment, and government purchases. To sustain any given level of production and income, say Y_f, total spending must add up to Y_f. Since consumption spending will amount only to C_f, non-consumption spending must make up the difference. If Y_f represents the full employment potential of the economy, failure of non-consumption spending to reach I_f would mean failure of production and income to attain Y_f. The result would be unemployment and excess capacity. (Likewise, should non-consumption spending exceed I_f, total demand would tend to exceed Y_f, causing inflation.)

Further, the consumption function enabled Keynes to say by how much national income would fall short, for a given shortfall in non-consumption expenditure. A difference of a dollar in non-consumption expenditure means a difference of more than a dollar in national income. The *multiplier* which expresses this relationship depends on the *mpc*. In Figure 29.1, for example, if non-consumption spending is equal to zero instead of to I_f, income will be at the break-even level Y_0 instead of at Y_f. The difference in income $(Y_f - Y_0)$ is $1/(1 - m)$ times the difference in non-consumption spending I_f. The multiplier is $1/(1 - m)$. Thus if the national mpc is $\frac{3}{4}$, the multiplier is 4; if the mpc is $\frac{2}{3}$, the multiplier is 3; and so on.

The multiplier is a measure of the response of total production, income, and employment to changes in non-consumption spending – whether these changes reflect natural volatility of private investment or conscious policy in public expenditure. It was in the latter context that the concept of the multiplier was first advanced, by Kahn (1931), as a means of estimating the response of employment to public works expenditure during the depression.

The dynamics of the multiplier can be exhibited by assuming, along with Kahn and many other writers, a lag in the adjustment of consumption to income. Suppose non-consumption spending was initially zero, and income and consumption were in equilibrium at $C_0 = Y_0$. Now non-consumption spending rises to I_f and stays there. Initially income and production rise by a like amount, i.e., to $Y_1 = C_0 + I_f$. But then consumption adjusts to Y_1 along the consumption function, and rises to C_1. This raises income to $Y_2 = C_1 + I_f$. The process converges to income Y_f, where the consumption function indicates consumption of C_f, leaving just enough room for the new level of non-consumption spending I_f.

Table 29.1

"Round"	ΔI	$\Delta C = \frac{3}{5} \Delta Y_{-1}$	$\Delta Y = \Delta I + \Delta C$
0	0	0	0
1	10	0	10
2	10	6	16
3	10	9.6	19.6
4	10	11.76	21.76
5	10	13.06	23.06
6	10	13.83	23.83
7	10	14.30	24.30
.	.	.	.
.	.	.	.
∞	10	15	25

For an example with numerical concreteness, take $m = \frac{3}{5}$ and suppose the sustained increase ΔI in non-consumption spending to be 10. Then the process is as presented in Table 29.1, where ΔY, ΔI, and ΔC are the increases in these variables over their *initial* levels.

The dynamic formulation serves to make two points. First, stability requires that the national *mpc* be smaller than one. Otherwise the multiplier process would never converge. An initial stimulus would keep spending and income rising indefinitely. (It is a mistake, therefore, to conclude from the formula, multiplier $= 1/(1 - m)$, that the multiplier is negative if m exceeds one. Rather the whole multiplier concept is inapplicable in that case.) Second, assuming the *mpc* to lie in the normal stable range, as Keynes assumed, a one-shot injection of investment or government expenditure cannot lift income more than temporarily. A sustained higher level of income requires a sustained higher level of non-consumption spending. Multiplier theory offers no comfort for "pump-primers". Temporary stimulus can work only if there are some unstable elements in national spending which can be set into sustained motion by an initial surge in economic activity. According to Keynes, consumption is not an unstable element of this kind.

4. Price and Population Adjustments

The consumption–income relation is intended to link *real* per capita magnitudes, measured in constant prices. An increase in national income in Figure 29.1, for example, represents an increase in production and purchasing power rather than an increase in the prices at which production is valued. The community cannot be expected to react to a doubling of money income in the same way when it reflects a doubling of prices and wages with real output constant as when it reflects a doubling of output with prices constant. Creating a new franc by deleting two zeros from the old one should not change anyone's basic behavior. Of course actual price movements are not so uniform, universal, and neutral as de Gaulle's decimal reform. Consequently both the level of prices and their rate of change may affect the relation between real consumption and real income; some of these possible effects will be mentioned below.

For somewhat similar reasons, the variables in the consumption function must also be corrected for changes in population. The logic of the argument that the average propensity to consume is lower when society is better off implies that an increase in real national income accompanied by an equal proportionate rise in prices or in population would leave the average propensity to consume unchanged. Consequently the variables in Figure 29.1 should be regarded as *per capita* measures. (The theoretically appropriate correction for population change is somewhat more complicated. Presumably persons of different age, sex, and family status have different consumption requirements and should receive different weights, as in the "equivalent adult" procedures used in studies of food consumption.) However, this gross correction for population change is not the end of the story, any more than simple "deflation" for price changes disposes entirely of price effects.

Both price and population changes play important roles in recent theories of the consumption function, as will be noted below.

5. The Reliability of the Multiplier

Although the propensity to consume and the multiplier have become standard items in the tool kits of economists, they have not gone un-challenged. When quarterly income and consumption data became available in the U.S.A. after the Second World War, they showed erratic fluctuations in the response of consumption to quarter-to-quarter changes in income. And at times, notably during the Korean War, there have been wide swings in the propensity to consume. Some critics, e.g., Burns (1954), have questioned the view that consumption is a particularly stable or predictable element in national expenditure, that consumers respond passively to shocks originating in business investment and government expenditure. In their view the multiplier is not a reliable tool of analysis and prediction, certainly not one that can be applied mechanically. It should be noted that the multiplier multiplies error as well as truth in translating fluctuations of non-consumption expenditure into predicted changes in national product.

In a series of statistical studies, most recently Friedman and Meiselman (1963), Friedman has argued that multiplier analysis performs less well in explaining fluctuations of national product than an alternative model of equal simplicity relating national product to the quantity of money. In a different vein, Katona, e.g., in (1960), has contended that consumers in a modern rich society possess sufficient discretion and autonomy to originate, not just respond to, fluctuations in overall economic activity. Consequently he has pioneered in conducting surveys of consumer intentions and attitudes, which can be used to improve the short-run forecasts of consumer behavior made from conventional economic variables. (See Katona and Mueller, 1953, 1956.) The record suggests that these surveys contain useful forecasting information, at least for the short-run timing of the durable goods component of consumer expenditures.

A doubt of somewhat different import concerns a possible ambiguity in the direction of causal influence between income and consumption. Keynes, and virtually all subsequent writers on the consumption function, take income to be the determining, and consumption the determined, variable. The income of an individual or household or corporation is assumed to be outside its control, at least in the short run. It is a datum, determined by market forces, constraining consumption and saving decisions. But there are many opportunities in an advanced economy for households to adjust their incomes, by working more or less, by movement of wives and other secondary earners in or out of the labor force. A study by Rosett (1958), for example, shows the influence of the financial position of the household on the labor force participation of wives. It is possible that many households adjust their incomes to their consumption standards, rather than vice versa. One way of looking at this difficulty is to attribute it to the failure to count leisure, and other uses of time alternative to gainful employment, as both income and consumption. An analogous opportunity is presumably available to some corporations; that is, if they are in need of profits to pay dividends or to make investments, they can take steps to increase them.

6. National versus Household Propensities to Consume

Keynes was concerned with the propensity to consume of a whole society, the relation of its consumption to its net national product. The difference between these magnitudes takes various forms: household saving, the retained earnings of enterprises, the receipts of governments. Accordingly, the national consumption function reflects a variety of social institutions and patterns of behavior, a mixture of family, business, and political habits and decisions. If it is based on any psychological law, the law must be founded in social psychology rather than in the psychology of individual consumers and savers.

Personal saving proper is defined as the difference between private consumption and *personal disposable income* – the *income* of which individuals and households have wholly free disposition. This differs from net national product by the sum of (a) taxes and other government receipts, net of government "transfer payments", which are in the nature of negative taxes (pensions, benefits, subsidies, etc. for which no current productive services are rendered); and (b) the net earnings, after taxes, retained by corporations. The national *mpc* depends not only on the response of consumers to an increase in disposable income, but also on the response of personal disposable income to an increase in net national product. The latter response, in turn, reflects (a) the sensitivity of government tax receipts (net of transfer payments) – state and local as well as federal – to increases in national product; and (b) the share of corporate profits after taxes in such increases, together with the "propensity" of corporate directors to retain these earnings rather than to disburse them as dividends. In the analytical framework of the *General Theory*, a change in any of this complex of relationships would shift the consumption function, changing its level and perhaps its slope and shape. For example, tax rate reductions, increases in public welfare payments, increases in corporate dividends, reductions in the share of profits in national product – these would all raise the national propensity to consume. This could happen even though the thriftiness of households, as measured by their propensity to consume from disposable income, remained unchanged.

The practical quantitative importance of this observation can be illustrated from recent experience in the U.S.A. In the short run at least, both the *apc* and *mpc* from disposable income appear to be between 0.90 and 0.95. But the *apc* with respect to net national product is about 0.70, and the *mpc* about 0.55. Thus the gap between disposable income and net national product accounts for the major part of the gap between consumption and net national product.

Of course not all the difference between net national product and private consumption is saving in the sense of augmenting national wealth and future consumption possibilities. On the expenditure side, the counterpart of this gap includes government purchases of goods and services as well as net private investment. Some government expenditure is investment in the future, and some is collective consumption. Unfortunately our present government accounting techniques do not permit a useful quantitative classification. But, as observed above, this is not crucial for the purpose for which Keynes designed the consumption function.

Subsequent theoretical and empirical investigation has not followed Keynes in postulating a single stable relationship linking consumption to national product. Instead "the consumption function" has come to have a narrower meaning: the relationship of consumption to disposable income and other variables. The linkages between disposable income and national product have been set to one side for independent investigation. Despite the fact that they are of greater quantitative importance than household saving proper, less theoretical and statistical effort has been expended on them. See, however, Ruggles and Ruggles (1956).

It is true that to a certain extent the structure of government taxes and transfer payments is a matter of economic stabilization policy, to be regarded not as an institutional datum, but as a counterweight to be deliberately adjusted for variations in private spending. But this is true to only a limited degree even of many central governments, and hardly at all of subordinate governments. Functions relating tax revenues and transfer payments to national product and its components, on the basis of given legislation, are of course computed for government budgetary purposes. This is only half the job of the economic analyst, for he must assume that legislation itself will respond to changes in national product and other economic magnitudes.

In respect to corporate saving, Lintner (1953) has pioneered with an empirically tested theory of dividend pay-outs in lagged response to after-tax profits. But much remains to be done on the determinants of disposable corporate income itself, in relation to national product, tax rates, depreciation accounts, and other variables. It is clear, however, that profits – and therefore corporate saving – are highly sensitive to cyclical fluctuations of national product.

Although this division of labor is probably an advance over Keynes's global approach, the propensity to save from disposable income is surely not entirely independent of corporate saving or of certain tax payments. Retained earnings do not enter disposable income, but they are reflected in the value of corporate stocks and thus in the wealth of households and individuals. Accumulation of wealth by this route may substitute for personal saving; evidence that wealth affects the household propensity to save is noted below. Tax payments connected with social security programs are excluded from both disposable income and personal saving, even though private withholdings from wages and salaries for similar purposes are counted as both income and saving. One may suspect that socialization of saving for retirement, medical emergencies, and unemployment would lower the apparent propensity to save from personal disposable income. But it is hard to support this suspicion empirically.

What follows will concern the consumption function in the narrower sense, the division of disposable income between consumption and personal saving.

7. The Postwar Reappraisal of the Keynesian Function

The Keynesian consumption function, typified in Figure 29.1, fits admirably two kinds of empirical data. First, economy-wide time series of consumption and income for the period between the two world wars lie along a function of the Keynesian type; there are even observations of negative private saving in the depths of the Great Depression. Second, any cross-section survey of household budgets appears to confirm the "psychological law" at a microeconomic level. When households are classified into income brackets, and the average consumption for a bracket is plotted against income, the scatter of points traces out a path (Engel curve) like the consumption function of Figure 29.1. Dissaving in low brackets gives way to positive saving at higher levels. Indeed some survey evidence suggests that the *mpc* falls in high brackets.

After the Second World War, however, several pieces of evidence combined to cast doubt on the Keynesian consumption function. The reappraisal that followed led to new theories and deeper empirical investigation of the determinants of household consumption.

First, extrapolations of statistical consumption functions based on prewar U.S. data to potential postwar income levels greatly underestimated the postwar propensity to consume. These extrapolations led some analysts to pessimistic views of postwar economic prospects in the U.S.A., which were in the event quite unjustified. These extrapolations were based either on interwar time series, e.g., Smithies *et al.* (1945), or on the Engel curves relating household consumption and income in prewar budget studies, e.g. Cornfield *et al.* (1947).

The Keynesian propensity to consume is primarily a tool for the short run, for analysis of the determination of income and employment during a business cycle or a period of underemployment. The failure of the postwar forecasts did not impair its usefulness for this primary purpose. Moreover, Keynes certainly did not exclude shifts in the consumption function, and no doubt he himself would have understood the significance of the artificial shortages of consumers' goods and the abnormal accumulations of liquid savings which a great war leaves in its aftermath. At the same time, many of his *obiter dicta* suggest that he expected rich capitalist societies to face in the long run a chronic and increasing excess of potential saving at full employment. Experience since the war, persisting beyond its immediate legacy of backlogs and liquidity, compels a considerable modification of this expectation.

Second, just as the interwar Keynesian consumption function forecasts too much saving after the Second World War, it "backcasts" too little saving before the first. Indeed it would not indicate any positive saving until about 1908, when per capita income reached the break-even point observed during the depression. One does not require data to know that U.S. economic growth in the 19th and early 20th centuries was not generated from dissaving. But a statistical study by Kuznets (1946) provided the data, showing that the share of capital formation in U.S. output, averaged for overlapping decades, has been roughly constant since the Civil War. Moreover, Brady and Friedman (1947) took the trouble to look at earlier household budget studies, going as far back as 1901. They found that, while any one survey indicates the same kind of Keynesian consumption–income relationship observed in the 1935–36 study, the relationship shifts upward in successive surveys. A family with, say, an income of $3000, corrected for price changes, will in general be observed to save much less in 1918 than in 1901, still less in 1935, and, as it has later turned out, less in 1950 than in 1935 or 1941. This finding, of course, undermines the simple use of the Engel curve of a cross-section survey for prediction or aggregation. The hypothesis which Brady and Friedman offered to explain the finding anticipates that of Duesenberry, which will be discussed below.

Recognition of these facts led a number of investigators to formulate and test hypotheses which would explain them – broadly speaking, hypotheses which would reconcile the short-run or cyclical success of the Keynesian consumption function with its long-run or secular failure. Indeed as early as 1943 Samuelson (1943) proposed a "ratchet" model: Consumption grows in the long run roughly in proportion to income; but during cyclical interruptions of long-run growth consumers defend living standards already attained, and consequently consumption follows a flatter (lower *mpc*) Keynesian path. In independent but similar contributions, Duesenberry (1948) and Modigliani (1949) formalized the ratchet idea and tested it statistically, making the *apc* depend inversely on the ratio between current income and previous peak income. Brown (1952), proposed a slight modification, using previous peak consumption rather than peak income.

These formulations do the trick in a statistical sense. They do it by eliminating absolute real income from the determination of the long-run average propensity to consume, which becomes a constant. Why should this be so?

8. Relative Income

Duesenberry (1949) offered one explanation, his "relative income" hypothesis. Consumer utility depends, he reasoned, not on absolute amounts of consumption but on the relation of these amounts to the consumption of others with whom the consumer feels in social competition or under pressure to conform. This hypothesis has obvious support in many findings of modern sociology and psychology, and in some older ideas of Veblen. Duesenberry's hypothesis rationalizes the Brady–Friedman findings, in much the same way they themselves suggest. The pattern of any one cross-section reflects the fact that the consumption leaders, in the upper ranks of the income distribution, can "afford" high propensities to save, while the followers in the lower ranks respond to social pressures by high propensities to consume. A general increase in absolute incomes, leaving the relative income distribution unchanged, will leave unchanged both these social pressures and the responses to them in terms of shares of income consumed. Most of the differences between successive budget surveys disappear when consumption ratios are plotted not against absolute incomes but against relative income positions. The broad conclusion is that while substantial changes over time in the inequality of incomes might alter the aggregate consumption ratio – contrary to the usual view, equalization would tend to increase the saving ratio – sheer growth in per capita income will not.

A basic theoretical difficulty with the relative income hypothesis is that it ignores the essential intertemporal nature of the consumption-saving choice. If high current consumption is the means to social status today, high future consumption is the means to social status tomorrow. Just like the individualistic consumer of traditional theory, Duesenberry's consumer must consult his expectations of future income and his time preference in balancing consumption now against consumption later. The relative income hypothesis is not really a substitute for the intertemporal analysis explicit in the permanent income and life cycle theories discussed in the next section. The pressures of interpersonal comparison seem more central to other choices: visible and conspicuous consumption against other goods and services, work versus leisure.

9. Permanent and Lifetime Income

Friedman (1957) and Modigliani and Brumberg (1954) have in independent contributions offered an alternative explanation of the same phenomena. Students of household consumption behavior, e.g., Mack (1948), have long observed that incomes other than current incomes affect current consumption. Consumers suffering income declines resist departures from their previous consumption standards; and those enjoying income gains generally consume less than other households who long ago achieved the same income level. Similarly, the Katona–Mueller studies (1953, 1956), and other investigations of Katona and his colleagues at the Survey Research Center, indicate that optimistic expectations of future incomes encourage current consumption, while pessimistic expectations have the reverse effect.

According to Friedman's "permanent income hypothesis", the consumption of a household is proportional to its *permanent income*, i.e., the average income it expects to earn over its planning horizon. Friedman is not definite about either the factor of proportionality – which might vary with the household's stage in the life cycle, its wealth, the interest rate, and other variables – or about the length of the planning horizon. On these matters the *lifetime income* hypothesis of Modigliani is much more explicit, as will be seen below. In any case, Friedman employs his hypothesis to explain both the evidence of cross-section budget surveys and the ratchet effect observed in aggregate time series.

In budget surveys the low-income brackets are bound to be abnormally loaded with families temporarily below their permanent incomes, while the high brackets naturally have more than their share of families temporarily above their permanent status. This is the reason that the low brackets in any cross-section exhibit a higher propensity to consume, relative to measured current incomes, than the high brackets – even though the propensity to consume from permanent incomes, unobserved, may be the same for all groups. When the households of a cross-section are classified, not by current incomes but by other observed attributes – occupation, educational attainment, residence, age – better correlated with permanent income status, the scatter of points relating average consumption to average income gives a better approximation of the long-run consumption function. It starts from the origin – after all, groups with low permanent income status cannot do much dissaving – and shows a higher marginal propensity to consume than the usual Engel curve. (See Watts, 1958.) Whether this *mpc* is a constant or diminishing function of income is, however, an open empirical question.

As for the ratchet effect, many households are below their permanent incomes in recessions and depressions; therefore their consumption is high relative to their current incomes. Like the "previous peak" hypotheses discussed above, this explanation is more satisfactory for recessions clearly believed to be temporary than for prolonged depression periods like the thirties when the memory of the preceding peak grows faint.

The Modigliani–Brumberg model is in the same spirit. But by being bolder in its assumptions it is more specific in its conclusions. In its most stark formulation, the planning horizon of the individual consumer is his whole lifetime. And the factor of proportionality between consumption and permanent income is simply one. Individuals are assumed to plan no net lifetime saving; they transfer to their heirs no more and no less than they inherited. Subject to this constraint, they try to spread their lifetime consumable resources evenly over their lives. In particular, they seek to accumulate enough savings during their earning years to maintain the same consumption standard during their years of retirement. The division of life between work and retirement is taken, somewhat implausibly, as an institutional fact, a constant independent of national and individual incomes. The model has several interesting implications:

(a) In a society with stationary population and income, aggregate net personal saving would be zero. The dissaving of the retired would exactly offset the saving of the workers, whose only purpose in saving is to provide for their own future retirement.

(b) In a society with growing population or growing per capita income or both, aggregate net personal saving will be positive. Indeed the higher are these rates of growth, the higher will be the ratio of saving to aggregate income. For in a growing economy, the retired of the future always exceed, in number or in lifetime income or in both, the retired of the present. Consequently the saving necessary to provide for future retirements always exceeds the dissaving of the currently retired. See Farrell (1959) and Modigliani and Ando (1963) for precise calculations.

(c) Changes in this year's income affect this year's consumption only to the extent that current consumption benefits, equally with consumption in all future years, from a general recalculation of lifetime consumable resources. This effect will not be large unless current income changes are regarded as permanent. This is the counterpart of Friedman's more extreme contention that all temporary income gains will be saved and none consumed, and symmetrically that temporary income losses will be wholly offset by dissaving.

This implication of the two models has attracted widespread attention and controversy. One reason is that it casts doubt on the efficacy of temporary changes in tax rates or income transfers as measures of economic stabilization. Some caution is required in drawing this inference from the permanent income or lifetime income hypotheses. Strictly speaking, these theories concern consumption rather than expenditures on consumers' goods, e.g., the use of an automobile rather than its purchase. It may be that temporary windfalls are used to purchase durables but do not appreciably increase their use. But from the standpoint of economic stabilization, the stimulus of such expenditure is equally good whether it is properly classified as saving or as consumption. The pure theories assume, moreover, that there are no obstacles in financial markets to borrowing against expected future incomes. In actual fact many households are at the limits of their lines of credit and are therefore prevented from adjusting current consumption fully to their permanent incomes. Temporary windfalls may increase their consumption expenditures simply by adding to their liquid resources.

Empirical measurement of the *mpc* from temporary income has not been conclusive. But Bodkin (1959) concluded that the households of veterans who received unexpected national service life insurance dividends during the 1950 budget survey spent significantly more than households similar to them in income and in other respects. Using different methods and data, Watts (1958) estimated the *mpc* from temporary income to be significantly positive, though perhaps only half of the *mpc* from permanent income. Watts's results also indicated that household reaction to temporary income changes may not be symmetrical for positive and negative changes.

(d) An individual whose life proceeds according to plan will gradually build up his wealth, so that at any age his wealth plus his remaining expected earnings during working years just suffice to maintain his consumption throughout his lifetime, including his years of retirement. To every age corresponds a normal ratio of wealth to income. But unexpected income changes, consumption emergencies, or capital gains and losses on past savings may cause an individual's wealth to deviate from its normal relation to income. A high wealth–income ratio permits the individual to consume more, both now and in retirement, while a low wealth–income ratio requires him to consume a lower fraction of his current income in order to provide for undiminished consumption in retirement. Extended to the whole population, this argument suggests that the aggregate saving ratio depends inversely on the wealth–income ratio. Along with the effects of growth rates mentioned in (b), this is the major aggregative implication of the lifetime income hypothesis.

Although the *relative* and *permanent*, or *lifetime*, income hypotheses are alternative explanations of many of the same phenomena, there is no reason in principle why the two theories cannot be married. (See Fellner, 1959.)

10. Wealth and the Propensity to Consume

The importance of wealth in the consumption function had been urged by several earlier writers, e.g., Ackley (1951). They based their view on more general considerations than those involved in the Modigliani–Brumberg model. In particular, saving may be motivated by the desire to make bequests or other transfers of wealth to the next generation, as well as by the need to even out consumption over the savers' lifetimes. The adequacy of wealth to meet a bequest target – which may itself be a function of lifetime income, of course – will then be one of the determinants of current saving and consumption.

Keynes himself alluded to the possible influence of "unforeseen changes in the money value of wealth". (There are indeed few hypotheses which Keynes cannot be found to have foreshadowed. He even catalogued, though "only for the sake of formal completeness", what he called "changes in expectation of the relation between the present and the future level of income".)

Pigou (1947) emphasized the wealth effect in the course of an abstract theoretical attack on the whole structure of Keynes's *General Theory*. Keynes had contended that in certain circumstances no amount of wage and price deflation could restore aggregate real demand to full employment levels. Pigou pointed out that the real value of private wealth can be indefinitely increased by price deflation. The reason is that deflation would increase the purchasing power of gold, government-issued currency and interest-bearing government debt, all of which are fixed in money value. As the owners of these assets become saturated with real wealth, their propensity to consume is bound to increase. Via what has come to be known as "the Pigou effect", the absolute price level – because of its effect on the real value of private wealth – has a bearing on the propensity to consume.

Quite apart from the theoretical context of Pigou's argument, a general wealth effect is an alternative explanation of some of the same phenomena explained by the other hypotheses under review. Over the long run disposable income and private wealth tend to grow in step, with wealth five to six times income. Recent empirical calculations – see Arena (1963) and Modigliani and Ando (1963) – suggest a marginal propensity to consume from income of 0.5 to 0.7 and from wealth of 0.05 to 0.07. When income and wealth grow in step, estimates in these ranges explain how consumption can consistently take about 90 per cent of increases in disposable income. But the apparent *mpc* from income can be quite different when cyclical fluctuations break the normal long-run linkage of wealth and income. Assuming that the real value of wealth fluctuates less than real income, consumption will appear less sensitive to income in the short run than in the long.

At the level of individual households in budget surveys, the dissaving recorded for the lower brackets is of course supported by past savings. As pointed out by Tobin (1951, here reprinted as Chapter 30), differences in the wealth available to households at a given real income can help to explain the differences observed in different surveys in their propensities to save or to dissave. This explanation is not inconsistent with those by which Duesenberry, Friedman, and Modigliani explain the same phenomenon.

Sometimes the wealth effect on saving and consumption has been attributed to a particular kind of wealth, liquid asset holdings, rather than to total net worth. In theory net worth is the relevant variable. This is the constraint which the past and the market impose on consumers, a constraint which they can change only slowly, and to which they must meanwhile adjust. In contrast, many households can, within wide limits, decide for themselves at each moment of time how much of their wealth they wish to hold in liquid form; and they can implement such decisions very quickly by purchases or sales of other assets and debts. It is not helpful for explanation or prediction to attribute one type of discretionary behavior, saving decisions, to the outcomes of another type of equally discretionary behavior, portfolio choices. (See Tobin, 1952, reprinted as Chapter 5 in Vol. I.) But for many households below the top brackets, liquid assets (bank deposits, savings accounts, savings bonds) are virtually the only assets held; their total serves as a good proxy for total wealth. In other cases, the remaining constituents of net worth are not easily convertible into current purchasing power – home real estate, consumers' durable goods, pension rights. Consumption functions fitted to survey data indicate a positive effect of liquid asset holdings on consumption, especially for households suffering income reverses. See Klein *et al.* (1954) and Guthrie (1954).

11. Income and Wealth Distribution

Aggregate consumption can be affected not only by changes in aggregate income and wealth, but also by changes in the distribution of a given aggregate income or wealth. However, these distributional effects are commonly exaggerated by observers who are struck by the wide discrepancies in average propensities to consume among different economic and social groups. Redistribution will affect total consumption only to the extent that the *marginal* propensities of the affected groups differ. And these appear to differ much less than average propensities. See, for example, Lubell (1947). Nevertheless the prevailing evidence is that certain redistributions of income and wealth would increase saving: for example, from low or middle to top income brackets (see Kuznets, 1953), from employees to self-employed, from urban residents to farm operators.

It is necessary to beware of another frequently heard argument, namely that reduction in taxes levied on individuals with high saving propensities, in particular those in the upper brackets of income and wealth, will by itself increase saving. This increase in disposable income will doubtless increase *personal* saving, and probably by more than equal tax reductions benefiting other groups. But it will increase consumption too. By raising disposable income relative to net national product, it raises the propensity to consume with respect to national product and leaves less room in the economy for non-consumption expenditures.

The hypothesis that "capitalists" save while "workers" spend has a long history, and it has recently been revived in connection with certain analyses of economic growth and development. See, for example, Kaldor (1955, 1961). He has gone so far as to build a theory of the functional distribution of income on the differences between capitalists and workers in marginal propensities to save. Houthakker, who has conducted some pioneering studies of intercountry differences in saving propensities, finds (1957) that the saving ratio appears to be higher in countries where the property share of income is higher. This statistical result can, however, be alternatively rationalized.

This hypothesis may be more relevant to underdeveloped economies with a well-defined division of the population between high-income property-owners and low-income workers than to advanced economies like the U.S.A., where ownership of property is widely diffused and some *rentiers* are poor while some "workers" are rich. But if "capitalists" are identified with corporations and their saving with retained corporate earnings, the proposition has some applicability to the U.S.A.

The importance of the distribution of income has also been stressed in the analysis of "forced saving" during inflation. If wages lag behind prices, and the marginal propensity to consume from profits is less than from wages, the process of inflation suppresses some demand for consumption goods which would occur if prices were stable. The same effect can occur without a change in income distribution if consumers are slow to adjust their money expenditures to rising prices and money incomes. See Keynes (1940), Koopmans (1942) and Smithies (1942).

12. The Rate of Interest

Prior to Keynes the economic variable which economists usually stressed in analyzing the choice between consumption and saving was the interest rate. The classic exposition of the theoretical relation of saving decisions to the rate of interest is Fisher's (1930), and Conard (1959) provides a good review of doctrine on this subject. An increase in the rate of return on saving was expected to tip the balance of choice in favor of the future. But it was recognized that for many positive savers, an increase in interest rates means an overall increase in consumable resources, from which current as well as future consumption might benefit.

Whether because of this real ambiguity or because of the narrow range of variation of observed interest rates, econometricians have not been able to detect significant interest rate effects on saving. Perhaps these effects would be more evident if it were possible to relate net saving not merely to rates paid on savings accounts and bonds, but to the effective rates at which consumers can borrow and the rates of return on business capital, corporate equities, houses, other real estate, and consumer durables. These assets, after all, absorb the bulk of national saving; but their returns are difficult to measure. The positive correlation internationally between saving and the property share of income could be interpreted to mean that saving is higher in those countries where its yield is greater.

13. Other Variables

Observed differences among households in consumption and saving behavior are, of course, attributable to a long list of differences in their circumstances, habits, and preferences. Some of these are, like income and wealth, variables whose influence is the major interest of economists. Others are, like demographic characteristics, variables which can differ widely among households even though their distribution over the population changes only very slowly. It is nonetheless important to measure their effects, if only to disentangle them from the measurement of the influence of variables more important in economic fluctuations and economic policy. Considerable statistical effort has been devoted to the "life cycle" variables (age, marital status, family size and composition) and other demographic characteristics (educational attainment, occupation, race, geographical location). See for example Klein *et al.* (1954) and Lydall (1955).

A set of variables of a different nature are the "psychological" ones – attitudes, intentions, expectations, personality attributes – which Katona and his associates seek to measure. Unlike demographic variables, the distribution of some of these psychological variables in the population may change radically in the short run, in ways that can be ascertained in our present state of knowledge only by new surveys. If household surveys are to contribute further to our understanding of the propensity to consume and make possible more powerful tests of competing theories, they will have to take a longer perspective. To measure the effects of past and expected levels of income and wealth and of retirement and bequest objectives, it is necessary to observe not only the current status of households but their lifetime histories, plans, and aspirations.

References

Ackley, Gardner, "The Wealth-Saving Relationship," *Journal of Political Economy*, 59 (1951), 154-61.

Arena, John, "The Pigou Effect and Consumption: A Statistical Inquiry," *Yale Economic Essays*, Vol. 3, No. 2 (1963).

Bodkin, Ronald, "Windfall Income and Consumption," *American Economic Review*, 49 (1959), 602-14.

Brady, Dorothy S. and Rose D. Friedman, "Savings and Income Distribution," in *Studies in Income and Wealth*, Vol. 10 (New York: National Bureau of Economic Research, 1947).

Brown, T.M., "Habit Persistence and Lags in Consumer Behavior," *Econometrica*, 20 (1952), 355-71.

Burns, Arthur F., *The Frontiers of Economic Knowledge* (Princeton: Princeton University Press, National Bureau of Economic Research, 1954).

Conard, Joseph W., *An Introduction to the Theory of Interest* (Berkeley: University of California Press, 1959).

Cornfield, Jerome, W. Duane and Marvin Hoffenberg, *Full Employment Patterns, 1950* (Washington, D.C.: U.S. Bureau of Labor Statistics, 1947).

Duesenberry, James S., "Income-Consumption Relations and Their Implications," in *Income, Employment and Public Policy, Essays in Honor of Alvin H. Hansen*, Lloyd A. Metzler *et al.* (Eds.) (New York: W.W. Norton & Co., 1948).

Duesenberry, James S., *Income, Saving and the Theory of Consumer Behavior* (Cambridge, Mass.: Harvard University Press, 1949).

Farrell, M.J., "The New Theories of the Consumption Function," *Economic Journal*, 69 (1959), 678-96.

Fellner, William J., "Relative Permanent Income: Elaboration and Synthesis," *Journal of Political Economy*, 67 (1959), 508-11.

Fisher, Irving, *The Theory of Interest* (New York: Macmillan Co., 1930).

Friedman, Milton, *A Theory of the Consumption Function* (Princeton: Princeton University Press, National Bureau of Economic Research, 1957).

Friedman, Milton and David Meiselman, "The Relative Stability of Monetary Velocity and the Investment Multiplier in the United States 1897-1958," in Commission on Money and Credit, *Stabilization Policies* (Englewood Cliffs, N.J.: Prentice-Hall, 1963).

Guthrie, Harold, Changes in the Ratio of Liquid Asset Holdings to Income among Groups of American Consumers between 1947 and 1951 and Some Effects of Liquid Assets on Spending. Unpublished doctoral dissertation, University of Michigan, 1954.

Houthakker, Hendrik S., "An International Comparison of Household Expenditure Patterns, Commemorating the Centenary of Engel's Law," *Econometrica*, 25 (1957), 532-51.

Kahn, Richard F., "The Relation of Home Investment to Unemployment," *Economic Journal*, 41 (1931), 173-98.

Kaldor, N., "Alternative Theories of Distribution," *Review of Economic Studies*, 37 (1955), 94-100.

Kaldor, N., "Capital Accumulation and Economic Growth," in *Theory of Capital*, F.A. Lutz (Ed.) (New York: St. Martin's Press, 1961), pp. 177-222.

Katona, George, *Psychological Analysis of Economic Behavior* (New York: McGraw-Hill, 1951).

Katona, George, *The Powerful Consumer* (New York: McGraw-Hill, 1960).

Katona, George and Eva Mueller, *Consumer Attitudes and Demand, 1950-52* (Ann Arbor: University of Michigan, Survey Research Center, Institute for Social Research, 1953).

Katona, George and Eva Mueller, *Consumer Expectations 1953-56* (Ann Arbor: University of Michigan, Survey Research Center, Institute for Social Research, 1956).

Keynes, J.M., *The Géneral Theory of Employment, Interest and Money* (New York: Harcourt, Brace & Co., 1936).

Keynes, J.M., *How to Pay for the War* (New York: Harcourt, Brace & Co., 1940).

Klein, Lawrence R., George Katona, John B. Lansing, and James N. Morgan, *Contributions of Survey Methods to Economics* (New York: Columbia University Press, 1954).

Koopmans, T.C., "The Dynamics of Inflation," *Review of Economics and Statistics*, 24 (1942), 53.

Kuznets, Simon, *National Product since 1869* (New York: National Bureau of Economic Research, Inc., 1946).

Kuznets, Simon, *Share of Upper Income Groups in Savings* (New York: National Bureau of Economic Research, Inc., 1953).

Lintner, John, "The Determinants of Corporate Savings," in *Savings in the Modern Economy*, Walter W. Heller, Francis M. Boddy and Carl L. Nelson (Eds.) (Minneapolis: University of Minnesota Press, 1953).

Lubell, Harold, "Effects of Redistribution of Income on Consumer's Expenditures," *American Economic Review*, 37 (1947), 930.

Lydall, Harold, "The Life Cycle in Income, Saving, and Asset Ownership," *Econometrica*, 23 (1955), 131-50.

Mack, Ruth P., "The Direction of Change in Income and the Consumption Function," *Review of Economics and Statistics*, 30 (1948), 239-58.

Modigliani, Franco, "Fluctuations in the Saving-Income Ratio: A Problem in Economic Forecasting," in *Studies in Income and Wealth*, Vol. 11 (New York: National Bureau of Economic Research, Inc., 1949).

Modigliani, Franco and Albert Ando, "The Life Cycle Hypothesis of Saving," *American Economic Review*, 53 (1963), 55.

Modigliani, Franco and Richard Brumberg, "Utility Analysis and the Consumption Function: An Interpretation of Cross Section Data," *Post Keynesian Economics* (New Brunswick, N.J.: Rutgers University Press, 1954).

Pigou, A.C., "Economic Progress in a Stable Environment," *Economica*, 14 (1947), 180.

Rosett, Richard N., "Working Wives: An Economic Study," *Studies in Household Economic Behavior* (New Haven: Yale University Press, 1958).

Ruggles, Richard and Nancy Ruggles, *National Income Accounts and Income Analysis* (New York: McGraw-Hill, 1956).

Samuelson, Paul A., "Full Employment after the War," in *Postwar Economic Problems*, Seymour E. Harris ed. (New York: McGraw-Hill, 1943).

Schultz, T.W. *et al.*, "Symposium: Investment in Human Beings," *Journal of Political Economy*, 70 (1962), 1.

Smithies, Arthur, "The Behavior of Money National Income under Inflationary Conditions," *Quarterly Journal of Economics*, 57 (1942), 113-28.

Smithies, Arthur, S. Morris Livingston and Jacob L. Mosak, "Forecasting Postwar Demand I, II, and III," *Econometrica*, 13 (1945), 1.

Tobin, James, "Relative Income, Absolute Income and Saving," in *Money Trade and Economic Growth, Essays in Honor of John Henry Williams* (New York: Macmillan Company, 1951) (Chapter 30 below).

Tobin, James, "Asset Holdings and Spending Decisions," *American Economic Review*, 42 (1952), 109-23 (Vol. 1, chapter 5).

Watts, Harold W., "Long Run Income Expectations and Consumer Saving," in *Studies in Household Economic Behavior, Yale Studies in Economics*, Vol. 9 (New Haven: Yale University Press, 1958).

RELATIVE INCOME, ABSOLUTE INCOME, AND SAVING

1. Two Hypotheses Concerning Consumption Behavior

1.1. Important recent contributions to the study of the consumption function [1] have raised an interesting and crucial question concerning the determination of family consumption behavior. The issue arises most strikingly in the interpretation of family budget data. Does the array of income–consumption points obtained from simultaneous observations of different families represent a relationship between family consumption and family income measured in dollars? Or does it represent a relationship between family consumption and relative income, measured by the position of a family in the income distribution? Students of family budgets, from Engel on, have taken the first interpretation for granted. And in recent years, budget data have frequently been "blown up", on that assumption, to yield predictions of national demand. [2] The assumption has not been employed without misgivings and criticism. But, until the development of the second interpretation, there has been neither a systematic explanation of how the traditional interpretation errs nor a determinate alternative.

The two interpretations give widely differing predictions of family consumption when incomes change, prices and other variables relevant to consumption remaining the same. Under the first interpretation, which will be called the "absolute income" hypothesis, the expected value of the consumption of a family whose new income is y is the observed average consumption of families who formerly received income y. Under the second interpretation, which will be called the "relative income"

Reprinted from *Money, Trade, and Economic Growth* (*Essays in Honor of John Henry Williams*) (New York: Macmillan, 1951).

hypothesis, the expected value of the proportion of income devoted to consumption by a family whose new income is y is the proportion observed for families who formerly stood in the same percentile of the income distribution as families with y do now.

To this difference in prediction of family consumption corresponds, of course, a difference in prediction of national consumption. According to the "absolute income" hypothesis, national consumption can be predicted from a budget survey for any distribution of income, and consequently for any level of national income, merely by weighting appropriately the average consumption observed at every income level. The "relative income" hypothesis denies the validity of this procedure. Indeed, if the distribution of families by relative income – the ratio of family income to mean income – remains unchanged, the new hypothesis predicts that national consumption will be a constant proportion of national income, whatever the level of national income. The number of families at each percentile of the distribution will be the same, and consequently the distribution of families by proportion of income devoted to consumption will be unchanged.

1.2. The "relative income" hypothesis has been developed to explain the division of income between saving and consumption, and it is in this connection that it will be considered here. Presumably it would not be applied without modification to individual consumption goods. However, it has wide implications for the interpretation of budget data. Demand relationships, whether for consumption as a whole or for individual commodities, cannot usually be estimated satisfactorily from time series of national totals alone. If estimates can be obtained from microeconomic data, the statistical difficulties of evaluating the parameters in demand functions from macroeconomic time series are reduced. Such estimates can be derived from budget data on the "absolute income" hypothesis. But if the "absolute income" interpretation is incorrect in regard to saving and total consumption, it cannot be used with any confidence in estimating the demand for components of consumption.

1.3. This paper will be concerned with empirical evidence relevant to a choice between the two hypotheses. There is, of course, a third possibility: that family consumption behavior depends on both absolute income and relative income. Indeed, the intermediate position is very appealing. Each of the two hypotheses rests on an extreme proposition regarding the interdependence of families in consumption behavior. One denies all interdependence, and the other asserts that in a family's preference function consumption is always measured in units of other families' consumption.[3] Nevertheless, the third possibility will be ignored. In the absence of data which would permit the effects on absolute income and relative income to be distinguished, it does not yield determinate predictions.

2. Testing the Two Hypotheses on Continuous Budget Data

2.1. By what test could a choice between the two hypotheses be made? An ideal test would require a socially self-contained group of families, so that any social influences on consumption come from within the group. It would require constancy in all variables affecting consumption, other than incomes. Initially the relationship of family consumption to family income within the group would be observed. Then family incomes and the total group income would be changed. For the new constellation of family incomes, there would be two predictions of the consumption of each family. One would be based on the "absolute income" interpretation, and the other on the "relative income" interpretation, of the initially observed consumption–income relationship. The relative success of the two predictions would provide the basis for choosing between the hypotheses.

2.2. In practice the best approximation to a test of this kind is provided by continuous budget data for identical samples of families. For two samples of Corn Belt farm families, budget records are available over the three years 1940–42.[4] During these three years, most families in these two samples enjoyed large increases in money and real income. Given no information other than the 1940 records, which method would predict more accurately the consumption behavior of these families in 1941 and 1942?

2.3. First, consider the history of the Farm Security Administration (FSA) sample as a whole; this is the larger and, according to the authors, the more reliable of the two. Table 30.1 shows, for this sample, average money and real incomes and percentages consumed over the three years. It also compares the movement of average income for the sample with

Table 30.1
Income and consumption 1940-42

	(1) Average income (FSA sample) (dollars)	(2) Cost of living index (1940 = 100)	(3) Average real income (FSA sample) (1940 = 100)	(4) Real per capita farm income (U.S.A.) (1940 = 100)	(5) Consumption as per cent of income (FSA sample)
1940	2172	100	100	100	53
1941	2792	108	119	134	48
1942	3790	127	137	174	43

Sources and explanation:

Column 1: Net cash farm income, plus off-farm income, plus value of home-produced consumption and imputed rent. Average per family. Cochrane and Grigg, *op. cit.*, Tables 5, 7, 9.

Column 2: Bureau of Agricultural Economics index of prices paid by farmers for family living. Cochrane and Grigg, *ibid.*, p. 38, footnote 12.

Column 3: Column 1 ÷ column 2, converted to index.

Column 4: Net income from farm marketing to persons on farms, per capita, adjusted for changes in cost of living. *Economic Report of the President*, January 1948 (Washington: U.S. Government Printing Office, 1948), Table VI, p. 114.

Column 5: Consumption includes money expenditures plus value of home-produced consumption and imputed rent. Cochrane and Grigg, *op. cit.*, Tables 5, 7, 9.

changes in national farm income over the same period. The decline in the consumption ratio with increases in real income conforms to the "absolute income" hypothesis. On the "relative income" interpretation this ratio should not have decreased. If anything, it should have increased. This sample of farmers did not enjoy as large income gains as farmers in general. On the whole, the position of the sample families in the income distribution of farmers probably declined.

2.4. Second, consider the relationship of family consumption to family income within the sample over the three years. Figure 30.1 shows three scatters, one for each year, of the percentage of income consumed against absolute real income. The coincidence of the three scatters indicates that, not only for the sample as a whole but for families in every income class, the "absolute income" hypothesis yields a good prediction of the consumption ratio.

In testing the "relative income" hypothesis, the ratio of family income to the mean family income of the sample has been taken as the measure

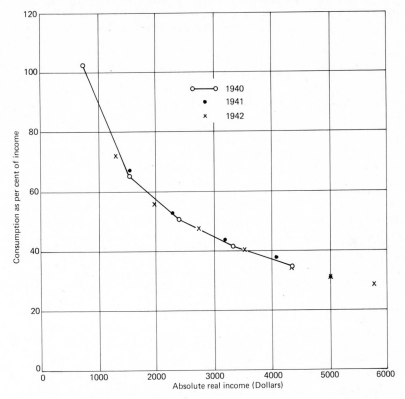

Fig. 30.1. Consumption ratio and absolute real income, FSA sample, 1940-42.

of relative income. That is, family real incomes in the three years have been "deflated" by column 3 of Table 30.1. The use of a measure of relative income of this type is compelled by the absence of yearly income distributions for farmers of this region. The income distributions of the sample cannot be taken to be representative. This measure of relative income probably results in an overstatement of the relative incomes of these families in 1941 and 1942. If their real incomes were deflated by column 4 – average farm income for the nation – their "relative incomes" would be considerably lower. Figure 30.2 embodies the same basic data as Figure 30.1, but here the consumption ratio is plotted against "relative income". The scatters do not coincide, but are progressively lower. Had family incomes been measured in terms not of the sample mean but of the

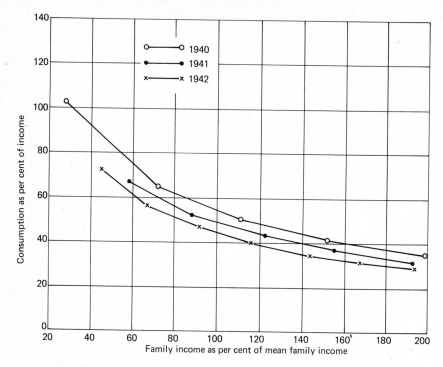

Fig. 30.2. Consumption ratio and relative income, FSA sample, 1940-42.

national mean, the discrepancies would have been even larger. Clearly the "absolute income" hypothesis gives a closer prediction of the consumption behavior of this sample, income group by income group, than the rival interpretation.

2.5. Third, it is possible to follow through the three years three sub-samples of families with common income histories. Table 30.2 gives the history of these sub-samples, along with predictions of their behavior made by the two methods. These predictions are based on the relationships observed for the whole sample in 1940 (Figures 30.1 and 30.2). Errors in the 1940 "prediction" by either method represent deviations of the sub-sample from the average consumption ratio of all families in the same 1940 income class. Thus in the case of sub-samples I and III, if the predictions for 1941 and 1942 by the "absolute income" method were corrected for the fact that in 1940 these groups had higher than average

Table 30.2
Observed and predicted consumption ratios 1940-42
(three sub-samples of the FSA sample)

	(1) Absolute real income (1940 dollars)	(2) "Relative income"	(3) Observed consumption ratio (%)	Predicted consumption ratio	
				(4) "Absolute income" method (%)	(5) "Relative income" method (%)
I (30 families)					
1940	2507	1.15	51	49	49
1941	3300	1.25	44	41	47
1942	3730	1.18	42	38	49
II (50 families)					
1940	2371	1.09	50	50	51
1941	2420	0.87	53	50	60
1942	2920	0.77	47	45	63
III (22 families)					
1940	2480	1.14	54	49	50
1941	3340	1.26	42	41	46
1942	3020	0.96	50	44	56

Sources and explanation:
   Column 1: Cochrane and Grigg, *op. cit.*, Table 41. Money incomes deflated by column 2, Table 1.
   Column 2: Money incomes ÷ column 1, Table 1.
   Column 3: Computed from Cochrane and Grigg., *ibid.*, Table 41.
   Column 4: Found graphically from 1940 scatter in Figure 1, using column (1).
   Column 5: Found graphically from 1940 scatter in Figure 2, using column (2).

propensity to consume, they would be improved. A similar correction would worsen the predictions by the "relative income" method. Again, the "absolute income" hypothesis makes the better predictions.

2.6. It is, of course, possible that the apparent success of the "absolute income" hypothesis and failure of the "relative income" hypothesis are due to lags in the adjustment of consumption to relative income. Perhaps families are guided in making consumption decisions not by their position in the current income distribution but by the position in which their current income would place them in a previous income distribution. The only way of testing this possibility in the FSA sample is to measure family incomes in 1941 and 1942 in terms not of current mean income, but of mean income in the previous year. The results of plotting the

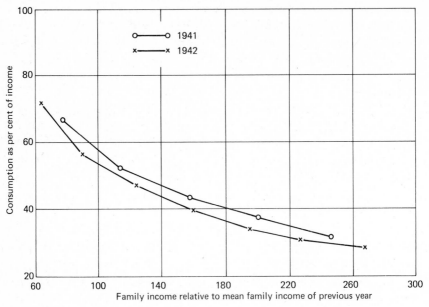

Fig. 30.3. Consumption ratio and lagged relative income, FSA sample, 1941-42.

consumption ratio against relative income, so measured, are displayed in Figure 30.3. Although a lag of this kind improves the prediction the "relative income" hypothesis would make for 1942 from 1941 and 1940 data, it is still not as good as prediction by the other method. The possibility of a lag longer than one year cannot be tested with data for three years.

As has been noted elsewhere,[5] the data for this sample do indicate a lag in the adjustment of consumption to absolute income. At given levels of 1942 income, the consumption ratio is higher the larger the 1940 income. The agreement of the three scatters in Figure 30.1 probably depends, therefore, on the fact that these families generally enjoyed income gains not only during the period of observation but before. That is, the 1940 scatter presumably reflects the influence not only of observed 1940 incomes but also of unobserved but lower 1938 and 1939 incomes. Had incomes in the years before 1940 been at the 1940 level or higher, the 1940 scatter would have been higher and predictions based on it by either method would have been worse.

2.7. The results of performing the same experiments on the other set of data – the "college" sample – are similar and need not be reported here. In the "college" sample, the consumption ratio corresponding to a given level of family real income declines somewhat over the three years. This decline means that neither hypothesis works as well as it does in the FSA sample.

2.8. The value of this test is open to question on the ground that 1942, at least, was a war year in which consumption was low simply because goods were unavailable at quoted prices. From Figure 30.2 it can be seen that the curtailment of consumption on this account would have to be substantial to explain the apparent failure of the "relative income" hypothesis. Moreover, for reasons given in paragraph 2.4 above, Figure 30.2 is a conservative statement of that failure.

In any case, a test based on one small sample of farmers for so short a period cannot decide the issue. For this and other purposes, additional continuous budget data are badly needed, covering urban as well as rural families and extending over a longer and more nearly normal period of years.

3. Testing the Hypotheses by Negro–White Budget Comparisons

3.1. In the absence of additional data on the behavior of an identical group of families at different times, a test of the two hypotheses may be based on a comparison of different groups at the same time. Two groups to be compared for this purpose should differ in and only in the income distributions relevant, under the "relative income" hypothesis, to their consumption behavior. Then, according to one theory, consumption ratios in the two samples should be the same at the same absolute incomes. According to the opposing theory, consumption ratios in the two samples should be the same at the same relative incomes. These statements cannot both be true.

3.2. The conditions of this test are approximately met by Negro and white samples in the same city. The conditions are met, that is, provided the possibility of inherent racial difference in "thriftiness" is rejected in advance. For the purposes of the "relative income" hypothesis, the important fact is that the two races form separate enough communities so that any social influences on consumption can be assumed to spring from within the racial group. Thus the distribution of income relevant to the behavior of Negro families is only the distribution among Negroes, and similarly for whites.

3.3. Two comparisons will be considered here, for Columbus, Ohio, and for New York City in the survey of 1935–36. In these two cities, as elsewhere, the saving of Negro families was considerably higher than that of white families with the same absolute incomes. It has been shown [6] that this apparent difference in the propensity to save is fairly well explained on the "relative income" hypothesis. A verdict in favor of the "relative income" hypothesis, so far as this evidence goes, must be returned unless an alternative explanation of Negro–white differences, consistent with the "absolute income" hypothesis, can be offered. Such an explanation must attribute the differences to one or more variables other than incomes.

3.4. There is, in fact, a plausible alternative explanation of Negro–white saving differences in these two cities. It is simply that Negroes had, on the whole, smaller financial resources other than income. Consequently, Negroes were unable to dissave as frequently or as much as whites. This difference in wealth between the two groups seems very probable, but unfortunately there are no figures for the asset holdings of the two groups. However, there is indirect evidence in the budget statistics themselves that nearly all of the higher saving of Negro families can be attributed to their lack of financial reserves.

3.5. In any sample of families, white or Negro, the net average saving for every income group conceals a wide variation in saving by individual families. At almost every income level, there are some families who save and some who dissave. The proportion of savers rises and the proportion of dissavers falls as income increases. The average surplus of positive savers rises with income, but the average deficit of negative savers shows little systematic variation with income.

A certain proportion of families at all income levels are each year below their break-even points; they have incomes less than the income above which they would save. A higher proportion fall short of the level above which they would save more than their contractual saving – insurance and debt repayment. The variation in break-even points among families is in part due to differences in consumption standards. It is also in part due to unexpected losses of income or occasions for expenditure which develop during the year, e.g., sickness, unemployment, wage cuts, price rises. Further, some families will have large non-recurrent expenditures, e.g., for durable goods; the burden of such expenditures will not be placed entirely on other current consumption but in part on future consumption.

The saving behavior of families below their break-even points will depend on the financial resources at their command. If they have no asset holdings or credit, their saving will be zero or positive to the amount of their contractual saving. But if they have asset holdings or credit, they will dissave, or at least save less than their contractual saving. Availability of credit is to a large extent dependent on asset holdings; and families are, if only because of the costs of borrowing, more willing to draw on their own savings than to go into debt. Therefore, the asset holdings of the families below their break-even points will determine the amount of their dissaving.

Suppose that we have observations of saving and dissaving for two samples of families, one rich in assets and the other poor. Assume that the distribution of family break-even points, at each income level, is the same in the two samples. What would be the statistical symptoms of the difference in wealth? What would be the observable effects of the difference in wealth on the saving patterns of the two samples?

(a) Clearly the average deficit of non-saving families will be larger, at every income level, in the rich sample than in the poor sample. Because of the correlation within each sample between income and asset holdings, the difference in average deficit will be most marked at low incomes.

(b) The average surplus of saving families at each income level should differ, between the two samples, much less than the average deficit of dissavers. Families above their break-even points will be less affected by differences in wealth than families below. However, if contractual saving is important in both groups, the average surplus in the rich sample will be lower than in the poor sample because families with assets can offset positive contractual saving by dissaving in other forms.

(c) Net average saving will be lower, for each income class, in the rich sample than in the poor sample. This will be particularly true in the low-income groups, where the largest proportions of both samples are below their break-even points. The scatter of income-saving points for the poor sample will be nearly flat over a considerable range of low incomes, while the scatter of these points for the rich sample will show less net dissaving as income increases. The apparent break-even points for the two samples as a whole should not be very different, but net positive saving will emerge sooner for the poorer group.

3.6. With these symptoms in mind, let us examine the records for Negroes and whites in 1935–36 in New York City.[7] Figure 30.4 shows the average surplus for saving families, the net average saving for all families,

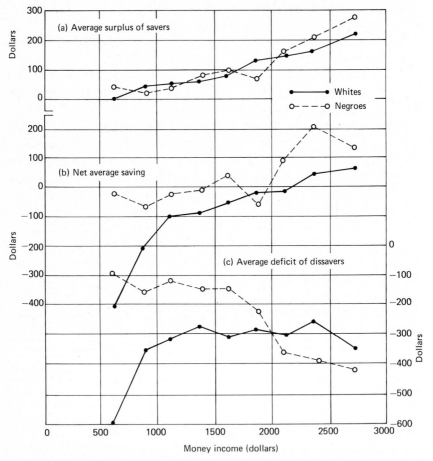

Fig. 30.4. Saving patterns of whites and Negroes, New York City, 1935-36.

and the average deficit for dissaving families, separately for the Negro and white samples in New York City. It is evident that the differences between the two samples can be explained by the hypothesis that they are due to differences in wealth. First, the average deficits of dissavers are much greater for whites than for Negroes, except in two of the three highest income brackets. Second, the average surpluses of saving families differ very little. Only at the two highest income levels is there evidence that Negroes are more "thrifty". The average size of Negro families in these income groups was appreciably lower than that of white families: 2.5 and 2.9 persons per Negro family and 3.4 and 3.5 persons per white family. Differences of this amount did not occur at any other income level. Third, the relationship of net saving to income for Negro families is erratic, reversing its direction four times. In this respect, it contrasts with the comparable scatter for whites and with the income-surplus scatters for both samples. This is understandable on the theory that the apparent relationship of Negro net saving to income is strongly influenced by an unsystematic distribution of assets by income level in the sample. Fourth, up to an income level of $2000 the scatter for Negro families is flat and oscillates about zero saving. The break-even point for the Negro sample as a whole cannot be placed more than one income class below that for the white sample.

Further evidence that the higher propensity to save of Negroes was due to their poverty of assets is provided by the details of changes in assets and liabilities in the two samples. A large amount of contractual saving was done by both groups, somewhat larger in most income classes for whites than for Negroes. As pointed out above, the existence of contractual saving will tend to make even the positive saving of the poorer sample larger than that of the richer group. The deficits of Negro families were financed more by increases in debt than by decreases in assets. The reverse is true of white families, who drew substantially on bank deposits.

The effects of differences in family composition between the two groups may be avoided by comparing separately sub-samples of the same family type. The conclusions from the comparison of the two complete samples are reinforced. For Type 1 (two-person, husband and wife) families, the average surplus of positive savers is actually greater for whites than for Negroes at five of the eight income levels available for comparison, including the highest four. Even the net saving of whites is higher at two income levels, including the highest bracket. For Types 2 and 3 combined (husband, wife, and one or two children under 16), Negroes show small but constant net dissaving up to the highest reported income level. Whites show large but decreasing net dissaving which turns into net saving at the two highest brackets. At only two of the seven income levels do Negro positive savers have a higher average surplus than whites.

3.7. The story is similar for Columbus.[8] Figure 30.5 is comparable to Figure 30.4. Again most of the difference in the propensity to save between the two groups may be attributed to greater ability of white families to run deficits. Only in the highest income bracket is the average amount of saving by surplus families more than $42 greater for Negroes than for whites.

3.8. So far as these two cities are concerned, therefore, racial differences in the propensity to consume may be explained without the help of the "relative income" hypothesis. Indeed the "absolute income" hypothesis, supplemented by the "assets" theory, explains more about the saving differences between whites and Negroes than its rival. For it would not be expected, on the "relative income" interpretation, that positive saving by the two groups would be nearly the same at equivalent absolute incomes and that the differences in net saving would be almost wholly due to differences in dissaving.

4. Testing the Hypotheses by Geographical Budget Comparisons

4.1. A test similar to the comparison of Negro and white samples can be made by comparing geographically distinct samples. As between two cities, for example, it will be the local income distributions which represent the social influences on consumption contemplated in the "relative income" hypothesis. It may be possible to see whether there is greater agreement among cities in the saving ratio at equivalent percentiles or at equivalent absolute incomes. Such a test assumes, of course, that there are no inherently geographical differences in "thriftiness".

4.2. The "relative income" hypothesis has been used to explain the following geographical differences in saving patterns:

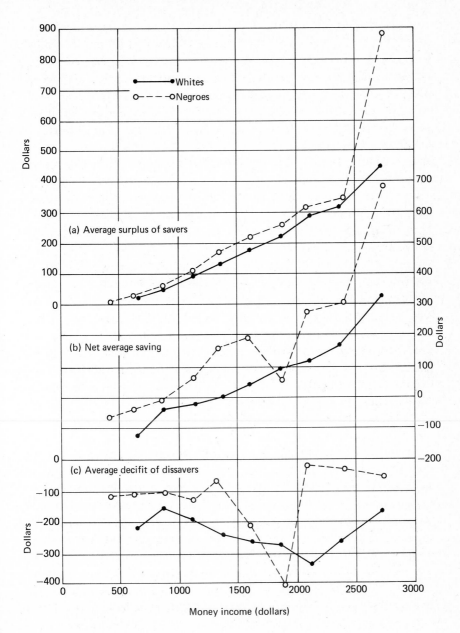

Fig. 30.5. Saving patterns of whites and Negroes, Columbus, 1935-36.

(a) In both the 1935–36 and 1941 surveys, village families reported higher saving than city families of the same money incomes. The difference is substantially eliminated, especially in the 1935–36 data, by relating village saving ratios to the village income distribution and city saving ratios to the city income distribution.[9]

(b) Both in 1935–36 and in 1941, farm families reported higher saving than non-farm families at comparable money incomes. This difference is reduced but by no means eliminated by relating farm and non-farm saving ratios, respectively, to farm and non-farm income distributions.[10]

(c) In the 1935–36 survey, saving from given money income varied, among non-farm families, inversely with size of community. Village families were the biggest savers, and metropolitan families the largest spenders. These differences are not eliminated by the hypothesis. The saving pattern for metropolitan families is brought closer to the rest, but the four other samples disagree as much as before, only with the order of thriftiness changed.[11]

(d) Similar calculations for finer geographical groups yield varying results. Intercity and interregional differences are not eliminated, as can be seen by the heterogeneity of the values of parameters in Duesenberry's Table 2 or of the charted curves in Brady's and Friedman's Charts 2 and 5. Whether this heterogeneity is greater or less than on the "absolute income" hypothesis will be considered, for a limited group of cities, in the following section.

Geographical differences in the propensity to save are exaggerated by the use of money income. If money income and saving were corrected for geographical price differentials, some of the discrepancies in saving behavior would vanish. The inverse relationship between propensity to save and size of community corresponds to a direct relationship between cost of living and size of community. Mendershausen [12] obtained for cities for which he had comparative cost-of-living figures a high negative correlation (0.95) between the propensity to save and cost of living. He also found, among urban samples, a negative correlation between propensity to save and mean income. This result is in agreement with the "relative income" hypothesis. However, mean income and cost of living were highly correlated; and mean income did not have a significant net influence on saving.

4.3. The two hypotheses can be compared with greater precision for six cities (including one pair of western cities which were merged in the 1935–36 budget survey): Columbia, Providence, Denver, Chicago, Omaha, and Butte-Pueblo. For each of these cities a regression of the consumption ratio against the percentile in the city income distribution has been computed.[13] For the same cities, regressions of the saving ratio against absolute money income are also available.[14] These regressions can be converted into relationships to absolute real income – money income in, say, Columbus dollars – by intercity cost-of-living comparisons cited in the same source. Both types of regression give excellent fits for all six cities. It is convenient to use the regressions rather than the original observations in judging on which hypothesis saving behavior is the more nearly uniform among the six cities.

Suppose that, given the consumption pattern of one city, we wish to predict consumption in the other cities. Take as the base city Denver, which occupies a middle position in both sets of regressions. Find the percentile, x of the Denver income distribution for which the consumption ratio, according to the Denver regression, has a given value y. For another city, say Chicago, find the value y' of the consumption ratio corresponding, on the Chicago regression, to the same percentile x of the Chicago income distribution. The difference between y' and y measures the success of the prediction by the "relative income" hypothesis. Similarly, find the absolute real income z for which the consumption ratio, according to the other Denver regression has the given value y. Find the value y'' of the consumption ratio corresponding, on the Chicago regression, to the same real income z. The difference between y'' and y measures the success of the prediction by the "absolute income" hypothesis. Table 30.3 shows the results of calculations of this kind for four values of y, for all cities. The four values of y are representative of the range of both kinds of regressions. At each of them, the "absolute income" hypothesis gives, on the whole, better predictions than the "relative income" hypothesis. In each of the four comparisons, the dispersion of the values corresponding to a given real income is less than the dispersion of the values corresponding to a given percentile.

Table 30.3

Intercity predictions of consumption by two methods

		Consumption ratio						
		Den-ver	Colum-bus	Provi-dence	Chi-cago	Omaha	Butte-Pueblo	Coefficient of variation(%)
Percentile	90.2	100.0	100.5	104.4	100.8	95.8	105.7	3.2
Real income	$1470	100.0	98.0	100.2	99.0	97.8	102.2	1.5
Percentile	1.0	72.3	65.1	75.0	75.4	78.5	74.4	5.7
Real income	$9800	72.3	69.3	74.5	73.2	76.7	66.1	4.8
Percentile	3.4	79.8	74.7	82.9	82.3	83.2	82.8	3.7
Real income	$5000	79.8	77.0	83.1	78.6	78.8	80.4	2.4
Percentile	30.2	93.2	91.9	97.2	94.6	91.6	98.1	2.6
Real income	$2380	93.2	90.9	94.4	91.9	90.5	92.8	1.5

Sources and explanation:

Percentile rows: Values of consumption ratio obtained for indicated percentile from regressions given by Duesenberry, *op. cit.*, Table 2, p. 54.

Real income rows: 100 minus the values of saving ratio obtained for indicated income from regressions given by Mendershausen, *op. cit.*, modified as follows: Mendershausen's regressions are of the form $S/Y = a + bY + c(1/Y)$, where S/Y is the saving ratio and Y is money income. The modified regression for each city is of the form $S/Y = a + (b/k)kY + (kc)1/kY$, where $k = \dfrac{\text{cost of living in Columbus}}{\text{cost of living in city}}$. Thus kY measures income in "Columbus dollars". If a, b, c are the parameters fitted by least squares using money income, $a, b/k, kc$ are the corresponding parameters using "real income".

5. The Secular Invariance of the Aggregate Saving Ratio

5.1. On none of the three kinds of tests to which the two hypotheses have been subjected does the "relative income" interpretation prove to be a better tool of prediction than the "absolute income" interpretation. Indeed the contrary is true. However, the major appeal of the "relative income" hypothesis is that it explains the relative constancy over the last 70 years of the percentage of national income saved.[15] This invariance cannot be explained on the simple Keynesian theory that the saving ratio is a unique function of absolute real income. For, if it is such a function, the evidence both of budget data, and of interwar aggregate time series, is that it must be an increasing function. And an increasing function is bound to under-estimate the pre-World War I saving ratio and to over-estimate the post-World War II saving ratio.

5.2. The "relative income" hypothesis is one explanation of the secular invariance of the saving ratio. An alternative explanation must introduce variables other than incomes into the consumption functions of families, and consequently into the national function. Under such a solution, the dependence of the saving ratio on absolute real income, as in the simple Keynesian function, would still hold, but only provided other variables

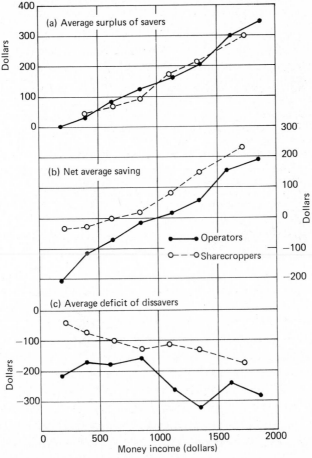

Fig. 30.6. Saving patterns of farm operators and sharecroppers, North Carolina–South Carolina, 1935-36.

were constant. The historical constancy of the saving ratio must then be explained by balancing the operation of the new variables against the growth of real income. The fate of the "absolute income" hypothesis is logically tied to the existence of an alternative explanation of this nature. If the "absolute income" hypothesis could be independently validated, then the explanation of the invariance of the saving ratio would have to involve variables other than incomes. Conversely, if such variables can explain the facts, the "absolute income" hypothesis need not be rejected.

5.3. In Section 3, reasons were advanced why the propensity to save of a group of families should be inversely related to its ability to finance deficits, i.e., to its holdings of assets. Negro–white differences in saving were attributed to differences in asset holdings. The same symptoms of the effects of differences in asset holdings which were detected in the Negro–white budget data can be found elsewhere:

(a) Figure 30.6 shows the average surplus of savers, net average saving, and average deficit of dissavers for two rural samples in the same counties of North and South Carolina in 1935–36.[16] One sample consists of white farm operators, and the other of white sharecroppers. We should expect in advance that the operators would have the greater resources for financing dissaving, if only because of their investment in the farm enterprise. Similar comparisons can be made for Negro operators and sharecroppers and for the Georgia–Mississippi area.

(b) There are repeated examples in budget surveys of large families running lower net deficits than small families of the same low family income class. Table 30.4 shows the net saving of urban families of various

Table 30.4
Net saving of urban families of various sizes, 1941

Income class (dollars) Family size (number of persons)	0-500	500-1000 Average saving (dollars)	1000-1500
1	−122	17	40
2	−139	−32	−38
3	−517	−65	−38
4	no data	−103	−43
≧ 5	5	−83	−12

Source: *Family Spending and Saving in Wartime*, Bureau of Labor Statistics Bulletin 822 (Washington: U.S. Government Printing Office, 1945), Table 19.

sizes in the three lowest income groups in the 1941 survey. It is difficult to imagine in this, and in similar cases which can be found in the 1935–36 survey, that the largest (≥ 5) families were for any reason less willing, in spite of their greater needs, to run deficits than single individuals. In the higher income ranges, their consumption exceeded that of smaller families, and their break-even point did not occur until $5000. It seems much more likely that they simply lacked the means to finance deficits, perhaps because they had previously exhausted their resources.

5.4. The principal means of deficit financing, at least for urban families, is drawing on holdings of liquid assets – currency, bank deposits, and, in recent years, savings bonds. There is little doubt that over time the supply of these assets has increased more rapidly than income. The ratio of national product to the total money supply – demand and time deposits plus currency in circulation – fell from roughly 2.5 in the eighties to 1.5 in the twenties. Recently the war has spectacularly increased liquid asset holdings relative to income.

Is it possible that the growth of asset holdings over time has lifted the propensity to consume secularly and contributed to the failure of the saving ratio to rise with the growth of real income? Two samples of families widely separated in time may differ in their holdings of assets in a manner similar to Negroes and whites or sharecroppers and operators. Because of this difference in asset holdings, the later sample will appear to have a lower propensity to save than the earlier. For this conjecture only the sketchiest of evidence can be presented.

(a) Compared with 1941, the postwar patterns of saving and dissaving reported in the annual *Surveys of Consumer Finances* exhibit the usual symptoms of a wealthy sample. Differences of definition preclude exact quantitative comparisons. But it is clear that the main reason for the low level of postwar net saving was a large increase in the average deficit of dissavers. Measured in dollars of constant purchasing power, the average deficit was about twice as large in 1947 and 1948 as in 1941. This increase in average dissaving is almost exactly proportional to the rise in liquid asset holdings. The average surplus of positive savers was, in real terms, roughly the same before and after the war. The proportions of savers and dissavers in the population changed only slightly. The data on which these statements are based are summarized in Table 30.5.

Table 30.5
Savings, dissaving, income and asset holdings, 1941, 1947, 1948

	1941	1947	1948
1. Disposable income per capita, 1948 dollars	1117	1280	1295
2. Liquid asset holdings per capita, 1948 dollars	650	1230	1170
3. Net saving per family, 1948 dollars	355	320	240
4. Percentage of families saving	62	64	63
5. Average surplus of saving families, 1948 dollars	820	860	750
6. Percentage of families dissaving	33	28	31
7. Average deficit of dissaving families, 1948 dollars	445	885	775

Sources and explanation: Conversion to 1948 dollars, in all cases, by Bureau of Labor Statistics consumers' price index.

1. Department of Commerce revised series, divided by midyear population.

2. Based on personal holdings at end of previous year, *Federal Reserve Bulletin*, 34, No. 7 (July 1949), 794.

3-7. 1941: Bureau of Labor Statistics Bulletin 822, Table 4, p. 73.

    1947: *1948 Survey of Consumer Finances:* Part IV, *Federal Reserve Bulletin*, 34, No. 8 (August 1948), 914-27.

    1948: *1949 Survey of Consumer Finances:* Part VIII, *Federal Reserve Bulletin*, 36, No. 1 (January 1950), 14-34.

(b) The propensity to save evidenced in the 1901 survey of workers' family budgets [17] was substantially higher than in any subsequent survey. Whether at the same absolute real income or at the same relative income, workers in 1901 saved more than urban families in later years.[18] The 1901 sample, compared to later surveys, exhibits the symptoms associated with poverty of asset holdings. Of the more than 25 000 families, half had surpluses, 16 per cent deficits, and the remaining third broke even. Here, breaking even was defined as covering mortgage and insurance payments as well as consumption expenditures. On the more usual definition, somewhat more surpluses and even fewer deficits would have been reported. The low percentage of deficits and the high proportion of break-evens are consistent with the hypothesis that the average net saving reported from this sample was strongly influenced by inability to dissave. This conjecture is further supported by the means by which the few deficits which did occur were financed. Only a fifth of the dissavers, in a smaller sample for which these details were obtained, drew on former savings.

6. Conclusion

Two hypotheses concerning the determination of family saving have been considered. According to one, the ratio of saving to income depends on absolute family income. According to the other, the saving ratio of a family depends on the size of its income relative to other families' incomes. These two hypotheses were tested on three kinds of budget data: in Section 2, budgets of the same families over three successive years; in Section 3, budgets of Negro and white families in the same cities in the same year; in Section 4, budgets of families in different cities in the same year. In all three tests, the "absolute income" interpretation proved to explain the observations better than the alternative theory. In Section 3, however, it required the help of the hypothesis that net saving depends on asset holdings as well as on income.

The major appeal of the "relative income" hypothesis is its success in explaining the long-run constancy of the nation's saving ratio. In Section 5 the possibility that this invariance could be explained alternatively by the growth of asset holdings was briefly examined. This factor has certainly operated in the right direction, but it is impossible to say whether or not it is strong enough to offset the effects on the saving ratio which the "absolute income" hypothesis attributes to the growth of real income. Since growth of assets and growth of income are necessarily highly correlated, the economy will seldom perform the experiments necessary to choose between an explanation of saving based solely on income and using the "relative income" hypothesis and an explanation based on both variables and employing the "absolute income" theory. In this case, as in many others, microeconomic data offer a more promising field for testing competing hypotheses than time series of aggregates. But the required microeconomic data are more complex than the conventional one-year cross-section budget survey.

Notes

[1] James S. Duesenberry, *Income, Saving, and the Theory of Consumer Behavior* (Cambridge, Mass.: Harvard University Press, 1949).

Dorothy S. Brady and Rose D. Friedman, "Savings and the Income Distribution," *Studies in Income and Wealth*, 10 (New York: National Bureau of Economic Research, 1947), 247-65.

[2] For example, J. Cornfield, W.D. Evans, and M. Hoffenberg, "Full Employment Patterns, 1950: Part I," *Monthly Labor Review*, 64 (February 1947), 163-90.

[3] Duesenberry, *op. cit.*, 32-37.

[4] Willard W. Cochrane and Mary D. Grigg, *The Changing Composition of Family Budgets for Selected Groups of Corn Belt Farmers 1940-1942* (Washington: Bureau of Agricultural Economics, 1946).

[5] Ruth P. Mack, "The Direction of Change in Income and the Consumption Function," *Review of Economics and Statistics*, 30 (November 1948), 241-42.

[6] Duesenberry, *op. cit.*, 50-52.

[7] *Family Income and Expenditure in New York City, 1935-36*, Bureau of Labor Statistics Bulletin 643 (Washington: U.S. Government Printing Office, 1941).

[8] *Family Income and Expenditure in Nine Cities of East Central Region 1935-36*, Bureau of Labor Statistics Bulletin 644 (Washington: U.S. Government Printing Office, Vol. I, 1939, Vol. II, 1941).

[9] Brady and Friedman, *op. cit.*, Chart 3, p. 259.

[10] *Ibid.*, p. 262.

[11] *Ibid.*, Chart 1, p. 254.

[12] Horst Mendershausen, "Differences in Family Saving between Cities of Different Sizes and Location, Whites and Negroes," *Review of Economic Statistics*, 22 (August 1940), 122-37.

[13] Duesenberry, *op. cit.*, Table 2, p. 54. It should be noted that Duesenberry does not join Brady and Friedman in claiming geographical uniformity in the relationship of saving ratio to relative income.

[14] Mendershausen, *op. cit.*, Table 1.

[15] See Section 1.1 above for an explanation how the "relative income" hypothesis leads to the conclusion that aggregate saving will be a constant proportion of aggregate income. For the detailed argument, see Duesenberry, *op. cit.*, 32-37.

[16] *Family Income and Expenditures*, U.S. Department of Agriculture Miscellaneous Publication 465 (Washington: U.S. Government Printing Office, 1941).

[17] *Eighteenth Annual Report of the Commissioner of Labor* (Washington: U.S. Department of Commerce and Labor, 1903).

[18] See Duesenberry, *op. cit.*, Chart II, p. 80 and Brady and Friedman, *op. cit.*, Chart 4, p. 261.

CHAPTER 31

MILTON FRIEDMAN'S THEORY OF THE
CONSUMPTION FUNCTION

Milton Friedman's book setting forth his "permanent income hypo-thesis" concerning the relation between household income and consump-tion is a major event.[1] This is one of those rare contributions of which it can be said that research and thought in its field will not be the same henceforth. Other students of household behavior may not agree with the theoretical basis of Friedman's hypothesis or grant it the whole-hearted affirmative verdict which Friedman believes justified by the empirical evidence. But their future work will be influenced by Fried-man's approach and they will have to account for the kinds of phenomena to which Friedman calls attention.

Since the book was available only a week before the conference, my comments are based on a much more cursory study than the work deserves, and my remarks must be regarded as tentative questions rather than mature criticisms. In particular, a thorough consideration of the consistency of the hypothesis with the statistical evidence presented by the author and with other evidence would be a major investigation. Consequently, my remarks concern mainly the logic and *a priori* plausibility of the hypothesis and the general method of testing it. I have little to say about the details of the supporting empirical evidence.

1. Concept of Permanent Income

The hypothesis begins with a division of the observed income of a household into two unobservable components, permanent income and

Reprinted from *Consumer Behavior*, Lincoln H. Clark (Ed.) (New York: Harper, 1958). The paper was originally given in October 1955 at the Universities–National Bureau Conference on Consumption and Economic Growth.

transient income. Fundamental though this division is, Friedman is far from clear and consistent in defining it.

1.1. The concept is introduced in Chapter II with reference to an individual with an indefinitely long horizon and advance knowledge of the entire stream of his future earnings. How the concept applies to a household containing more than one individual is not considered. Uncertainty about future earnings is discussed only briefly. The author concludes (p. 15) that uncertainty "establishes no presumption against" his form of consumption function. But he does not demonstrate that his concept of permanent income retains any meaning under conditions of uncertainty.

1.2. Even within the world of certainty or of certainty equivalents, the concept of permanent income has important ambiguities as soon as the individual's horizon is limited to his lifetime. If events develop according to the individual's expectation, is his permanent income constant throughout his lifetime? In particular, is the size of his permanent income independent of his saving behavior? When Friedman comes to analyze available data on the relation of savings to age and to claim them in support of his hypothesis (Chapter IV, Section 3), he starts with the presumption that permanent income is constant over the lifetime. He modifies this presumption (footnote 51) only to allow for some imperfection in the capital market.

The definition of permanent income with which Friedman begins (p. 11) is the amount that the individual could consume and still maintain the value of his total wealth, including his human wealth, i.e., the capitalized value of his expected future earnings from labor. His permanent income would be the interest on his total wealth. If the individual increases or decreases his total wealth, his permanent income will change. This conclusion seems inescapable, but it is ignored throughout the book.

An alternative definition of permanent income for a mortal individual is hinted in the example Friedman gives (pp. 7–11) for a two-year horizon. On this definition, permanent income is the constant rate of consumption that would, over a lifetime, maintain intact only the initial non-human wealth of the individual. His initial human wealth would be exhausted at the end of his life. It is clear that, on this definition too, permanent income will depend on the rate of accumulation of non-human wealth.

If the individual consumes less than his permanent income, thus defined, he is increasing his future permanent income.

1.3. Clarity in the concept of permanent income is essential to an understanding of the implications of estimated values of Friedman's k, the ratio of permanent consumption to permanent income. If the first of the two definitions just discussed is adopted, a k of 1.00 means that during a lifetime an individual will accumulate enough non-human wealth to replace entirely the initial value of his human wealth. A k of 0.90, for example, would imply an even greater amount of accumulation. On the second definition, a k of 1.00 would mean merely that the individual would, over a lifetime, neither accumulate nor decumulate non-human wealth.

1.4. Most of the empirical argument in the book is dominated by a concept of permanent income with a much shorter time horizon than either of these two theoretical concepts. According to this concept, permanent income is something like a moving average of observed incomes over a period of two to five years. Permanent income is the expected value of income for the individual, taking into account his age as well as his occupation, ability, non-human wealth, etc. The transitory component is a deviation from this expectation, owing to circumstances that change at random from year to year, e.g., health, weather, fashion. On this definition, changes in observed income related systematically to age are regarded as changes in permanent income rather than as transient components.

This is a difference of considerable significance. According to the lifetime concept of permanent income, the consumption of both the very young and the very old should greatly exceed their observed incomes. According to the short-horizon concept, this need not be the case. The implications of the short-horizon concept are considerably less novel, and also considerably more widely accepted, than those of the lifetime concept. With the short-horizon concept, the Friedman hypothesis says that consumers will tend to maintain their consumption in the face of declines in observed incomes when these declines are regarded as temporary. No student of the consumption function would deny the existence of such a tendency, although Friedman may exaggerate its strength.

In discussing this problem, Friedman takes the view that "intuitive plausibility gives little guidance to the exact kind of average [lifetime income], or length of horizon. For this, we must rely on the empirical evidence" (p. 25). As I hope to make clear below, the empirical evidence is already heavily burdened. It cannot be expected both to test Friedman's hypothesis and to determine how the hypothesis ought to be formulated.

2. Relation of Permanent Consumption to Permanent Income

Like observed income, observed consumption is subject to a myriad of transient influences that vary randomly from one year to the next. Consumption, too, according to Friedman, can be divided into permanent and transitory components. The ratio of permanent consumption to permanent income is asserted to be independent of the level of permanent income. The ratio may, however, vary from individual to individual and from time to time for the same individual. According to Friedman, the ratio will depend on the rate of interest, the ratio of non-human to human wealth, and such demographic variables as age, size of family, and education.

Why is the consumption ratio independent of the level of income? This fundamental question receives surprisingly meager discussion. In Chapter II Friedman uses an illustrative example of a consumer with a two-year horizon. He *assumes* that the individual will consume all this wealth over the two periods, and he then addresses himself to the question how this consumption will be apportioned between the two years. The relative apportionment, he argues, will depend on the interest rate (the higher the interest rate, the greater will be first-year consumption relative to second-year consumption) but not on the absolute amount of wealth. Acceptance of this argument does, it is true, remove one possible source of a relationship between first-year consumption and total wealth or permanent income. But this is surely of minor importance compared to the question which Friedman begs by his assumption that the terminal wealth of the individual is zero. Terminal wealth, the amount an individual leaves to his heirs, is surely related to the initial human and non-human wealth of the individual. Is it plausible to believe that this relationship is one of proportionality? Do both the millionaire and the unskilled worker pass on, say 10 per cent of their initial wealth? The answer depends on aspects of human behavior, cultural values, and social institutions, that Friedman does not mention: attitudes concerning responsibility for the economic status of the next generation.

This is an important unsolved question of social science, on which we have all too little guidance either from theory or from empirical observation. It is not to be solved by a glib dimensional argument such as Friedman gives in the footnote on page 13: "... the ratio of consumption to permanent income is dimensionally free from any absolute units. ... One would expect this ratio to depend on dimensionally similar variables ... (like the rate of interest ...). Why should it depend in any obvious way on such a dimensionally different variable as the absolute level of income ...?" Economics abounds with functional relationships between variables different in dimensionality: for example, the relation of average or marginal cost to rate of output. To choose an example more closely related to the issue in dispute, the proportion of time devoted to leisure rather than to work (a pure number) is historically related to the real wage (with dimension units of physical goods per hour).

The assertion that permanent consumption is proportional to permanent income must be distinguished from the assertion that the relationship between the two variables goes through the origin. The first proposition implies the second, but the second does not imply the first. The second proposition has much more support in common sense and in empirical evidence than the first. Since the means available to consumers to finance dissaving are limited, consumption cannot long exceed income even if income is very low. It was foolish to think that the dissaving associated with depression incomes in the 1930s would also have occurred at the same levels of income in prosperity before the First World War. We are indebted to Paul Samuelson, Simon Kuznets, Dorothy Brady and Rose Friedman, James Duesenberry, and Franco Modigliani for their parts in combating this foolishness. But neither their evidence and their arguments nor those of the present book are sensitive enough to choose between the hypothesis that the long-run consumption ratio is invariant with income and the hypothesis that the consumption ratio, though never greater than one, declines with income.

3. Relation of Transitory Consumption to Transitory Income

The assumption that the marginal propensity to consume out of transitory income is zero is undoubtedly the most implausible component of Friedman's hypothesis. It is especially implausible if permanent income is regarded as a lifetime constant and deviations from this constant due to age as transitory components. But even on the short-horizon interpretation of permanent income, Friedman finds it difficult to defend the assumption.

Against the observation that windfalls are likely to be spent in part on durable luxuries, Friedman argues that accumulation of durable goods should be counted as saving rather than consumption. As James Morgan has argued, this method of accounting may indeed make more sense in terms of household motivations than the conventional concepts of national income accounting. But even this definition of savings does not entirely rescue Friedman's assumption. Use of durable goods must be counted as consumption. Is it not likely that temporary good fortune will lead to a more intensive use of existing stocks of durables as well as to acquisition of new durable goods?

In any case, virtually all the budget study data introduced as evidence in support of the permanent income hypothesis use data employing the conventional definitions of consumption and saving.[2] What do checks against this evidence mean when there is such a wide discrepancy between the concepts appropriate to the hypothesis and those used in the data?

There are many reasons for doubting the assumption that the marginal propensity to consume from transitory income is zero. Two important ones are: (1) Dissaving to maintain consumption in the face of temporary declines in income requires wealth or borrowing capacity. Since some individuals are bound to lack these in sufficient quantity, there is necessarily a positive correlation between transitory consumption and transitory income. (2) Temporary needs or desires for greater consumption are a motivation for a household to supply more labor, either by overtime or by the entry into the labor force of secondary earners. This source of positive correlation between income and consumption is surely more frequent than Friedman's example of a negative correlation where increased hours of work leave less time for consumption.

4. Methodology of the Empirical Tests

Elsewhere in *Essays in Positive Economics*, Friedman placed his methodological views emphatically on record. The influences of two of these views on this book are not hard to find. In my opinion, one of the views has a very salutary influence and the other an unfortunate effect. The salutary view is that a theory should lead to implications that are capable of refutation by empirical evidence. Friedman is justly scornful of theories that are so general, so trivial, so tautological that they cannot conceivably be wrong. He has the courage to construct a theory which results in meaningful propositions and to suggest a list of tests, beyond the ones he has made in this book, on which his hypothesis might fail. This list is an admirable practice, and our science would advance faster if Friedman's example were more widely followed. At the same time, the question arises why Friedman himself did not perform some of these tests. For some, it is true, the necessary data were not available to him; but this was not the case for all.

The less salutary methodological view is that a theory should be tested only by its ultimate implications, that the postulates and intermediate deductions of a theory need not, and indeed should not, be subjected to informal or formal empirical test. Friedman's ultimate answer to possible doubts about his assumptions is always that they will be implicitly tested along with the propositions deduced from them. If these propositions give useful predictions, then all worries about the plausibility of the assumptions can be dispelled.

The trouble is that this methodological practice places too great a burden on the evidence and techniques available for empirical testing. Our means of distinguishing among hypotheses on the basis of empirical evidence are so meager that we must welcome any opportunities for testing, wherever they may arise in the logical structure of a theory. Given the limited kind of tests available for the final propositions of a theory, there is bound to be ambiguity in the interpretation of the test results. If a test indicates rejection, we cannot ascertain whether the fault is with the central content of the theory or with auxiliary assumptions maintained only to make the data relevant. If a test indicates acceptance, we are also faced with ambiguities of interpretation. The result will indicate acceptance of the central proposition only if it is taken for granted that the data meet all the auxiliary requirements of the test. Thus when Friedman finds a negative result, he is led first to look for failures of the data to match his auxiliary assumptions. Ordinarily, Friedman is content to assume that, for a group of families observed at the same time, mean transient consumption and mean transient income are both zero. When cross-section data fail to accord with the predictions of his theory, he finds the explanation in the failure of this assumption. And he argues that plausible corrections for this failure would eliminate the inconsistency of the data with his theory. But when the results of a test are favorable, Friedman is seldom led to worry about the accuracy of the assumption that the means of transient consumption and income are both zero.[3] Moreover, Friedman adopts quite a different assumption when he comes [Chapter V, Section 3(b)] to test his hypothesis on aggregate time series. There he no longer assumes that mean transient income is zero except in unusual years like 1944. On the contrary, he identifies mean permanent income for the whole nation with a weighted average of past mean measured incomes; thus only if it should happen that current mean measured income equaled this weighted average would mean transient income be zero. In particular, it would not be zero in 1917, 1935–36, 1941 and other budget study years; nor would it be the same in all these years.

Another example is the treatment of age, wealth, size of family, and other variables that Friedman thinks may influence the propensity to consume, although they are extraneous to his central hypothesis. Constancy from one cross-section to another in the average propensity to consume supports Friedman's hypothesis only if the extraneous variables have in fact stayed the same or changed in such a way as to offset one another. In his discussion of the secular constancy of the aggregate average propensity to consume in the U.S.A. (Chapter V, Section 1b), Friedman argues that there have been offsetting changes in the relevant variables. Among the factors he cites as important in the direction of reducing the propensity to consume is the secular reduction in average size of family. However, the budget data Friedman uses as the principal evidence for his hypothesis are data in which households are grouped together regardless of size of family, age, wealth, location, and other characteristics. The failure to take account of these variables has unknown but potentially serious consequences for the calculations Friedman cites in support of his hypothesis.

Economic theorists have traditionally shown a disposition to use basic concepts and basic axioms that cannot be observed or tested directly, but it has remained for Friedman to claim that this disposition is a virtue rather than a fault or, at best, a regrettable necessity. Given Friedman's preference for ingenious indirect tests over simple direct tests, it is not surprising that he assumes without question that his concepts of permanent and transient income are unobservable. He does not include in his list of potential tests of his hypothesis the possibility of asking individuals questions about their long-range and short-range income expectations. If such questions were asked of the same households for whom consumption and current income were measured, some fairly direct tests of Friedman's central hypothesis might be possible. To this proposal it may be objected that many respondents would not have sufficiently well-formed expectations to give useful answers. If this objection is correct, one would also have to doubt that their expectations are sufficiently well formed to influence their consumption.

The data on which Friedman tests his hypothesis must in virtually every case be regarded as sample observations from some statistical universe. Consequently allowance should be made for chance variations in observed statistics in judging whether they confirm or refute the hypothesis. Logically Friedman's tests are of two kinds. Sometimes his theory implies that two statistics are estimates of a common population parameter, or that a statistic is an estimate of a parameter with an *a priori* known value. His most interesting and compelling tests, for example, concern the agreement between two methods of estimating the proportion of variances of measured income due to variance of permanent income: one method depending on the apparent elasticity of consumption with respect to income in budget data, the other depending on the income histories of identical households. In such cases, Friedman quite properly demands less than exact agreement. He claims in effect that the agreement is close enough so that he does not have to reject the hypothesis that the difference is due only to sampling variation. Unfortunately, he does not support such claims by any calculations of sampling errors. In a different set of cases, Friedman's theory implies that two statistics are estimates of parameters that differ in value in a specified direction. Thus many of his tests concern the proposition that the consumption–

income scatter of a group is less steep the more homogeneity of permanent income there is within the group. Once two groups have been ranked by this criterion of homogeneity, Friedman is testing the hypothesis that the slopes of the consumption–income relation are the same, against the alternatives that the slope for the more heterogeneous group is larger than the other slope. In these cases, Friedman is looking for statistically significant differences, to enable him to reject the null hypothesis. But here again his failure to compute any sampling errors makes it impossible to judge whether the differences he displays are significant or not. It is surprising that Friedman, who in other contexts – even within this same book – is a sophisticated statistician, should not have viewed the problem of testing his permanent income hypothesis against empirical evidence as a statistical problem.

5. Concluding Comment

One of the great appeals of Friedman's hypothesis, both to author and to reader, is its simplicity. We should certainly welcome any single principle that can reveal unity and system in data that otherwise appear variable and chaotic. According to Friedman, the labors of investigators who search for complex multivariate explanations of consumption are misguided. But a considerable multivariate effort would be needed to test Friedman's own hypothesis with proper allowance for the variables that ought to be held constant. Until such tests are made, I doubt that the hypothesis has been sufficiently proved so that it might be used, as Friedman suggests, to derive from consumption–income relations in budget data information about the variability of permanent and transient incomes. It is certainly better to be simple than complicated. But is it better to be simple than right?

Notes

[1] These comments are based on a preliminary version of the book. In the published version (National Bureau of Economic Research, Princeton University Press, 1957) the author has made some changes, partly in response to these and other comments. But I have not altered my original discussion. References are to the published book.

² Friedman's time series data do conform to his preferred definition of saving, but his time series tests are not as crucial as his budget study tests. See below, pp. 452-53.

³ In Chapter IV, Section 2(a) Friedman argues, plausibly, that the failure of 1944 to fall in place in Figure 4 may be explained by non-zero transient mean income and consumption in that year. This explanation raises a question about the apparent congruence of 1917-18 observations with expectation, and Friedman has to look for another *ad hoc* explanation.

CHAPTER 32

LIFE CYCLE SAVING AND BALANCED GROWTH

Irving Fisher provided the foundations of the theory of saving and interest a half-century ago. Much recent and contemporary work is rediscovery or elaboration of what Fisher knew and wrote. Certainly this is true of the fruitful idea of relating saving and dissaving to the personal life cycle. Fisher showed clearly [1] how an individual with a fluctuating lifetime stream of income could and would even out his consumption by alternately lending and borrowing, and how his decisions would depend on the market rate of interest. He also showed, of course, how these savings decisions interact with investment decisions – exploiting opportunities to alter income streams – to determine market interest rates.

This study is very much in the spirit of Fisher's work on saving and interest. But it applies his fundamental approach to contemporary macroeconomic theory of growth and therefore ignores the diversity of individual circumstances, time preferences, and investment opportunities that Fisher's general equilibrium approach handled so elegantly. The chapter tries to show how the life cycle saving theory can complete and close aggregative growth models and help to determine the equilibrium interest rate and saving rate in steady balanced growth. It also engages in some speculation concerning the amount of capital accumulation which life cycle saving, unaided by saving for subsequent generations, can account for. This numerical speculation is based partly on *a priori* assumptions and partly on some observed characteristics of the contemporary U.S. population and economy.

Reprinted from *Ten Economic Studies in the Tradition of Irving Fisher* (New York: John Wiley & Sons, Inc., 1967).

1. Saving and Wealth in Balanced-growth Equilibrium

In the familiar one-commodity two-factor growth model with constant returns to scale and purely labor-augmenting (Harrod-neutral) technical progress, the technology permits a variety of balanced-growth paths or "golden ages". Along any path, output, capital stock, and effective (augmented) labor all grow at the same rate g; natural labor grows at an exogenously determined rate n; income per capita and the wage rate grow at the rate of technical progress $\gamma = g - n$; the marginal productivities of capital and of effective labor are constant. Assuming competitive determination of factor prices, these marginal productivities are, respectively, the rates of return on capital and the wage of a unit of effective labor. Alternative paths differ in capital intensity; those with higher ratios of capital to effective labor also have higher ratios of capital to output, higher per capita incomes and wages, and lower rates of return on capital. Similarly, the more capital-intensive paths require higher ratios of investment to output. If μ is the ratio of capital to output, and if both output and capital are growing at rate g, the share of output that must be invested in new capital is $g\mu$. Or, to put the same relationship the other way around, if the share of output the community is willing to invest in new capital is s, the equilibrium path is the one with a capital–output ratio μ equal to s/g.

In a full equilibrium, the saving and wealth-holding propensities of the society must be satisfied at the same time as the technological constraints on production and on factor prices. A balanced-growth path is an equilibrium path only if the society continuously desires the capital–output and investment–output ratios characteristic of the path. It is not obvious that there is any path along which the amounts people wish to invest in new capital are continuously and perpetually just enough to maintain the required capital–output ratio. This question is begged in models which assume a constant investment ratio s or a constant desired capital–income ratio μ. We need to know whether such an assumption makes sense in terms of more basic determinants of saving behavior. If so, we can then look for a golden-age path that induces the constant investment ratio necessary to support it.

This study shows how the life cycle theory of saving leads to an equilibrium balanced-growth path. That is, the conditions of a balanced growth generate a demand by savers for a constant ratio of wealth to income and, correspondingly, a constant ratio of new saving to income. In a one-asset world, physical capital is the only kind of wealth and real investment is the only kind of saving. Therefore an equilibrium balanced-growth path is one along which the desired wealth–income ratio is the same as the required capital–output ratio, and correspondingly, the desired saving–income ratio is the same as the required investment–output ratio. Of course, there are many other theories of saving with similar implications.

The ratio of private wealth to income may diverge from the capital–output ratio and private saving from capital formation. For example, the government may own a share of the capital stock. Or the government may provide assets – "outside" money or public deadweight debt – that can be substituted for capital in satisfying the demand for wealth and saving. Government financial activity thus enlarges the number of golden-age paths that are possible equilibria, paths that could simultaneously satisfy technological requirements and thrift propensities.

Anticipating results presented later in the chapter, the life cycle theory of saving suggests that along a golden-age path the community will desire a constant ratio of wealth to income, and that this ratio depends on three characteristics of the path. Two of these are fixed parameters of the economy, the same for every path: the rate of growth of the labor force n and the rate of labor-augmenting technical progress γ. The third varies from path to path: the rate of return on capital r. The desired wealth–income ratio is smaller the more rapid is labor force growth and technical progress, and is greater the higher the interest rate r.

It is convenient to consider the ratio of capital or wealth to *labor income* rather than to total income. This is because the golden-age demand for wealth as a ratio of labor income turns out to be a function of only two variables rather than of three. The two are the rate of labor force growth n and the difference between the interest rate r and the rate of technical progress γ. The determination of an equilibrium path, from among the family of technologically possible golden-age paths, may then be described as follows.

In Figure 32.1, the rate of return on capital r is measured vertically,

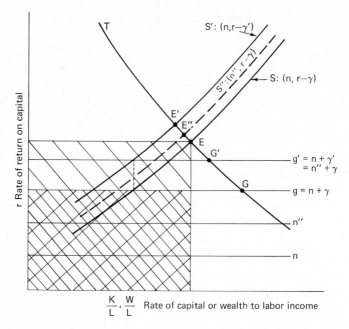

Fig. 32.1.

and the ratio of the capital stock to the competitively determined real wage bill is measured horizontally. The horizontal axis may also be used to measure the ratio of wealth to labor income – which in a one-asset economy coincides with the ratio of capital stock to wage bill. The horizontal lines n and $g (= n + \gamma)$ indicate, respectively, the rate of labor force growth and the natural rate of growth of the economy; their difference γ is the rate of (labor-augmenting) technical progress. Curve S then indicates the supply of savings – the ratio of wealth to labor income which would be desired at different interest rates. It should be understood that each point on the curve represents a hypothetical golden-age path, along which the interest rate is, and is expected to be, constant at the indicated level r. The curve does not apply to other situations. If the rate of technical progress should increase to γ', and the total rate of growth similarly to $g'(= n + \gamma')$, the curve moves up vertically by the same amount, to S'. The desired wealth–labor income ratio remains the same if r rises by the amount $\gamma' - \gamma$. However, if the same increase in g came instead from an increase in the rate of growth of the natural labor force, from n to n'', the upward shift in the savings curve, this time to S'', would be less.

The other side of the scissors is a relationship between the same two variables derived from the economy's production function, taking the interest rate r to be the marginal productivity of capital and the wage bill to reflect a wage rate equal to the marginal productivity of labor. This relationship, illustrated by curve T in Figure 32.1, is uniquely determined by the technology of the economy – assuming, as always, that the technology obeys constant returns to scale and changes over time only by labor-augmenting technical progress. The shape of this curve may be considered by noting that the product of the ordinate and abscissa is Kr/L, the ratio of capital income to labor income. For a Cobb–Douglas function this measure of competitive income distribution is of course constant. In that case, therefore, curve T is a rectangular hyperbola, that is, has an elasticity of -1. The curve will be more elastic if the elasticity of substitution in production is greater than 1: a lowering of r, accompanying an increase in the capital–labor ratio K/N, means that if the elasticity of substitution is greater than 1 there is a rise in capital's relative share Kr/L. If the elasticity of substitution is smaller than 1, then a rise in capital intensity K/N will produce a decline both in r and in capital's relative share. The curve T will be steeper than the Cobb–Douglas rectangular hyperbola. Indeed, it may actually be positively sloped. In Figure 32.1 the curve is drawn with a negative slope and approximates the Cobb–Douglas case. Unlike the S curve, the technological relationship T is independent of the rates of growth n and γ. The equilibrium paths are indicated by the intersections of curve T with curve S at E, or with S' at E', or with S'' at E''.

These intersections are all above the corresponding natural growth rates g or g'. They illustrate equilibrium with capital intensity short of the golden rule amounts, G or G'. Incidentally, the amount of saving in the economy, relative to labor income, is given in the diagram by the rectangle $g \cdot W/L$. Thus at the equilibrium E capital's share of income, relative to labor's share, is indicated by the shaded rectangle with corners 0 and E. The amount of saving, relative to labor income, is indicated by the heavily shaded portion of that rectangle, below the horizontal line g. Here the interest rate exceeds the growth rate, so saving is smaller than

Table 32.1
Cobb–Douglas value of K/L

r	α			
	0.2	0.25	0.33	0.4
0.10	2.5	3.33	5.0	6.67
0.05	5.0	6.67	10.0	13.33
0.04	6.25	8.33	12.5	16.67

capital income. At capital intensities beyond the "golden rule" the reverse would be true.

Some rough estimates of the magnitudes on curve T will be relevant for comparison with estimates, to be produced later in the chapter, of curve S magnitudes. If the production function is Cobb–Douglas with capital's share α, then $K/L = 1/r \cdot \alpha/(1 - \alpha)$. Table 32.1 calculates K/L for various values of α and r.

2. The Life Cycle Theory of Saving

The theory of saving here considered as the underlying source of the S curve of Figure 32.1 is the life cycle theory proposed by Fisher and later by Modigliani and Brumberg.[2] Each individual fully consumes his lifetime income. Modigliani and Brumberg called particular attention to the effect of retirement on the lifetime income stream. The individual wants to spread his consumption evenly over earning and retirement years. He therefore saves first and then dissaves, and his net worth is never negative. Consequently, a society of individuals of all ages has a positive demand for wealth. In a growing economy, moreover, there is net saving in aggregate; young savers are relatively more numerous or more affluent or both than retired dissavers. An interesting question is whether the retirement motive alone suffices to explain observed magnitudes of saving and wealth, or whether a bequest motive is needed in addition.

Modigliani and Brumberg illustrated their theory by a specific model, a model that is highly suggestive but too simple to use as a basis for serious quantitative estimates. The stylized life cycle and the zero interest rate assumed are unrealistic. Consequently, the Modigliani–Brumberg (M–B) model is not a good basis for assessing Modigliani's assertion of the importance of retirement saving. This is no criticism. The authors did not intend their life cycle to be more than illustrative.

In this chapter I shall (1) suggest a generalization of the individual life cycle model to allow for positive interest rates, probabilistic life spans, any income profile, childhood as well as old age, and family structure, (2) show how to derive from the individual and family saving behavior described in (1) aggregate wealth and saving for golden-age paths with given rates of interest and rates of growth of population and per capita income, and (3) report some numerical calculations of ratios of wealth and saving to income, based on realistic income profiles.

Let $y(t, u)$ be the labor income earned by each person of age u at time t. It is assumed that technological progress steadily and uniformly increases the (marginal) productivity of all ages

$$y(t, u) = y(0, u) e^{\gamma t} \quad (0 \leqq u \leqq u^*). \tag{1}$$

Thus the actual lifetime path of an individual's income follows the stationary "cross-section" income profile $y(t, u)$ for given t modified by the general growth trend. The probability of surviving from birth to age u is given by $s(u)$; this function is assumed to remain unchanged with the passage of calendar time. u^* is a theoretical age such that $s(u^*) = 0$. The interest rate available to consumers, for both lending and borrowing, is r. Thus the expected value discounted to birth of the lifetime income of an individual born at time t is

$$Y(t, u^*) = \int_0^{u^*} y(t + u, u)s(u) e^{-ru} du$$

$$= e^{\gamma t} \int_0^{u^*} y(0, u)s(u) e^{(\gamma - r)u} du = e^{\gamma t} Y(0, u^*). \tag{2}$$

We shall also have need of the expected value, again discounted to birth, of the income an individual earns up to any arbitrary age u:

$$Y(t, u) = e^{\gamma t} \int_0^u y(0, x)s(x) e^{(\gamma - r)x} \, dx = e^{\gamma t} Y(0, u)$$

$$(0 \leq u \leq u^*). \quad (3)$$

Similarly, let $c(t, u)$ be the expected consumption by each individual of age u at time t. Then the expected cumulative consumption by age u, discounted to birth, of an individual born at time t is

$$C(t, u) = \int_0^u c(t + x, x)s(x) e^{-rx} \, dx \quad (0 \leq u \leq u^*). \quad (4)$$

The present value, at birth, of expected lifetime consumption is $C(t, u^*)$. The basic assumption that each cohort consumes its lifetime income, including interest on savings, is

$$C(t, u^*) = Y(t, u^*) \quad (5)$$

for all t. The present value at birth date t of the net worth accumulated by $t + u$ by an individual born at t, averaging both the deceased and living members of the cohort born at t, is simply

$$w_t(t + u, u) = Y(t, u) - C(t, u) \quad (0 \leq u \leq u^*). \quad (6)$$

It will also be necessary to evaluate the undiscounted value at time $t + u$ of the savings of a cohort born at t:

$$w_{t+u}(t + u, u) = e^{ru}w_t(t + u, u) = e^{ru}Y(t, u) - e^{ru}C(t, u). \quad (7)$$

A rule is required for the allocation of consumption over time, subject to the constraint (5) that the present values of expected lifetime consumption and expected lifetime income be equal. The rule assumed is

$$c(t + u, u) e^{-ru} = c^*(t) \quad (0 \leq u \leq u^*). \quad (8)$$

In words, each individual makes the present value, at birth, of his consumption equal at all ages. With a zero interest rate, this is the same as the M–B assumption that consumption is equal at all ages. With a positive interest rate, the lifetime consumption path is tilted upward to take advantage of the fact that total consumption can be greater if it is postponed. The particular formulation (8) seems a natural generalization of the M–B consumption path.[3] It can, if desired, be related to a particular utility maximization, as follows:

Suppose that the expected utility of a consumption path is simply $\int_0^{u^*} U[c(t + u, u)]s(u)\, du$, that is, the sum of utilities of consumptions at successive ages, weighted by the probabilities of surviving to each age. Suppose that $U(c)$ takes the following form:

$$U(c) = \log c. \tag{9}$$

We have also the constraint (5). The path of c which will maximize expected utility subject to the constraint is the one which will maximize

$$\int_0^{u^*} \log\left[c(t+u, u)\right]s(u)\, du - \lambda\left[\int_0^{u^*} c(t+u, u)s(u)\, e^{-ru}\, du - Y(t, u^*)\right].$$

Differentiating this maximand with respect to $c(t + u, u)$ gives

$$\frac{s(u)}{c(t + u, u)} - \lambda e^{-ru}s(u) = 0 \quad (0 \leqq u \leqq u^*) \tag{10}$$

from which (8) is derived, with $c^*(t) = 1/\lambda$.

Using (5), we find

$$c^*(t) = \frac{Y(t, u^*)}{\displaystyle\int_0^{u^*} s(u)\, du}. \tag{11}$$

An alternative rule for allocating consumption over time would be

$$c(t + u, u)\, e^{(\delta - r)u} = c^*(t), \tag{8$'$}$$

where δ represents a subjective rate of discount of future utility:

$$U(c) = e^{-\delta u} \log c. \tag{9$'$}$$

What is spread evenly over lifetime is not consumption discounted at the market rate of interest but consumption discounted at the difference between market interest rate and the subjective utility discount. This quantity will be

$$c^*(t) = \frac{Y(t, u^*)}{\int_0^{u^*} e^{-\delta u} s(u)\, du}. \tag{11'}$$

In other words, expected years of life are not to be counted equally but discounted at the subjective rate. Except where explicitly stated otherwise, δ is taken to be zero in the following discussion.

Interpretation of (11) may be easier if we begin with the simple case of an invariant and known life span

$$s(u) = \begin{cases} 1 & (0 \leq u \leq u^*) \\ 0 & (u \geq u^*). \end{cases} \tag{12}$$

Then $c^* = (1/u^*)Y(t, u^*)$. That is, the initial present value of lifetime income is spread evenly over all years of life. This is also what (11) says for the general case, except that years of life are not weighted equally but in proportion to the probability of lasting long enough to enjoy them.

Using (4) and (11), we have

$$C(t, u) = c^*(t) \int_0^u s(x)\, dx = Y(t, u^*) \frac{\int_0^{u^*} s(x)\, dx}{\int_0^{u^*} s(x)\, dx},$$

$$C(t, u) = Y(t, u^*) \frac{S(u)}{S(u^*)}, \tag{13}$$

where $S(u)$ is total expected years of life accounted for by years up to age u. Under the simple mortality assumption (12), $S(u)$ reduces to u.

From (7),

$$
\begin{aligned}
w_{t+u}(t + u, u) &= e^{ru}\left[Y(t, u) - Y(t, u^*)\frac{S(u)}{S(u^*)} \right] \\
&= e^{\gamma t} e^{ru}\left[Y(0, u) - Y(0, u^*)\frac{S(u)}{S(u^*)} \right] = e^{\gamma t} w_u(u, u).
\end{aligned} \tag{14}
$$

Obviously, $w_u^*(u^*, u^*) = 0$. That is, the savings of a cohort vanish u^* years after its birth. So also $w_v(u^*, u^*) = 0$ for $v > u^*$.

Figure 32.2 illustrates a relationship of wealth to age for an individual born at time zero. On the assumptions made, the same path will apply, with only a proportional vertical increase, to an individual born subsequently. The non-decreasing curve $Y(0, u)$ shows the present value at time zero of all the expected earnings of the individual up to age u. The straight line $C(0, u)$ shows the present value of all expected consumption up to age u. The vertical difference is the net worth, positive or negative, accumulated at age u. In the figure, these quantities are all discounted to birth date. The horizontal axis measures age, not linearly but weighted by the probability of survival.

Expression (14) gives the wealth of an individual of age u. For $\gamma > 0$, this is growing exponentially: a 40-year-old in 1965 has more wealth than a 40-year-old in 1960, by a factor related to the general growth of per capita income.

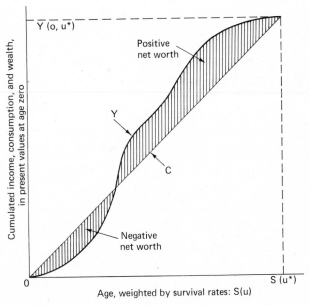

Fig. 32.2.

In the special case considered by M–B, it is easy to evaluate $w_u(u, u)$. The assumptions are

$$r = 0, \quad \gamma = 0, \tag{15}$$

$$S(u) = u,$$

$$\begin{cases} Y(0, u) = uy & (0 \leq u \leq \hat{u}) & \text{(earning years)}, \\ Y(0, u) = Y(0, \hat{u}) = \hat{u}y & (\hat{u} \leq u \leq u^*) & \text{(retirement years)}. \end{cases}$$

Therefore

$$w_u(u, u) = uy - \hat{u}y \cdot \frac{u}{u^*} = uy\left(1 - \frac{\hat{u}}{u^*}\right) \quad (0 \leq u \leq \hat{u}),$$

$$w_u(u, u) = \hat{u}y - \hat{u}y \cdot \frac{u}{u^*} = \hat{u}y\left(1 - \frac{u}{u^*}\right) \quad (\hat{u} \leq u \leq u^*). \tag{16}$$

In numerical examples, M–B take $\hat{u}$ as 40 and u^* as 50 (measuring "life" from beginning of work).

Figure 32.3 shows the M–B special case of Figure 32.2.

3. Aggregate Wealth and Saving

To find aggregate wealth and saving it is necessary to know the age distribution of the population. The net worths for various ages, as depicted in Figures 32.2 and 32.3, need to be weighted by the number of persons of each age and summed.

I am considering only "golden ages", in which age distribution is stationary. Survival probabilities are constant; the number of births is constant or growing exponentially; the total population is growing at the same rate.

Births at time t are

$$B(t) = B(0) \, e^{nt}. \tag{17}$$

In the following discussion we may without loss of generality take $B(0)$ equal to 1.

The number of people born at time t surviving at time $v \, (\geq t)$ is

$$N(v, v - t) = e^{nt}s(v - t). \tag{18}$$

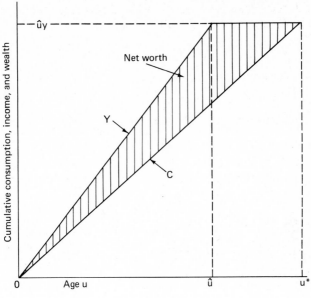

Fig. 32.3.

The size of the population at time v is

$$N(v) = \int_{v-u^*}^{v} e^{nt}s(v-t)\, dt = e^{nv}\int_{0}^{u^*} e^{-nu}s(u)\, du = N(0)\, e^{nv}. \quad (19)$$

The labor income at time v of an individual of age u is $y(v, u)$. Therefore aggregate labor income at time v is

$$L(v) = \int_{v-u^*}^{v} y(v, v-t)N(v, v-t)\, dt$$

$$= e^{(\gamma+n)v}\int_{0}^{u^*} y(0, u)\, e^{-n\dot{u}}s(u)\, du = e^{(\gamma+n)v}L(0). \quad (20)$$

From (2) it will be recognized that if $r = \gamma + n$, the condition for a golden rule path,

$$L(v) = e^{(n+\gamma)v}Y(0, u^*) = e^{rv}Y(0, u^*). \quad (21)$$

The consumption at time v of an individual of age u is

$$c^*(v - u)\, e^{ru} = \frac{Y(v - u, u^*)\, e^{ru}}{S(u^*)} = \frac{e^{\gamma v} e^{(r - \gamma)u} Y(0, u^*)}{S(u^*)}. \tag{22}$$

Therefore the consumption of the society at time v is

$$C(v) = \int_{v-u^*}^{v} c^*(t)\, e^{r(t - v)} N(v, v - t)\, dt = \int_{0}^{u^*} c^*(v - u)\, e^{ru} N(v, u)\, du$$

$$= \frac{e^{(n + \gamma)v} Y(0, u^*)}{S(u^*)} \int_{0}^{u^*} e^{(r - \gamma - n)u} s(u)\, du = e^{(n + \gamma)v} C(0). \tag{23}$$

Along a golden rule path $(r = \gamma + n)$, we have the familiar equality between aggregate consumption and labor income,

$$C(v) = e^{(n + \gamma)v} Y(0, u^*) = L(v) \tag{24}$$

Comparing (20) and (23), $C(v) \gtreqless L(v)$ according as $r \gtreqless \gamma + n$.

It should be emphasized that this is a tautological proposition about saving behavior, not a golden rule theorem about technology. The usual golden rule proposition is that along the golden rule path, capital formation is equal to non-labor income and the capital–output ratio thus maintained implies technologically a marginal efficiency of capital equal to the natural rate of growth. The present statement (24) follows simply from the fact that along a balanced-growth path, wealth grows at the natural rate of growth of the economy: $\dot{W} = (n + \gamma)W$. If, also, $r = n + \gamma$, then the income to wealth-owners rW is equal to the increase of wealth $\dot{W}$.

The wealth at time v of a cohort born u years before is, according to (14),

$$w_v(v, u) = e^{\gamma(v - u)} e^{r(u)} \left[Y(0, u) - \frac{Y(0, u^*) S(u)}{S(u^*)} \right].$$

In aggregating past savings to obtain the wealth of the society at time v we know we do not have to consider the savings of any cohort born before $v - u^*$, because their savings have all vanished. Any wealth left by early decedents of the cohort has been offset by the debts left by late decedents. The size of the cohort born at time $v - u$ is $e^{n(v - u)}$.

Therefore the total wealth of the society at time v is

$$W(v) = \int_{v-u^*}^{v} w_v(v, v - u)\, e^{n(v-u)}\, du$$

$$= e^{(n+\gamma)v} \int_{0}^{u^*} e^{(r-\gamma-n)u}\left[Y(0, u) - Y(0, u^*)\frac{S(u)}{S(u^*)}\right] du. \tag{25}$$

In the golden rule case ($r = \gamma + n$), the integral in (25), which is $W(0)$, is simply the algebraic sum of the vertical differences pictured as shaded areas in Figure 32.2. In the general case it is a weighted sum of these differences, the weights growing with u as the interest rate exceeds the natural growth rate.

From (20) and (25) we observe that the ratio of wealth to labor income is constant over time:

$$\frac{W(v)}{L(v)} = \frac{W(0)}{L(0)} = \frac{1}{L(0)} \int_{0}^{u^*} e^{(r-\gamma-n)u} Y(0, u)\, du$$

$$- \frac{Y(0, u^*)}{L(0)S(u^*)} \int_{0}^{u^*} e^{(r-\gamma-n)u} S(u)\, du. \tag{26}$$

We recall from (2) that $Y(0, u)$, including $Y(0, u^*)$, depends on $r - \gamma$, and from (20) that $L(0)$ depends on n. Therefore, the value of W/L depends on the parameters r, γ, and n. Specifically, it is a function of $r - \gamma$ and n. That is, for given n, only the difference between γ and r, not their absolute magnitudes, matters. And if, as for golden rule paths, $r - \gamma = n$, then the ratio depends only on n. It is not true that growth in per capita income, measured by γ, has the same effect as growth of population, measured by n.[4]

In golden rule cases $Y(0, u^*) = L(0)$ and

$$\frac{W(0)}{L(0)} = \frac{1}{Y(0, u^*)} \int_{0}^{u^*} Y(0, u)\, du - \frac{1}{S(u^*)} \int_{0}^{u^*} S(u)\, du. \tag{27}$$

In the M–B case we know from (16) that

$$\frac{W(0)}{L(0)} = \frac{1}{\hat{u}y}\int_0^{\hat{u}} uy\,du + \frac{1}{\hat{u}y}(u^* - \hat{u})\hat{u}y - \frac{1}{u^*}\int_0^{u^*} u\,du = \frac{u^* - \hat{u}}{2}.$$

(28)

The ratio of wealth to income is simply half the retirement span, for example, wealth is five-year income if the retirement span is ten years. This is true for $n = 0$ and for $\gamma = r$, regardless of the value of $\gamma = r$.

Sticking to golden rule paths, we may consider how $W(0)/L(0)$ varies with n when n exceeds zero. Here $Y(0, u) = (y/n)(e^{-nu} - 1)$ and $L(0) = Y(0, u^*) = Y(0, \hat{u}) = (y/n)(e^{-n\hat{u}} - 1)$. Therefore

$$\frac{W(0)}{L(0)} = \frac{1}{e^{-n\hat{u}} - 1}\left[\int_0^{\hat{u}} (e^{-nu} - 1\,du + (u^* - \hat{u})(e^{-n\hat{u}} - 1)\right] - \frac{u^*}{2}$$

$$= \frac{u^*}{2} - \frac{\hat{u}\,e^{-n\hat{u}}}{e^{-n\hat{u}} - 1} - \frac{1}{n} \quad \text{for} \quad n = r - \gamma.$$

(29)

In the general case $W(0)/L(0)$ depends on $(r - \gamma)$ as well as on n, as follows:

$$\frac{W(0)}{L(0)} = \frac{n[e^{-(r-\gamma)\hat{u}} - 1][e^{(r-\gamma-n)u^*} - 1]}{(r - \gamma)u^*(r - \gamma - n)^2(e^{-n\hat{u}} - 1)} - \frac{1}{r - \gamma - n}$$

$$\text{for} \quad \begin{aligned} &n, r - \gamma > 0, \\ &n \neq r - \gamma, \end{aligned}$$ (30)

$$\frac{W(0)}{L(0)} = -\frac{[e^{-(r-\gamma)\hat{u}} - 1][e^{(r-\gamma)u^*} - 1]}{u^*\hat{u}(r - \gamma)^3} - \frac{1}{r - \gamma}$$

$$n = 0, (r - \gamma) > 0,$$

$$\frac{W(0)}{L(0)} = \frac{1}{n} - \frac{\hat{u}(1 - e^{-nu^*})}{nu^*(1 - e^{-n\hat{u}})} \quad n > 0, (r - \gamma) = 0.$$

Table 32.2 gives values for $W(0)/L(0)$ for various values of n and $(r - \gamma)$, assuming $\hat{u} = 40$ and $u^* = 50$. Entries in diagonals are for golden rule paths.

Table 32.2.

$r - \gamma$ \ n	0	0.005	0.010	0.015	0.020	0.025	0.030
0	5.000	4.755	4.521	4.297	4.084	3.881	3.688
0.005	5.940	5.666	5.403	5.152	4.912	4.683	4.465
0.010	6.935	6.626	6.329	6.046	5.774	5.514	5.267
0.015	7.996	7.647	7.310	6.988	6.679	6.385	6.103
0.020	9.138	8.740	8.357	7.990	7.638	7.303	6.982
0.025	10.374	9.920	9.483	9.064	8.663	8.279	7.913
0.030	11.722	11.202	10.703	10.223	9.764	9.326	8.907

These computations concern the ratio of wealth to labor income, W/L. It is more usual to consider ratios of wealth to total income, X. Total income is larger than labor income by rW. Thus $W/X = 1/[1/(W/L)+r]$. The corresponding saving ratio is $(n + \gamma)W/X$. For example, if $n = 0.010$, $\gamma = 0.030$ and $r = 0.005$, the ratio of wealth to total income is $1/(1/8.357 + 0.005)$ or about 5.9, and the saving ratio is 0.236. To take another example with the same total growth rate, let $n = 0.020$, $\gamma = 0.020$, and $r = 0.005$. Then the ratio of wealth to total income is $1/(1/9.764 + 0.005)$ or about 6.6 and the saving ratio is 0.264.

The M–B life cycle does not allow for children. Presumably, their consumption is to be assumed to be squeezed from their parents' consumption. In this case, however, it is implausible to assume that parents spread consumption evenly over adult life, independently of the number of mouths to feed. A mechanical amendment to the model, which continues to treat individuals as individuals and to ignore their grouping in households, would simply tack the childhood years without income on at the beginning of the life cycle. Each person would then be consuming from birth in anticipation of his future adult earnings. He would accumulate debt during his childhood years, and he would have to use his earnings to pay back the debt as well as to provide for his second childhood. Clearly, the social wealth–income ratio for a cross-section of ages would then be smaller than in the M–B model. Indeed, it might very well be negative. In the simplest case of complete stationarity, $Y(0, u^*) = L(0) = (\hat{u} - \tilde{u})y$, where $\tilde{u}$ is the age at which earning of income begins. $Y(0, u) = 0$ for $u < \tilde{u}$, $Y(0, u) = (u - \tilde{u})y$ for $\tilde{u} \leq u \leq \hat{u}$, and $Y(0, u)$

$= (\hat{u} - \tilde{u})y$ for $\hat{u} \leq u \leq u^*$. Therefore

$$\frac{1}{Y(0, u^*)} \int_0^{u^*} Y(0, u)\, du = \frac{\displaystyle\int_{\tilde{u}}^{\hat{u}} y(u - \tilde{u})\, du + (\hat{u} - \tilde{u})y(u^* - \hat{u})}{(\hat{u} - \tilde{u})y}$$

$$= \frac{(\hat{u} - \tilde{u})}{2} + u^* - \hat{u} = u^* - \frac{\hat{u}}{2} - \frac{\tilde{u}}{2}.$$

To get $W(0)/L(0)$, Equation (29) says to subtract $u^*/2$. Hence $W(0)/L(0)$ $= (u^* - \hat{u} - \tilde{u})/2$. If the childhood span of years $\tilde{u}$ exceeds the retirement span $u^* - \hat{u}$, which is 10 years in the numerical example, then net social wealth is negative. Population growth will magnify this effect by giving more relative weight to the young and debtor years.

4. Toward More Realistic Calculations

In this concluding section I shall report some illustrative calculations designed to be somewhat more realistic than the simple M–B life cycle. The improvements in realism are the following: (1) Observed mortality and survival rates, for the U.S. population in 1963, are assumed. (2) Realistic income–age profiles, for males and females, are assumed. (3) Allowance is made, although in a simple and arbitrary way, for the combination of men, women, and children in households.

4.1. *Rate of Growth of Population*
Given (1) the survival rates of females to all ages, and (2) the number of female births per surviving female of every age, it is possible to compute a hypothetical steady-state growth rate for the female population. That is, assuming these survival and birth rates had always obtained and would continue to do so, they imply a particular constant growth rate for the female population. With given survival rates for males to all ages, and with a given and constant ratio of male to female births, the same growth rate applies to the male population and thus to the total population.

Let $s_f(u)$ be the survival rate of females to age u; let $b(u)$ be the number of births per surviving female: let f be the fraction of such births that are female. Let $B_f(t)$ be the number of female births at time t. In the hypothetical steady state, $B_f(t) = B_f(0)\,e^{nt}$. We can therefore calculate n as follows:

$$B_f(t) = \int_{t-u^*}^{t} B_f(v)s_f(t-v)fb(t-v)\,dv,$$

$$B_f(0)\,e^{nt} = B_f(0)\,e^{nt} \int_{0}^{u^*} e^{-nu}s_f(u)fb(u)\,du, \tag{31}$$

$$1 = \int_{0}^{u^*} e^{-nu}s_f(u)fb(u)\,du.$$

The equilibrium growth rate is that rate of "discount" which makes the "present value" of the expected stream of future female births from a newborn female equal to one. This calculation has been made, based on 1963 observations of survival and birth rates. The solution is $n = 0.016875$. This is the hypothetical growth rate used in subsequent calculations.

4.2. Income Profiles

The 1964 income profiles used are derived from the Current Population Survey.[5] The survey gives, separately for males and females, median incomes for income recipients, and percentages of population receiving income, for seven age brackets, beginning with age 14. The reported medians have been reduced by multiplying them by the percentage of the age–sex group receiving income. The corrected median has then been interpolated for each year of age. The open-ended final age bracket has been arbitrarily assumed to cover ages 65–74, with income becoming zero from age 75. These profiles are shown in Figure 32.4.

A defect in these income estimates is that they do not exclude property income. The calculation theoretically requires the profile of labor income only. However, the use of medians probably makes the distortion from this source very small. Only the shapes of the income profiles, not the dollar incomes, are used in the calculation.

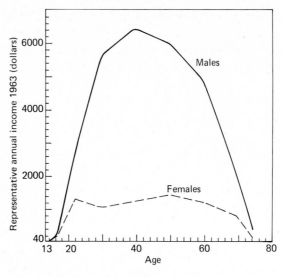

Fig. 32.4.

As would be expected, the computed profiles show income rising to a peak (at age 40 for males, age 50 for females) and then declining. It should be remembered that this is a cross-section profile. Any particular individual would reap over time the benefits of the general advance in per capita income, and this would postpone his peak income to a later age.

4.3. Households

It is assumed, as in the preceding sections, that lifetime income is on the average completely consumed and that expected present value of consumption is equal in all years. However, the unit to which these assumptions are applied is the household rather than the individual. A household is arbitrarily constructed. Its life begins with an "average" female aged 18. Associated with her are a certain number of males aged 20 (specifically, the number of surviving males aged 20 per surviving female aged 18 in a population growing steadily at the rate $n = 0.016875$; this number is approximately 1). Associated with her also are the numbers of male and female children (per surviving female) of various ages who have been born to all females of this cohort in its first 17 years. The size of the household changes as the female grows older: some of the adult women and men die; additional children are born, and some children die; female children leave the household when they become 18, male children when they become 20. Using the standard survival rate and birth rate tables, it is possible to compute, for each age of the "mother", the number of surviving adult women, number of surviving adult men, number of surviving children under 14, number of surviving "teenage" female children 14–17, and number of surviving male children 14–19.

Applying to these numbers the male and female income profiles makes it possible to compute a cross-section of household incomes across all ages of the "mother". From this cross-section the present value of expected lifetime income of a household, at its formation when the woman is 18, can be computed – given the discount rate r and the rate of growth of per capita income γ.

It is this present value which is assumed to be spread evenly in present value of consumption over the expected lifetime of the household. But of course this assumption does not have the same unambiguous inter-pretation it has when only a single individual is involved. Presumably,

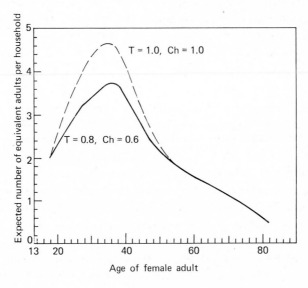

Fig. 32.5.

more of the household's lifetime occurs in years when the expected size of the household is large than when it is small. One assumption would be that each expected year of life of a household member counts the same, regardless of the age or sex of the household member. This would be extreme, as it follows for no economies of household scale and provides equally for the consumption of a small child and an adult. Alternatively, "equivalent adult" coefficients could be assumed – or preferably estimated from household budget data – for various age–sex categories.

Calculations have been made on a number of alternative assumptions, ranging from the extreme assumption that all persons count equally regardless of age and sex to the extreme assumption that children do not count at all.

Some of the calculations are interesting both at the level of the individual household and at the level of the population as a whole. In Figure 32.5 the expected number of equivalent adults per household during the household life cycle is shown for two of the four assumptions used: (a) teenagers $T = 1.0$, children $Ch = 1.0$, and (b) $T = 0.8$, $Ch = 0.6$. Figures 32.6 and 32.7, like Figures 32.2 and 32.3, show cumulated income, cumulated consumption, and net worth, all discounted to the "birth" of the household. Figure 32.6 assumes $T = Ch = 1$ and $r - \gamma = n = 0.0169$, the "golden rule" case. Figure 32.7 in contrast, assumes $T = Ch = 0$ and $r - \gamma = 0.05$. As the diagrams illustrate, the presence of children and the relative absence of interest incentive leads to high consumption fairly early in life in Figure 32.6, compared to Figure 32.7. Note that the C curves are not straight lines; they would be if the horizontal axis measured cumulative equivalent adult years rather than calendar years. As plotted, the fluctuations in C just reflect fluctuations in cumulative equivalent adult years.

The percentage of earned income saved at different ages is graphed in Figure 32.8 for the situations of Figures 32.6 and 32.7. The dip in net saving in the 30s in the curve for $T = Ch = 1$ reflects, of course, the need to provide for children's consumption in those years.

The calculations permit negative net worth. Credit markets are assumed perfect, so that families can borrow against future income at the same interest rate they earn on their assets. But very few years of negative net worth appear in the calculations. Those that do occur are in the first

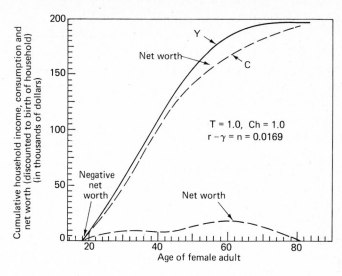

Fig. 32.6.

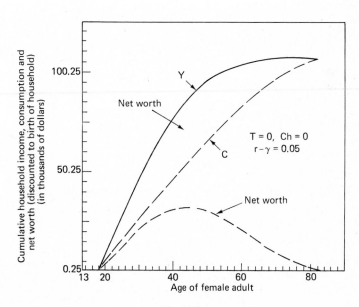

Fig. 32.7.

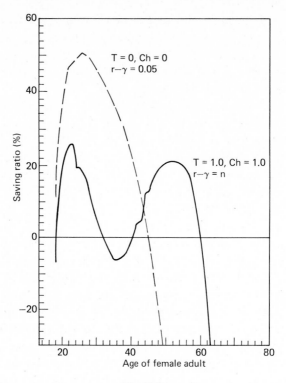

Fig. 32.8.

years of the household's life. The maximum number of years in debt, in the examples calculated, is four, when $T = Ch = 0$ and the interest rate is low: $r - \gamma = 0.02$. In these circumstances neither the future needs of

Table 32.3
Ratio of wealth to labor income

		Equivalent	Adult	Consumption	Weights
	Teenagers T	1.0	0.8	0.1	0.0
$r - \gamma$	Children Ch	1.0	0.6	0.1	0.0
$= n = 0.0169$		3.18	4.25	not computed	
$= 0.02$		3.82	4.91	6.97	7.52
$= 0.035$		7.11	8.45	11.10	11.79
$= 0.05$		11.24	12.97	16.52	17.44

children nor the incentive of a high interest rate keeps the household from anticipating higher future incomes by high present consumption.

The results of some aggregative calculations are shown in Table 32.3. All the calculations assume the same rate of natural population increase (0.0169), calculated in the manner described. The first row of Table 32.3 refers to "golden rule" paths, in which $r - \gamma$ is equal to this value of n. Other rows refer to higher values of $r - \gamma$. Clearly the interest rate has a powerful positive effect on the demand for wealth.

To what extent do these results depend on the assumption that there is no subjective discount of future utility? When the market interest rate r exceeds the subjective discount rate δ, the consumption stream (per expected equivalent adult) is tilted upward: consumption rises with age. If, however, r is equal to δ the consumption stream would be flat; if r is less than δ, it would be tilted downward. Alternative calculations have been made for positive values of δ, 0.01, 0.02, and 0.05 for one equivalent adult scale ($T = 0.8$, $Ch = 0.6$). As might be expected, given the market interest rate, a rise in δ lowers the demand for wealth. Indeed a high subjective discount rate so encourages high consumption by young people, financed by borrowing against future income, that the aggregate demand for wealth is negative. The results are shown in Table 32.4.

For comparison with Table 32.1 the reader might wish to assume a γ of 0.025 or 0.030, as an estimate of the rate of growth of per capita income. Table 32.5 makes such a comparison for illustration. The first column of Table 32.5 corresponds to the second column of Table 32.3, assuming $\gamma = 0.03$ and equivalent adult scales of 0.8 and 0.6 for teenagers and younger children, respectively. The second column corresponds to the

Table 32.4
Ratio of wealth to labor income ($T = 0.8$, $Ch = 0.6$)

$r - \gamma$	0	0.01	0.02	0.05
			δ	
$= n = 0.0169$	4.25	1.14	−1.63	−5.06
$= 0.02$	4.91	2.42	0.21	−4.91
$= 0.035$	8.45	5.54	3.01	−2.61
$= 0.05$	12.97	9.32	6.22	−0.38

third column of Table 32.1; that is, it assumes a Cobb–Douglas production function with elasticity of output with respect to capital equal to $\frac{1}{3}$. On the assumptions of Table 32.5 – and assuming capital to be the only form of wealth – a balanced-growth path with a rate of return to capital r of about 6% and a ratio of capital to labor income of about 8 would be an equilibrium path. The corresponding ratio of capital to output would be 5.4. This capital–output ratio may seem unrealistically high and the rate of return on capital unrealistically low for the U.S.A. But there is, after all, another major component of private wealth in the U.S.A. – the debt, monetary and otherwise, of the federal government, including its social security trust funds, to its citizens. There is also the net foreign wealth of U.S. citizens. Together these add up roughly to 1.0 times annual labor income ($\frac{2}{3}$ of national income) and reduce the demand for capital implied by column 1 of Table 32.5 by 1.0 at each interest rate. This means that the equilibrium interest rate would be of the order of 0.07, with a ratio of capital to labor income of 7.0, implying a capital–output ratio of somewhat less than 5. Raymond Goldsmith's estimates suggest that the actual ratio of productive tangible wealth, broadly inclusive, to net national income is of the order of 4.

In any case, it seems quite possible that life cycle saving can account for the U.S. capital stock. However, it appears unlikely that life cycle saving would be sufficient to give the economy a "golden rule" capital stock and interest rate.

Table 32.5
Ratios of wealth and capital to labor income

r	Wealth ratio ($\gamma = 0.03$; $T = 0.8$, $Ch = 0.6$)	Capital ratio ($\alpha = \frac{1}{3}$)
0.05	4.91	10.0
0.065	8.45	7.7
0.08	12.97	6.25

Notes

[1] See, for example, Chapter V of his *Theory of Interest.*

[2] Franco Modigliani and Richard Brumberg, "Utility Analysis and the Consumption Function: An Interpretation of Cross Section Data," *Post Keynesian Economics* (New Brunswick, N.J.: Rutgers Univ. Press, 1954).

[3] However, Ando and Modigliani assume a level stream of actual consumption whatever the interest rate. See Franco Modigliani and Albert Ando, "The Life Cycle Hypothesis of Saving," *American Economic Review*, 53 (1963), 55.

[4] Ando and Modigliani, *op. cit.*, p. 59, say that the parameters of the consumption function depend "only on the rate of return on assets and on the overall rate of growth of income, which in turn is the sum of population growth and the rate of increase of productivity". In a footnote they say: "Strictly speaking the values of the parameters would vary somewhat depending on whether the growth of income results from population or from productivity growth. However, for rates of growth within the relevant range, say 0 to 4 per cent per year, the variation turns out so small that it can be ignored for present purposes." Table 32.2 of this chapter indicates that γ and n have rather different effects on the desired wealth–income ratio. But Ando and Modigliani assume that *un*discounted consumption is spread evenly over lifetime, regardless of the market interest rate, while I assume that discounted consumption is evenly spread.

[5] Census Current Population Reports Series P-60 No. 44 (May 27, 1965), Table 6.

CHAPTER 33

WEALTH, LIQUIDITY, AND THE PROPENSITY TO CONSUME

The careers of the Consumption Function and George Katona have been intertwined since 1945. The consumption-saving decision has been a major subject of theoretical and empirical inquiry, to which no one has contributed more than Katona. A behavioral scientist by training and temperament, he brought to economic research quite a different bag of tools and insights from those of the technical economist. As a social psychologist, he was probably not surprised to find that he annoyed many of the brethren of his adopted scientific fraternity. What put them off was his disdain for utility-maximizing or profit-maximizing models of individual behavior, and his failure to base his statistical inferences and macroeconomic conclusions on explicit formal system-wide models. But today we can appreciate, even from the perspectives of economic theory and econometrics themselves, Katona's perception, prescience, and persistence.

Katona was the great entrepreneur of survey data collection, and for this alone the economics profession owes him an immense debt. In the early postwar years economists were still convinced that rigorous sophisticated methods could make time series of economic aggregates disclose simple reliable macrorelations. This optimistic faith dominated in particular economists' research on saving behavior, thanks initially to the apparent statistical success of the Keynesian consumption function. But as primitive Keynesian functions failed and competing hypotheses of greater complexity were advanced to fill the vacuum, the importance of household survey data came to be appreciated. Meanwhile Katona and his colleagues in Ann Arbor and Washington were busy

Reprinted from *Human Behavior in Economic Affairs* (*Essays in Honor of George S. Katona*), B. Strumpel, James N. Morgan, and Ernest Zahn (Eds.) (Elsevier Scientific Publishing Co., Amsterdam 1972), pp. 36–56.

providing, in the annual *Surveys of Consumer Finances*, an invaluable data base. Moreover, Katona and the Survey Research Center pioneered in reinterview surveys: the profession's appetite for panel data of this type is now almost insatiable.

Katona's other major enterprise in survey data collection has been the continuous monitoring of consumer attitudes, expectations, and intentions. Indeed these are the data closest to his own theoretical and methodological interests. Economists have been slower to appreciate and to use these data than the more conventional demographic and financial information of household surveys. But this situation, too, is changing. One reason is that contemporary theories of saving behavior, portfolio choice, and inflation place great emphasis on economic agents' perceptions of their environment and expectations of its future. There is precious little information on these psychological variables – what they are, what their behavioral implications are, how they are altered by experience and learning – except what George Katona has collected. As economists move beyond the stage of regarding expectations as unobservable and representing them by untested functions of past observations, they will have to rely heavily on Katona's data, and on his interpretations as well.

Imitation and extension are flattery in science as elsewhere. The federal government and other agencies now collect, regularly or *ad hoc*, many of the kinds of survey and panel data in which Katona and his organization pioneered.

Economists concerned with consumption and saving behavior owe Katona a debt for insights and ideas as well as for data. He has always expressed skepticism of the tight mechanical relation of consumption spending to cash income, into which the Keynesian propensity to consume had evolved in lesser hands than those of its inventor. Katona saw two major developments in America, and with a lag in other economies as well, which make consumption a less and less predictable function of cash income. One is general affluence; as consumption spending becomes further and further removed from basic subsistence, both its direction and its timing become more discretionary. The other is the improvement of credit markets, the appearance and growth of institutions enabling consumers to borrow against houses, other durable goods, or simply their names and earning prospects.

To these reasons one might add a special consequence of the growth of affluence: increase in life expectancies and retirement spans. These have been accompanied by a shift in the socially accepted financial responsibilities of generations. Most Americans now expect, and are expected, to provide for their old age with their own resources and social insurance rather than to become charges on their children. Faced with this requirement, a household cannot, and as a result need not, follow the simple rule of spending as it earns.

These developments, in Katona's view, liberate consumer spending from dependence on contemporaneous cash income and make consumption-saving decisions, like any other area of discretionary behavior, a matter of psychology. The conventional economists' reaction to the news that contemporaneous cash income alone does not explain consumption is to add other "objective" explanatory variables: lagged incomes, wealth, liquid assets, etc. Katona's reaction has been to try to measure directly the attitudes and expectations that proximately govern households in exercising their discretion, and to seek in turn explanations of the formation of these proximate variables.

The two approaches are not as antagonistic as they have often seemed. Indeed, in the context of the current theory and econometrics of consumption and saving, they are convergent and complementary. That, at any rate, is the theme I propose to argue in this paper in honor of George Katona, as much to justify economic theory to him as him to the economic theorists.

1. Income as Liquidity and as Wealth

Throughout its history the consumption function has been characterized by intellectual tension between a liquidity and a wealth interpretation of income as the primary determinant of consumption. Both interpretations are present in the *General Theory* (Keynes, 1936). But the wealth interpretation is dominant; Keynes, after all, discusses the propensity to consume as a "psychological law". Nevertheless the liquidity interpretation came to dominate early statistical and econometric work, textbook expositions of multiplier arithmetic, and practical models of fiscal policy. Recent emphasis on permanent and lifetime income has brought the wealth interpretation to the fore.[1]

Which is the effective constraint on the current consumption of a household? Its liquidity, the resources it can mobilize to spend within a short period, a month, a quarter, a year or two? Or its wealth, human as well as non-human, the total of its present and future consumable resources, including prospective earnings from work? For a liquidity-constrained household, income is a source of cash and changes in income will be almost completely reflected in changes in consumption spending in a short time. For a wealth-constrained household one year's income is by itself a small part of total wealth; like other variations in wealth, changes in current income will be shared among this year's consumption and all future years. Only if changes in current income inspire significant changes in estimates of future income and thus in total wealth will there be a large response in current consumption.

2. Volatility and Stability in the Marginal Propensity to Consume

Primitive evidence certainly supports Katona's observation that the *ex post* marginal propensity to consume is extremely volatile in the short run. In Figure 33.1 I have plotted, with apology for the use of so crude a device in this computer age, a scatter diagram of annual changes in per capita real personal consumption against contemporaneous changes in per capita real disposable income for the U.S.A., 1951–70. The reference line has a slope of 0.91, which is the ratio of the full 19-year change in consumption to the change in income over the period. The scatter speaks for itself. It would be even worse, of course, for quarterly data. Judicious expenditure of degrees of freedom on lag structure makes things better – see the consumption sector of any econometric model. But the obstacles to substantial improvement by lagging income alone are indicated on the diagram by the horizontal arrows, which indicate how the designated point would shift if the horizontal variable included last year's income with weight up to $\frac{1}{2}$. About half the arrows point the wrong way.

Whether the volatility is greater postwar than prewar is not so clear. Figure 33.2 presents the same data for 1929–40, on a scale that compensates roughly for the difference in the magnitudes of income and consumption changes between the two periods. The reference line has the slope 0.78, based on comparison of 1933 and 1940, the biggest income

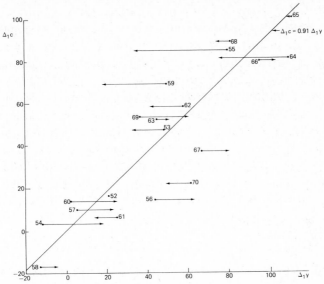

Fig. 33.1. Differences from previous year in per capita real disposable income ($\Delta_1 y$) and consumption ($\Delta_1 c$), 1951-70 (1958 dollars).

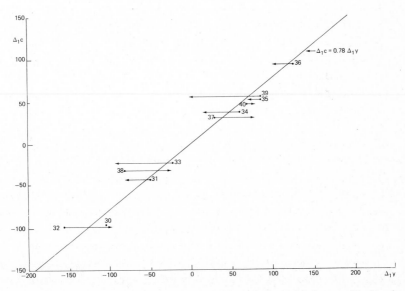

Fig. 33.2. Differences from previous year in per capita real disposable income ($\Delta_1 y$) and consumption ($\Delta_1 c$), 1929-40 (1958 dollars).

difference during the period. Prewar deviations of consumption from the reference line were smaller than postwar in average absolute magnitude, both in dollars and in relation to the average absolute size of income and consumption changes. But the prewar deviations were larger relative to average income and consumption levels.

Short-run volatility is consistent with a remarkable degree of long-run stability in the marginal propensity to consume. Figure 33.3 is derived from the same 1951–70 data as Figure 33.1, but plots average differences from 5 and 10 years earlier, instead of one year earlier. Since these deviations from the reference line in Figure 33.3 include averages of successive random elements in the one-year deviations of Figure 33.1, it is to be expected that they will have lower variance. But the improve-

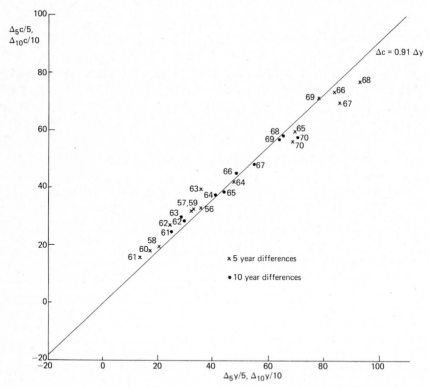

Fig. 33.3. Average annual differences from 5 or 10 years previous in per capita real disposable income ($\Delta_5 y/5$, $\Delta_{10} y/10$) and consumption ($\Delta_5 c/5$, $\Delta_{10} c/10$) (1958 dollars).

ment is greater than would be expected on this basis. For the 10-year differences, the standard deviation is 0.17 of that for the one-year differences, rather than $(\frac{1}{10})^{1/2}$. For the 5-year differences it is 0.27 rather than $(\frac{1}{5})^{1/2}$. Evidently short-run fluctuations in the marginal propensity to consume are not independent. Although timing is erratic, a correction mechanism seems to operate to keep consumption, saving, and income in fairly stable long-run relationship to each other. The task of theory is to explain both the short-run volatility and the long-run stability.

The role of disposable personal income (DPI) in consumption functions illustrates the vacillation of the profession between the wealth and liquidity models. Although the choice of this income concept might be justified on both grounds, it is not really appropriate for either one. As a liquidity measure it would be a proxy for cash inflow. As a wealth measure it would be a surrogate for lifetime income or total wealth. Its most characteristic feature, the omission of direct taxes, makes sense in either case.

Department of Commerce DPI handles many items on a cash rather than accrual basis, and excludes both employer and personal contributions for social insurance. In these respects it is more liquidity than wealth oriented, but Paul Taubman (1971) has recently pointed out that it is far from a thoroughgoing cash income measure. It is certainly a poor measure either of total wealth or of human wealth. It includes some but not all earnings of property; a major omission is corporate retained earnings. It omits earned supplements to wages and salaries. And of course it registers fluctuations of cash incomes of property and labor that households presumably smooth out in evaluating their wealth positions.

3. Wealth and Liquidity: a Two-period Example

Consider, for example, the Fisherian consumer of Figure 33.4, with a life "cycle" of two periods. Suppose his wealth is entirely human wealth: his labor will yield cash incomes of y_1 and y_2 in the two periods. He can convert first-period income into second-period consumption at an interest rate of r. In a perfect capital market he can also borrow at this rate and convert future income into current consumption. His opportunity locus would be the line C_2C_1, and let us suppose his chosen consumption sequence would be C^*. Should his initial income be y_1' instead, his opportunity locus will shift, parallel, to $C_2'C_1'$, and his chosen sequence will become $C^{*\prime}$. Normally, as in the illustration, both periods' consumption will share in the gain in total resources; the marginal propensity to consume from current cash income is less than one. [If preferences are scale-free, indifference curves homothetic, C^* and $C^{*\prime}$ are on the same ray. The marginal propensity is simply the ratio of c_1 to C_1, the household's total resources evaluated in terms of first-period consumption, $y_1 + y_2/(1 + r)$.] In this example the only constraint on the consumer is his wealth.

A pure and extreme case of liquidity constraint arises if the consumer of Figure 33.4 is not allowed to borrow against future income, to convert

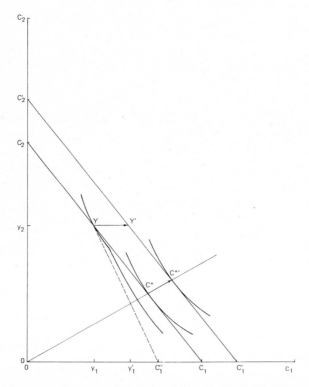

Fig. 33.4. Two-period consumption choice with and without liquidity constraints.

second-period income y_2 into first-period consumption c_1. This constraint forces the consumer to point Y, the consumption sequence $c_1 = y_1, c_2 = y_2$. His opportunity locus is $C_2 Y$, and in technical jargon he is at a "corner" instead of "interior" maximum of utility. The marginal propensity of current consumption with respect to current cash income is unity: $\partial c_1/\partial y_1 = 1$. This is indicated in Figure 33.4 by the horizontal path, YY', of response to an increase of initial income to y_1'.

The liquidity constraint need not be absolute. The consumer may be permitted to borrow against future income, but only at a penalty rate. The opportunity locus will be like $C_2 YC_1''$, and the consumer may still prefer the corner Y to any point interior to YC_1''. The current marginal propensity to consume is one, as before, at least for income decreases and small enough increases.

4. Wealth and Liquidity in the Life Cycle Model

The same points can be illustrated for a multi-period lifetime. I have set forth the life cycle model formally elsewhere (Tobin 1967; Dolde and Tobin, 1971), and here I will only sketch it and illustrate it graphically. In Figure 33.5 the age of a consuming household from its formation to its death is measured horizontally, and against it is plotted the cumulative discounted labor income $Y(a)$ of the household up to each age a. This is the present value as of age 0 of the stream of income from 0 to a, with discount rates equal to the lending or saving rates available to the household. The flow of income $y(a)$, discounted to age zero, is the slope of the curve $Y(a)$. The value, as of age zero, of total lifetime income is $Y(A)$. A similar path $C(a)$ may be drawn for discounted cumulative consumption. Assuming that the household begins and ends with zero net non-human wealth – or with the same amount in value as of age zero – its lifetime budget constraint is that $C(A) = Y(A)$. [This implies $C(a) \leqq Y(A)$ for all a – since consumption flow is non-negative, $C(a)$ is non-decreasing in a.]

In a wealth model of consumption this is the only budget constraint. The shape of $Y(a)$ does not matter; any path $C(a)$ is available provided it ends up at the proper point. All wealth, human and non-human, future yields of labor as well as future yields of bonds and stocks, is available

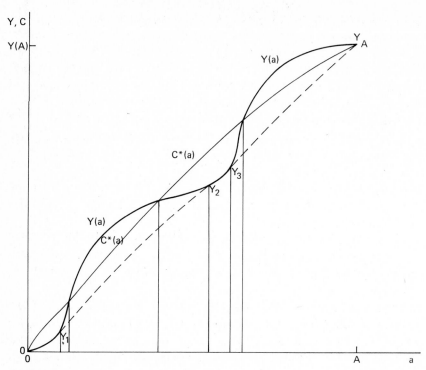

Fig. 33.5. Cumulative income Y and consumption C, constrained and unconstrained, in relation to household age a.

at its capitalized value for consumption now or any future time. Wealth is completely fungible between periods.

With this freedom of choice, what consumption path will the household choose? This will depend on several factors: (a) the smaller its *subjective rate of time preference* and the greater the *interest rated offered in the market,* the more the household will tilt its consumption stream [the slope of $C(a)$] in favor of later as against earlier consumption; (b) *household size and composition* vary over the life cycle, and there may be other age-related reasons for variation of consumption rates. With these factors taken into account, diminishing marginal utility of consumption in any one period is a strong force for equality of consumption between periods. The theory suggests a smooth consumption path $C(a)$. One with sharp changes of slope, that is of consumption rates, would probably be one with differences of marginal utility which the household could to its advantage erase by shifting consumption from a plush to a sparse year.

At this point a digression is in order to recall the role of Katona's Economic Behavior Program, especially the late John Lansing, in developing the "life cycle" concept and implementing it statistically. It was Jack Lansing who long ago saw the convenience and fruitfulness of regarding household age as a sovereign exogenous variable on which many other demographic and economic magnitudes were jointly dependent – family size and composition, labor force participation, income, consumption, wealth. (See Klein 1954.) He saw before many of the rest of us that in handling household survey data this approach would often make more sense than regarding some of the jointly dependent variables as predetermined and regressing others upon them, as in the fitting and interpretation of Engel curves. It is also noteworthy that the long series of *Surveys of Consumer Finances* provide the best available data for estimating age–income profiles, on both a cross-section and sequential basis, for people of various occupations and educational attainments.[2]

Returning to Figure 33.5, suppose that $C^*(a)$ represents the utility-maximizing path. The difference $Y(a) - C^*(a)$ is non-human wealth $W_n^*(a)$ at age a, discounted as usual to age zero. This may be negative at some ages, as in the illustration, because of borrowing against future labor incomes. The age–wealth profile $W_n^*(a)$ is also plotted in Figure 33.6.

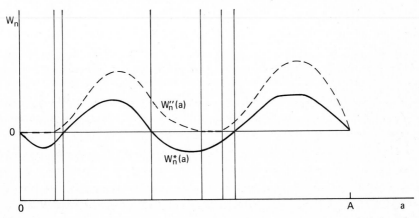

Fig. 33.6. Non-human wealth W, constrained and unconstrained, in relation to household age a.

According to the life cycle theory, a household dissaves, saves, and dissaves, in order to smooth out in consumption the age-related fluctuations of its earnings.

With liquidity constraints, however, the household would not ever be able to have negative W_n. To the general wealth constraint $C(A) = Y(A)$ would be added $C(a) \leq Y(a)$ for all a. Alternatively, as in the two-period example above, a high penalty rate for borrowing could have the same effect as an absolute prohibition. The best liquidity-constrained path – with no negative net worth positions at any age – is $OY_1Y_2Y_3Y_4$. Two segments of this path are liquidity-constrained, OY_1 and Y_2Y_3. A best constrained C-path will have, as illustrated, tangencies to the Y-path at the ages at which liquidity constraints become or cease to become effective, Y_1, Y_2, and Y_3 in the illustration. Otherwise there would be sharp discontinuities in consumption rates, inviting smoothing in order to bring marginal utilities closer together.

The liquidity-constrained age–wealth profile W_n'' is shown in Figure 33.6. It is of course always above the unconstrained age–wealth profile W_n^*.[3]

Here, even more than in the two-period example, the effectiveness of liquidity constraints makes a difference in the current marginal propensity to consume (*mpc*). In the constrained case, this *mpc* is 1 during the stages of the life cycle at which the constraint is effective, and less than 1 at other ages. In the absence of constraint, all consumption within the horizon, future as well as current, will share in any revision of the household's estimate of the present value of its resources. The horizon may be the remaining lifetime, as in the completely unconstrained case, or just the time until the liquidity constraint becomes binding, as in the interval Y_1Y_2 in, Figure 33.5. An increase in current disposable income alone will in these circumstances have only a fractional effect on current consumption; generally most of the increment in total resources will be saved for future consumption. Calculations for an unconstrained life cycle model for the U.S. population indicate an *mpc* from total wealth, human or non-human, of about 0.05–0.07 (Dolde and Tobin, 1971, Part IV). This would apply to a one-shot change in disposable income. It is a far cry from the estimate of 1 for liquidity-constrained consumers.

The wealth model and the liquidity model thus imply very different values of the short-run *mpc*, much smaller in the former case than in the latter. The mirror image is that they also imply very different responses to other parameters, larger for the wealth model than the liquidity model. Wealth-constrained households will, liquidity-constrained households will not, alter their current consumption in response to marginal changes in their illiquid resources – increases in expected future labor incomes, improvements in prospective retirement benefits, capital gains on houses and other imperfectly liquid assets. Wealth-constrained households will, liquidity-constrained households will not, respond to small changes in interest rates, either for lending or for borrowing. (In all these cases it is conceivable that large enough changes in the right direction will move a household from a corner to an interior point. For example, if future income declines enough the inability to borrow against it ceases to be a relevant concern.)

5. Current Income as an Index of Wealth

Current income, in addition to being a constituent of total wealth, a small one for households of most ages, is a source of information about future incomes. This role may greatly magnify the short-run *mpc*. Whether it does or not depends upon how people read the changes in income which they experience. If their expectations are extrapolative, obviously, the effects will be stronger than if they are regressive. Here is one point on which the life cycle model must appeal to George Katona and other students of expectations.[4]

To formulate the point more precisely, the life cycle theory says that current year's consumption of a household of age a is a certain fraction γ_a of its total human and non-human wealth $W_h + W_n$. Human wealth W_h is $\sum_{i=0}^{A}(d_i)^i y_{a+i}$, where $y_a, y_{a+1}, y_{a+2}, \ldots$ is the stream of current and expected disposable labor income, and the $(d_i)^i$ are the discount rates that convert these incomes to present values. Let the prior expectations of the income stream be y_{a+i}^*, and let W_h^* be the corresponding value of human wealth using the discount factors d_i. Suppose that the household obeys the following rule of revision of income expectations after learning the true value of y_a:

$$y_{a+i}/y_{a+i}^* = (y_a/y_a^*)_i^\beta \quad (i = 1, 2, \ldots). \tag{1}$$

Thus $W_h = y_a + \sum_{i=1}^{A}(d_i)^i \, y_{a+i}^*(y_a/y_a^*)_i^\beta$, and

$$\partial c_a/\partial y_a = \gamma_a\left[1 + \sum_{i=1}^{A} \beta_1(d_i)^i (y_{a+i}^*/y_a^*)(y_a/y_a^*)\beta_i^{-1}\right]. \qquad (2)$$

If all the β_i are zero, the *mpc* is simply γ_a, a parameter, as previously stated, of the order of 0.05–0.07 on average. If all the β_i are one, $W_h = (y_a/y_a^*)W_h^*$ and the short-run *mpc* is

$$\gamma_a(W_h^*/y_a^*) = (c^*/y_a^*)[W_h^*/(W_h^* + W_n)]. \qquad (3)$$

Blowing disposable labor income y_a up by the ratio of total wealth to human wealth gives approximately total disposable income. So the short-run *mpc* in this case is equal to the average propensity to consume.

But of course there are many other possibilities, within and beyond these two special cases. We have no reason to believe the β_i to be constant over time or to be independent of the sources and circumstances of income change. We must expect revisions of income expectations resulting from information other than that conveyed by current income. Unlike the liquidity model, therefore, the wealth model gives us plenty of reason to understand the observed short-run volatility of the marginal propensity to consume.

6. Liquidity Constraints and Horizons

The life cycle model has the substantial merit of providing an explanation of the long-run trend interrelations of consumption, saving, income and wealth. The theory predicts that in a demographic and economic growth equilibrium, in which households correctly foresee their lifetime income, their non-human wealth will follow a characteristic age profile. (See Figure 33.6.) The shape of the age–wealth profile will remain the same as incomes grow, assuming that technological progress raises proportionately the incomes of all age groups. Aggregate wealth is a weighted sum of the average wealth holdings of different ages, where the weights are the numbers of households of those ages. With a constant relative age distribution of the population, aggregate wealth will, just like aggregate income, rise at the natural rate of growth of the economy,

g, the sum of the rates of population growth and of technological progress. The aggregate wealth–income ratio will be a constant μ. The saving–income ratio will be $g\mu$. These ratios will be constant along any given demographic–economic growth path, but they will differ from path to path. The wealth–income ratio μ depends on, among other things, the interest rate, the rate of growth of population, and the rate of growth of per capita income.

The long-run aggregative implications of an unconstrained wealth model can be modified to allow for liquidity constraints of constant incidence, for example, always effective on typical consumers of certain ages. Such constraints will modify the characteristic age–wealth profile in the manner indicated in Figure 33.6 and raise μ above what it would be in the unconstrained case.

The merit of the life cycle model is to explain both (a) why the long-run saving–income ratio should be roughly constant, and (b) what determines the value at which it is constant. The model's essential properties hold even if a bequest motive for saving is introduced, provided that lifetime accumulation for transfer to the next generation is proportional to lifetime income. The model can probably also accommodate uncertainty and precautionary saving, a subject not discussed at all in this paper.

Critics complain that the model assumes a vastly unrealistic degree of foresight and rational calculus on the part of households. Similar criticisms are made of the maximize-present-value theory of the firm, which is in many respects analogous. In both cases theory assumes an objective and spells out its logical consequences. Real world households and firms doubtless employ many rules-of-thumb and shortcuts, and make many mistakes. That does not destroy the usefulness of the theory in pointing out the trends and relations implicit in the pursuit of these objectives. Perhaps the crucial assumption is that saving reflects purposeful behavior and is not just an unplanned random residuum. Purposeful saving is done for Christmas, taxes, vacations, college, retirement, and estates. Although households commonly speak of saving "what is left over", this is often a short-run technique of budget control rather than an indication that future and current needs are not balanced against each other.

There has been widespread agreement that purposeful foresight is involved in household consumption decisions, but disagreement about the length of the "horizon". Few consumers live literally hand-to-mouth in the sense that they are liquidity-constrained every hour or every day. People do smooth out their consumption and spending between pay-checks and anticipate seasonal gaps between needs and receipts. Further-more, there is plenty of evidence that horizons generally extend beyond one year. Friedman (1957) suggests 3 years or so for his permanent income horizon; Modigliani and Brumberg (1954) suggest a lifetime; others, emphasizing bequest motives, would span several generations. (Some dynasties, and some non-profit institutions counted in the house-hold sector in the national accounts, evidently have infinite horizons; consider the Rockefeller family and Yale University.)

The model expounded above and illustrated in Figures 33.5 and 33.6 may help to clarify the concept of horizon. In its most inclusive and vaguest sense the word refers to the future period over which outcomes are of current concern and interest. In its technical meaning for con-sumption theory, it refers to the period over which resources are pooled and, speaking loosely, averaged to determine rates of consumption. This is the interval between effective liquidity constraints, as was illustrated in Figure 33.5. This interval may be a month for some consumers, and for others a year or two or three, or a lifetime. Knowing that whatever happens you will hit a liquidity constraint in a few years greatly simplifies the estimates and calculations relevant for current consumption. Incomes that will occur after that date can be ignored; they will not arrive in time to relieve the constraints on current and near-term consumption anyway.

7. Concluding Remarks

The *mpc* for short-run variations of aggregate disposable income will evidently depend on how the change is split between liquidity-con-strained and wealth-constrained households. The liquidity-constrained households will contribute an *mpc* of one to the average. The contribu-tion of the remaining group will depend on their horizons and on how they re-estimate their human wealth as a result of changes in current income. Clearly it would be very desirable to identify the two groups and to collect relevant information from each. This would not be an easy task, but the model does provide a framework for the collection and organiza-tion of data.

Although the exposition and illustrations above stressed the possible illiquidity of future labor incomes, human wealth is not the only kind of wealth that may be illiquid. Future retirement benefits, under federal social security or private pension plans, cannot be turned into cash or pledged as security for loans. There are limits to the amounts that can be borrowed against houses, other consumer durable goods, and business proprietorships. These assets can be sold, it is true, but frequently only with sacrifices comparable to the penalty rate in the examples above. The reasons are familiar. Neither the markets for these assets nor those for rental of their services are perfect. Because of complementarities with the tastes or labor of their owners, durable goods and businesses often yield considerably more value in continued operation by their owners than they can realize in sale.

Liquidity constraint corners need not occur at zero current saving. They may occur with positive "contractual" saving, when a household is committed to accumulate illiquid wealth or to follow an agreed schedule of debt repayment. This will be true when these accumulations of equity fail to enlarge the household's credit lines, or do so only with interest penalties. Liquidity constraint corners may also occur with negative current saving, when a household is borrowing to the extent its credit line permits. Very likely there are a succession of credit lines with successively steeper penalties, and an effective liquidity constraint can occur at the threshold of any of them.

The unconstrained wealth model does not require, of course, that *all* human and non-human wealth be intertemporally fungible. It requires only that households always have sufficient liquid assets or credit lines so that they can offset as they wish the illiquidities of particular assets. Then they will never be forced into corners. Compelled to accumulate illiquid claims to retirement benefits, for example, they can if they please simply reduce other saving.

The desire to avoid liquidity binds in case of unfavorable surprises may induce more subtle and complex departures from hypothetical unconstrained consumption-saving paths. A well established finding from Michigan survey data is that among households suffering income reverses, those that have liquid assets reduce their consumption spending less than those that do not (Klein 1954). This observation conforms to the interpretation that the wealth model applies to the liquid asset holders while the others are liquidity-constrained. But it is conceivable that the fear of income decline previously led the first group to curtail consumption in favor of liquid saving.

No doubt there are still plenty of liquidity-constrained households in the U.S.A. We know, for example, that one-fifth of all households have no liquid assets and 45 per cent have less than $500 (Katona *et al.* 1970). Most of these households have low incomes and substantial installment debt. But households of this type certainly do not dominate, in dollars, marginal consumption and saving dispositions in our economy. Those dispositions are dominated by households who have considerable short-run discretion, even if many of them have horizons shorter than their lifetimes. The strength of consumer spending in the face of the temporary tax surcharge of 1968 is a recent reminder that American consumers are not slaves of their after-tax paychecks.

That is why we need George Katona. The wealth model offers him plenty of latitude. He is right that once consumption is not liquidity-constrained it is a highly psychological variable. Wealth itself is highly psychological. Recently something of an econometric identification problem has arisen, as between wealth and consumer confidence as variables explaining items of consumer expenditure (Fair 1971; Friend and Adams 1964; Hymans 1970). This is not really surprising. When Katona measures confidence, he is also measuring an important dimension of wealth.

But in the long run, attitudes and valuations are strongly governed by objective realities, and the purposes for which wealth is desired determine how much is accumulated. That is why the consumption–income relation is stable in trend while volatile quarter to quarter and year to year. That is why studies of consumer attitudes and behavior need to be embedded in a theoretical framework of rational accumulation.

References

Ando, Albert and Franco Modigliani, "The Life Cycle Hypothesis of Saving," *American Economic Review*, 53 (March 1963), 55-84.
Dolde, Walter and James Tobin, "Wealth, Liquidity and Consumption," in Federal Reserve Bank of Boston, *Consumer Spending and Monetary Policy: The Linkages* (1971). (Chapter 34 below.)

Fair, Ray C., "Consumer Sentiment, the Stock Market, and Consumption Functions," Econometric Research Program Research Memorandum No. 119 (Princeton University 1971) (mimeographed).

Friedman, Milton, *A Theory of the Consumption Function*, National Bureau of Economic Research Series General Series No. 63 (Princeton University Press 1957).

Friend, Irwin and Gerard Adams, "The Predictive Ability of Consumer Attitudes, Stock Prices, and Non-Attitudinal Variables," *Journal of the American Statistical Association*, 59 (December 1964), 987-1005.

Hymans, Saul H., "Consumer Durable Spending: Explanation and Prediction," *Brookings Papers on Economic Activity*, No. 2 (1970), 173-99.

Katona, George et al., *1969 Survey of Consumer Finances* (University of Michigan Survey Research Center, 1970).

Keynes, John Maynard, *The General Theory of Employment, Interest, and Money* (London: Macmillan, 1936).

Klein, Lawrence R. (Ed.), *Contributions of Survey Methods to Economics* (University of Michigan Survey Research Center, New York: Columbia University Press, 1954).

Modigliani, Franco and Richard Brumberg, "Utility Analysis and the Consumption Function: An Interpretation of Cross Section Data," in *Post-Keynesian Economics*, K. Kurihara (Ed.) (New Brunswick: Rutgers University Press, 1954), pp. 388-436.

Shuford, Harry L., "Subjective Variables in Economic Analysis: A Study of Consumers' Expectations." Unpublished Ph.D. dissertation, Graduate School, Yale University, June 1970.

Stearns, Robert, "Life Cycle Earnings and Consumption: Evidence From Surveys." Unpublished Ph.D. dissertation, Graduate School, Yale University, June 1971.

Taubman, Paul, "Monetary Policy and Consumption (or a Chain is only as Strong as its Weakest Link)," in Federal Reserve Bank of Boston, *Consumer Spending and Monetary Policy: The Linkages* (1971).

Tobin, James, "Relative Income, Absolute Income, and Saving," in *Money, Trade, and Economic Growth* (*Essays in Honor of John Henry Williams*) (New York: Macmillan, 1951), pp. 135-56. (Chapter 30 above.)

Tobin, James, "Life Cycle Saving and Balanced Growth," in *Ten Economic Studies in the Tradition of Irving Fisher*, W. Fellner (Ed.) (New York: Wiley, 1967), pp. 231-56. (Chapter 32 above.)

Watts, Harold W., "Long-run Income Expectations and Consumer Saving," in Thomas F. Dernburg et al., *Studies in Household Economic Behavior* (New Haven: Yale University Press, 1958), pp. 101-44.

Notes

[1] The standard references are Ando and Modigliani (1963), Friedman (1957), and Modigliani and Brumberg (1954).

[2] This has been painstakingly done by Robert Stearns (1971). Stearns has some success in showing that differences among households in current consumption are related to whole profiles, not just to current income. Some years earlier Harold Watts used SCF data for a similar purpose (Watts 1958).

[3] In emphasizing the importance of household differences in liquidity in explaining their differences in saving, I return to the theme of Tobin (1951) 20 years ago. There I

contended that simple lack of liquidity rather than lack of status aspiration explained the higher average propensity to save of Negroes. Their higher propensity as a group was largely due to the infrequency and limited amounts of dissaving among them, more likely the result of external constraints than of choice.

[4] Besides the studies of Katona and his colleagues, reference can be made to Fair (1971), Hymans (1970), and Shuford (1970).

CHAPTER 34

MONETARY AND FISCAL EFFECTS ON CONSUMPTION

1. Monetary Influences on Consumption and Saving

In discussion of the effects on aggregate demand of monetary policies
and events, investment spending has been the main focus of attention.
Economists have devoted a great deal of theoretical and empirical effort
to tracing monetary influences on plant and equipment expenditure and
residential construction. They have paid relatively less attention to
monetary effects on consumption and saving. One reason has been the
wide currency of a simple Keynesian consumption function, a mechanical
relation of consumption to disposable income. It has not been easy
empirically to improve on the approximation that consumption is a
constant fraction of disposable income, although the short-run volatility
of this fraction is a major source of uncertainty and error both in forecasting and – as the unhappy memory of the 1968 surcharge reminds us –
in policy.

In this paper we consider various monetary and fiscal influences on
consumption and attempt to estimate their importance. We do not have
a new aggregate consumption function to propose, and we cannot at this
point hope to explain the instability of the propensity to consume that
has been so troublesome to forecasters and policy-makers. Our approach
is semi-realistic simulation. Instead of postulating a macroeconomic
consumption function, we derive aggregate consumption explicitly from
a model of the decisions of individual households. We stimulate a population of households with semi-realistic demographic and economic
characteristics. We assume that these households make consumption

By Walter Dolde and James Tobin. Reprinted from *Consumer Spending and Monetary
Policy: The Linkages*, Federal Reserve Bank of Boston, Conference Series No. 5 (1971).

decisions and plans in accordance with certain rules of behavior and market constraints. More specifically, the households conform to a life-cycle model of consumption and saving.

Each of our simulations generates a hypothetical path of consumption and saving for the population as a whole. The simulations differ from each other in the economic environment to which the households are adapting. Some of the environmental differences can be associated with monetary and fiscal policies. Any change in policy alters the households' constraints and expectations, and its global impact is gauged by the difference in the resulting simulated aggregate path of consumption and saving.

The word "semi-realistic" means that the overall characteristics of the hypothetical population resemble those of the population of the U.S.A., and that parameters have been chosen so that the magnitudes of aggregate variables have a familiar ring. But we cannot of course begin to mimic the actual population in detail, and we have necessarily made many untested *a priori* assumptions. Compared with usual studies of consumption, our work contains a much greater and bolder theoretical component and a much weaker component of conventional statistical estimation and testing. We do not defend this methodology here, nor do we regard it as a substitute for customary econometric methods. But the conventional methods have not been dramatically successful, and we do believe that microeconomic simulations can provide some interesting macroeconomic insights.

There are two major recognized channels of monetary influence on consumption: (a) changes in wealth and in interest rates, (b) changes in liquidity constraints. We shall also address ourselves to (c) changes in taxes, temporary and permanent. The third would traditionally be regarded as an aspect of fiscal rather than monetary policy. But the impact of a tax change depends, in our model, on the monetary environment in which it occurs, and for comparative purposes it is instructive to examine it within the same general framework.

1.1. *Wealth and Interest Rates*

Wealth has, of course, frequently been proposed as an argument in theoretical and statistical consumption functions.[1] Early in the Keynesian controversy the wealth effect on the propensity to consume became prominent as the vehicle for the "Pigou effect". Currently popular econometric consumption functions for the U.S.A. are essentially, suppressing lags, of the form

$$C = aY_d + bW, \tag{1}$$

where C is real consumption, Y_d real disposable income, and W real net non-human wealth of households. With coefficients a and b of the order of 0.5–0.7 and 0.03–0.05 respectively, and with W normally five times Y_d, an equation of this kind is consistent with the observation that consumption is normally of the order of 90 per cent of disposable income. At the same time, the equation implies a much lower marginal propensity to consume from changes in disposable income unaccompanied by changes in wealth.[2] In this respect it appears to be consistent with the abundant evidence that the marginal propensity to consume from income is lower in the short run than in the long run.[3]

Monetary policy can affect household wealth by changing interest rates and the market values of securities and other assets. Evidently this mechanism was important in the 1969–70 decline in stock and bond prices, and in the 1971 recovery of these markets. In the MIT–Penn–SSRC model, the consumption consequence of such asset revaluations is a very important component of the power of monetary policy over aggregate demand.

There is, however, some danger in applying a consumption function like (1) in this context. The historical variations of W which yield an empirical estimate of the propensity to consume from wealth have not been solely or even principally the kind of variations generated by monetary policy. The historical path of household wealth results from: (a) planned accumulation, the consequence of the very saving behavior that wealth is supposed to help to explain, (b) unexpected gains or losses due to changes, actual or expected, in the capacity of the economy's capital stock to earn income for its owners, and (c) unexpected gains or losses due to changes in the discount rates at which the market capitalizes prospective earnings. These sources of changes in wealth should not be expected to have identical effects on consumption. In particular, the changes engineered by monetary policy are of type (c) and necessarily involve changes in interest rates, while the other types do not.

Interest rates determine the terms on which households can make substitutions between present and future consumption. In theory a change in wealth connected with a change in interest rates will have not only "income effects" on consumption but also intertemporal "substitution effects". These are not included in Equation (1), and indeed econometric studies of consumption and saving have been notably unsuccessful in detecting them.[4] But in view of the formidable identification problems involved, we are not entitled to assume that they do not exist. The model used in our simulations allows for a modest amount of intertemporal substitution. Therefore it is necessary and possible to specify various packages of changes in interest rates and asset valuations and to distinguish among their consumption effects.

The effects on current consumption of changes in wealth and in interest rates may depend on the importance of liquidity constraints, about to be discussed in Section 1.2. Capital gains which are realizable in cash or in enlarged credit lines may permit households to escape from constraints on their current consumption. In these circumstances the apparent marginal propensity to consume from wealth will be higher than in a perfect capital market.

1.2. Liquidity Constraints

In macroeconomics there has always been tension between "wealth" and "liquidity" theories of consumption and saving. Should the income variables in consumption functions be liquidity measures – disposable income, disposable income less contractual saving, etc. – or human wealth measures – permanent or lifetime income? Should the stock variables be liquidity measures – liquid assets – or wealth measures – net worth?

In a theoretical perfect capital market, the consumption plans of households are constrained only by their wealth, human as well as non-human. They can turn future income from the assets they own and from their own labor into current consumption on the same terms on which they can convert current income into future consumption. Within the bounds of solvency, they can dissave and borrow at the same interest rates at which they can save and lend. In such a world, the wealth of households, including the "permanent income" from their labor, is the only relevant measure of their consumable resources.

Additional constraints arise when households cannot substitute one kind of wealth for another, or can do so only with a penalty. Human wealth may be illiquid because households are not allowed to have a negative non-human net worth position even when it is offset by the value of their future labor incomes. Alternatively, they may be allowed to borrow against prospective wages and salaries, but only at a penalty rate. The threshold at which liquidity constraints apply may indeed be a positive level of non-human wealth. Borrowing is often possible, or possible without penalty, only on a fraction of the value of real estate, securities, and other assets. Mortgage contracts and retirement plans typically require the household to build up its non-human wealth at a prescribed rate. The market imposes penalties not just for dissaving but for saving at less than the contracted rates.

Monetary policy is one determinant of the tightness of such liquidity constraints. Easy money conditions induce lenders to liberalize their down payment and margin requirements, to reduce penalty rates, to make consumer credit available on easier terms, to take more chances on unsecured personal IOUs. In tight money periods lenders move in the opposite direction.

1.3. *Permanent and Temporary Changes of Taxes*

The effects of tax changes on consumption depend on the importance of liquidity constraints. In the hypothetical world of perfect capital markets, increases of tax rates reduce human and non-human wealth by lowering expected incomes from labor and property. They may also, by lowering after-tax interest rates, have substitution effects in favor of present consumption against future consumption. Temporary tax increases diminish wealth calculations very little and will have weak income effects.

The situation is quite different for taxpapers whose current consumption is constrained by liquidity. An increase in taxes withheld or required to be paid in cash will have a powerful effect; in principle the marginal propensity to consume will be 1.0. This will be true whether the tax increase is permanent or temporary, a distinction that is much less important in a "liquidity" theory of consumption than in a "wealth" theory.

One of the difficulties of aggregation that confronts macroeconomic specifications of the consumption function is that there are undoubtedly both liquidity-constrained and liquidity-unconstrained households in the economy, in proportions that vary from time to time. The younger and poorer households are more likely to be liquidity-constrained. One advantage of the microeconomic simulation method of this paper is that differential incidence of liquidity constraints can be systematically introduced and its consumption effects calculated.

2. The Life-cycle Model as a Framework of Analysis

Our framework for analysis of the questions raised in Section 1 is the life-cycle model of household consumption.[5] We begin with a simplified exposition of this model, in two stages. Many of the essential points can be illustrated by the familiar textbook example of a consumer with a two-period lifetime. This is done in Section 2.1; Section 2.2 sketches the extension of the model to multi-period consumption and saving decisions; Section 2.3 points out some of its aggregate implications.

2.1. Two-period Consumption Decisions

Consider a consumer with a two-period lifetime. In Figure 34.1 the horizontal axis measures first-period consumption c_0 and the vertical axis second-period consumption c_1. Labor incomes in the two periods are (y_0, y_1), marked as point y. Coordinate axes are also shown with origin at y. On these axes, W_0 is the value in first-period consumption of the consumer's non-human wealth, and W_1 is its value in second-period consumption. W_0 and W_1 are related by the one-period interest rate: $W_1 = W_0(1 + r)$. The point $(y_0, y_1 + W_1)$, labelled W_1, represents one feasible consumption combination, one involving zero current saving. In the assumed perfect capital market, the household can move in either direction from this point, on terms of $1 + r$ units of deferred consumption for one unit of initial consumption. The point Y_0 measures the present value of total consumable resources, equal to $y_0 + (y_1 + W_1)/(1 + r)$ $= y_0 + y_1/(1 + r) + W_0$. The point Y_1 is the value of total resources in terms of second-period consumption. The consumer can choose any point on the opportunity locus Y_0Y_1. In the illustration he chooses point c.

A liquidity constraint would be illustrated by a kink in the opportunity

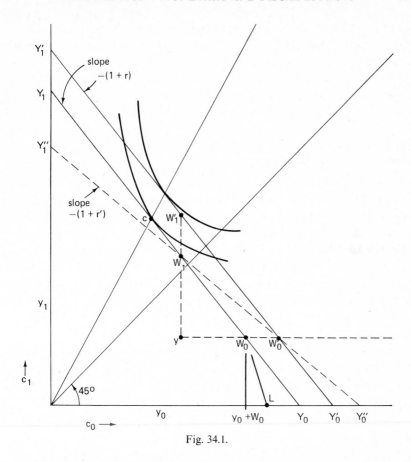

Fig. 34.1.

locus. For example, if the consumer could not consume in period 0 more than $y_0 + W_0$, the locus would be vertical from point W_0 to the horizontal axis. If he could exceed $y_0 + W_0$ only by borrowing at a rate $r_b > r$, the locus $Y_1 W_0 L$ would have a steeper slope, $-(1 + r_b)$ instead of $-(1 + r)$, from W_0 to the horizontal axis at L. The kink could occur further to the left if the consumer were required to carry a positive amount of wealth into period two, or penalized to the extent he did not.

The consumer is assumed to have a preference ordering of consumption points (c_0, c_1) with the usual properties, and to choose a point on the highest attainable indifference curve. In the later sections of the paper we have represented these preferences by a particular utility function, and we will introduce that representation here. We assume that the consumer's prospective utility U is a discounted sum of utilities of amounts consumed in each period:

$$U = \sum_{i=0}^{a^*} u(c_i)\left(\frac{1}{1+\delta}\right)^i.$$ (2)

The same one-period utility function u applies to every period; the marginal utility $u'(c_i)$ is positive and declines with c_i. Future utility is discounted at a subjective rate δ, the pure rate of time preference. In Figure 34.1, for example, the slope of an indifference curve is $-[u'(c_0)]/[u'(c_1)](1+\delta)$, and in particular it is $-(1+\delta)$ for $c_1 = c_0$, i.e., along the 45° ray. The curvature of the indifference curves is related to the substitutability between consumption in different periods. We take for marginal utility

$$u'(c_i) = Bc_i^{-\rho} \quad (\rho > 0),$$ (3)

so that $-\rho$ is the elasticity of (undiscounted) marginal utility with respect to c_i. The slope of a (c_0, c_1) indifference curve is then $-(c_0/c_1)^{-\rho}(1+\delta)$. The larger the value of ρ, the faster the slope of the indifference curve changes as the ratio c_1/c_0 moves to the left or right of the 45° ray. A high value of ρ means high curvature and low intertemporal substitutability. Following Fellner (1967) and others, we take $\rho = 1.5$ in our calculations below.[6]

In a perfect capital market, a consumer maximizes U subject only to the budget constraint

$$\sum_{i=0}^{a^*} (c_i - y_i)\, d_i - W_0 = 0,$$

$$\sum_{i=0}^{a^*} c_i d_i - \sum_{i=0}^{a^*} y_i d_i - W_0 = 0,$$ (4)

where the d_i are the market discount factors that convert consumption and income in period i to present values. In the two-period illustration $d_0 = 1$ and $d_1 = 1/(1+r)$. The first-order conditions of the constrained maximum are:

$$u'(c_i)\left[\frac{1}{(1+\delta)}\right]^i - \lambda d_i = 0 \quad (i = 0, 1, 2, \ldots, a^*),$$ (5)

where λ, the Lagrange multiplier, is the marginal utility of consumable resources. If market interest rates are constant, so that $d_i = [1/(1 + r)]^i$, we have

$$\frac{u'(c_{i+j})}{u'(c_i)} = \left(\frac{1 + \delta}{1 + r}\right)^j. \tag{6}$$

From (6) we know that undiscounted marginal utility must rise, fall, or remain constant with age according as δ is greater than, smaller than, or equal to r. If, for example, the market interest rate r exceeds the subjective discount rate δ, second-period consumption must exceed first-period consumption. The chosen combination will be to the left of the 45° line, as in Figure 34.1.

For our specific utility function, condition (5) becomes:

$$c_i = \left[\frac{B}{\lambda} d_i \frac{1}{(1 + \delta)^i}\right]^{1/\rho} \quad (i = 0, 1, 2, \dots a^*). \tag{7}$$

For example, in the two-period case

$$c_1 = c_0\left(\frac{1 + r}{1 + \delta}\right)^{1/\rho}.$$

The elasticity of c_1/c_0 with respect to $1 + r$ is $1/\rho$, or 0.67 for our numerical assumption. This means roughly that a 100-basis-point rise in the interest rate will increase c_1 relative to c_0 by two-thirds of 1 per cent.

An increase in consumable resources with no change of interest rates would be represented in Figure 34.1 by a parallel outward shift of the budget constraint. On our assumptions it would lead to a proportionate increase in c_1 and c_0, because the slope of an indifference curve derived from (3) depends only on the ratio of the two consumptions, not their absolute amounts. The same implication – proportionate shift in all c's – holds for the multi-period case.

A fall in the interest rate will tilt the opportunity locus counterclockwise and lead to intertemporal substitution. In general an interest rate decline will also have an income effect, enlarging the opportunity set for dissavers and restricting it for savers.

Both income and substitution effects are different if liquidity constraints are operative. So long as the consumer is at a kink in his opportunity locus, he will consume immediately 100 per cent of any increment in currently available resources. The substitution effect, however, will be zero for small changes in interest rates.

As our discussion in Section 1.1 indicated, changes in wealth induced by monetary policy are associated with interest rate changes, while other changes in wealth need not be. In Figure 34.1 the shift of locus from $Y_0 Y_1$ to $Y_0' Y_1'$ reflects pure capital gain, with no change of interest rates. W_0 and W_1 increase in the same proportion, to W_0' and W_1'. However, the shift of locus from $Y_0 Y_1$ to $Y_0'' Y_1''$, involves the same capital gain from W_0 to W_0', but provides no increase in W_1.

In the first case, the income effect is positive, and proportionately of the same magnitude whether the initial consumption choice was c or any other point on the budget constraint $Y_0 Y_1$. In the second case, whether the income effect is positive, zero, or negative depends on whether the initial consumption choice was to the right of W_1, at W_1, or to the left of W_1. Only if the initial choice was to the right of W_1, involving dissaving in the first period, does the income effect work in favor of current consumption. In the illustration of Figure 34.1 c was to the left of W_1 and the income effect is negative. But while there is no substitution effect in the case of pure capital gain, the reduction of the interest rate in the second case always favors current consumption.

Obviously there are other possibilities. In the second case, $(Y_0'' Y_1'')$, wealth consists entirely of claims that mature in the second period, claims that do not outlive the household. To the extent that claims are longer-lived, a smaller reduction of the interest rate will suffice to accomplish the given gain in initial wealth $W_0' - W_0$, and there will be a positive increment in W_1.[7] The two-period example does not permit us to exhibit the opposite case, where wealth consists of claims which mature short of the household's horizon. There will be some periods for which W_i is reduced – as if the budget constraints cut below W_1 in Figure 34.1. Saving for consumption in late periods is less fruitful because of the low yield at which maturing claims must be reinvested.

A case similar to the shift of opportunity locus to $Y_0'' Y_1''$ arises when asset revaluations in security markets are regarded as temporary. This means that they are associated with temporary rather than permanent changes in discount rates. Consider, for example, consol-like claims that rise in value because of a decline in the interest rate connecting period zero and period one, while subsequent rates remain unchanged. These claims will revert to their old value after period one. The value of the household's wealth in current consumption is increased, but its value in future consumption is not.

It is possible that capital gains may accompany *increases* in interest rates, so that substitution effects oppose, while income effects favor, current consumption. This combination would be the result not of monetary policy but of optimistic revisions of expected future profits.

Finally, the modeling of tax changes in the two-period illustration is obvious. A permanent tax on labor income reduces both y_0 and y_1, while a temporary tax lowers only y_0. The income effect on current consumption is obviously greater for the permanent tax except when the household is liquidity-constrained. Taxes on property incomes are like interest rate reductions.

2.2. *Multi-period Lifetime Consumption Decisions*

Consider a household at the beginning of its career, anticipating a sequence of labor incomes and deciding on a sequence of consumption rates within the limits set by its income prospects. In Figure 34.2 an expected income sequence is illustrated, and along with it a chosen consumption plan. Both the income sequence and the consumption plan are pictured in two ways, in current real dollars (dashed curves) and in dollars discounted to the decision date (solid curves).

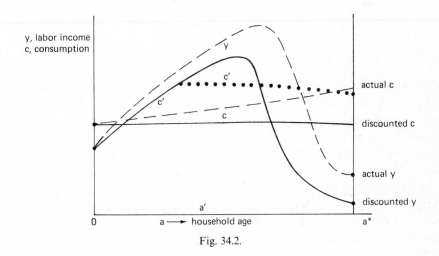

Fig. 34.2.

The consumption plan is shown as smoother than the income sequence. The spirit of the life-cycle hypothesis is that consumers prefer steady consumption to fluctuating consumption. The one-period marginal utility of consumption, like (3) above, is declining. Households save and dissave in order to smooth out their income paths. Saving for retirement is the clearest example of such behavior, but certainly not the only one. Another example is debt financing by young people to obtain a standard of life beyond their current means but consistent with their occupational status and income prospects. Of course the household is not free to choose any paths for c that it desires. It is limited by its income sequence. Specifically, the sum of the differences between discounted y_i and discounted c_i – the present value of its savings and dissavings from labor income, must add up to zero over the lifetime [as in Equation (4) above].

Figure 34.3 provides the same information as Figure 34.2 in different form. The curves are the integrals of the "discounted y" and "discounted c" curves. The Y curve shows for each age the cumulative total of labor income earned until that age, discounted to household age zero. Similarly the C curve shows the present value, as of age zero, of consumption through age a. At the terminal age a^* Y and C meet. This is the budget constraint: the present value of lifetime consumption must be the same as the present value of lifetime income. Actual consumption, cumulated at current dollars, will generally exceed actual labor income summed over the whole life. The household will earn and consume some interest.

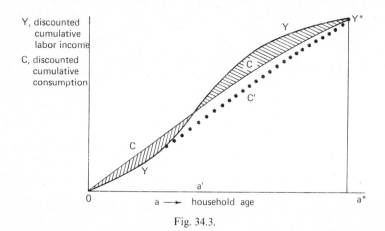

Fig. 34.3.

From the income and consumption paths the wealth profile of the household can be easily derived. In present value terms, non-human wealth W is just the vertical difference, positive or negative, between Y and G. These differences are shaded in Figure 34.3 and plotted in Figure 34.4 as "discounted wealth". By putting the discounting process in reverse, this present value wealth profile can be converted into a current dollar wealth profile – the dashed curve "actual W" in Figure 34.4. If the household's expectations are realized, this is the course its wealth will follow as its plans are carried out.

This account has assumed that the household can save and dissave in a perfect capital market – in particular, that the household can borrow against future labor income at the same interest rates at which it can save. The only constraint has been the lifetime budget constraint. Terminal wealth must not be negative, a restriction that limits total lifetime consumption but not its allocation among ages. In Figure 34.3 curve C must start at 0 and end at Y^*, but in between it may have any shape the household desires.

Consider, on the other hand, a simple liquidity constraint, that non-human wealth W can never be negative. The best the household, so constrained, can do is to consume its cash income in early years until a' and then follow the dotted curves c' and C' in Figures 34.2 and 34.3. Correspondingly, in Figure 34.4, discounted W will be 0 until age a' and then follow the dotted path. The less drastic constraint of a penalty borrowing rate, finite instead of infinite, would move the household in

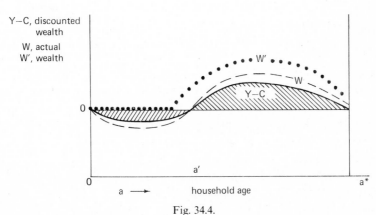

Fig. 34.4.

the same direction. In general, as the example illustrates, liquidity constraints *raise* the household's wealth profile.

In the illustration, the household begins and ends with zero wealth. The model can easily accommodate other assumptions. For a household beginning with inherited wealth, the Y and W curves of Figures 34.3 and 34.4 will start with positive intercepts. Inheritances anticipated at later ages would be shown as jumps in the Y curve. Similarly any planned or required bequest at a^* would be indicated by a positive difference between Y^* and C at a^*.

The plan made at age zero can be reconsidered and remade in the same manner at every subsequent age a. If external constraints and market interest rates conform to original expectations, and if the household's preferences are unchanged, the new decisions simply confirm the old, and the original plan will be executed. But if conditions and expectations change, the household will make a new plan for the remainder of its life.

In this introductory exposition of the model for a single household we have ignored some complications which we have to face in the applications of the model described later in the paper. These include allowance for life-cycle variation of the size and composition of the household, as children are born, grow up, and leave, and actuarial allowance for mortality.

2.3. *Macroeconomic Implications*

The life-cycle model has interesting implications for the economy as a whole. The income, consumption, saving, and wealth of a household depend on what profiles it is following and on its age. Aggregates of these variables can be obtained by summing over all households. Households differ both in profile and in age, but of course their age differences are much easier to observe. Specific results can be obtained by calculating the aggregate income, consumption, saving, and wealth of a population of households of different ages, all following essentially the same life-cycle profiles. The aggregate value of any variable is the sum of the profile variables for different ages, weighted by the number of households of each age. The aggregates will change from year to year as the population grows and its age distribution changes.

Allowance can also be made for steady growth of labor productivity. The expected income profiles of Figures 34.2 and 34.3 take general gains in labor income into account, as well as increases which are simply related to experience and seniority. A similar household starting a year later would face a higher income profile, shifted upward, as a first approximation, by the proportion γ at every age. With everything else equal, the model of consumption choice implies a similar proportionate shift in every other profile of Figures 34.2–34.4. The income, consumption, saving, and wealth of 10-year-old households in 1975 will all be $(1 + \gamma)$ times as large as those of the 10-year-old households of 1974. The aggregate consequence is that all the macro variables will grow at the rate γ per year, plus any changes that may occur because of changes in the population of households of various ages.

In a demographic "golden age", the population is growing at a steady rate n per year and its relative age distribution is constant. Consequently the number of households of each age is growing at rate n. If it is also an economic "golden age", interest rates are constant and so likewise is the growth of labor productivity γ. The model then implies that all the aggregates are growing at the rate $n + \gamma$. Since this is the natural growth rate of the economy, the life-cycle model provides an explanation of saving behavior which is consistent with a neoclassical growth equilibrium.[8]

3. Description of the Simulations

In this section we describe more specifically the modeling of the consumption decision and the variables which influence it. The Appendix contains a more complete mathematical treatment and indicates our data sources.

3.1. *Demographic Assumptions*

We distinguish among individuals by only three characteristics. The first of these is age, the central variable of the life-cycle model. The second distinguishing characteristic is sex. Realistic calculations require some recognition of family structure and of the work habits and consumption requirements of different family members.

Finally we have divided the population into two income classes. The relative proportions of the population in the groups are those that existed in 1963 between the population above and below the poverty line.

If different income groups face different opportunity sets (e.g., differential ease of access to capital markets), then aggregate consumption may depend on the income distribution. We have assumed that the two income classes differ only in the relative levels of their income profiles, not in the time shapes of the profiles or other demographic and economic circumstances.

The basic behavioral unit is the cohort, which consists of all adult females of a given age plus associated adult males and children of various ages. All cohorts are actuarially average. There are no unattached individuals or families of larger or smaller size.

An individual lives with his parental family until age 21 (in the case of males) or 18 (in the case of females). Any income earned as a teenager is contributed to the household, which in turn makes provision for the child's consumption needs until he leaves the household. At 18 the females form the nucleus of a new cohort, to which a complement of males, including newly matured 21-year-olds, are assigned. As the cohort ages it will gain some adult males from each new group of 21-year-olds. Some of the current crop of 21-year-old males is, in turn, assigned to older cohorts.

With a minor exception discussed in the Appendix, the cohort loses its adult members only by death. Each cohort is disbanded when the females become 85. A specific, unchanging, perfectly anticipated mortality table is assumed. All people expect to die before age 85. The cohort will include some adult males who are younger than the females and thus outlive the cohort. These men are assigned to new cohorts. No children are reassigned in this manner since the last age at which females bear children – 49 according to the birth table assumed – is such that all children have matured and left the cohort before it disbands. It is assumed for convenience that women do not bear children before age 18. The birth vector has been adjusted accordingly.

Although a number of demographically unrealistic simplifications have been made, none of them is quantitatively significant. The simplifications are necessary to make the computational burden manageable.

3.2. Income Expectations and the Consumption Allocation

In making its lifetime consumption plan the cohort is constrained not to allocate more than the present value of its lifetime resources. These total resources consist of human and non-human wealth. The former is the accumulated savings – including capital gains – of the cohort;[9] the latter is the present value of future labor income.

The evaluation of both sources of wealth involves expectations about their future income streams. For a number of reasons these income streams may be expected to vary with time.

Because of age-related differences in participation rates and in productivity, labor earnings vary with age, generally rising to about age 40 or 50 and then declining. For women, on the average, there is a slight decline related to reduced participation in the primary child-rearing years. We assume that the labor earnings of an individual of a given age and sex in any year will be a constant proportion of the labor income of a 40-year-old male in that year. Thus the relative income profile by age, for both men and women, will be assumed constant over time.

The absolute level of the profile, however, will change. We assume labor-augmenting technological change at a constant annual rate γ. Although factor rewards might be expected to be influenced by variations in the capital–labor ratio, we have not assumed an explicit production technology and such effects will not be considered.

A final source of variation in income streams will be changes in tax rates, both on property and on labor income. It is disposable labor income which is to be allocated to consumption or to saving, and it is after-tax property yields which are relevant to this allocation.

Having estimated the present value – at current and expected rates of discount – of its lifetime resources, the cohort then allocates these resources among all its members for all the years that they are expected to live.

The optimal allocation will be one for which the prospective marginal utility of a unit of consumption is the same in every year, so that total utility cannot be increased by shifting a unit from one year to another. We assume, of course, that the marginal utility of consumption in a given year declines with the amount of that consumption. That is why the household seeks to avoid large differences in consumption between years. The marginal utility of a unit of consumption will also vary with the year in which it is to occur: we assume a pure rate of time preference of δ. Thus the value of a unit of utility from consumption t years hence has only $1/(1 + \delta)^t$ times the value of a unit of utility today.

The utility of consumption will also vary from year to year with household size and composition. This variation reflects economies of scale in household life and differences in the needs and priorities of various household members. To allow for these phenomena we weight the utility of consumption for children and teenagers differently from adults. In this calculation of household size, adults receive a weight of $w_a = 1.0$, while the weights for teenagers and children, w_t and w_c, are 0.5 and 0.2 respectively. Thus a consumption-year for a child is equal to $w_c = 0.2$ "equivalent adult years".[10]

Barring the complications discussed in Section 3.3, the cohort maximizes its utility if it allocates its consumption – discounted by a transformation of the difference between the expected interest rate and the rate of time preference – so as to equalize consumption per equivalent adult year, where the equivalent adult years, too, are discounted by transformations of the interest rate, the rate of time preference, and birth and death rates.

3.3. *Capital Gains and Interest Rate Changes*

In the two previous sections, 3.1 and 3.2, we have explained our model of the household sector of the economy. The households make the consumption decisions, and our purpose is to see how those decisions are affected by monetary policies and other events exogenous to the household sector. In Part 2 we discussed in general terms the policy and environmental changes of interest, and now we explain how we have modeled these "shocks" in our simulations. In this section we discuss capital gains and interest rate changes. In the two sections following we discuss how we have modeled liquidity constraints and their relaxation or tightening, and how we have modeled tax changes.

As we pointed out in Part 2, capital gains and interest rate changes are intimately bound together. It is not possible to trace the effects of shocks of this kind without being explicit about the nature of the assets whose yields are assumed to change, and about the expected asset prices and interest rates.

We are assuming that the wealth of the household sector consists of various direct and indirect claims on the economy's capital stock. Monetary policies and events can change the valuation of the stock, and so can changes in the real earnings of capital due to technological or macroeconomic developments. But in the long run adjustments in the size of the capital stock or in monetary interest rates, or in both, keep market valuations of capital in line with reproduction costs. We do not provide a model of those adjustments, but we assume that our households know that they will occur and we provide them accordingly with a plausible mechanism of expectations.

The present discounted value of the earning stream of capital per dollar of reproduction cost is

$$q = \frac{R_1^e}{(1 + r_1^e)} + \frac{R_2^e}{(1 + r_1^e)(1 + r_2^e)} + \cdots$$

$$+ \frac{R_n^e}{(1 + r_1^e)(1 + r_2^e) \cdots (1 + r_n^e)} + \cdots,$$

where R_1^e is the expected net earnings i years hence, and r_1^e is the expected one-year rate of interest in the ith year. The R_i^e are net of depreciation and operating costs.

For a finite-lived piece of capital directly owned the R_i^e become zero at some point. If the R_i^e represent earnings on equity shares in a firm, however, they may not be expected to be zero. Rather it may be expected that the firm's shares will yield earnings in perpetuity. In the special case in which both R_i^e and r_i^e are expected to be constant forever at R and r, respectively, we know that $q = R/r$.

In long-run equilibrium q must equal one, i.e., the market value of a unit of capital stock must equal its reproduction cost.

Both R_i^e and r_i^e represent expectations about the future. For generating expectations we have assumed a mechanism which distinguishes between long-run and temporary phenomena. Essentially, expectations are assumed to be regressive in the short run and adaptive in the long run. Suppose that rates of return have been constant for some time at a level $\bar{r}$. This $\bar{r}$ will come to be regarded as a normal level. Suppose, however, in some period, r rises above $\bar{r}$. It might then seem reasonable to believe that r will stay above $\bar{r}$ for a while but will eventually decline to $\bar{r}$: expectations in the short run are regressive. If r continues to exceed $\bar{r}$ for some time, however, it will be less reasonable to expect a return to $\bar{r}$. In fact, $\bar{r}$ will no longer be regarded as the normal level, and estimates of the normal level will be revised upward.

If earnings on equities (the capital stock) R diverge from what has been a normal level, an entirely analogous mechanism operates. The two processes are linked, in fact, since as we have noted above, long-run equilibrium requires $R = r = \bar{R} = \bar{r}$ (i.e., $q = 1$). Thus the normal level of earnings on capital and the normal level of interest rates must be identical.

We will asume that R and r, if they differ from $\bar{R}$, will be expected to converge geometrically to $\bar{R}$ with 85 per cent of the remaining difference expected to be eradicated in each year. We assume an adaptive mechanism for $\bar{r}$, where 80 per cent of the weight is on $\bar{R}_{-1}$ and 10 per cent each on the current levels of R and r:

$$R_i^e = \bar{R} + \theta_R^i(R - \bar{R}), \tag{8}$$

$$r_i^e = \bar{R} + \theta_r^i(r - \bar{R}), \tag{9}$$

$$\bar{r} = (1 - \eta_R - \eta_r)\bar{R}_{-1} + \eta_R R + \eta_r r, \tag{10}$$

where we assume $\theta_R = \theta_r = 0.85$ and $\eta_R = \eta_r = 0.10$.

Actual values of R and r are assumed to be known and to be exogenously determined. Monetary policy will influence r in the first instance, while changes in R will be due to capital-augmenting technical change and other factors affecting the earnings of firms. Such effects are dynamically interrelated, as both affect $\bar{r}$ and hence each other. In part because they are interrelated, differences are viewed as temporary, since there exist natural forces in the economy causing R and r to reconverge to each other. As we have indicated above, however, there may be times when a permanent change in the earnings on capital is expected. This corresponds to a shift in $\bar{R}$ overriding the adaptive expectations of Equation (10). In our simulations we will investigate the effects of changes in $\bar{R}$ as well as of changes in R and r.

3.4. Liquidity Constraints

Monetary policy will affect consumption through its effects on borrowing conditions and liquidity constraints as well as through its influence on wealth. The monetary authority's ability to affect such credit conditions will be parameterized in two variables in our simulations. One of these will be a borrowing rate r_b charged on funds borrowed.

In general r_b will exceed r, the market rate of interest (lending rate for individuals). The second instrument will involve quantitative restrictions as discussed below.

Foreseen dissaving, for example in the retirement years, presumably does not pose a liquidity problem, there having been sufficient time to reallocate the portfolio to provide necessary liquidity. It is in the younger years that liquidity constraints may be of consequence, forcing the household to save more, or dissave less, than it desires.

For the purposes of our simulations it will be assumed that a cohort undertakes at age $u_a = 25$ an illiquid investment of amount A, financed by debt on which the cohort commits itself to make annual payments of principal of A/T in each of T consecutive years.[11] Cohorts are not permitted to make advanced payments on their contracts. Both the illiquid investment and the debt bear the market rate of interest.

We introduce the concept of contractual saving, $\hat{s}$, saving required of the cohort in a given year. The contractual payments of principal, A/T, are one source of obligatory saving, but not the only one. If in some year the cohort wishes to save less than $\hat{s}$, it will have one borrowing option available to it. It will borrow at a penalty rate r_b, the principal to be reduced in $\hat{T}$ equal payments of $1/\hat{T}$ times the amount borrowed. We have used $\hat{T} = 5$.

$\hat{s}$ may differ from A/T, the amount due on the initial agreement, for two reasons. First, if any secondary borrowing has occurred in the past $\hat{T}$ years, the current obligation is the sum of the amounts due on the primary and such secondary obligations. Note that any borrowing in the last $\hat{T}$ of the T years of the initial contract extends the period in which the cohort is susceptible to saving constraints, since the secondary obligations are subject to the same stipulations as the primary contract.

The second reason $\hat{s}$ may differ from A/T is related to a second credit rationing instrument. Suppose E, possibly zero, is the currently due amount at secondary loan repayments, so that the total due is $A/T + E$. Lenders may require that only a fraction ϕ of the amount due actually be paid. Equivalently, lending institutions make available loans at the market rate of interest r in the amount $(1 - \phi)(A/T + E)$.

ϕ cannot exceed one if advanced prepayment cannot be required. On the other hand, in order not to be a constraint under any circumstances, ϕ must equal negative infinity, or else r_b must equal the market interest rate r. For $\phi > -\infty$, any borrowing in excess of $(1-\phi)(A/T+E)$ occurs at the penalty rate r_b.

Monetary policies operate on consumption through these two parameters, the penalty rate for borrowing r_b and the range of its applicability ϕ. Presumably by altering policy mix and institutional structure the two parameters can be varied relative to one another. In our simulations, such variations create a wide range of credit market opportunity loci facing cohorts. Borrowing can be prevented altogether with $\phi = 1$ and r_b set prohibitively high. Algebraically smaller ϕ with r_b still prohibitively high corresponds to direct quantitative limits on borrowing. A lower r_b will permit price allocation beyond $(1 - \phi)(A/T + E)$.

The discussion has been in terms of a liquidity constraint faced only in the current period, and this is the basis on which our calculations have been made. But very likely a household expects also to be bound by similar constraints in the future. Calculation of the truly optimal consumption plan would then require explicit recognition of all possible future constraints and their costs. Indeed the timing of the undertaking of large illiquid investments should also be endogenous. The solution of such a non-linear dynamic programming problem, however, is not computationally feasible for the present investigation.

3.5. Tax Rate Changes

A final element of the economic environment which affects consumption decisions is tax policy. All of the income streams above, both property and labor, are after-tax disposable incomes. We will consider uniform percentage reductions in incomes from each source separately and from the two together. We also examine the effects of temporary and permanent taxes. In both cases it will be assumed that the timing of the tax changes are perfectly anticipated. Interest payments are assumed tax deductible. Capital gains are taxed on an accrual basis.[12]

4. Results of Specific Simulations

In this section we discuss the simulated effects of changes in policy instruments and of changes in expectations about the earnings stream of capital. Simulation 1, termed the "neutral" case for shorthand reference, represents the standard against which the other cases will be compared. The various simulations are defined in Table 34.1 and their differences relative to simulation 1 are noted. The actual time paths of r, R, q, and $\bar{R}$ for those cases in which they vary are presented in Table 34.2. The resulting time paths of aggregate consumption (C), aggregate wealth (W), and the personal saving ratio (S) are presented in Table 34.3.

Table 34.1

Description of exogenous changes defining the various simulations

Simulation	Description
1	"Neutral", $r = R = \bar{R} = 0.0525$, $q = 1$ throughout. $r_b = 0.07$, $\phi = 1.0$. No tax surcharges.
2	Interest rate changes. Starting in fourth period r declines, then rises back to initial level by ninth period.
3	Profit rate changes, short run. Starting in fourth period R rises, then declines to initial level by ninth period.
4	Profit rate changes, long run. Same short-run movement of R as in case 3. In addition, in sixth period long-run expectations change, $\bar{R}$ rises.
5	Eased liquidity constraint. $\phi = 0.5$.
6	Differential liquidity constraints, $\phi = 0.5$, $r_b = 0.07$ for higher income group. $\phi = 1.0$, $r_b = 0.10$ for lower income group.
7	Tax surcharge plus capital gains. Five-period increase in taxes on all income, reducing disposable income by 2%, coupled with an increase in R in the second period, later followed by a return to its initial level.
8	Temporary labor income tax surcharge. Labor income reduced by 2 per cent for five periods.
9	Temporary property income tax surcharge. Property income reduced by 2 per cent for five periods.
10	Temporary income tax surcharge. Combination of cases 8 and 9.
11	Permanent labor income tax surcharge, of same size as in case 8.
12	Permanent property income tax surcharge, of same size as in case 9.
13	Permanent income tax surcharge, of same size as in case 10.
14	Eased liquidity constraint. $\phi = 0$.
15	Temporary labor income tax surcharge, of same size as in case 8, plus eased liquidity constraint. $\phi = 0$.
16	Interest rate changes, same as case 2, plus eased liquidity constraint. $\phi = 0$.
17	Profit rate changes, same as case 3, plus eased liquidity constraint. $\phi = 0$.

Table 34.2

Time paths for r, R, q, $\bar{R}$ in the simulations where they are not constant*

Simulation	Variable	Year										
		1969	1970	1971	1972	1973	1974	1975	1976	1977	1978	1979
2, 16	r	0.0525	0.0525	0.0525	0.0425	0.0325	0.0325	0.0325	0.0425	0.0525	0.0525	0.0525
	q	1.0	1.0	1.0	1.043	1.089	1.089	1.090	1.044	1.0	1.0	1.0
	$\bar{R}$	0.0525	0.0525	0.0525	0.0515	0.0497	0.0483	0.0471	0.0472	0.0483	0.0491	0.0491
3, 17	R	0.0525	0.0525	0.0525	0.0625	0.0725	0.0725	0.0725	0.0625	0.0525	0.0525	0.0525
	q	1.0	1.0	1.0	1.042	1.083	1.083	1.083	1.041	1.0	1.0	1.0
	$\bar{R}$	0.0525	0.0525	0.0525	0.0535	0.0553	0.0567	0.0579	0.0578	0.0568	0.0559	0.0559
4	R	0.0525	0.0525	0.0525	0.0625	0.0725	0.0725	0.0725	0.0625	0.0525	0.0525	0.0525
	q	1.0	1.0	1.0	1.042	1.082	1.082	1.082	1.041	1.0	1.0	1.0
	$\bar{R}$	0.0525	0.0525	0.0525	0.0535	0.0625**	0.0625	0.0625	0.0615	0.0597	0.0583	0.0575
7	R	0.0525	0.0625	0.0725	0.0725	0.0725	0.0625	0.0525	0.0525	0.0525	0.0525	0.0625
	q	1.0	1.042	1.083	1.083	1.083	1.041	1.0	1.0	1.0	1.0	1.0
	$\bar{R}$	0.0525	0.0535	0.0553	0.0567	0.0579	0.0578	0.0568	0.0559	0.0552	0.0547	0.0545

* In other simulations these variables have the constant values they have in simulation No. 1, namely $r = R = \bar{R} = 0.0525$, $q = 1$, except that in simulations 9, 10, 12, 13 after-tax yields are 98 per cent of 0.0525.

** Represents a change in long-run expectations other than as represented by the adaptive expectations mechanism of Equation (10).

Table 34.3

Time paths for aggregate consumption (C), market value of wealth (W), and the saving ratio (S), for various simulations

Simulation number and type	1 Neutral			2 Easy money			3 Capital gains short run			4 Capital gains long run			5 Eased liquidity constraint			6 Differential liquidity constraints		
Year	C	W	S	C	W	S	C	W	S	C	W	S	C	W	S	C	W	S
1969	592.5	1894.8	0.061	592.5	1894.8	0.061	592.5	1894.8	0.061	592.5	1894.8	0.061	596.2	1894.8	0.056	592.0	1894.8	0.062
1970	607.9	1933.3	0.066	607.9	1933.3	0.066	607.9	1933.3	0.066	607.9	1933.3	0.066	614.3	1930.1	0.057	607.2	1934.0	0.068
1971	624.2	1976.3	0.071	624.2	1976.3	0.071	624.2	1976.3	0.071	624.2	1976.3	0.071	633.0	1967.4	0.059	623.5	1978.2	0.073
1972	641.3	2023.8	0.076	655.4	2111.2	0.054	650.6	2108.6	0.089	650.6	2108.6	0.089	652.1	2007.0	0.061	640.7	2027.5	0.079
1973	660.1	2076.3	0.079	687.2	2243.5	0.038	681.3	2258.9	0.103	676.2	2256.1	0.109	671.8	2049.2	0.063	659.7	2082.1	0.083
1974	683.4	2133.2	0.078	706.2	2271.4	0.042	705.6	2336.4	0.101	701.7	2339.3	0.107	693.4	2094.4	0.064	683.0	2141.5	0.081
1975	707.6	2190.8	0.076	729.5	2302.9	0.040	730.7	2415.8	0.101	727.7	2423.6	0.105	715.9	2141.6	0.064	707.2	2202.1	0.080
1976	732.1	2249.2	0.075	738.5	2234.8	0.057	744.9	2402.0	0.088	742.7	2414.4	0.092	739.3	2190.7	0.065	731.8	2263.5	0.079
1977	756.8	2308.6	0.075	748.3	2184.5	0.076	758.0	2376.0	0.077	756.4	2391.8	0.080	763.2	2241.8	0.065	756.6	2326.3	0.079
1978	781.5	2369.8	0.075	772.5	2246.0	0.077	782.7	2439.1	0.077	781.6	2457.6	0.080	787.8	2294.9	0.065	781.5	2391.1	0.079
1979	806.8	2433.1	0.075	796.6	2310.4	0.079	807.9	2504.4	0.077	807.2	2525.3	0.080	812.9	2350.1	0.066	807.0	2458.2	0.079

Table 34.3 (continued)

Simulation number and type	1 Neutral			7 Temporary surcharge plus capital gains			8 Temporary labor income tax			9 Temporary property income tax			10 Temporary general income tax			11 Temporary labor income tax		
Year	C	W	S	C	W	S	C	W	S	C	W	S	C	W	S	C	W	S
1969	592.5	1894.8	0.061	590.0	1894.8	0.046	589.5	1894.8	0.050	593.0	1894.8	0.057	590.0	1894.8	0.046	584.6	1894.8	0.058
1970	607.9	1933.3	0.066	612.9	2002.9	0.066	604.4	1925.6	0.054	608.1	1930.8	0.063	604.5	1923.1	0.051	599.5	1930.6	0.063
1971	624.2	1976.3	0.071	637.4	2127.2	0.084	620.3	1960.4	0.059	624.0	1971.4	0.068	620.1	1955.5	0.056	615.3	1970.7	0.068
1972	641.3	2023.8	0.076	654.9	2185.7	0.089	637.0	1999.1	0.063	640.7	2016.8	0.073	636.4	1992.1	0.060	631.9	2015.4	0.073
1973	660.1	2076.3	0.079	674.5	2250.1	0.093	654.4	2042.1	0.067	658.7	2067.4	0.078	653.3	2033.2	0.065	649.6	2065.0	0.077
1974	683.4	2133.2	0.078	692.6	2230.9	0.092	678.7	2089.8	0.081	682.2	2122.9	0.079	677.5	2079.1	0.082	672.1	2119.4	0.076
1975	707.6	2190.8	0.076	706.4	2209.7	0.078	702.9	2149.7	0.079	706.5	2181.3	0.077	701.7	2139.6	0.080	695.7	2175.0	0.075
1976	732.1	2249.2	0.075	731.0	2269.8	0.077	728.1	2210.5	0.078	731.2	2240.2	0.076	727.0	2201.0	0.078	719.7	2231.3	0.074
1977	756.8	2308.6	0.075	755.4	2331.0	0.077	753.5	2271.8	0.076	756.0	2300.1	0.075	752.6	2263.0	0.077	744.0	2288.6	0.073
1978	781.5	2369.8	0.075	780.0	2394.1	0.077	778.9	2334.2	0.076	780.8	2361.7	0.075	778.1	2325.9	0.076	768.2	2347.5	0.073
1979	806.8	2433.1	0.075	805.0	2459.6	0.078	804.3	2398.2	0.076	806.1	2425.3	0.075	803.6	2390.2	0.076	792.8	2408.4	.074

Table 34.3 (*continued*)

Simulation number and type	1 Neutral			12 Permanent property income tax			13 Permanent general income tax			14 No liquidity constraint			15 No liquidity constraint labor tax			16 No liquidity constraint easy money			17 No liquidity constraint capital gains		
Year	C	W	S	C	W	S	C	W	S	C	W	S	C	W	S	C	W	S	C	W	S
1969	592.5	1894.8	0.061	594.3	1894.8	0.055	586.3	1894.8	0.052	597.7	1894.8	0.054	595.2	1894.8	0.041	597.7	1894.8	0.054	597.7	1894.8	0.054
1970	607.9	1933.3	0.066	609.4	1929.5	0.060	600.9	1926.8	0.057	617.0	1928.7	0.053	614.4	1920.6	0.040	617.0	1928.7	0.053	617.0	1928.7	0.053
1971	624.2	1976.3	0.071	625.5	1968.6	0.065	616.5	1963.2	0.062	637.0	1963.4	0.053	634.3	1946.4	0.040	637.0	1963.4	0.053	637.0	1963.4	0.053
1972	641.3	2023.8	0.076	642.3	2012.3	0.070	632.8	2004.0	0.067	657.7	1998.9	0.053	654.9	1972.4	0.038	675.7	2085.2	0.027	665.5	2082.6	0.068
1973	660.1	2076.3	0.079	660.0	2060.8	0.075	649.9	2035.4	0.072	679.0	2035.4	0.053	676.1	1998.5	0.038	717.3	2196.3	−0.002	694.8	2216.3	0.084
1974	683.4	2133.2	0.078	682.6	2114.4	0.075	671.5	2100.3	0.074	700.9	2073.1	0.053	697.9	2025.0	0.054	740.2	2195.4	−0.005	717.0	2279.0	0.085
1975	707.6	2190.8	0.076	706.2	2169.6	0.074	694.4	2153.0	0.072	723.5	2112.1	0.053	720.5	2064.4	0.054	763.4	2192.6	−0.006	740.2	2345.1	0.086
1976	732.1	2249.2	0.075	730.9	2225.8	0.072	718.2	2206.9	0.071	746.8	2152.5	0.053	743.8	2105.4	0.054	766.7	2095.5	0.019	755.6	2322.5	0.073
1977	756.8	2308.6	0.075	755.7	2282.8	0.071	742.7	2262.1	0.070	770.7	2194.5	0.054	767.7	2147.9	0.055	768.2	2021.8	0.046	771.6	2287.3	0.058
1978	781.5	2369.8	0.075	780.6	2341.2	0.071	767.0	2318.3	0.070	795.2	2238.2	0.054	792.1	2192.3	0.055	790.9	2059.0	0.049	797.3	2335.0	0.057
1979	806.8	2433.1	0.075	805.7	2401.4	0.072	791.7	2376.3	0.070	820.2	2283.6	0.054	817.1	2238.3	0.055	814.5	2099.3	0.050	823.3	2383.4	0.057

The simulations are hypothetical even though they are labeled with real calendar years. The first year corresponds to 1969. In particular, actual disposable income of historical 1969, $631.6 billion, will be disposable income for our 1969 as well, except in those simulations where tax surcharges are imposed. The eleven periods of each simulation are labelled 1969–79.

It is assumed that in the years prior to the start of the simulations r and R have been constant at 0.0525 long enough for 0.0525 to be regarded as the normal level for both. Hence $\bar{R} = 0.0525$ and $q = 1$ initially. With regard to the obligatory saving required of younger cohorts, it will be assumed that all previous payments have been made on schedule and that no secondary borrowing has occurred.

Comparisons of certain of the simulations below will permit us to obtain approximate estimates of the marginal propensity to consume from total resources and its components. For reference we have calculated the average propensity for 1969 in our simulations. This average, the ratio of aggregate consumption to the present value of aggregate total lifetime resources, is 0.055. In a world from which liquidity constraints are absent, the marginal and average propensities are equal for a life-cycle model.

An examination of simulations 1, 2, and 3 indicates that both lower interest rates and higher capital incomes stimulate consumption. In the former case (2) the actual disposable income of individuals has not changed (relative to case 1). Income streams from capital and from labor have not changed, though they are discounted at a new interest rate. In the latter case (3) disposable income has increased, since R, the earning stream from capital, has risen.

In both cases there has been an unanticipated increase in W, having a positive income or wealth effect on present consumption. The substitution effect works in opposite directions in cases 2 and 3, favoring current consumption in the former, where r declines, and working against current consumption in the latter case, where r rises.[13]

Because we have observations on the two different cases we can derive approximate magnitudes for an aggregate marginal propensity to consume from wealth and for an interest-elasticity of consumption. Our technique as demonstrated in the Appendix indicates that the marginal propensity to consume from wealth is of the order of 0.09 to 0.12.

This is our second estimate of the marginal propensity to consume from total resources. It is considerably higher than our finding above, affirming the theoretical reasoning about the effects of liquidity constraints. Some caution is required in attaching significance to the magnitude of the difference, however, since the current estimate, for reasons indicated in the Appendix, is perhaps the least precise we have attempted. The indicated interest-elasticity of consumption is between -0.02 and -0.43.

In an attempt to evaluate the influence of liquidity constraints on the marginal propensity to consume from wealth, we have repeated simulations 1, 2, and 3 in simulations 14, 16, and 17 with the liquidity constraint relaxed sufficiently to insure that no cohorts were constrained in the years 1969–72. Repeating the calculations described in the Appendix, we find the probable values of the marginal propensity to consume out of wealth to be bracketed by 0.08 to 0.14. The interest-elasticity is -0.04 to -0.72.

The changes in r and R in cases 2 and 3 occur in two equal steps in 1972 and in 1973 in the simulations. The percentage capital gains, measured by $\Delta q/q$, are roughly the same in both cases and roughly equal in the two years. Consumption also is increased in two roughly equal steps, but more in case 2 than in case 3. The consumption increments over the neutral case are $14.1 billion for 1972 and $27.1 billion for 1973 for case 2; $9.3 billion for 1972 and $21.2 billion for 1973 for case 3. As q declines in two steps in 1976 and 1977, the excesses of C over the neutral case also decline. Why does simulation 3 exhibit a smaller impact on consumption? The difference is in the direction of the substitution effects. It is shown even more dramatically by the saving ratios (0.103 in 1973 for case 3 as against 0.038 for case 2). The correspondingly greater capital formation in case 3 eventually leads to greater consumption there despite the substitution effect favoring saving.

Simulation 4 differs from 3 only in that in 1973 long-run profit expectations change. The substitution effect favoring current saving is greater, but certainly more moderate than the difference between the long-run profits rates (72 bases points in 1973) might superficially indicate. The explanation lies in the fact that the current levels – and hence the expected levels for the immediately following years – of R and r are the same in the two cases ($R = 0.0725$, $r = 0.0525$ in 1973). Since the expected rates in the near future have more influence than those further distant, the effects on consumption are not too dissimilar.

Simulations 5, 6, and 14 examine the influence of changes in the instruments affecting liquidity. Case 5 differs from case 1 only in that ϕ is 0.5 in the former rather than 1.0. In case 14, ϕ is zero. That is, it is possible in case 5 (14) for individuals to borrow up to half (the entirety) of their contractually required saving at the market rate of interest r rather than at a penalty rate r_b. In case 1 all of the borrowing incurs the penalty rate. The result in case 5 is to increase consumption by 4 to 11 billion dollars in various years, with wealth accumulation suffering a concomitant decrease ($83 billion over the 10-year period). In case 14 consumption exceeds that of case 1 by $5.2 billion to $18.9 billion. Accumulated wealth is less by $149.5 billion.

In simulation 6 the two income groups face different liquidity constraints. As in case 5, the higher income group is assumed to be able to forgo half of their required saving costlessly ($\phi = 0.5$) and to be able to borrow beyond that at a rate of 7 per cent ($r_b = 0.07$). The lower income group may not borrow costlessly ($\phi = 1.0$), and they must pay more for the funds they do borrow ($r_b = 0.10$). Relative to those in case 1, the credit market conditions are eased for the higher income group and are more stringent for the lower income group. The negative incentive on the consumption of the poorer group has a stronger influence, as aggregate consumption declines slightly relative to case 1.

The savings ratios are better indicators of the effects in the later years. By then greater disposable income due to more capital accumulation permits more absolute consumption. By 1979 wealth in case 6 exceeds that in case 1 by $15.1 billion.[14]

A comparison of cases 8–13 with case 1 indicates that a labor income tax reduces consumption, a property income tax increases it, and a general income tax – a combination of labor and property income taxes – decreases consumption, but less than the labor income tax alone initially. In these simulations the time paths of other variables, including the before-tax rates of return, r, R, and $\bar{R}$, are the same as in the reference simulation, case 1. The variable q remains at par, in the face of the tax on property income, because it is assumed that R and r are lowered in the same proportion.

The taxes on labor income have only wealth or income effects on consumption. They do not affect rates of return, do not have a substitution effect. The property income tax has both, with the substitution effect in favor of current consumption (since after-tax rates have declined) being stronger than the effect of the income lost in tax payments.

In principle a tax surcharge that is expected to be temporary should have little effect on current consumption, the effect being spread over the remaining years of life. Comparing cases 1 and 8 for 1969, we find consumption reduced by $3.0 billion. The aggregate expected reduction of lifetime resources is $47.8 billion (not shown). Thus our third estimate for the marginal propensity to consume from total resources is 0.063.

To test our theoretical proposition that operative liquidity constraints may increase this marginal propensity, we have duplicated the comparison of cases 1 and 8 with a relaxed liquidity constraint ($\phi = 0$) in cases 14 and 15. We find a reduction in first-period consumption of $2.5 billion, indicating that the tighter credit market conditions of simulation 8 enhance the effectiveness of the tax increase by about 20 per cent. The corresponding marginal propensity to consume is 0.052, close to the average propensity (and theoretical unconstrained marginal propensity) of 0.055 and somewhat lower than the liquidity-constrained 0.063 found in simulations 1 and 8.

In simulation 11, in which labor income streams are reduced uniformly for all years, a $162.4 billion decrease in total resources leads to a $7.9 billion decrease in first-period consumption. The corresponding marginal propensity, which is roughly the marginal propensity to consume out of total resources, is 0.049.

As we noted above, a general income tax increase does not initially lower consumption as much as a labor income tax alone because of the disincentive effect on saving of lower expected rates of return. The decreased capital accumulation eventually leads to a reversal, however, with more consumption occurring in the case of the labor income tax alone. It must be recalled, however, that we do not attempt to take into account the system-wide response of before-tax rates of return to variations in the size of the capital stock.

One of the explanations offered for the apparent ineffectiveness of the tax surcharge of the 1960s is that capital gains enjoyed by individuals had a more than offsetting effect on consumption. We have found results consistent with this explanation in simulation 7. There we have imposed a temporary (5-year) reduction of 2 per cent on all income as in case 10. The corresponding tax revenue is $12.6 billion for 1969. In addition, we have assumed increases in capital earnings starting in the second year, as indicated in Table 34.2. In the first year, before the first increments to wealth, consumption is less than in the standard case by $2.5 billion. With the first capital gains, however, consumption increases by $5.0 billion, and ultimately by $14.4 billion, relative to case 1.

5. Conclusions

(1) The method is promising. The model generates aggregates which are realistic and plausible in magnitude and in their simulated time paths. We are certainly not entitled to conclude that American households are actually conforming to the life-cycle model, much less to our specialization of it. But assuming that they are doing so gives reasonable results. In further work more attention should and can be paid to sources of differences among households other than age, to the effects of uncertainties on consumption and accumulation plans, to the diversity of assets available for saving, and to other features of the "real world" that the model of the present paper omits or oversimplifies.

(2) Revaluations of non-human wealth do, according to the model, have important effects on consumption and saving. But these effects depend significantly on the nature of the revaluation, in particular on the concomitant changes in current and expected interest rates. In our "easy money" simulation 2, a reduction of interest rates brought about by monetary policy increased consumption by 16.1% of the increase in wealth it. accomplished. In simulation 4, wealth and consumption both rise because of a non-monetary shock: profits and expected profits rise. The increase of consumption is 8.8 per cent of the increment of wealth.

(3) Liquidity constraints make a difference. In our simulations they are binding on younger and poorer segments of the population. In their absence, the marginal propensity to consume currently from an increase in consumable resources – current wealth plus the present value of labor income – would be the same as the average, about 0.055. Our simulations indicate the marginal propensity to consume from current wealth to be

0.09–0.12. The excess is attributable to the role of realizable capital gains in relieving liquidity constraints on current consumption.

For the same reason, the marginal propensity to consume from current disposable income is higher than it would be in a perfect capital market. Our simulations of tax changes give permanent changes 2.6 times as much effect on current consumption as temporary (5-year) changes. This difference is in the expected direction, but in a model without liquidity constraints it would be larger, 3.4 times instead of 2.6 times. These comparisons would be more striking if our "temporary" tax rise lasted a shorter time.

(4) Monetary policies tighten or relax liquidity constraints. Changes in those constraints, including the differential between borrowing and lending interest rates, have important effects in themselves, as comparison of simulations 1, 5, 6, and 14 indicates. Moreover, the tightness of liquidity constraints helps to determine the effectiveness of other policy instruments. A temporary tax increase, for example, is 1.2 times as powerful in the tight credit simulation (8 relative to 1) as in the easy credit simulations (15 relative to 14).

To construct a complete story of the linkages of monetary policy to the propensity to consume, it would be necessary to specify how given Federal Reserve operations simultaneously change interest rates, capital values, and liquidity constraints. We have not attempted to provide those links in the chains of causation.

Appendix

Data Sources and Initial Conditions

The initial population was that of the U.S.A. on July 1, 1969 as estimated in *Current Population Reports* (Series P-25, 1970, Table 1, p. 12) for ages 0–84. The estimated 1.29 million people aged 85 and above were ignored. The birth rates by single age of mother were interpolated from grouped data for 1967 reported in the *Statistical Abstract of the United States* (1969, p. 48). As noted in the text the birth rates for women younger than 18 were set at zero. To compensate, birth rates for ages 18–21 were increased slightly.

Mortality rates for 1967 for ages 0–69 also came from the *Statistical*

Abstract (1969, p. 54). For ages 70–84, mortality rates were interpolated from crude death rates calculated from grouped data in *Demographic Yearbook of the United Nations* (1969, pp. 169, 603). The interpolations from the two sources were constrained to be continuous at age 69.

The simulations required the assigning of all males and of females younger than 18 to cohorts. No direct observations were available on the initial values of the $N_{pm}(x, a)$, $N_{pmc}(x, a)$, $N_{pmt}(x, a)$, $N_{pfc}(x, a)$, or $N_{pft}(x, a)$ (number of adult males, male children, male teenagers, female children, female teenagers, respectively, aged a in cohorts with adult females aged x). The $N_{pm}(x, a)$ were approximated by frequency distributions $\pi_m(x, a)$ of husbands aged a by age of wife (x).

Unmarried males were assigned with the same distribution used for husbands. Thus for $N_m(a)$ the total number of males aged a, $N_{pm}(x, a)$ is given by

$$N_{pm}(x, a) = \pi_m(x, a) \cdot N_m(a).$$

Note

$$\sum_x N_{pm}(x, a) = \sum_x \pi_m(x, a) \cdot N_m(a)$$

$$= N_m(a) \sum_x \pi_m(x, a) = N_m(a),$$

since for the frequency distribution $\pi_m(x, a)$ the sum $\sum_x \pi_m(x, a) = 1$. The $\pi_m(x, a)$ were interpolated from tables grouped both by x and by a in *Current Population Reports* (Series P-20, 1969, Table 17, p. 83).

The distributions for children and teenagers were interpolated from tables in *Current Population Reports* (Series P-20, 1969, Table 6, p. 51), which strictly applied only to age distributions of youngest children. This distortion was somewhat offset, however, by the fact that the distributions as used were assumed to apply to the age of the mother (cohort age) while the reported distributions were by age of head of household. Further, the distributions were restricted to be consistent with the assumptions that females do not bear children before age 18 nor after age 49.

The preceding discussion applies to the derivation of the initial distributions among cohorts. Distributions for later years of the simulations are generated through the use of the appropriate birth and mortality rates as the simulations progress. The only additional demographic assumptions required concern the assignment of new 21-year-old males and 18-year-old females, and of the males surviving the disbanding of the 84-year-old cohort. It is assumed that the initial distribution of 21-year-old males, $\pi_m(x, 21)$ applies in all future years as well. Similarly, the new cohort forming with 18-year-old females is assigned $\pi_f(a) \cdot N_f(18)$ $= N_{pm}(18, a)$ males, where the π_f are constant over time and are interpolated from *Current Population Reports* (Series P-20, Table 17, p. 83).

The implication of assigning to the new cohort a full complement of males of various ages is that some males originally assigned to one cohort are reassigned to a younger cohort. A more realistic model of household formation would of course resolve the problem, but such completeness is not feasible. The current simplification has only minor effects and only on the younger cohorts.

The two income groups correspond to groups above and below the Level 1 Poverty Line as defined in Projector and Weiss (1966, p. 37) (roughly $3000 for a family of four in 1963). The indication there, and the assumption we have used, is that 70 per cent of the population is in the higher income group and that their income is four times as great as that of individuals of the same age and sex in the lower income group. After approximate adjustment for omitted items (life insurance cash balances, pension rights, annuities) the average net worth of group I was also about four times that of group II.

The actual wealth profiles by age used as initial conditions were interpolated from Projector (1968, Table S17, p. 316), then scaled up to give a wealth–disposable income ratio of 3.0 for the first year simulated. The four-to-one ratio between net worth of individuals in the two groups was maintained. In interpolating, net worth of zero for cohorts aged 18 and 85 was assumed.

In a similar manner, interpolated labor earnings by age for 1967 from Projector and Weiss (1966, pp. 162–66) were scaled up to $532.1 billion. This is the labor share of disposable income in 1969 consistent with the wealth–disposable income ratio and rate of return on capital assumed. Again the four-to-one ratio between the earnings of the two groups was maintained. Thus a male aged i in group j ($j = 1, 2$) earns $\beta_{ji}^m \cdot y_{1,40}^m$ and a female earns $\beta_{ji}^f \cdot y_{1,40}^m$, where $y_{1,40}^m$ represents the labor income of a 40-year-old male in the first group. We have $\beta_{2,i}^m = \frac{1}{4} \cdot \beta_{1,i}^m$ and $\beta_{2,i}^f = \frac{1}{4}\beta_{1,i}^m$.

The β^m and β^f are assumed constant over time, while $y^m_{1,40}$ grows exponentially at the rate γ:

$$y^m_{1,40}(t + 1) = (1 + \gamma)y^m_{1,40}(t).$$

In deriving the β^m and β^f from *Current Population Reports* (Series P-60, 1969, Table 3, p. 26), the median incomes reported there were multiplied by the percentage of the age–sex group receiving income to account for participation rates. Since the estimates do not exclude property income, we have the set β^m_{ji}, β^f_{ji} for $i \geq 65$ equal to zero.

Derivation of an Allocation Rule: No Liquidity Constraints

For ease of explication we shall present the analysis of this section in terms of a behavioral unit consisting of a single individual. The grand utility function of a cohort will be a sum of individual utility functions, weighted by appropriate equivalent adult weights.

We assume the utility function $u(c_0, c_1, \ldots, c_{a^*-x})$ for an individual aged x has the specific form

$$u(c_0, c_1, \ldots) = \sum_{i=0}^{a^*-x} u(c_i)(1+\delta)^{-i}\, \frac{s(x + i)}{s(x)}, \qquad (A.1)$$

where

$$u(c) = A - Bc_i^{-\rho+1} \qquad (A.2)$$

and a^* is the last age to which individuals survive given the mortality table assumed, δ is the pure rate of time preference, $s(x)$ is the probability of surviving from birth to age x, A and B are arbitrary constants of no consequence (except that B must be positive), and $-\rho$ is the (constant) elasticity of marginal utility. We assume $-\rho = -1.5$. [Assuming a form for u of $u(c) = \log c$ as in Tobin (1967) is equivalent to choosing $\rho = 1$.]

Assuming first a world of perfect capital markets with no constraints on dissaving and no divergence between the borrowing and lending rate, the optimal consumption plan results from maximizing the Lagrangian

$$\mathcal{L} = \Sigma\, u(c_i)(1 + \delta)^{-i}\, \frac{s(x + i)}{s(x)}$$

$$+ \lambda\left[W(1 + r_0) + W_h - \Sigma\, c_i(1 + \tilde{r}_i)^{-i}\, \frac{s(x + i)}{s(x)}\right]. (A.3)^{15}$$

W is the market value of non-human wealth

$$W = \left[\sum_{i=1}^{\infty} R_i^e (1 + \tilde{r}_i)^{-i} \right] K = qK, \qquad (A.4)$$

and W_h is human wealth

$$W_h = \sum_{i=0}^{a^* - x} y_i (1 + \tilde{r}_0)^{-i} \frac{s(x + i)}{s(x)}. \qquad (A.5)$$

The expected labor income i years hence is y_i. $\tilde{r}_i$ is the expected i period rate of interest

$$(1 + \tilde{r}_i)^i = (1 + r_1^e)(1 + r_2^e) \cdots (1 + r_i^e), \qquad (A.6)$$

where r_j^e is the expected one-period rate of interest j periods hence. Differentiating (A.3) and eliminating λ from the resulting first-order conditions yields

$$c_i = \left(\frac{1 + \tilde{r}_i}{1 + \delta} \right)^{i/\rho} \cdot \frac{W(1 + r_0) + W_h}{\sum \left[(1 + \tilde{r}_i)^{\frac{\rho - 1}{\rho}} (1 + \delta)^{1/\rho} \right]^{-i} \frac{s(x + i)}{s(x)}}. \qquad (A.7)$$

The second factor on the right of (A.7) is a constant independent of i. Consumption per person-year in the ith year exceeds (is the same as, is less than) c_0 if $\tilde{r}_i > \delta$ ($\tilde{r}_i = \delta$, $\tilde{r}_i < \delta$). Since recalculation occurs every year, only the first year of the consumption plan need be actually realized.

Derivation of an Allocation Rule: With Liquidity Constraints

Let $\hat{s}$ represent the amount of saving the individual is obligated to do in the current period. As indicated in the text, $\hat{s}$ will equal a fraction ϕ of A/T plus any payments due on secondary loans undertaken. If an individual wishes to save less than $\hat{s}$, he has only one option. He may borrow at a rate r_b, paying back by making equal payments against the principal of $1/\hat{T}$ in each of the next $\hat{T}$ years.

Let $\hat{c}$ be the amount of consumption which would result if exactly $\hat{s}$ were saved out of current income. Then the Lagrangian is

$$\mathcal{L}' = \Sigma \, u(c_i)(1 + \delta)^{-i} \frac{s(x + i)}{s(x)}$$

$$+ \lambda_1 \left[W + W_h - (c_0 - \hat{c}) \Sigma \, (r_b - r_i^e) \frac{\hat{T} - i}{\hat{T}} (1 + \tilde{r}_i)^{-i-1} \right.$$

$$\left. - \Sigma \, c_i (1 + \tilde{r}_i)^{-i} \frac{s(x + i)}{s(x)} \right] + \lambda_2(c_0 - \hat{c}). \tag{A.8}$$

The term $(c_0 - \hat{c}) \Sigma \, (r_b - r_i^e)(\hat{T} - i)/\hat{T}(1 + \tilde{r}_i)^{-i-1}$ represents the net interest loss on new borrowing, $c_0 - \hat{c}$. The constraint associated with the multiplier λ_2 insures that individuals cannot lend at the higher borrowing rate r_b, i.e., $c_0 - \hat{c}$ must be non-negative. Differentiating and solving for the c_0 yields

$$c_0 = \left(\frac{1}{1 + Q} \right)^{1/\rho}$$

$$\times \frac{W + W_h + \hat{c}Q}{\Sigma \dfrac{s(x + i)}{s(x)} \left[(1 + \tilde{r}_i)^{\frac{\rho-1}{\rho}} (1 + \delta)^{1/\rho} \right]^{-i} + \left[1 + Q \right]^{\frac{\rho-1}{\rho}} - 1},$$

$$\lambda_2 = 0, \tag{A.9}$$

or

$$c_0 = \hat{c}, \quad \lambda_2 \gtreqless 0,$$

where

$$Q = \Sigma \, (r_b - r_i^e) \frac{\hat{T} - i}{\hat{T}} (1 + \tilde{r}_i)^{-i-1}.$$

An Approximate Estimate of the Marginal Propensity to Consume from Wealth and the Interest-elasticity of Consumption

Let us summarize the influence of $r_1^e, r_2^e, \ldots, r_n^e, \ldots$ on aggregate consumption by a single variable r^e. Similarly let us indicate the impact of the R_i^e by R^e. Let W denote aggregate wealth. Then we can write current aggregate consumption as

$$C = C[W(R^e, r^e), r^e, \pi, \ldots]. \tag{A.10}$$

π, the current aggregate earnings on capital enter separately because, as noted above, W as a valuation of the earning stream from non-human sources does not include earnings in the current period. We need not specify the other variables affecting consumption since they will be held constant in obtaining our estimates.

Differentiating (A.10) with respect to R^e, r^e, and π yields

$$dC = C_W(W_R\, dR^E + W_r\, dr^e) + C_\pi\, d\pi + C_r\, dr^e, \qquad (A.11)$$

where C_W, W_R, W_r, C_π, C_r represent partial derivatives of the functions C and W with respect to the subscripted variables. Now $C_\pi = C_W$ since an extra dollar of market value of wealth and an extra dollar at income – income in the present period only – both command the same consumption value today and hence both augment the present value of cohort lifetime resources by the same amount.

Assume that the various partial derivatives C_W, etc. are approximately constant in the neighborhood of variation of the values of C, W, π, r^e, and R^e involved in our simulations. Then we may apply equation (A.11) to the non-infinitesimal changes in variables between two of our simulations for which all other variables are unchanged. The 1972 values of the variables for simulations 1, 2, and 3 meet this criterion. Thus dC is the difference in the 1972 values of aggregate consumption between cases 2 and 1: $dC = 655.4 - 641.3 = 14.1$. For case 3, $dC = 9.3$. The expression $(W_R\, dR^E + W_r\, dr^e)$ is dW, and is 87.4 and 84.8 for the two cases respectively. $d\pi$ is zero for case 2 and 20.3 (not shown) for case 3. Since $C_\pi = C_W$, we may write

$$14.1 = 87.4 C_W + C_r\, dr_2^e, \qquad (A.12)$$

$$9.3 = 105.1 C_W + C_r\, dr_3^e, \qquad (A.13)$$

where dr_2^e and dr_3^e are the changes in r^e from case 1 for cases 2 and 3 respectively.

The dr_i^e are unobservable, but we can bracket their values. From Table 34.2 we see that in case 2, the current interest rate in 1972 is 0.0425, which is less than that in case 1 by 0.01. $\bar{R}$, the normal rate to which future rates are expected to return, is less in case 2 than in case 1 by $0.001 = 0.0525 - 0.0515$. The differential between the two cases in expected one-period rates of return in 1972 is nearly -0.01 for early periods and is closer to -0.001 for later periods. dr_2^e is some weighted average of these differentials, and is thus bounded by -0.01 and -0.001.

Similarly dr_3^e is a weighted average of 0.0 (differential between cases 1 and 3 in r) and 0.001 (differential in $\bar{R}$). Solving the two equations (A.12, A.13) by using the four sets of boundary values $dr_2^e = (-0.01, -0.001)$, $dr_3^e = (0, 0.001)$ yields the solutions for C_W and $C_r \cdot r/C$ presented in the text. In converting to the interest-elasticity, values of r and C for 1972 in simulation 2 were used.

References

Ackley, G., *Macroeconomic Theory* (New York: MacMillan Co., 1961).

Ando, A. and F. Modigliani, "The Life Cycle Hypothesis of Saving," *American Economic Review*, 5 (1963), 53.

Arena, J., "Capital Gains and the 'Life Cycle' Hypothesis of Saving," *American Economic Review*, 5 (1964), 54.

Fellner, W., "Operational Utility: The Theoretical Background and a Measurement." in *Ten Economic Studies in the Tradition of Irving Fisher*, W. Fellner (Ed.) (New York: John Wiley and Sons, Inc., 1967).

Fisher, I., *The Rate of Interest* (New York 1907).

Fisher, I., *Theory of Interest* (New York 1930).

Modigliani, F. and R. Brumberg, "Utility Analysis and the Consumption Function: An Interpretation of Cross Section Data," in *Post-Keynesian Economics*, K. Kurihara (Ed.) (New Brunswick: Rutgers University Press, 1954).

Projector, D., *Survey of Changes in Family Finances* (Board of Governors of the Federal Reserve 1968).

Projector, D. and G. Weiss, *Survey of Financial Characteristics of Consumers* (Board of Governors of the Federal Reserve 1966).

Tobin, J., "Life Cycle Saving and Balanced Growth," in *Ten Economic Studies in the Tradition of Irving Fisher*, W. Fellner (Ed.) (New York: John Wiley and Sons, Inc., 1967). (Chapter 32 above.)

United Nations, *Demographic Yearbook*, 1969.

United States Department of Commerce, *Current Population Reports*, Series P-20, No. 191, October 20, 1969.

United States Department of Commerce, *Current Population Reports*, Series P-25, No. 441, March 19, 1970.

United States Department of Commerce, *Current Population Reports*, Series P-60, No. 60, June 30, 1969.

United States Department of Commerce, *Statistical Abstract of the United States*, 1969.

Notes

[1] See Ackley (1961), pp. 554-61 for a good summary.

[2] Ando and Modigliani (1963) and Arena (1964) have estimated consumption functions of this form. The consumption function of the MIT–Penn–SSRC econometric model is also essentially of this type.

One difficulty with the equation is that, although it requires a W/Y_d ratio of the order of 5 or more in order to obtain a realistic C/Y_d ratio, it does not generate enough saving to maintain so high a wealth–income ratio. If the normal saving ratio is 0.10 and the growth rate of the economy is 0.035-0.04 the equilibrium wealth–income ratio is only $2\frac{1}{2}$ or 3. The answer may be that household wealth grows by capital gains, some of which reflect corporate saving, as well as by personal saving as measured in the national income accounts. In principle these gains should be included in the disposable income used in the equation, but Arena's attempts to do so were not successful.

[3] This is not always true. In some cyclical fluctuations, the market value of household wealth has moved as much as, or more than, disposable income. Stickiness of consumption must then be attributed to inelasticity of income expectations rather than to stability in non-human wealth.

[4] As, for example, assumed by Ando and Modigliani (1963).

[5] The basic idea goes back to Fisher (1907, 1930). Its modern elaboration begins with Modigliani and Brumberg (1954). Our approach in this paper is a sequel to Tobin (1967), Chapter 32 above.

[6] Tobin (1967) assumed $\rho = 1$, as would follow from a logarithmic utility function. Ando and Modigliani (1963, p. 59), on the other hand, assumed perfect complementarity, i.e., L-shaped indifference curves with the corner on the 45° line.

[7] If wealth takes the form of consol-like claims the new discount rate is

$$r' = \frac{rW_0}{W_0'}, \quad \text{and} \quad \frac{W_1'}{W_1} = \frac{(1 + r')W_0'}{(1 + r)W_0} = \frac{W_0'/W_0 + r}{1 + r}.$$

In this case W_1 increases almost in proportion to W_0.

[8] See Tobin (1967), Chapter 32 above.

[9] Inheritances and bequests are ignored.

[10] For our purposes teenagers are defined as those children who earn incomes, aged 15-17 (female) or 15-20 (male).

[11] A will be assumed to be $30,000 per adult female for new group 1 cohorts and $7500 for new group 2 cohorts in the first year of the simulations. It will be assumed to grow at the constant rate γ, the rate of growth of per capita income. The simulations assume $T = 20$.

[12] For computational convenience, taxes on future labor income of teenagers are not anticipated, though such taxes are imposed at the time the income is actually earned.

[13] Recall that because expectations are such that equilibrium will be reestablished with $R = r = \bar{R}$, and because $\bar{R}$ is influenced by R, r is expected to rise even in the case where it is R that has changed initially.

[14] Most of this, however, reflects an artificiality in the simulations. In our calculations, not only reduced consumption but also reduced penalty interest payments permit greater accumulation. The institutions engaging in lending are considered exogenous to the household sector. Hence disposable income equals not just consumption plus saving, but rather consumption plus saving plus penalty interest premiums on loans. We intend in further calculations to redistribute these payments as incomes to wealth-owners.

[15] W is multiplied by $(1 + r_0)$ since in this discrete model there is a distinction between beginning of period and end of period stocks. W is interpreted as the beginning of period stock and thus earns r_0W in the current period. The model is recursive rather than simultaneous: first production occurs, using the beginning of period capital stock, then the savings decision allocates output between consumption and investment.

CHAPTER 35

CONSUMER DEBT AND SPENDING: SOME EVIDENCE FROM ANALYSIS OF A SURVEY

1. The Approach and the Data

A survey of the consumer debt position of a sample of households at the beginning and end of a year provides an opportunity for statistical analysis of variables associated with the size of a household's consumer debt and with the amount and direction of change in that debt during the year. The objective of such analysis is to assist in the estimation of stable economic behavioral relationships which can serve as tools in forecasting and in assaying the effects of alternative policies. As will become amply clear in the course of the paper, this objective is a difficult one to achieve; the results of statistical analysis of cross-section data are likely to be susceptible to a variety of possible interpretations. Still the attempt must be made; the ambiguities of econometric analysis of aggregate time series are, if anything, even greater than those confronting the analyst of cross-sections of individual economic units.

Households differ from each other in economic behavior for a great variety of reasons, some of which are measured in surveys and some of

Reprinted from National Bureau of Economic Research, *Consumer Installment Credit*, Part II, Volume 1 (Washington: U.S. Government Printing Office, 1957) and from *Studies of Portfolio Behavior*, Donald Hester and James Tobin (Eds.), Cowles Foundation Monograph 20 (New York: Wiley 1967), pp. 40-65.

I am indebted to the Social Science Research Council for a Faculty Research Fellowship under which the research, of which this is a part, was begun; to the Board of Governors of the Federal Reserve System and the Survey Research Center of the University of Michigan for cooperation in making the data available and in guiding their use; to Donald Hester and Harold Watts for making the computations; to George Katona, Ruth Mack, and Guy Orcutt for useful comments on the first version of this paper presented at the Conference on Consumer Credit Regulation, October 12-13, 1956.

which are not. Many of the relevant differences among consumers – e.g., age of head, location, occupation, personality – may be of very little interest to the economist. His central interest is in the effects on economic behavior of differences in economic variables such as income and wealth. Yet he ignores the other variables at his peril. Expenditure on some commodity, for example, may appear to be positively related to income. But suppose it is also positively related to size of family, age, size of city, and educational attainment. Income happens to be positively related to all these things too. Perhaps the apparent positive effect of income on expenditure is only an illusion, mirroring the effects of the demographic variables with which income is associated. If so, the economist will be fooled when national income rises the next year. He will expect a rise in expenditure that does not occur; it does not occur because, even though income fluctuates, the basic demographic determinants change very little from year to year.

To avoid this kind of pitfall, the approach of the analyst of survey data must be resolutely multivariate. Two- and three-variable frequency tables are interesting and suggestive. But it is *net* or *ceteris paribus* effects rather than gross associations that we wish to estimate. For this reason, the present paper relies heavily on the technique of multiple regression. An attempt is made to estimate, by this technique, the effects of the size of existing debt on three kinds of subsequent behavior, holding constant a variety of other variables relevant to this behavior. Likewise, the *net* effects of a variety of factors on change in consumer debt are estimated.

1.1. *The Nature of the Sample*

The data for the calculations reported in this chapter came from the 1952 and 1953 *Surveys of Consumer Finances* conducted by the Survey Research Center, University of Michigan, for the Board of Governors of the Federal Reserve System. The sample used in this analysis consists of spending units who were interviewed both in the 1952 *Survey* in early 1952 and in the 1953 *Survey* a year later. The number of spending units reinterviewed was 1036, roughly a third of the entire *Survey* in either year. The reinterview sample is somewhat unrepresentative of the national population of spending units. Certain kinds of units are systematically excluded from the sample: units which were formed or dissolved during the year, and in this case, units which moved from one dwelling unit to another. This disadvantage is outweighed, for the purpose of studying behavior relationships, by the analytic advantages of having two observations of each unit. Reinterviewing increases the accuracy of relevant financial data. Income in 1951, and such stock variables as asset holdings and outstanding debt as of January 1, 1952, can be obtained more reliably in February 1952 than in February 1953. Accordingly, financial flow variables for 1952 can be estimated, with less reliance on respondent's memory, by comparing the stock reported in the 1953 interview with the stock reported by the same respondent a year earlier.

For the purpose of the statistical analysis, farm spending units and secondary spending units are excluded. (A secondary spending unit is a unit of one or more persons who maintains his own finances but shares the dwelling unit of some related or unrelated primary spending unit.) In addition, spending units who did not give responses on one or more of the relevant variables are excluded. The remaining units are then divided into two groups for separate analytic treatment, as follows:

1952 income greater than $1000	652
1952 income less than $1000	55

The reason for treating spending units with low incomes separately is as follows: In general, it is desirable, for statistical and economic reasons, to use as variables ratios in which income is the denominator. Income is a powerful variable, with which both the dependent variable and the other independent variables in a regression are likely to be highly correlated. The use of ratios to income focuses attention on explaining, by means of other variables, the share of income devoted to some particular purpose. From a statistical point of view, the use of ratios to income diminishes *heteroskedasticity* in a sample of households; the variance of the dependent variable, expressed in dollars, is roughly proportional to income, and dividing by income tends to make the variance homogeneous. This procedure, however, leads to extreme values when the income denominator is small or negative. Consequently the low-income spending units are here analyzed in terms of dollar variables, rather than fractions of income.

The spending units in this sample did not have equal probabilities of being included. Some were deliberately given a greater probability of selection than others. These differentials in sampling rate were designed to compensate for anticipated differentials in the variance of the attributes the sample was intended to measure. Thus high-income households had a greater probability of selection than low-income households, because it was believed to require more observations to get an estimate with given accuracy for high- than for low-income units. In addition to deliberate differentials in sampling rate, there are unintended differences due to failures to obtain responses from spending units drawn for the sample. As a consequence, each observation in the sample stands for a different number of spending units in the population; an observation of a low-income unit represents more unobserved households than an observation of a high-income unit. For some purposes, it is important to weight the observations in the sample accordingly. It is important to do so whenever the sample is used to estimate a population parameter which might be expected to differ among the differentially sampled population groups. This will be true of almost all characteristics of single-variable distributions: averages and frequencies of incomes, expenditure, debt, liquid-asset holdings, and other financial and economic variables. It is also important to use the weights whenever the sample is used to estimate a parameter of the distribution of a variable whose variance is in fact inversely proportional to the weights. If the observations are not weighted in such a case, the less reliable observations will have too great an influence on the estimate.

In the calculations of the present chapter, the weights were not used. The objective was to estimate regression coefficients and other characteristics of multivariate distributions, not to estimate parameters of univariate distributions. Thus the single-variable means and frequencies calculated here as by-products are unweighted and, therefore, biased estimates of population means and frequencies; this should be remembered in interpreting any single-variable statistics. This bias does not extend, it is believed, to the regression coefficients and other multivariate parameters. While expenditures for durable goods, for example, are obviously different for high-income than for low-income groups, the marginal propensity to spend for durable goods is not necessarily different for one group than for the other. If it is, the remedy is not weighting to obtain a properly averaged slope but fitting a non-linear relationship that allows for differences in slope. The other reason for weighting – to avoid heterogeneity of variances – also does not apply, provided other measures to avoid this malady are employed. As explained above, the use of ratios to income is an attempt to produce homogeneity of variance. It is, in effect, a more systematic and, for many observations, a more drastic weighting scheme than the use of the sampling weights; to use the sampling weights also would be to make an overcorrection for heterogeneity of variance.

1.2. *Regression Variables*

The variables used in the analysis are as follows:

Y	1952 income of the spending unit, after estimated federal tax liability, as reported in the 1953 *Survey*.
Y_{-1}	1951 income of the spending unit, after estimated federal tax liability, as reported in the 1952 *Survey*.
E	Expenditure, net of trade-ins and sales, of the spending unit on cars and major household goods during 1952, as reported in the 1953 *Survey*, regardless of how financed.
E_{-1}	The same for 1951, as reported in the 1952 *Survey*.
L	Total holding of liquid assets January 1, 1952, reported by the spending unit in the 1952 *Survey*, including checking accounts, savings accounts, and savings bonds.
L_{+1}	The same for January 1, 1953, as reported in the 1953 *Survey*.
$\Delta L = L_{+1} - L$	Change in liquid-asset holding during 1952.
D	Outstanding personal debt (debt other than business and real estate indebtedness) as of January 1, 1952, as reported in the 1952 *Survey*.
D_{+1}	The same for January 1, 1953, as reported in the 1953 *Survey*.
$\Delta D = D_{+1} - D$	Change in outstanding personal debt during 1952.
$N = L - D$	"Net asset position" at January 1, 1952.
$\Delta N = \Delta L - \Delta D$	Change in "net asset position" during 1952.

A   Age of the head of the household as reported in the
                    1953 *Survey*, on the following scale:
                    Age 18–24 $A = 1$
                        25–34 $A = 2$
                        35–44 $A = 3$
                        45–54 $A = 4$
                        55–64 $A = 5$
                        65– $A = 6$
M   Marital status of the head of household:
                    $M = 1$ if married and spouse present,
                    $M = 0$ otherwise.

In the analysis of spending units with incomes over $1000, the three
dependent variables are as follows:

E/Y Ratio of expenditure on durable goods to disposable income.
$\Delta L/Y$ Ratio of change in liquid-asset holding to disposable income.
$\Delta D/Y$ Ratio of change in personal debt to disposable income.

In the analysis of the units with incomes under $1000, the three
dependent variables are simply E, ΔL, ΔD.

1.3. *The Regression and Correlation Calculations*

Regressions of the three dependent variables on a common set of
independent variables were calculated, and the correlations among the
three dependent variables were examined. The purpose is (1) to estimate
the effects of certain predetermined variables on the durable-goods
spending, liquid saving, and debt behavior of households, and (2) given
these effects, to determine the pattern of association among these three
kinds of behavior. Results of the regression calculations for the 652
primary spending units with income above $1000 are given in Table 35.1,
and regressions for the 55 units with lower income are shown in Table
35.2.

In Table 35.1 income change enters each regression in two forms: as a
continuous variable, and as a three-way principle of classification. The
reason for introducing it in the second form is to allow for interaction
effects between income change and the other explanatory variables, as
well as additive effects.

Primary non-farm spending units with 1952 incomes $1000 or greater

Dependent variable	Income change	Regression coefficients (estimated standard errors) M	A	L/Y $Y_{-1}/Y < 0.8$	L/Y $0.8 \le Y_{-1}/Y < 1.3$	L/Y $1.3 \le Y_{-1}/Y$	D/Y $Y_{-1}/Y < 0.8$	D/Y $0.8 \le Y_{-1}/Y < 1.3$	D/Y $1.3 \le Y_{-1}/Y$	Y_{-1}/Y $Y_{-1}/Y < 0.8$	Y_{-1}/Y $0.8 \le Y_{-1}/Y < 1.3$	Y_{-1}/Y $1.3 \le Y_{-1}/Y$	Constants $Y_{-1}/Y < 0.8$	Constants $0.8 \le Y_{-1}/Y < 1.3$	Constants $1.3 \le Y_{-1}/Y$	R^2	Standard error of estimate
E/Y	Up	+0.020 (0.014)	*−0.020 (0.004)	−0.003 (0.010)			+0.056 (0.093)			+0.026 (0.077)			*+0.113 (†)			0.23	0.125
	Little change				−0.004 (0.001)			+0.010 (0.029)			*−0.117 (0.052)			*+0.240 (†)			
	Down					+0.012 (0.010)			+0.006 (0.097)			*+0.032 (0.008)			*+0.070 (†)		
ΔL/Y	Up	*−0.213 (0.082)	*+0.072 (0.023)	*−0.311 (0.082)			*−2.64 (0.58)			−0.113 (0.633)			*+0.377 (†)			0.38	0.768
	Little change				*−0.289 (0.031)			−0.075 (0.200)			−0.097 (0.270)			*+0.186 (†)			
	Down					*−0.214 (0.095)			−0.212 (0.232)			*+0.367 (0.044)			−0.560 (†)		
ΔD/Y	Up	+0.019 (0.012)	*−0.006 (0.002)	*−0.027 (0.009)			*−0.733 (0.059)			*−0.070 (0.041)			*+0.117 (†)			0.35	0.155
	Little change				−0.011 (0.007)			*−0.573 (0.051)			−0.032 (0.023)			+0.093 (†)			
	Down					−0.024 (0.020)			*−0.886 (0.104)			+0.010 (0.011)			+0.104 (†)		

* Significant at 10 per cent level.

† The significance of the three constants may be considered jointly, by testing the hypothesis that they are, except for sampling variation, equal: i.e., that classification by income change does not really affect the level of the relationship. This hypothesis would be rejected for E/Y (F-ratio of 5.2 with 2 and 638 degrees of freedom) and ΔL/Y (F-ratio of 7.3, 2 and 638 degrees of freedom). But it cannot be rejected for ΔD/Y (F-ratio of 0.05).

224 CONSUMER DEBT AND SPENDING

Table 35.2
Primary non-farm spending units with 1952 incomes under $1000

Dependent variable	M	A	L	D	Y_{-1}	Y	R^2	Standard error of estimate
E	−6.04 (14.61)	−3.53 (3.95)	*+0.005 (0.002)	−0.079 (0.067)	*+0.043 (0.007)	−0.092 (0.263)	†0.68	$53.5
ΔL	+370.0 (348.0)	−21.9 (94.1)	*−0.153 (0.044)	+1.28 (1.60)	*−0.778 (0.160)	+3.73 (6.27)	†0.65	1273
ΔD	*+79.5 (15.6)	+2.07 (4.21)	−0.002 (0.002)	*−0.672 (0.076)	*+0.068 (0.007)	*−1.04 (0.28)	†0.82	56.8

* Significant at 10 per cent level.

† These represent the proportions of the variances of the dependent variables *about zero* explained by the regressions, which include no constant term. Of these same variances about zero, the means of the variables would explain the following proportions: 0.05, 0.04, and 0.00.

Table 35.3 presents coefficients of correlation among the three dependent variables, computed for the households with incomes above $1000. The correlations were first computed on the variables as reported "before" regression; then they were computed on the residuals from the

Table 35.3
Correlations among dependent variables

	ΔL/Y		ΔD/Y		
E/Y	†0.219 †0.206	0.028 0.026	†0.212 †0.199	†0.305 †0.305	Simple Partial
ΔL/Y	Before regression	After regression	*0.089 0.044	0.011 0.002	Simple Partial
			Before regression	After regression	

* Significant at 10 per cent level.
† Significant at 1 per cent level.

regressions of Table 35.1. Both simple and partial correlations are presented; the partial correlations are net of the third variable in every case. Table 35.3 shows that debt accumulation and durables expenditures are significantly positively correlated; this correlation is greater on the residuals than on the original variables. However, this is the only pair among the three kinds of behavior for which a significant association exists. The apparent correlations among other pairs turn out to reflect no more than the common effects of the independent variables, removed by the regressions.

2. Difficulties in the Interpretations of Cross-section Data

Does large personal indebtedness deter consumers from buying durable goods, from further borrowing, and from depleting their liquid reserves? Given their incomes and their other circumstances, are consumers more likely to make net reductions in their indebtedness and to curtail their spending when their existing debt is large than when it is small? Are they more likely to borrow, and to buy durable goods, when they are relatively debt free?

Answers to these questions would greatly contribute to an appraisal of the economic consequences of a given volume of consumer debt. If the answers are affirmative, a high ratio of debt to income would have to be interpreted as a deflationary sign, an indication that consumer spending would decline. If there is no such relationship between debt and consumer spending and borrowing, a student of business cycles could not view a high debt level as itself a cause of subsequent recession. He might, however, wonder about the longer run social and economic consequences of heavy debt in case a recession developed from other causes. If there is no automatic tendency for debt to deter further borrowing and spending, consumers and their expenditures will be highly vulnerable to drastic reductions of income.

Surveys of cross-sections of households, such as the survey which is the basis for the calculations of this chapter, may help to answer these questions. But the essential limitations of single-time cross-sections must be borne in mind. The use of cross-section data for the estimation of economic relationships depends on a crucial assumption. The assumption is that economic behavior in response to changes in circumstances over time can be inferred from differences in observed behavior among individuals in differing circumstances at the same moment of time. For many purposes this assumption is justified, especially when account can really be taken of the many relevant respects in which the circumstances of individuals differ. But the assumption can be a treacherous one in attempting to estimate relationships between stocks and flows, as in the present case, where we seek to estimate the dependence of spending, debt change, and liquid-asset change on outstanding debt. The reason that the assumption may be treacherous in such a case is that stocks are the resultant of the past behavior of households, and flows represent their current behavior. Any correlation, positive or negative, between the past behavior and current behavior of individual households will tend to be reflected in a correlation between stocks and flows in a cross-section of households. There are several possible sources of such correlations.

2.1. *Periodicity in Durable Goods Expenditure*

Since some durable goods purchases are large "lumpy" expenditures, they do not occur every year for a given household. In a year when such a purchase does occur, the household's total expenditure for durable goods is large; but in the following year it is small. Suppose that the large purchase is financed by incurring installment debt. Then debt will rise in the year of the lumpy purchase and fall in the subsequent year. A cross-section "snapshot" of households at a single year will find some making a large lumpy purchase and other households repaying debt incurred for such purchases in the previous year. In the cross-section, therefore, small current expenditure and debt repayment will tend to be associated with high levels of outstanding debt, while large expenditure and large additions to debt will be associated with low levels of debt. But it would be a mistake to conclude from these negative relationships between D and E and between D and ΔD that *for the economy as a whole*, debt is a deterrent to durable-goods expenditure and to further increase in debt. That conclusion would be justified only if it could be shown that the negative correlations still exist among households at the same phase in the lumpy-expenditure cycle; e.g., that, within the group of households who are making a large lumpy purchase, more is spent by those who are relatively free of debt than by others.

This kind of nuisance correlation would be more likely to occur the narrower the range of commodities included in the category of expenditures E. The variety covered by the category in the present survey means that the household has considerable scope for smoothing even within a single year. It should also be remembered that expenditure is measured *net* of trade-ins, and includes expenditure for secondhand as well as new items. Thus there is a greater divisibility in E than one might conclude from concentrating his attention on periodic purchases of new automobiles. The personal-debt concept of the survey is also quite comprehensive, so that the relations of D, ΔD, and E should not be dominated by the mechanical correlation due to periodicity in lumpy expenditures.

Fortunately the data of the reinterview survey on durable-goods expenditure in the previous year E_{-1} make it possible to guard against this kind of correlation. If we find that, holding E_{-1} constant, there is a negative relationship between D and E or ΔD, we can conclude that this is not due merely to periodicity in durable-goods purchases.

2.2. Persistent "Personality" Differences among Households

It is reasonable to expect that there are persistent differences among households in respect to a set of attributes suggested by such words as thriftiness, foresight, conservatism, self-restraint, venturesomeness. People differ in the degree of calculation and care with which they arrive at decisions. They differ also in the contingencies that they foresee and attempt to allow for, from obsessive concern with improbable catastrophes at one extreme to a happy-go-lucky disregard of the future at the other. These differences are reflected in their behavior toward consumers' goods and personal debt. Some households regard such debt as a convenience to be continuously exploited in order to increase their collection of durable goods at the fastest possible rate. Households of a more "thrifty" disposition, at the other extreme, regard buying on time as sinful. Most households, of course, are located at intermediate positions of a continuous spectrum. Differences in location along the spectrum – let us call them "personality differences" – are not directly measured in the usual economic survey of households. (There is no insuperable obstacle to measuring them, and recent *Surveys of Consumer Finances* have made attempts in this direction.) Neither are "personality differences" adequately represented by the variables that economic surveys generally do measure.

These persistent "personality differences" tend to produce a positive correlation between existing debt, D, and either change in debt, ΔD, or expenditure on durable goods, E, and a negative correlation between D and liquid-asset change, ΔL. The same attitudes and values that led a household to accumulate a large debt in the past in order to buy durable goods continue to dispose the household to borrow and to spend in the current year. The same scruples that kept a family out of debt before continue to inhibit it from going into debt, and possibly also to give the accumulation of liquid reserves priority over the acquisition of consumers' durables.

Correlations of this kind between stocks and flows – let us call them "personality correlations" – are of interest in the broadest contexts of the study of human behavior. But for such a purpose as appraising the economic effects of the burden of consumer debt over time, they are quite irrelevant. For a given family, or within a group of families of common personality traits, the economic behavior relationship may go in the opposite direction – the more debt the less borrowing and spending, and the more repayment and liquid saving. But the "behavior relationship" may be partially or completely obscured, in a single-time cross-section, by the "personality correlations".

3. Effects of Outstanding Debt on Expenditures on Durable Goods

According to Tables 35.1 and 35.2, the regression coefficients representing the effect of debt on durable-goods expenditure are insignificantly different from zero. For households with 1952 incomes under $1000 (Table 35.2), the coefficient is negative in sign; this is the only one of the four coefficients that is greater in absolute value than its estimated standard error. The three coefficients of D/Y in the E/Y regression, for households with incomes greater than $1000, are all small positive numbers. But the significance of the regression would have been increased by the omission of D/Y; the F-ratio for testing the significance of its inclusion is 0.17 (3 and 638 degrees of freedom).

In order to eliminate any effect due to periodicity in lumpy purchases of durable goods, E_{-1}/Y was introduced as an additional independent variable in the E/Y regression. The net relationship of E/Y to E_{-1}/Y turned out to be positive rather than negative, and insignificantly different from zero. The estimated coefficients of D/Y were moved somewhat closer to zero.

These results can be interpreted to mean that there may be in fact a negative behavioral relationship between debt and durable-goods expenditure, a relationship which has been prevented from displaying itself in this cross-section of households by the positive personality correlation. To this interpretation two objections might be made.

First, it might be objected that the "personality correlation", if at all important, would have shown up in a significantly positive relation of E/Y to E_{-1}/Y. However, E_{-1}/Y is a very imperfect representative of personality. There are many reasons other than its location on the thriftiness spectrum for a household to have made high or low durable-goods expenditures in the previous year. It would be better to have, as an indicator of position on this spectrum, the residual of E_{-1}/Y_{-1} from a regression for 1951 similar to the one shown for 1952 in Table 35.1, but the data do not permit calculation of such a regression. In any case, the relevant personality traits would be better measured by a summary of a considerable range of past behavior than by behavior in the immediately preceding year alone.

Second, it might be objected that the variable D may stand not only for the stock of debt but also for the stock of durable goods, since the acquisition of durable goods is associated with going into debt. Any negative relationship between D and E which we detect may, according to the objection, represent the deterrent effect of a large stock of durable goods on further purchases of durables rather than the deterrent effect of consumer debt *per se*. It is unfortunate that a direct measurement of the stock of durable goods could not be included in the regression, so that "saturation effects" could be estimated separately and disentangled from other relationships. But even so, the objection does not seem too serious. Although it is true that there is positive correlation between debt change, ΔD, and expenditure on durables, E (see Table 35.2), this correlation is too loose to permit the summation of ΔD over a period of past years, which is D, to represent the stock of durable goods, which is the summation of E less depreciation over the past period. Age, A, and marital status, M, almost certainly constitute together a better proxy for the stock of durable goods than D. Saturation effects, if any, have probably entered the regression through these variables rather than through debt.

4. Effects of Outstanding Debt on Change in Personal Debt

The regressions reported in Tables 35.1 and 35.2 indicate a highly significant negative relationship between change in debt, ΔD, and initial debt, D. Other things equal, households with large debts tend to reduce, and households with small or zero debts to increase, their indebtedness. According to these results, there are certain average equilibrium debt levels, to which households tend to adjust their debt if their circumstances remain unchanged.[1] For example, consider households with stable incomes above \$1000, in which the head is married and in the 35 to 44 age group. Suppose that the household holds liquid assets equal to three months' income. According to the second of the three $\Delta D/Y$ regressions in Table 35.1, inserting the values $M = 1$, $A = 3$, $L/Y = \frac{1}{4}$, $Y_{-1}/Y = 1$,

$$\frac{\Delta D}{Y} = 0.059 - 0.573 \frac{D}{Y}.$$

The equilibrium ratio of debt to income – the level at which $\Delta D/Y$ will be zero – is thus $0.059/0.573$, or about 0.10. If the existing debt is greater or smaller than 10 per cent of income, the household will move about 57 per cent of the distance to the equilibrium level in the course of a year.

However, we must use caution in interpreting the negative coefficients in these regressions. There are several reasons why such results might be expected. One is the possible periodicity in debt-financed expenditure, discussed above. Such periodicity would result in a cross-section pattern showing repayment by last year's heavy borrowers and large additions to debt by households who enter this year relatively free of debt. There is no evidence of this pattern in the data. The variable E_{-1}/Y does not make a significant addition to the $\Delta D/Y$ regression reported in Table 35.1, and its inclusion would not change the values of the coefficients of D/Y.

A second reason for a negative relation between D and ΔD may be found in the constraints within which households operate, rather than in behavior reflecting their own choices. A household does not have an unlimited line of credit. Households whose debt is the maximum available to them have only one direction in which to move, though it is conceivable that some of them would gladly increase their debt if more credit were available.[2] At the other end, debt is by definition a non-negative quantity; one cannot pay off more debt than he owes. Indeed in some cases repayment of debt ahead of the schedule of installments may be difficult or impossible, or the possibility may not occur to the household. Thus among households who are inclined by circumstances and preferences to reduce debt, there are mechanical reasons why the size of the reduction will be positively related to the size of the initial debt.

The upper limit, imposed by the line of credit, does not appear to have a serious influence on our results. Since the credit limit depends on income, it should apply least to households with rising incomes. These households, even if they were previously in debt to the limit of their credit line, should now be able to borrow more if they choose. In fact, however, they show a greater tendency to reduce their debt (a coefficient of $\Delta D/Y$ on D/Y of -0.733) than households of stable income (coefficient of -0.573).

The effect of the lower limit on the statistical pattern displayed by a cross-section is more difficult to evaluate, but it does not seem sufficient to account for the observed negative coefficients relating ΔD to D. Those negative coefficients evidently reflect both a greater willingness to add to debt and a willingness to add larger amounts when initial debt is low than when it is high; they do not reflect merely the mechanical fact that households who reduce debt have greater repayments to make when their initial debt is high. Of the 322 spending units who had no personal debt at the beginning of 1952, about 25 per cent added to debt during 1952 (Table 35.4). Of the 330 spending units who began the year in debt, 41 per cent added to debt during the year. However, as Table 35.4 shows, these additions were concentrated in spending units with low initial debt ratios; those with initial debt higher than 10 per cent of income were not likely to add to debt. It must also be remembered that other variables (age, income "personality", etc.) are more likely to be favorable to use of debt by the group already in debt than by the debt-free group. Therefore these figures do not support the conclusion that willingness to add to debt is independent of initial debt level. Further evidence is provided by

Table 35.4
Primary non-farm spending units with 1952 incomes greater than $1000
(number of spending units)

Change in debt during 1952	Debt at beginning of 1952 as ratio of 1952 income				
	$D/Y = 0$	$0 < D/Y < 0.1$	$0.1 \leq D/Y < 0.3$	$0.3 \leq D/Y$	All
Decrease in debt		93	69	27	*189
No change in debt	245	1	1	1	248
Increase in debt	77	105	28	5	215
All	322	199	98	33	652

* Of these 189 spending units, 81 made complete repayment of their debt.

the regressions of Table 35.5. For households who are already in debt and are not short of gross liquidity, category IV, the regression shows an even stronger negative relationship of ΔD to D than the regression for the whole sample, shown in Table 35.1. The coefficient is too high to reflect merely the mechanical relation of repayments to initial debt among the debt reducers.

The conclusion is that there is a real behavioral relationship between outstanding debt and subsequent change in debt. High initial debt deters further use of debt, while low initial debt encourages borrowing. This conclusion is indicated by the regression coefficients, whose significant negative values do not appear to be due, in any great degree, to irrelevant special characteristics of the cross-section sample.

5. Interrelations between Debt and Liquid-asset Holdings

The regressions and correlations in Tables 35.1 to 35.3 indicate that liquid-asset holdings and debt are virtually independent in consumer decisions. Only in the highest income-change group does initial debt seem to affect significantly the value of change in liquid-asset holdings ΔL. That group is also the only one for whom initial liquid-asset holdings influence measurably the subsequent change in debt. The correlation between $\Delta D/Y$ and $\Delta L/Y$ is very low even before any account is taken of

Table 35.5

Primary non-farm spending units with 1952 incomes $1000 or greater

Category	Number of cases	Dependent variable	Regression coefficients (estimated standard errors)							Coefficients of correlation between $\Delta D/Y$ and $\Delta L/Y$	
			M	A	L/Y	D/Y	Y_{-1}/Y	Constant	R^2	Before regression	After regression
I. $D/Y = 0$, L/Y below median	103	$\Delta L/Y$	+0.064 (0.058)	+0.026 (0.018)	−0.782 (0.473)		*−0.065 (0.039)	+0.030 (0.097)	0.068		
		$\Delta D/Y$	−0.010 (0.014)	−0.000 (0.014)	−0.484 (0.395)		+0.006 (0.032)	+0.092 (0.081)	0.019	−0.005	−0.021
II. $D/Y = 0$, L/Y above median	232	$\Delta L/Y$	*−0.395 (0.190)	*+0.127 (0.061)	†−0.358 (0.057)		†+0.425 (0.037)	−0.179 (0.310)	0.375		
		$\Delta D/Y$	0.007 (0.015)	0.003 (0.005)	−0.005 (0.004)		+0.002 (0.003)	+0.007 (−0.024)	0.007	+0.046	+0.037
III. $D/Y > 0$, L/Y below median	223	$\Delta L/Y$	−0.016 (0.017)	†+0.011 (0.004)	+0.159 (0.105)	†−0.863 (0.031)	*−0.026 (0.013)	†+0.168 (0.023)	0.794		
		$\Delta D/Y$	+0.034 (0.048)	*−0.022 (0.011)	*+0.614 (0.294)	†+0.297 (0.086)	−0.035 (0.038)	+0.008 (0.066)	0.084	−0.031	†+0.355
IV. $D/Y > 0$, L/Y above median	94	$\Delta L/Y$	+0.074 (0.183)	+0.029 (0.053)	*−0.431 (0.042)	*−0.380 (0.183)	*+0.395 (0.220)	−0.397 (0.331)	0.581		
		$\Delta D/Y$	+0.014 (0.062)	−0.008 (0.018)	*−0.024 (0.014)	†−0.766 (0.062)	−0.063 (0.074)	+0.160 (0.112)	0.659	†+0.286	+0.090

* Significant at 10 per cent level.
† Significant at 1 per cent level.

their joint dependence on a common set of independent variables. Between residuals from the $\Delta D/Y$ and $\Delta L/Y$ regressions there is no correlation at all. The impression of independence given by these calculations suggests the desirability of a closer look at the interrelations between debt and liquid-asset holdings, both initial stocks and changes in stocks.

5.1. Some Theoretical Considerations

A given net asset position N for a household is consistent with a range of alternative amounts of liquid-asset holdings, L, and debt, D. For example, a net asset position of $+\$100$ may represent $\$100$ in liquid assets and $\$0$ of debt, or $\$1000$ of liquid assets and $\$900$ of debt, or $\$550$ of liquid assets and $\$450$ of debt. What factors may be expected to determine one of these alternatives rather than the others?

The costs of borrowing a dollar are greater than the earnings on a dollar of liquid assets. The financial costs of borrowing are reinforced, for many individuals, by psychological costs. These cost considerations would lead a household with a given net asset position to minimize its debt. However, the minimum would by no means always be at zero debt. There are minimal requirements of *gross* liquid-asset holdings, transactions balances to handle normal expenditures in between periodic income payments and precautionary balances to meet contingencies requiring extraordinary expenditures or entailing losses of expected income. These requirements may make it worthwhile to incur the cost of simultaneous holding of liquid assets and debt. They will make it worthwhile to the extent that the opportunity to borrow is not always available when a contingency that requires extra liquidity occurs. It is, for many households, easier to borrow at the time of purchasing new durable goods than later, because "easy" credit is offered by the seller to facilitate the sale; if the opportunity is passed up, borrowing to obtain needed liquidity later may be impossible, or may entail much greater costs.

If calculations of this nature lay behind a household's behavior, there would be an optimal level of gross liquid-asset holdings for the household. Since the household's income could stand as a measure of the scale of the transactions and contingencies for which liquidity is required, this optimum could be expressed as a proportion of income. Some households would set the optimum ratio higher than others, because of differences in striking the subjective balance between costs of borrowing and risks of illiquidity. By and large, the optimum gross liquid-asset ratio would be higher, the greater the net asset position of the household. Households who have to borrow to obtain liquidity would settle for less gross liquidity than wealthier spending units.

This pattern of behavior would have some observable consequences, depicted in idealized fashion in Figure 35.1. For households similar to each other in income and in other respects, Figure 35.1 shows debt out-standing, D, on the vertical axis and liquid asset holding, L, on the horizontal axis. A set of parallel 45° lines is shown; each line represents a locus of combinations L and D such that the net asset position $N = L - D$ is constant. A line lower and to the right represents a higher net asset position. Points A and A' and other points on the curve connecting them represent optimal combinations of D and L. As argued above, the optimal gross liquid-asset holding L will be greater the higher the house-

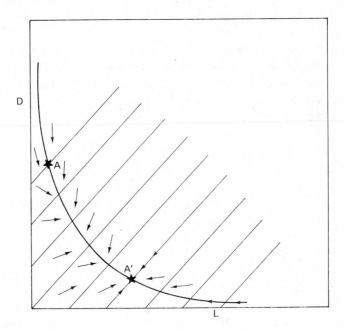

Fig. 35.1.

hold's net asset position. Strictly speaking, since the optima differ for different households, the locus AA' describes the average of optimum positions. There will be, according to the hypothesis, a general tendency for actual observations of D and L to cluster about the locus AA'. However, there will always be some households who, by virtue of changes in income or other circumstances, are out of adjustment. These will move toward AA'.

If households were always satisfied with their *net* asset position, these movements toward AA' would always be along a given 45° line, like the arrows toward A' in the figure. But presumably changes in net asset positions will be occurring at the same time as adjustments in the balance between debt and liquidity. Suppose that households with negative or low net asset positions seek to improve them and that households with high net asset positions reduce them in favor of consumers' durables and other expenditures. Then the adjustments of D and L will be in the general directions indicated by the arrows in Figure 35.1.

This pattern of behavior may, however, be less important than some irrational elements in household debt behavior. Households may be unaware of the costs of borrowing, or may consider them to be of minor importance. At the same time, they may find installment debt a desirable means of self-discipline. If they use up liquid assets to buy a washing machine, they will never restore their net asset position; income will be frittered away in current luxury expenses rather than saved. But if they hang on to the liquid assets and go into debt to get the washing machine, the pressure of paying installments will prevent the frittering away of income and restore their net asset position. This implies that somehow the liquid assets are less accessible for these dispensable expenditures than current income. Once segregated as a contingencies fund, say, savings deposits and bonds are untouchable except for real emergencies. It requires a deliberate decision to violate this self-imposed restraint, and this makes the restraint more enforceable.

If this trend of behavior is significant, the pattern of rational behavior may be completely canceled or even reversed. The possession of large liquid assets may be an encouragement to acquire debt, rather than a stimulus to its repayment. If one has assets, one can afford to buy things with debt financing, because certain contingencies that might otherwise compete with the installment payments are already provided for.

5.2. *The Empirical Test*

To test for the presence of the "rational" pattern of behavior of which Figure 35.1 is an idealized representation, the 652 observations with incomes greater than $1000 have been divided into four classes. The median ratio L/Y of liquid assets to income was determined, and those below the median were separated from those above the median. Then each of these categories was divided between those who had no debt at the beginning of the year and those who had some positive debt. Let us consider what Figure 35.1 would lead us to expect for each of these classes.

(I) *No Debt, Low Liquidity Ratio.* These households should show pre-dominantly positive changes in debt, ΔD, and in asset holdings, ΔL, positively correlated in amount with each other and inversely related in amount to the initial liquid asset holding, L.

(II) *No Debt, High Liquidity Ratio.* These households should show predominantly negative changes in asset holdings, ΔL, inversely related in amount to the initial liquid asset holding, L. They should show little if any change in debt, and little systematic relation of ΔD to L or correlation between ΔL and ΔD.

(III) *Positive Debt, Low Liquidity Ratio.* These households will be dominated by the need to improve their net asset position, largely by repayment of debt. The amount of debt change will depend negatively on the initial amount of debt, D, and will bear little relation to L. These households will show little systematic relation of ΔL to D and L.

(IV) *Positive Debt, High Liquidity Ratio.* Households in this position will tend to diminish their costs by using their liquid assets to reduce their debt. This tendency will overshadow any tendency to change the *net* asset position. Thus both ΔD and ΔL will be negatively related to D and L, and ΔD and ΔL will be positively correlated with each other.

On the whole, the calculations reported in Table 35.5 conform to *a priori* expectations derived from the "rational" pattern.

The 103 spending units in category I increased their debt by an average of 6.7 per cent of their incomes, and their asset holdings by an average of 7.7 per cent of income. As Table 35.5 shows, there is some evidence that the amounts of increase of debt and asset holdings were inversely related to initial asset holdings, but the coefficients are not significant. There was, moreover, no significant correlation between $\Delta D/Y$ and $\Delta L/Y$. The 232 households in category II showed, as expected, an inverse relation of $\Delta L/Y$ to initial liquid-asset position L/Y and, again as expected, no significant effect of L/Y on $\Delta D/Y$. These spending units showed little tendency to change debt; the average change was an increase of 2.2 per cent of income. They also added to liquid assets an average of 7.9 per cent of income. The fact that the average increase in liquid-asset holdings is greater in category II than in I may reflect some "personality correlation" effects, even though such effects are not evident within the categories.

Spending units in category III sought to improve their net asset position, increasing liquid assets an average of 5 per cent of income while leaving debt virtually unchanged, on the average. However, the expected inverse relation between existing debt and subsequent debt change did not materialize; perhaps because of "personality correlation" effects, the relationship was the other way. The most striking result for category III is the inverse relation between liquid asset change and initial debt. Households with high initial debt were more likely to borrow than small debtors, but evidently the large debtors borrowed for expenditure purposes while the small debtors borrowed to improve their liquidity. The pattern of borrowing to improve liquidity is reflected in the positive correlation between the residuals of $\Delta D/Y$ and $\Delta L/Y$. The force of the desire to improve liquidity, within this group, was independent of the initial liquidity position. Households in category IV seem to behave as expected, and this is the most crucial test of the "rational" pattern. As anticipated, both $\Delta D/Y$ and $\Delta L/Y$ were inversely related to D/Y and L/Y; the four coefficients are all significant. Both debt and asset holdings were decreased by this group, debt by an average of 7.7 per cent of income and assets by an average of 19.1 per cent.

It may fairly be concluded that the hypothesis of "rational" behavior with respect to debt and liquid assets is not refuted. If "personality correlation" effects could be eliminated, the hypothesis should stand up even better. The "irrational" self-discipline pattern does not show up in these results. The initial impression, from the over-all regressions, that debt and liquid assets are treated independently in consumer decisions has to be revised. The overall independence conceals several important interrelationships, which are revealed when the sample is broken into the four categories based on initial debt and asset positions.

6. Other Factors Associated with Change in Debt

Decisions to increase or reduce debt are, of course, affected not only by the initial debt and liquid-asset levels but also by other economic and demographic circumstances of the household. The present section will discuss estimation of the effects of these other variables.

6.1. Income and Income Change

The regressions that have been calculated allow for effects both of current year's income, Y, and previous year's income, Y_{-1}. It is necessary, therefore, to distinguish between long-run and short-run income effects. A "long-run effect" is the change in ΔD associated with a dollar change in Y, or Y_{-1}, on the assumption that the household's income is stable ($Y_{-1} = Y$). A "short-run effect" is the change in ΔD associated with a dollar change in Y, for fixed level of previous year's income, Y_{-1}. The long-run effect is the relevant one for such purposes as projecting the effects of secular growth in income on the propensity to go into debt. The short-run effect is the relevant one for models that attempt to forecast year-to-year changes in business activity.

For spending units with incomes above \$1000, the long-run effect can be estimated from the regression coefficients shown for D/Y in Table 35.1. By definition, Y_{-1}/Y is to be set equal to 1, and this means that the applicable coefficients are the ones for "little change" in income. If we then multiply the regression through by Y, we have

$$\Delta D = (0.061 + 0.019M - 0.006A)Y - 0.011L - 0.573D.$$

For married spending units with the head aged 18 to 24 ($M = A = 1$), this says that every dollar of permanent increase in income leads to an increase of 7.4 cents in ΔD. For single-person spending units in the highest age bracket ($M = 0$ and $A = 6$), however, the long-run income effect would be only 2.5 cents for every dollar of income.

For spending units with incomes below \$1000, the ΔD regression shown in Table 35.2 indicates an income effect in the opposite direction. An increase of a dollar in income is associated with a decline of 97 cents in additions to debt. In this income range, borrowing is evidently often an emergency measure rather than a means of obtaining luxuries; in consequence, additions to debt are greater the worse off the household.

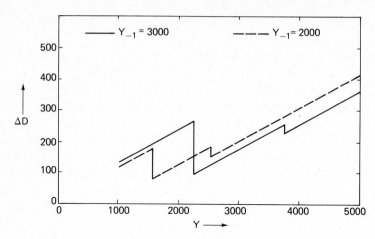

Fig. 35.2. Estimated short-run effects of income on change in debt: spending units with incomes over $1000.

The short-run income effect takes past income Y_{-1} as given and measures the change in ΔD due to change in current income Y alone. The regression for low-income spending units estimates \$1.04 more increase in debt for every \$1 increase in current income. For units with incomes over \$1000, short-run income effects are more complicated. They are plotted in Figure 35.2, drawn for $M = 1$, $A = 3$, $L = 0$, $D = 0$ and for two alternative assumptions regarding Y_{-1}, \$2000 and \$3000.

The effects of previous year's income, Y_{-1}, appear to differ in direction depending on current income level. For incomes below \$1000, additions to debt will be greater the higher the previous income level; the coefficient is small but significant. Its sign probably reflects differences among households in pressure to maintain accustomed consumption standards and in access to credit, both of which will vary with past income. At current income levels above \$1000, Figure 35.2 illustrates the change in direction of the effect of Y_{-1}. At low current income, additions to debt are smaller when previous income was \$2000 than when it was \$3000. But the opposite is true for incomes above \$2308 (\$3000 divided by 1.3). At higher income levels, borrowing is less a symptom of distress than a means of speeding the acquisition of worldly possessions appropriate to the household's economic and social status. This is likely to be a more urgent order of business for families for whom this status is newly achieved than for those whose present income represents little increase over previous levels.

6.2. *Other Independent Variables*

The independent variables in the regressions of Table 35.1 are financial, economic, or demographic characteristics of the spending unit. There are, of course, other characteristics that might be expected to affect the debt behavior of households. Some of these are further details of the economic, demographic, and geographic circumstances of the spending unit. Others are answers to questions designed to elicit the respondent's feelings of optimism or pessimism regarding his personal economic situation and the national economic picture.

Change in debt may appear to be significantly related to one of these variables when we examine the correlation without taking account of any others. But our multivariate approach teaches us to beware of simple correlations. The variable under test may, like change in debt, be related to variables in the regression of Table 35.1. A more meaningful way of testing the influence of additional variables, either singly or in combination, is to examine their correlation with the residuals from the regressions in Table 35.1. If there is no significant relationship, one may conclude that the tested variables contain no information relevant to explanation of the dependent variable beyond what is already contained in the regression independent variables. It is still possible, of course, that the candidates under test could substitute for one or more of the regression independent variables. If the test reveals a significant relationship with the residuals, then *a fortiori* the variables tested are significantly related to the dependent variables. To measure this relationship, it would be necessary to recompute the regression, introducing the additional variables and allowing for their correlations with the other independent variables.

A number of tests of this kind, both on the original variables and on the residuals from the regressions of Table 35.1, have been computed. Table 35.6 reports the results. The technique used is analysis of variance. That is, the hypothesis under test is that the mean value of the dependent variable (or residual) is the same regardless of the value or class of the independent variable. The test statistic is an F-ratio, and it is this which is reported in Table 35.6. A high F-ratio indicates that the hypothesis of

Table 35.6
Tests of significance of relation of $\Delta D/Y$ to selected variables

Variable	Number of classes into which observations were divided (k)	F-ratios Original variable (d. f. $k-1$ and $652-k$)	Residuals from Table 35.1 regression (d. f. $k-1$ and $638-k$)
I. Economic, demographic, geographic variables:			
1. Net worth brackets, early 1953	11	*4.7	†8.0
2. Education of head of household	5	0.8	0.1
3. Occupation of head of household	7	0.7	1.3
4. Region	4	0.5	2.6
5. Size of locality	5	1.1	0.8
II. Attitudinal variables:			
1. Would you say you folks are better off or worse off financially now than you were a year ago? Asked in 1952	4	0.4	0.1
2. Are you folks making as much money now as you were a year ago, or more or less? Asked in early 1952	4	1.2	0.6
3. How about a year from now – do you think you people will be making more money or less money than you are now, or what do you expect? Asked in early 1952	4	1.5	0.5
4. Same question as 3, but asked in early 1953	4	1.4	1.0
5. Do you think this is a good time or a bad time to buy automobiles and large household items? Asked in early 1952	6	0.9	0.8
6. Now, speaking of prices in general, I mean the prices of the things you buy, do you think they will generally go up during 1952, or go down, or stay about where they are now? Asked in early 1952	9	0.8	0.7
7. Linear regression on ratio of total anticipated 1952 expenditure on cars and large household items to realized 1952 income	‡2	*5.8	†9.5
8. Linear regression on attitudinal index (see text)	‡2	0.5	0.0

* Significant at 5% level.
† Significant at 1% level.
‡ Parameters estimated.

no influence should be rejected. Cases in which significantly high ratios have arisen are marked with an asterisk (5 per cent level) or a dagger (1 per cent level).

Among the financial, demographic, or geographic variables tested in Table 35.6, net worth at the beginning of 1953 was significantly related to change in debt during 1952. The lower the net worth bracket, the higher the ratio of 1952 addition to debt to 1952 income. The phenomenon is more pronounced for the regression residuals than for the raw variable. Unfortunately, it is not possible to tell how much of this relationship is a spurious correlation, due simply to the fact that persons who went into debt during 1952 would automatically tend to have high debt and low net worth at the beginning of 1953. This spurious correlation is probably not the whole story, since one would expect it to have more influence on the original variables than on the residuals. But net worth information is not available for early 1952; hence the question remains in doubt.

None of the demographic and geographic variables tested proved significant.

Of the attitudinal variables tested, only the question on intentions to buy durable goods during 1952 (II.7) proved to be significantly related to change in debt. Similar calculations for E/Y show that the predictive value of information on intended expenditure is even greater for that variable. Since E/Y and $\Delta D/Y$ are fairly highly correlated, it is not surprising that intended expenditure is also a useful predictor of debt change. It is noteworthy that intentions to buy add significantly to the information contained in the regression variables. Indeed, intended expenditure is complementary to the "objective" variables included in the regression; its F-ratio is greater for the regression residuals than for the original variables, indicating that it is a better predictor in combination with the regression variables than alone.

None of the more diffuse attitudinal questions appeared to be significantly related to change in debt. In order to test the possibility that a combination of attitudes, rather than individual attitudes considered singly, might be important for debt behavior, a test (II.8) was made of a 1952 attitudinal index, constructed from questions 1, 2, 3, and 5, as follows: For each question, the answer of a respondent was valued as optimistic ($+1$), neutral or no answer (0), or pessimistic (-1). These values were summed over the four questions to give each respondent a score, some integer from -4 to $+4$, inclusive. In Table 35.6, II.8, a test of linear regression on the index score is reported. A test for the significance of differences in the dependent variable for the nine possible scores was also carried out, with similar results. This index is similar in construction to the index the Survey Research Center has computed to summarize its periodic attitudinal surveys and to indicate the over-all trend of attitudes over time, but the index here tested has fewer components.

It is possible that further tests of attitudinal variables will yield different results. With the exception of II.4, the attitudes here tested were responses to questions at the beginning of the year. Conceivably some households who made optimistic responses in early 1952 may already have acted on their optimism by borrowing in 1951; these optimists may have been repaying debt during 1952, while others were borrowing. Debt behavior might, for this and other reasons, turn out to be more closely related to attitudes expressed at the middle or end of the year, or to some combination of attitudes held during the year. It is also possible that the optimism–pessimism dimension, to which the attitudinal questions of this survey were mainly directed, is not a particularly relevant dimension for debt behavior, whatever its importance may be for other aspects of household economic behavior. While optimism may lead some households to go into debt, secure in their anticipation of their ability to carry the burden, it may lead others to clear up their debts, confident that in the future they can get along without them.

7. Summary

Calculations on this cross-section of households suggest the following conclusions regarding household behavior in relation to consumer debt:

(1) The evidence suggests that, other things being equal, high debt levels deter expenditure on durable goods. Otherwise, it is hard to understand why a positive association between these variables, which would be expected in a cross-section of households as a result of persistent differences in thriftiness and related characteristics, failed to appear.

(2) The evidence is more clear cut that high debt levels deter further use of debt in financing purchases. Household behavior displays a

genuine inverse relationship between initial stock of debt and subsequent change in debt.

(3) There are important interrelations between debt and liquid assets in consumer behavior. These result from balancing the cost of borrowing against the needs for liquidity to handle normal and emergency transactions. The economic consequences of a given distribution of consumer debt in the population cannot be adequately appraised without considering simultaneously the distribution of liquid assets.

(4) Additions to debt are negatively related to current income and positively related to previous income among low-income spending units, where borrowing is frequently an emergency measure. These relationships are reversed at higher income levels. Single individuals are less apt to add to debt than married spending units; and, except among low-income units where distress borrowing reverses the relationship, young heads of households are more disposed to add to debt than older consumers. There may be a negative relationship between net worth and changes in debt, but the absence of *ex ante* net worth information leaves this question in doubt. Change in debt is significantly correlated with both actual and anticipated purchases of durable goods. But it does not appear to be significantly related to attitudes of economic optimism or pessimism.

Notes

[1] Guy Orcutt pointed this out very effectively in his illuminating comments on this paper.

[2] I am again indebted to Guy Orcutt for pointing out the possible statistical consequences of this upper constraint.

CHAPTER 36

CONSUMER EXPENDITURES AND THE CAPITAL ACCOUNT

1. Introduction

Like a business firm, a household may be imagined to have two related accounts, an income account and a capital account. The income account comprises *flows* over a period of time; the items in the capital account are *stocks* at a moment of time. The shape of the household income account is determined by decisions concerning work and leisure; consumption and saving; food, shelter, recreation, and other categories of consumption; insurance premiums, mortgage payments, and other forms of saving. A second set of decisions determines the shape of the household balance sheet; amounts of various kinds of indebtedness; proportions of wealth held in securities, life insurance, cash, business or professional assets of self-employed, residence, automobiles, household appliances, and so on. Traditionally both theoretical and statistical analyses of household economic behavior have concentrated on the income account and on the corresponding decisions regarding flows. The present paper,

By Harold W. Watts and James Tobin. Reprinted from *Proceedings of the Conference on Consumption and Saving*, vol. 2, Irwin Friend and Robert Jones, (Eds.) (University of Pennsylvania 1960), pp. 1-48, and from *Studies of Portfolio Behavior*, Donald Hester and James Tobin (Eds.), Cowles Foundation Monograph 20 (New York: Wiley, 1967), pp. 1-39.

This paper is based on research undertaken in connection with a broad Study of Consumer Expenditures, Incomes and Savings at the Wharton School of Finance and Commerce of the University of Pennsylvania. The Study is based largely on the 1950 survey of the Bureau of Labor Statistics of 12 500 families in 91 representative cities. It is financed by a grant from the Ford Foundation.

The authors wish to thank the Yale University Computing Center for its support of the lengthy computational work. Thanks are also due to Sylvester Berki, Donald Hester, John Nagle, and Alvin Puryear for their assistance in performing the calculations. The helpful comments of Arthur M. Okun and Robert Summers of the Cowles Foundation are gratefully acknowledged.

following a less common but growing practice, emphasizes the capital account and investment decisions of the household.

The bridges between the two accounts are of two kinds: accounting and behavioral. By an elementary accounting identity, the increase in net worth of the household over a period must – apart from capital gains and losses – equal net saving during the period. More important are the connections in economic behavior. The over-all division of income between saving and consumption is conditioned by the household's current net worth viewed in relation to its goals of accumulation – next summer's vacation, children's college education, retirement, legacies. Furthermore, the composition of current savings and investment depends on the structure of the capital account, as well as on net worth, and on the pattern, as well as the magnitude, of future consumption plans and aspirations. Many items of consumption, and many occupational pursuits as well, are either wholly inaccessible or available only at considerable extra expense to households who have not acquired specific assets. Accordingly many assets in the household's capital account – both durable consumption goods and business or professional capital – serve a dual purpose: they facilitate the desired pattern of consumption and work, and they help to meet at least some of the goals of wealth accumulation.

In perfect markets, it is worth noticing, only the over-all bridge between saving and net worth would be necessary. The household's decision problem would be less complex, and the analytic task of the interested econometrician would be easier. Decisions regarding the pattern of consumption could be taken without regard for the structure of asset holdings. By the same token, investment decisions could be reached with sole regard for capital appreciation, unconstrained by the household's consumption, or occupational, preferences. Thus the owner of a car and a washing machine would be able to consume the yields of these investments even if he chose, perhaps only temporarily, neither to ride nor to wash clothes – either by renting them out or by selling them, perhaps for later repurchase, and investing the proceeds in assets of liquid yield. Similarly the household wishing to include car mileage and washing-machine-service hours in its consumption program would not need to include the equipment in its asset portfolio but could buy the desired services. But in fact markets for rental and sale of durable goods are imperfect, so that it is both difficult to realize their value as an investment except by consuming their services directly, and expensive to consume the services without owning the goods. The rent a car owner can command by letting his car to someone else is much lower than what he would have to pay to hire the same service, from taxi or drive-yourself companies. Likewise, the price he could realize by selling his car is smaller than what he would have to pay a dealer for a car of the same age and quality. There are similar discrepancies – less for houses, more for smaller goods – between the buying and selling prices and rents of all consumers' durables, and indeed of business and professional equipment as well. These imperfections complicate the investment and consumption decisions of households, connecting the structures, as well as the net totals, of wealth and consumption.

They also complicate the accounting itself. In principle, no matter when a durable good was bought, the use of its services during a period – nothing more nor less – ought to be reckoned as consumption. The same services enter the other side of the account as income, offset to the extent perhaps of 100 per cent or more by the decline in the value of the good due to age and use. The capital account would carry the value of the good; purchase of a new good would be an item of saving and investment rather than a consumption outlay. Were there perfect rental and sale markets, there would be unambiguous money values to assign to the consumption, net income, and capital values of durable goods. An approximation to this principle is attempted, both at a household level in budget studies and at an aggregative level in national income accounts, for houses, where rental and sales markets, though far from perfect, are better developed than for lesser consumers' durables. By and large, the margins of indeterminacy between buyers' and sellers' prices and rents are too great to permit the application of these principles of valuation and accounting. It is not, as often thought, simply the difficulty of collecting the necessary information about use and depreciation that is responsible for the unsatisfactory handling of durable goods in household budgets and national accounts. The essential imperfections of their markets make it impossible to express and to aggregate all items on balance sheets and income accounts in terms of a single homogeneous unit of value.

As a result, there are two approaches, both valid and both incomplete, to analysis of the demand for durable goods. From the standpoint of the income account, expenditures on consumers' durables, which provide for consumption of the related services sooner or later, compete with consumption outlays for food, recreation, services, etc. From the standpoint of the capital account, ownership of durables competes with the holding of cash or other financial assets, or with freedom from debt. On both counts, there are reasons to expect households to maintain some balance between their investments in durable goods and other forms of holding wealth. Consumption of the services of durable goods competes with more distant consumption objectives, which are better provided for by financial assets – securities, insurance, retirement programs. As investments, durable goods share the advantages and risks, with respect to changes in price level and relative prices, of business equities; but they are less liquid and offer less scope for reduction of risk by diversification. A prudent household will wish to balance a position in durable goods by ownership of assets of assured stability of money yield and money value. This motive will be stronger if the durable goods position is financed by mortgage or installment debt.

A rational household will not persistently hold cash and short-term liquid assets beyond transactions requirements when these could be used to reduce outstanding indebtedness. Simultaneous holding of liquid assets of low yield and debt of high interest cost can be explained by the fear that the opportunity to borrow might not be available later if and when funds were needed, and by restrictions imposed by lenders on the speed of debt repayment. It is, of course, rational to balance against debt investments of relatively fixed money value if they promise a higher rate of return or if they are, like life insurance and pension rights, imperfectly liquid means of meeting future goals of accumulation.

The basic hypothesis underlying the calculations to be reported in this paper is that households endeavor to maintain a certain equilibrium or balance among the various items of the capital account: goods, cash and liquid assets, long-term financial assets, debts. The desired structure of assets and debts will be different for different households, depending, among other things, on: (a) their requirements and tastes for the services of consumers' durable goods; (b) their needs for balances of cash and liquid assets to meet transactions and to provide for contingencies due to fluctuations of income and outlay; (c) the investment requirements of their occupations; (d) the nature and remoteness of future demands on wealth, for retirement and for children; (e) their ability to borrow; (f) the extent of their information about capital markets, their estimates of the prospects, in terms of purchasing power, of various available assets, and their attitudes toward the associated risks; and (g) the difficulty and cost to them of making capital transactions. Since these factors are not directly observed, their influence must be sought in terms of observed variables with which they are likely to be related. Thus the desired structure of assets and debts may be expected to be different for households differing with respect to age, education, family size and composition, occupation, and location. It will be different for households at different levels of income or of "living"; as a determinant of fairly durable patterns of consumption, current income seems less relevant than a longer-run standard of living or "permanent income". Further, the relative proportions of different assets and debts can be expected to vary, for any given income level, with the general level of household wealth. For most households, a major decision affecting the structure of the balance sheet is whether or not to own a home. This decision depends on the factors already enumerated and, in addition, such unobserved considerations as frequency of occupationally required moves and attitudes toward the risk and effort specific to home ownership. Once this major decision is made, many other features of the balance sheet follow, e.g., mortgage debt and home furnishings. Home ownership is thus another observed variable to which the structure of the capital account is related. There will, of course, be residual differences in circumstances and tastes that are not measured by any of these observed variables; accordingly there will be unsystematic and unexplained differences in asset–debt patterns.

One implication of the hypothesis is the possibility of an imbalance in the actual asset and debt structure of households – too much of some assets, too little of others. (Throughout this discussion debts should be regarded as negative assets, high in value when low in absolute amount.) The structure cannot be changed overnight, given the imperfection of asset markets and the illiquidity of many assets. But circumstances and tastes can change so that a set of assets and debts that was once an equilibrium becomes a disequilibrium. Economists, at least until the vogue of *The Affluent Society*, have rightly been scornful of popular and journalistic notions of saturation and have emphasized that wants are unlimited and that households can never have too many durable goods, for example, in any absolute sense. But relative saturation there can be. Consumers can have too many durable goods, not in any absolute sense, but relative to their net holdings of financial assets. The opposite phenomenon, relative saturation with liquidity, no doubt characterized household balance sheets immediately after the war. Quite apart from dramatic shifts of circumstance or taste, the capital-account adjustments of a household are necessarily a continuing dynamic process; the appropriate amount and composition of wealth varies over the "life cycle". The adjustment process can be estimated by observing the relations of changes in assets and debts during the year to the levels of the same assets and debts at the beginning of the year. The hypothesis implies, generally speaking, that the change in each stock will be negatively related to the initial level of the stock itself but positively related to the initial level of other stocks.

 The basic hypothesis suggests two sets of calculations, one in which stock levels are the variables to be explained, and a second in which changes in stocks, or flows, take this role. Each set of calculations consists in turn of two parts: regressions of the dependent variables on various combinations of explanatory variables; and calculations of the correlations, simple, partial, and multiple, among the dependent variables before and after the regressions. In the case of the regressions of the stock variables, the explanatory variables are those enumerated above – indicators of the biological, geographical, social, and economic circumstances of the household. The purpose is to measure the influence of each explanatory variable on asset and debt holdings, and to test their significance in explaining differences among households in these holdings. The hypothesis suggests not only that these variables will be significant explanatory factors for the stocks individually but also that much of the consistency in the structure of stocks will turn out to be due to their common dependence on these explanatory variables. This suggestion is the reason for the calculation of correlations among the stocks before and after the regressions; to the extent that the suggestion is correct, the correlations will be smaller after regression. The regressions and correlations computed for the flows are similar in purpose. However, the flow regressions have, in addition to the explanatory variables used in the stock regressions, the initial values of the stocks themselves. Their inclusion is designed to test the implications of the hypothesis regarding adjustment of the capital account and to estimate the parameters of the adjustment process.

2. The Observations and the Variables Used

Since the objectives of the study did not include exhaustive description of consumer behavior no attempt was made to use the entire 12,500 observations available. The hypotheses under consideration, while perhaps relevant to all kinds of consumers, can be fairly examined only by comparing behavior among relatively homogeneous households. Some categories of households were eliminated entirely, leaving several sub-samples which meet the homogeneity requirement and at the same time are large enough to warrant the use of statistical analysis and inference. The body of data used can be concisely described as a sample of house-holds including an employed, male head between 25 and 74 years of age as well as one or more other persons for at least part of the year. All households not meeting those specifications were dropped from the sample. In addition households headed by a "professional" with less than 8 years of education and those headed by "unskilled" workers with more than 12 years of education were eliminated. Finally, a few house-holds were removed because of missing information on a variable used in the analysis.

The remaining households were divided on the basis of tenure status at the end of 1950. Households owning homes at the end of the year comprised one category and all other households a second. These classes will be referred to subsequently as home owners and renters respectively. All calculations and analyses have been carried out separately for home owners and renters. There are two reasons for this. First, as has already been mentioned, ownership of a home has a large impact on a house-hold's capital account and can be expected to influence the amount as well as the composition of expenditures and assets. Second, housing level is used as one of the variables in the analysis and there is no clear solution to the problem of defining a measure of housing level which renders home owners and renters comparable.

Table 36.1
Sample frequencies by tenure, age, and education classes

Age	25-34	35-44	45-54	55-74	All
Home owners:					
Education (yrs)					
0-8	117	343	490	684	1634
9-12	539	672	437	348	1996
13 or more	228	354	226	135	943
All	884	1369	1153	1167	4573
Renters:					
Education (yrs)					
0-8	297	356	388	357	1398
9-12	780	539	232	145	1696
13 or more	368	176	117	73	734
All	1445	1071	737	575	3828

Further subdivisions of the sample by age and education were made at some points in the analysis. For this purpose 4 age classes and 3 education classes were recognized. In the case of age the endpoints were 25 to 34, 35 to 44, 45 to 54, and 55 to 74. For education the classes were defined as less than 9 years, 9 to 12 years, and more than 12 years. The class frequencies by tenure, age, and education are shown in Table 36.1.

Ideally an analysis of household capital accounts would start with data showing an exhaustive enumeration of major balance sheet items for each household. Such complete information is not available in the *Survey of Consumer Expenditures* and probably will not be available in surveys of comparable size and coverage for some time to come. Although a complete balance sheet is not available, an attempt has been made to glean as much of it as possible from the available data.

The information on inventories of durable goods has been used to build 8 of the stock variables used in this study. The inventory data show the ages of specific durable goods in 5 age classes. To form the new variables approximate values were assigned for each good owned by a household on the basis of its age, and the values thus obtained were combined under seven general headings. The seven variables are:

A_1: Furniture;
A_2: Basic kitchen appliances (range and refrigerator);
A_3: Laundry appliances (washer, ironer);
A_4: Deep freeze;
A_5: Miscellaneous appliances (vacuum cleaners, sewing machines);
A_6: Radios and phonographs;
A_7: Television.

An eighth variable, A_f, was formed by adding A_1 through A_7 together and, since this sum represents inventory value at the end of the year, the expenditures on durables during the year were deducted to arrive at a beginning-of-year value of durable goods. The schedule of values used in the assignment process are shown in Table 36.2. They were arrived at by

Table 36.2
Assignment schedule for valuation of durable goods

Year of purchase	1950-51	1946-49	1941-45	Pre-1941
A_1 Living room suite	$300	$250	$200	$100
Dining room suite	300	250	200	100
Dinette set	100	80	60	20
Bedroom suite	300	250	200	100
Upholstered chair	100	80	60	20
Rugs and carpets	200	150	100	50
Pianos and organs	750	600	500	300
A_2 Range	200	120	40	30
Refrigerator	300	180	60	45
A_3 Automatic washer	250	150	50	38
Non-automatic washer	150	90	30	22
Ironer	175	105	35	26
A_4 Deep freeze	300	180	60	45
A_5 Sewing machine	200	120	40	30
Upright cleaner	75	45	15	11
Tank-type cleaner	75	45	15	11
A_6 Phonograph	75	45	15	11
Radio	50	30	10	8
Radio-phono. comb.	250	150	50	38
A_7 Television	300	180	60	45
Television comb.	400	240	80	60

Table 36.3
Assignment schedule for value of automobile

| Year of purchase | Price class | | | |
	Low	Medium	High	Not ascertained*
1950-51	1500	2000	2800	1700
1946-49	1000	1200	1600	1100
Pre-1946	300	400	600	300
Not ascertained*	500	600	800	500

* Pertains only to age or price class – not to whether household owns a car or not.
Note: Schedule value above multiplied by 1.5 in the case of multicar households.

applying "reasonable" depreciation rates to approximate prices of new goods in 1950 as shown in catalogs, *Consumer Reports*, etc.

Two dimensions of the automobile stock are given in the data: the age and the price class. Here, again, an assigned value was placed on each possible combination of age and quality of automobile. The variable T is this assigned value minus the net cost of automobiles purchased during the year to transform it to a beginning-of-year basis. The assignment schedule is shown in Table 36.3.

The variables, cash in bank C and mortgage debt M, were available directly in dollar amounts as of the beginning of the year. Installment debt, I, was punched in classes and was transformed into dollar amounts by assigning approximate "midpoint" values to the class codes. The "midpoints" used are shown in Table 36.4.

Table 36.4
"Midpoints" for installment debt
classes used for assigning dollar amounts to I

Class intervals	"Midpoints"
0-0	0
1-100	50
100-200	150
200-300	240
300-400	330
400-500	420
500-1000	600
1000 and over	1200

One other variable was, for all purposes, treated as a stock. Life insurance premiums can in some cases be interpreted as a proxy for the value of the policy – a proper balance sheet item for all non-term insurance. For this reason the reported premiums on personal insurance Z, was added to the list of variables to be analyzed.

As far as possible, flow variables were chosen and defined to correspond to stock variables. The reported expenditures on furnishings and equipment, E_f, thus corresponds to the stock variable A_f on total durable goods. Net cost of automobile purchases ΔT, change in mortgage debt ΔM, change in installment debt ΔI, and change in cash balances ΔC, similarly correspond to the stocks T, M, I, and C, respectively. It must be admitted that the correspondence is less than perfect for some of the paired stocks and flows but it does not seem that the differences are great enough to hamper seriously the modest objectives of the investigation.

In addition to these flows, change in total assets ΔA, and change in total debts ΔD, have been added to the list; both variables were directly reported in the *Survey*. Also the difference between the two, S $(= \Delta A - \Delta D)$, has been used. Although this difference will be called saving, it should be explicitly noted that it is different from the saving figure that would result from simply computing the difference between disposable income and consumption expenditures. It is difficult to say which measurement more closely approximates the "change in net worth" measure which would be ideal for the purposes of this study; there are considerations pointing in both directions. In any case, the nominal "net worth" measure was chosen here.

The group of variables upon which the stocks and flows are dependent according to the hypothesis may be described as a set of indicators of social status, economic status and prospects, life-cycle standing, and environment. The independent or determining variables to be used in the analysis to follow are: age (A), education (E), occupation (O), family size (N), region (R), community size (L), disposable income (Y), and housing level (H). It is claimed that these variables, as a group, provide a reasonably good description of a household's location with respect to the relevant dimensions mentioned above. Unfortunately the observable variables are not related in any simple way to those dimensions. For example, a variable such as education may be relevant because of its relation to social status or because of its effect on income prospects. This consideration will complicate matters later when an attempt is made to interpret the empirical findings.

The variables age and education have been introduced in two ways. At some points the sample was classified by age and education and separate regressions fitted within each subgroup. This procedure allows age and education to interact freely with each of the other variables in the regression. When the two tenure groups were not subdivided, additive age and education effects were allowed for by introducing dichotomous dummy variables. Dummies A-2, A-3, and A-4 represent the older three of the four age classes, and E-2 and E-3 represent the two higher education classes. The coefficients of these variables must be interpreted as differential effects relative to the youngest age class or the lowest education class, as the case may be.

Occupation also has been represented through the dummy variable device. Six occupation classes have been formed from the nine employed classes recognized in the "original" occupation of head code used by the B.L.S. The salaried professional class (dummy O-1) is parallel to the first "original" class. The self-employed class (O-2) also is the same as the second "original" class; it includes self-employed professionals, business-men, managers, and officials. The third and fourth "original" classes are combined in the clerical and sales class (O-3). The fifth "original" class has become the skilled worker class (O-4) and the sixth is now the semi-skilled worker class (O-5). Finally, the seventh, eighth, and ninth classes are combined in the unskilled worker category (O-6). As in the cases of age and education, one of the dummy variables is redundant and must be left out of regressions. O-4 has been chosen for this purpose; as a consequence the effects of the other occupation dummies will be relative to the skilled workers.

Family size (N) has been measured by the average number of persons in the household. N takes on fractional values when some persons are a part of the household for a part of the year.

The three regions and three community size classes are based on the city area code used in the *Survey of Consumer Expenditures*. The regions are North (R-1), South (R-2), and West (R-3). The size classes are: large cities (L-1), suburbs of large cities (L-2), and small cities (L-3). For purposes of establishing dummy categories R-1 and L-1 were left out.

The last two independent variables, disposable income (Y) and housing level (H), are to be considered together as measures of the budget constraint on a household's decisions. In recognition of the deficiencies of current income as a measure of the theoretically relevant permanent or expected income, housing level has been introduced as a variable. The argument in favor of this practice is that a household's housing level is related to its permanent or expected income and is not likely to be freely adjusted to allow for short-run variations in income. Clearly a measure of housing level will not provide an exact measure of permanent income but to the extent that errors in the "housing" measure of permanent income are uncorrelated with the errors in the current income measure of permanent income (i.e., transitory income) the use of housing level can provide useful information. Disposable income and housing level can both be regarded as imperfect proxy variables for permanent income. They are both used because for present purposes two poor substitutes are better than one if they are partially independent of each other.

Disposable income was, of course, directly available in dollar amounts. Housing level was coded by classes; the measure being based on market value of home in the case of home owners and on annual rent for renters. The codes were transformed to dollar amounts according to the schedule of "midpoints" shown in Table 36.5.

For convenience the variables will often be referred to by symbol. Table 36.6 lists the variables and the symbolic equivalents.

3. The Stock Calculations

Multiple linear regression functions were fitted for each of the stock variables on some or all of the independent variables. Table 36.7 shows F-ratios for testing, by analysis of variance, the significance of selected groups of independent variables. Test (9) in Table 36.7 shows results of the analysis in which each of the two tenure classes were subdivided by age and education and separate regressions fitted to each class. In the other tests age and education are included, if at all, in simple dummy variable form, and the regressions are fitted to the whole tenure class. Tables 36.8 to 36.20 show, for two of the "pooled" regressions, regression coefficients, their respective estimated standard errors, the standard

Table 36.5
"Midpoints" for housing level classes
used for assigning dollar values to H

Class intervals	"Midpoints"
Home owners:	
$1-4999	$4000
5000-7499	6500
7500-9999	8500
10 000-12,499	11 250
12 500-14 999	13 750
15 000-17,499	16 250
17 500-19 999	18 500
20 000-24 999	22 000
25 000 and over	30 000
Renters:	
$0-249	$200
250-499	400
500-749	650
750-999	825
1000-1249	1125
1250-1499	1375
1500-1999	1750
2000-2999	2250
3000 and over	3600

Table 36.6
List of variables used and their symbolic equivalents

Stocks:	
Furniture	A_1
Kitchen appliances	A_2
Laundry appliances	A_3
Deep freeze	A_4
Misc. appliances	A_5
Radio-phonograph	A_6
Television	A_7
Total durable goods	A_f
Automobile	T
Mortgage debt	M
Installment debt	I
Cash balances	C
Insurance	Z

Table 36.6 (*continued*)

Flows:

Durable goods purchases	E_p
Auto purchase	ΔT
Change in mortgage debt	ΔM
Change in installment debt	ΔI
Change in cash balances	ΔC
Change in assets	ΔA
Change in debts	ΔD
Saving	S

Independent variables:

Education:	E
0-8 years	E-1
9-12 years	E-2
13 or more years	E-3
Age:	A
25-34 years	A-1
35-44 years	A-2
45-54 years	A-3
55-74 years	A-4
Occupation:	O
Salaried professional	O-1
Self-employed	O-2
Clerical and sales	O-3
Skilled workers	O-4
Semi-skilled workers	O-5
Unskilled workers	O-6
Family size	N
Region:	R
North	R-1
South	R-2
West	R-3
Community size:	L
Large cities	L-1
Suburbs to large cities	L-2
Small cities	L-3
Disposable income:	Y
Housing level:	H
A_f, T, M, I, and C collectively as used in flow regressions	Σ

Table 36.7
"F"-tests for stock variables

Variable		(1) Simple effect of occupation		(2) Effect of N, R, and L when added to occupation		(3) Effect of N, R, and L added to A, E, and O		(4) Effect of Y and H when added to O, N, R, and L	
		Owners	Renters	Owners	Renters	Owners	Renters	Owners	Renters
Furniture	(A_1)	26.24†	25.22†	17.48†	16.80†	12.43†	15.69†	86.09†	40.91†
Kitchen appliances	(A_2)	1.75	3.39†	7.38†	11.45†	7.29†	9.09†	17.59†	4.15*
Laundry appliances	(A_3)	13.09†	7.10†	21.23†	27.04†	11.80†	21.27†	45.36†	68.84†
Deep freeze	(A_4)	21.42†	2.52*	3.36†	2.14	3.00*	2.00	88.05†	2.63
Miscellaneous appliances	(A_5)	11.54†	18.51†	12.66†	14.60†	9.12†	12.40†	6.80†	13.94†
Radio-phonograph	(A_6)	7.96†	5.09†	24.22†	8.42†	15.95†	6.42†	44.13†	48.88†
Television	(A_7)	6.91†	8.76†	82.68†	73.74†	90.19†	73.17†	53.38†	34.92†
Total durables	(A_f)	4.70†	10.63†	3.96†	25.20†	2.80*	23.62†	74.89†	7.40†
Automobile	(T)	9.34†	9.54†	0.87	1.47	0.032	1.52	13.87†	9.19†
Mortgage debt	(M)	35.40†	1.62	22.60†	3.74†	13.99†	3.74†	158.92†	13.61†
Installment debt	(I)	6.03†	4.99†	9.99†	3.92†	6.50†	3.06†	0.82	1.54
Cash in bank	(C)	22.04†	23.84†	6.58†	9.15†	3.52†	6.39†	89.87†	87.80†
Insurance premiums	(Z)	51.57†	26.76†	16.35†	6.62†	16.44†	7.77†	641.57†	1965.00†
Housing level	(H)	187.21†	99.36†	28.63†	7.45†	25.88†	6.42†	–0–	–0–
Degrees of freedom: used/remaining		5/4567	5/3822	5/4562	5/3817	5/4557	5/3812	2/4560	2/3815

Table 36.7 (continued)

	(5) Effect of Y and H when added to A, E, O, N, R, and L		(6) Additive effect of A and E when added to occupation		(7) Additive effect of A and E when added to O, N, R, and L		(8) Additive effect of A and E when added to O, N, R, L, Y, and H		(9) Interaction of A and E with O, N, R, L, Y, and H minus additive effects of age and education	
	Owners	Renters	Owners	Renters	Owners	Renters	Owners	Renters	Owners	Renters
(A_1)	83.74†	36.33†	30.45†	7.28†	25.30†	6.19†	24.00†	4.40†	1.83†	2.23†
(A_2)	20.24†	1.95	58.83†	16.47†	58.68†	14.74†	59.78†	13.96†	1.12	1.48†
(A_3)	49.12†	2.79	39.86†	22.72†	30.22†	17.00†	31.76†	17.40†	2.07†	1.32†
(A_4)	77.26†	1.87	5.57†	1.96	5.21†	1.87	1.07	1.57	1.28*	6.71†
(A_5)	14.20†	13.09†	32.94†	11.25†	29.31†	8.74†	29.80†	8.62†	1.56†	1.42†
(A_6)	39.62†	9.16†	35.17†	17.83†	26.84†	15.79†	24.99†	15.82†	1.51†	1.31†
(A_7)	64.98†	35.34†	8.70†	6.24†	8.11†	5.71†	12.71†	5.89†	2.13†	1.52†
(A_f)	70.97†	6.80†	14.59†	7.39†	13.41†	5.34†	11.90†	5.14†	2.57†	1.87†
(T)	11.89†	7.19†	2.67*	2.84*	2.64*	2.87*	1.86	2.07	1.14	1.01
(M)	185.94†	13.32†	86.06†	1.36	76.79†	1.36	139.96†	1.25	2.14†	1.41†
(I)	0.67	2.12†	28.21†	9.32†	24.55†	8.45†	24.24†	8.68†	1.44†	1.34†
(C)	75.04†	80.63†	14.07†	9.59†	10.90†	6.84†	5.15†	5.00†	1.43†	2.18†
(Z)	525.25†	1880.00†	44.68†	20.68†	44.75†	21.84†	10.37†	45.35†	2.35†	3.73†
(H)	–0–	–0–	70.69†	14.46†	67.78†	29.84†	–0–	–0–	–0–	–0–
D.f.	2/4555	2/3810	5/4562	5/3817	5/4557	5/3812	5/4555	5/3810	130/4425	130/3680

Note: * denotes significance at 0.05 level; † denotes significance at 0.01 level.

deviation of residuals (S_u), and R^2 (coefficient of multiple determination). One of the regressions (I) includes Y and H, and the other (II) omits them; both include age, education, occupation, family size, region, and community size.

Table 36.7 gives the impression that nearly everything is significantly related to everything else – as any good general equilibrium model suggests. A word of deflation seems in order and for this it is probably sufficient to call attention to the R^2's and S_u's in Tables 36.8 to 36.20. Only in the case of insurance premiums has as much as 20 per cent of the variation been explained. The explanation is that tests based upon large samples are quite powerful and variables which are statistically significant may have very little ability to predict individual cases.

Among the stocks, deep freeze (A_4) and automobile (T) were least related to the set of independent variables. The reasons for the poor

Table 36.8
Regression coefficients for furniture (A_1)

Independent variable	I		II	
	Home owners	Renters	Home owners	Renters
E-2	37.48 (11.24)	25.06 (12.78)	59.15 (11.31)	39.55 (12.77)
E-3	36.08 (15.92)	36.86 (18.42)	93.42 (15.55)	64.55 (18.30)
A-2	−11.48 (13.31)	25.25 (12.86)	5.74 (13.48)	34.75 (12.93)
A-3	−77.91 (14.20)	−13.67 (14.89)	−46.52 (14.24)	4.06 (14.88)
A-4	−104.10 (15.02)	−30.57 (16.66)	−74.96 (15.11)	−19.16 (16.75)
O-1	27.34 (20.11)	57.91 (23.20)	43.95 (20.40)	69.18 (23.37)
O-2	4.72 (13.77)	23.21 (17.52)	47.99 (13.59)	46.64 (17.46)
O-3	−5.16 (15.17)	17.91 (17.47)	2.29 (15.42)	24.02 (17.60)
O-5	−19.87 (14.14)	−16.04 (15.25)	−31.25 (14.35)	−20.94 (15.38)
O-6	−41.55 (16.58)	−68.88 (16.78)	−60.98 (16.80)	−83.28 (16.85)
1	552.17 (22.31)	359.50 (23.73)	608.40 (21.60)	442.10 (21.74)
N	6.49 (3.38)	13.96 (3.81)	9.80 (3.38)	15.58 (3.84)
R-2	−16.66 (11.86)	−72.61 (12.69)	−32.86 (12.00)	−80.87 (12.76)
R-3	60.08 (10.50)	−51.18 (12.70)	55.73 (10.68)	−51.57 (12.81)
L-2	−11.95 (10.75)	37.94 (14.31)	−4.50 (10.92)	40.50 (14.44)
L-3	−4.00 (12.48)	−17.68 (14.60)	−17.52 (12.65)	−24.29 (14.71)
$Y/1000$	10.73 (1.70)	6.25 (1.83)	—	—
$H/1000$	7.98 (0.97)	131.18 (21.66)	—	—
S_u	303.63	312.58	309.03	315.46
R^2	0.105	0.078	0.072	0.060

Note: All coefficients are in dollars. Estimated errors in parentheses.

Table 36.9
Regression coefficients for kitchen appliances (A_2)

Independent variable	I				II			
	Home owners		Renters		Home owners		Renters	
E-2	−8.56	(4.51)	−6.52	(6.06)	−6.85	(4.48)	−7.69	(6.00)
E-3	1.57	(6.39)	−16.34	(8.73)	7.94	(6.16)	−17.92	(8.60)
A-2	−61.47	(5.34)	−34.36	(6.10)	−59.78	(5.34)	−34.99	(6.08)
A-3	−82.25	(5.70)	−49.73	(7.06)	−79.50	(5.64)	−50.71	(6.99)
A-4	−91.21	(6.03)	−46.79	(7.90)	−89.12	(5.98)	−47.78	(7.87)
O-1	2.37	(8.07)	−1.94	(11.00)	1.83	(8.08)	−3.18	(10.98)
O-2	9.40	(5.53)	−12.81	(8.31)	12.86	(5.38)	−14.57	(8.20)
O-3	1.41	(6.09)	−1.08	(8.28)	0.89	(6.11)	−1.96	(8.27)
O-5	9.68	(5.67)	1.19	(7.23)	9.58	(5.68)	1.48	(7.23)
O-6	10.22	(6.65)	−15.51	(7.95)	8.19	(6.65)	−14.60	(7.92)
1	272.54	(8.96)	188.48	(11.25)	275.43	(8.55)	182.00	(10.21)
N	−5.17	(1.36)	5.40	(1.81)	−3.54	(1.34)	5.36	(1.80)
R-2	12.16	(4.76)	17.49	(6.01)	10.68	(4.75)	17.74	(5.99)
R-3	17.36	(4.22)	13.04	(6.02)	16.55	(4.23)	12.77	(6.02)
L-2	−4.08	(4.32)	11.61	(6.78)	−4.28	(4.32)	11.40	(6.78)
L-3	11.58	(5.01)	23.98	(6.92)	11.47	(5.01)	24.25	(6.91)
Y/1000	4.33	(0.68)	0.77	(0.87)	—		—	
H/1000	−0.89	(0.39)	−18.35	(10.27)	—		—	
S_u	121.86		148.17		122.37		148.19	
R^2	0.078		0.036		0.070		0.035	

Table 36.10
Regression coefficients for laundry appliances (A_3)

Independent variable	I				II			
	Home owners		Renters		Home owners		Renters	
E-2	1.72	(3.10)	2.80	(3.31)	6.33	(3.10)	3.86	(3.28)
E-3	7.96	(4.39)	5.21	(4.78)	20.12	(4.26)	7.17	(4.70)
A-2	−18.15	(3.67)	−10.96	(3.34)	−14.50	(3.69)	−10.27	(3.32)
A-3	−33.71	(3.92)	−25.64	(3.86)	−27.04	(3.90)	−24.39	(3.83)
A-4	−43.58	(4.14)	−31.08	(4.32)	−37.37	(4.14)	−30.24	(4.31)
O-1	−3.34	(5.54)	4.85	(6.02)	0.24	(5.58)	−3.99	(6.01)
O-2	1.72	(3.80)	−0.98	(4.54)	10.93	(3.72)	0.73	(4.49)
O-3	0.12	(4.18)	−4.12	(4.53)	1.74	(4.22)	−3.63	(4.52)
O-5	−6.16	(3.90)	−5.08	(3.96)	−8.60	(3.93)	−5.43	(3.95)
O-6	−6.71	(4.57)	−16.19	(4.35)	−10.83	(4.60)	−17.22	(4.33)
1	67.26	(6.15)	44.44	(6.15)	85.07	(5.91)	50.49	(5.59)
N	5.61	(0.93)	8.74	(0.99)	6.28	(0.92)	8.85	(0.99)
R-2	0.73	(3.27)	−4.26	(3.29)	−2.72	(3.29)	−4.83	(3.28)
R-3	9.59	(2.90)	7.56	(3.29)	8.67	(2.92)	7.57	(3.29)
L-2	−2.10	(2.97)	12.28	(3.71)	−0.49	(2.99)	12.47	(3.71)
L-3	1.86	(3.44)	4.82	(3.79)	−1.04	(3.46)	4.36	(3.78)
Y/1000	2.20	(0.47)	0.32	(0.48)	—		—	
H/1000	1.74	(0.27)	10.47	(5.62)	—		—	
S_u	83.72		81.05		84.60		81.09	
R^2	0.087		0.065		0.067		0.064	

Table 36.11

Regression coefficients for deep-freeze (A_4)

Independent variable	I		II	
	Home owners	Renters	Home owners	Renters
E-2	−0.74 (1.93)	1.44 (1.20)	2.72 (1.94)	1.65 (1.18)
E-3	1.69 (2.74)	3.18 (1.72)	11.19 (2.67)	3.67 (1.70)
A-2	1.98 (2.29)	2.13 (1.20)	4.79 (2.32)	2.29 (1.20)
A-3	0.80 (2.45)	1.12 (1.39)	5.86 (2.45)	1.44 (1.38)
A-4	−2.47 (2.59)	3.32 (1.56)	2.14 (2.60)	3.47 (1.55)
O-1	−6.02 (3.46)	0.04 (2.17)	−3.72 (3.51)	0.16 (2.17)
O-2	6.39 (2.37)	2.38 (1.64)	13.30 (2.34)	2.74 (1.62)
O-3	−1.39 (2.61)	1.61 (1.63)	−0.41 (2.65)	1.64 (1.63)
O-5	−1.39 (2.43)	0.26 (1.43)	−3.05 (2.47)	0.17 (1.43)
O-6	−3.92 (2.85)	−0.65 (1.57)	−7.11 (2.89)	−0.89 (1.56)
1	−11.14 (3.84)	−3.92 (2.22)	1.44 (3.72)	−2.71 (2.02)
N	−1.06 (0.58)	0.46 (0.36)	−0.27 (0.58)	0.50 (0.36)
R-2	4.74 (2.04)	0.97 (1.19)	2.11 (2.06)	0.79 (1.18)
R-3	7.38 (1.81)	3.40 (1.19)	6.60 (1.84)	3.35 (1.19)
L-2	0.93 (1.85)	0.70 (1.34)	1.97 (1.88)	0.73 (1.34)
L-3	3.30 (2.15)	−0.74 (1.37)	1.32 (2.18)	−0.87 (1.36)
Y/1000	2.37 (0.29)	0.28 (0.17)	—	—
H/1000	0.99 (0.17)	0.71 (2.03)	—	—
S_u	52.28	29.24	53.15	29.25
R^2	0.064	0.009	0.032	0.008

Table 36.12

Regression coefficients for miscellaneous appliances (A_5)

Independent variable	I		II	
	Home owners	Renters	Home owners	Renters
E-2	7.73 (2.26)	5.36 (2.64)	9.05 (2.24)	7.04 (2.63)
E-3	9.47 (3.21)	7.73 (3.81)	13.00 (3.08)	11.14 (3.76)
A-2	−12.83 (2.68)	2.06 (2.66)	−11.78 (2.67)	3.20 (2.66)
A-3	−23.30 (2.86)	−10.60 (3.08)	−21.38 (2.82)	−8.41 (3.06)
A-4	−26.26 (3.03)	−12.48 (3.45)	−24.48 (3.00)	−11.17 (3.44)
O-1	0.57 (4.05)	−0.20 (4.80)	1.55 (4.04)	1.01 (4.80)
O-2	1.48 (2.78)	−7.33 (3.63)	4.12 (2.69)	−4.58 (3.59)
O-3	0.05 (3.06)	−3.53 (3.61)	0.48 (3.06)	−2.93 (3.62)
O-5	1.04 (2.85)	−14.41 (3.16)	0.35 (2.85)	−15.01 (3.16)
O-6	−9.48 (3.34)	−17.74 (3.47)	−10.68 (3.33)	−19.48 (3.46)
1	65.77 (4.50)	37.94 (4.91)	70.78 (4.28)	47.58 (4.47)
N	0.20 (0.68)	2.67 (0.79)	0.43 (0.67)	2.88 (0.79)
R-2	−2.00 (2.39)	−13.27 (2.62)	−2.99 (2.38)	−14.35 (2.62)
R-3	9.64 (2.12)	3.85 (2.63)	9.37 (2.12)	3.72 (2.63)
L-2	8.74 (2.17)	4.88 (2.96)	9.18 (2.17)	5.18 (2.97)
L-3	2.08 (2.52)	6.03 (3.02)	1.27 (2.51)	5.19 (3.03)
Y/1000	0.72 (0.34)	1.09 (0.38)	—	—
H/1000	0.46 (0.20)	13.01 (4.48)	—	—
S_u	61.19	64.66	61.28	64.87
R^2	0.060	0.060	0.056	0.053

Table 36.13
Regression coefficients for radio-phonograph (A_6)

Independent variable	I				II			
	Home owners		Renters		Home owners		Renters	
E-2	2.01	(2.51)	0.96	(2.74)	4.92	(2.50)	2.19	(2.73)
E-3	9.33	(3.56)	10.00	(3.96)	17.70	(3.44)	12.73	(3.90)
A-2	−7.11	(2.98)	−6.52	(2.76)	−4.67	(2.99)	−5.64	(2.76)
A-3	−12.90	(3.17)	−16.21	(3.20)	−8.58	(3.15)	−14.44	(3.18)
A-4	−30.16	(3.36)	−25.23	(3.58)	−26.32	(3.35)	−24.30	(3.57)
O-1	−0.88	(4.49)	4.20	(4.99)	0.68	(4.52)	4.97	(4.99)
O-2	0.45	(3.08)	3.14	(3.77)	6.28	(3.01)	5.21	(3.73)
O-3	3.45	(3.39)	3.10	(3.75)	4.05	(3.42)	3.39	(3.75)
O-5	−1.84	(3.16)	0.05	(3.28)	−3.08	(3.18)	−0.42	(3.28)
O-6	0.91	(3.71)	0.24	(3.61)	−1.88	(3.72)	−1.12	(3.60)
1	37.78	(4.99)	47.24	(5.10)	47.61	(4.78)	54.34	(4.64)
N	2.43	(0.76)	1.78	(0.82)	3.38	(0.75)	1.97	(0.82)
R-2	7.85	(2.65)	−1.37	(2.73)	5.60	(2.66)	−2.31	(2.72)
R-3	12.76	(2.35)	3.23	(2.73)	12.00	(2.37)	3.02	(2.73)
L-2	−2.03	(2.40)	−0.81	(3.07)	−1.32	(2.42)	−0.60	(3.08)
L-3	14.07	(2.79)	14.09	(3.14)	12.60	(2.80)	13.38	(3.14)
Y/1000	2.72	(0.38)	1.29	(0.39)	—		—	
H/1000	0.52	(0.22)	6.55	(4.66)	—		—	
S_u	67.87		67.17		68.45		67.31	
R^2	0.078		0.042		0.062		0.038	

Table 36.14
Regression coefficients for television (A_7)

Independent variable	I				II			
	Home owners		Renters		Home owners		Renters	
E-2	−4.83	(4.81)	13.24	(5.15)	2.91	(4.82)	17.83	(5.15)
E-3	−27.63	(6.81)	−4.91	(7.43)	−6.15	(6.63)	5.21	(7.38)
A-2	−4.78	(5.69)	−3.08	(5.19)	1.55	(5.74)	0.21	(5.22)
A-3	−20.56	(6.07)	−10.17	(6.01)	−9.19	(6.07)	−3.61	(6.00)
A-4	−40.50	(6.43)	−21.44	(6.72)	−30.19	(6.44)	−17.98	(6.76)
O-1	−13.09	(8.60)	−13.11	(9.36)	−8.13	(8.69)	−10.23	(9.42)
O-2	−5.19	(5.89)	8.05	(7.07)	10.31	(5.79)	15.74	(7.04)
O-3	−4.60	(6.49)	−9.93	(7.04)	−2.52	(6.57)	−8.82	(7.10)
O-5	−11.79	(6.05)	−2.33	(6.15)	−15.43	(6.12)	−4.10	(6.20)
O-6	−20.99	(7.09)	−21.78	(6.77)	−28.21	(7.16)	−26.85	(6.79)
1	104.60	(9.54)	76.83	(9.57)	132.41	(9.20)	103.32	(8.77)
N	1.58	(1.45)	3.37	(1.54)	3.49	(1.44)	4.08	(1.55)
R-2	−28.01	(5.07)	−46.88	(5.12)	−33.91	(5.11)	−50.36	(5.15)
R-3	−46.67	(4.49)	−50.03	(5.12)	−48.48	(4.55)	−50.77	(5.16)
L-2	0.70	(4.60)	−0.10	(5.77)	2.94	(4.65)	0.70	(5.82)
L-3	−77.40	(5.34)	−68.58	(5.89)	−81.73	(5.39)	−71.22	(5.93)
Y/1000	5.69	(0.73)	4.68	(0.74)	—		—	
H/1000	2.05	(0.42)	25.16	(8.74)	—		—	
S_u	129.85		126.09		131.67		127.22	
R^2	0.130		0.122		0.105		0.105	

Table 36.15

Regression coefficients for total durables (A_f)

Independent variable	I Home owners	I Renters	II Home owners	II Renters
E-2	53.32 (21.99)	51.19 (19.25)	36.01 (22.07)	55.44 (19.11)
E-3	26.41 (31.15)	41.02 (27.76)	−35.79 (30.35)	44.05 (27.37)
A-2	−80.74 (26.05)	18.31 (19.39)	−97.46 (26.31)	20.03 (19.34)
A-3	−128.71 (27.79)	−54.75 (22.45)	−156.21 (27.79)	−53.10 (22.26)
A-4	−171.52 (29.40)	−39.04 (25.11)	−193.02 (29.50)	−35.12 (25.06)
O-1	106.52 (39.34)	18.91 (34.97)	109.63 (39.81)	24.80 (34.95)
O-2	48.36 (26.95)	20.31 (26.41)	13.32 (26.52)	26.18 (26.11)
O-3	22.22 (29.69)	14.83 (26.32)	26.07 (30.10)	19.72 (26.32)
O-5	−29.39 (27.66)	−22.19 (22.99)	−27.40 (28.02)	−22.79 (23.01)
O-6	−82.44 (32.44)	−108.49 (25.28)	−62.45 (32.80)	−110.81 (25.20)
1	970.12 (43.66)	537.61 (35.76)	936.13 (42.16)	560.63 (32.52)
N	26.11 (6.61)	42.57 (5.74)	11.33 (6.59)	42.30 (5.74)
R-2	−30.36 (23.21)	−120.12 (19.12)	−15.64 (23.43)	−119.30 (19.08)
R-3	17.82 (20.55)	−70.90 (19.14)	25.46 (20.85)	−68.66 (19.15)
L-2	−7.61 (21.04)	79.92 (21.56)	−6.58 (21.32)	80.71 (21.59)
L-3	−77.70 (24.42)	−28.23 (22.00)	−75.38 (24.68)	−28.12 (22.00)
$Y/1000$	−39.55 (3.32)	−8.34 (2.76)	—	—
$H/1000$	7.06 (1.90)	100.18 (32.65)	—	—
S_u	594.12	471.08	603.18	471.80
R^2	0.053	0.056	0.024	0.053

Table 36.16

Regression coefficients for automobile (T)

Independent variable	I Home owners	I Renters	II Home owners	II Renters
E-2	59.04 (32.12)	11.58 (28.11)	71.16 (31.83)	25.98 (27.88)
E-3	118.51 (45.49)	56.04 (40.51)	140.05 (43.76)	80.28 (39.94)
A-2	59.50 (38.05)	79.89 (28.29)	67.21 (37.95)	88.65 (28.23)
A-3	40.71 (40.58)	62.71 (32.76)	56.72 (40.07)	78.03 (32.49)
A-4	43.74 (42.94)	62.82 (36.64)	61.19 (42.53)	74.54 (36.57)
O-1	−54.47 (57.46)	70.06 (51.04)	−34.65 (57.41)	82.93 (51.01)
O-2	90.77 (39.36)	144.41 (38.54)	114.67 (38.25)	167.05 (38.11)
O-3	97.70 (43.36)	78.53 (38.41)	108.18 (43.40)	86.60 (38.41)
O-5	−27.67 (40.40)	3.09 (33.55)	−38.60 (40.40)	−1.25 (33.58)
O-6	−60.45 (47.38)	16.41 (36.91)	−68.44 (47.30)	3.33 (36.78)
1	−44.32 (63.76)	−77.36 (52.19)	23.12 (60.80)	3.95 (47.47)
N	2.77 (9.66)	−6.33 (8.37)	−3.18 (9.50)	−5.20 (8.38)
R-2	−4.72 (33.90)	−52.65 (27.90)	−12.64 (33.79)	−58.77 (27.86)
R-3	13.40 (30.01)	−21.26 (27.93)	13.63 (30.07)	−20.13 (27.96)
L-2	19.71 (30.73)	33.22 (31.47)	28.37 (30.74)	35.78 (31.51)
L-3	75.04 (35.67)	51.61 (32.11)	62.03 (35.59)	46.35 (32.12)
$Y/1000$	−13.91 (4.85)	−0.35 (4.04)	—	—
$H/1000$	13.10 (2.78)	170.20 (47.65)	—	—
S_u	867.72	687.48	869.79	688.61
R^2	0.019	0.022	0.014	0.018

Table 36.17
Regression coefficients for mortgage debt (M)

Independent variable	I		II	
	Home owners	Renters	Home owners	Renters
E-2	180.95 (93.24)	36.58 (29.21)	423.76 (95.85)	52.34 (29.02)
E-3	382.65 (132.08)	−18.39 (42.10)	953.26 (131.81)	2.72 (41.57)
A-2	−635.26 (110.46)	−33.02 (29.40)	−455.40 (114.27)	−24.56 (29.38)
A-3	−1537.63 (117.82)	−0.66 (34.04)	−1196.43 (120.68)	12.35 (33.82)
A-4	−2085.66 (124.65)	−44.79 (38.08)	−1751.13 (128.09)	−31.37 (38.06)
O-1	334.26 (166.82)	30.02 (53.04)	592.50 (172.89)	46.84 (53.09)
O-2	−146.33 (114.28)	47.75 (40.04)	336.52 (115.19)	71.45 (39.67)
O-3	428.76 (125.87)	−16.64 (39.92)	555.40 (130.70)	−4.53 (39.98)
O-5	53.02 (117.30)	−11.81 (34.86)	−105.75 (121.66)	−15.67 (34.95)
O-6	−116.26 (137.56)	−6.12 (38.35)	−314.28 (142.44)	−18.41 (38.28)
1	1042.97 (185.13)	−109.27 (54.24)	2118.63 (183.09)	−21.58 (49.40)
N	93.63 (28.03)	10.76 (8.71)	77.37 (28.62)	11.20 (8.72)
R-2	−12.32 (98.42)	11.70 (29.00)	−186.14 (101.75)	8.45 (28.99)
R-3	127.23 (87.14)	112.26 (29.02)	96.67 (90.54)	115.98 (29.10)
L-2	140.45 (89.22)	−0.92 (32.70)	254.69 (92.57)	1.93 (32.80)
L-3	−474.24 (103.55)	−21.25 (33.37)	−663.08 (107.19)	−24.83 (33.43)
Y/1000	−15.96 (14.09)	−11.17 (4.19)	—	—
H/1000	148.52 (8.08)	251.65 (49.52)	—	—
S_u	2519.11	714.44	2619.35	716.74
R^2	0.199	0.015	0.133	0.009

Table 36.18
Regression coefficients for installment debt (I)

Independent variable	I		II	
	Home owners	Renters	Home owners	Renters
E-2	−12.10 (3.85)	−3.38 (4.79)	−11.55 (3.80)	−2.92 (4.75)
E-3	−17.75 (5.45)	−10.76 (6.91)	−16.15 (5.23)	−9.28 (6.80)
A-2	−32.05 (4.56)	−21.40 (4.82)	−31.58 (4.53)	−20.97 (4.81)
A-3	−43.82 (4.86)	−27.84 (5.58)	−43.00 (4.79)	−26.86 (5.53)
A-4	−54.07 (5.14)	−32.52 (6.25)	−53.35 (5.08)	−32.23 (6.22)
O-1	0.27 (6.88)	−11.26 (8.70)	0.53 (6.86)	−11.20 (8.68)
O-2	−14.37 (4.71)	−15.13 (6.57)	−13.28 (4.57)	−14.26 (6.49)
O-3	−3.27 (5.19)	−2.30 (6.55)	−3.18 (5.18)	−2.47 (6.54)
O-5	1.85 (4.84)	5.84 (5.72)	1.63 (4.83)	5.58 (5.72)
O-6	1.43 (5.67)	−8.65 (6.29)	0.89 (5.65)	−9.33 (6.26)
1	58.78 (7.64)	44.42 (8.90)	60.56 (7.26)	47.20 (8.08)
N	2.42 (1.16)	4.40 (1.43)	2.63 (1.14)	4.53 (1.43)
R-2	15.50 (4.06)	10.23 (4.76)	15.08 (4.04)	9.59 (4.74)
R-3	16.57 (3.59)	0.59 (4.76)	16.42 (3.59)	0.30 (4.76)
L-2	2.62 (3.68)	−3.46 (5.36)	2.74 (3.67)	−3.38 (5.36)
L-3	−7.84 (4.27)	−1.98 (5.47)	−8.10 (4.25)	−2.43 (5.47)
Y/1000	0.57 (0.58)	1.39 (0.68)	—	—
H/1000	0.07 (0.33)	−3.03 (8.12)	—	—
S_u	103.92	117.18	103.91	117.22
R^2	0.043	0.023	0.043	0.022

Table 36.19
Regression coefficients for cash in bank (C)

Inde-pendent variable	I		II	
	Home owners	Renters	Home owners	Renters
E-2	67.73 (92.39)	102.62 (61.28)	219.25 (92.81)	164.60 (61.99)
E-3	181.33 (130.87)	48.12 (88.33)	612.47 (127.63)	204.42 (88.80)
A-2	162.93 (109.45)	78.64 (61.69)	288.78 (110.66)	127.21 (62.76)
A-3	245.00 (116.75)	194.92 (71.42)	468.98 (116.86)	297.13 (72.22)
A-4	585.18 (123.51)	380.40 (79.89)	785.75 (124.04)	424.98 (81.30)
O-1	172.51 (165.30)	178.08 (111.27)	258.60 (167.42)	207.11 (113.39)
O-2	262.24 (113.24)	116.85 (84.04)	565.71 (111.54)	224.55 (84.73)
O-3	−156.10 (124.73)	204.81 (83.76)	−121.99 (126.56)	208.01 (85.39)
O-5	−161.89 (116.23)	−85.13 (73.15)	−228.45 (117.81)	−112.24 (74.65)
O-6	−85.33 (136.31)	−138.37 (80.47)	−299.36 (137.93)	−214.13 (81.76)
1	137.99 (183.45)	218.94 (113.80)	660.37 (177.29)	581.33 (105.52)
N	−141.09 (27.78)	−107.48 (18.27)	−95.65 (27.71)	−95.06 (18.63)
R-2	−67.60 (97.52)	−9.40 (60.83)	−184.20 (98.53)	−68.81 (61.92)
R-3	80.83 (86.34)	−36.49 (60.89)	42.75 (87.68)	−55.60 (62.15)
L-2	16.47 (88.41)	76.90 (68.61)	55.77 (89.64)	87.58 (70.05)
L-3	136.02 (102.61)	−29.44 (70.02)	57.03 (103.79)	−72.90 (71.40)
Y/1000	131.92 (13.96)	102.19 (8.80)	—	—
H/1000	31.13 (8.01)	103.52 (103.89)	—	—
S_u	2496.18	1498.92	2536.41	1530.80
R^2	0.073	0.080	0.042	0.040

Table 36.20
Regression coefficients for insurance premiums (Z)

Independent variable	I		II	
	Home owners	Renters	Home owners	Renters
E-2	9.11 (8.79)	12.30 (5.96)	44.40 (9.64)	39.67 (8.31)
E-3	77.67 (12.46)	37.45 (8.59)	181.12 (13.26)	107.89 (11.91)
A-2	15.72 (10.42)	9.90 (6.00)	45.58 (11.49)	31.64 (8.42)
A-3	28.09 (11.11)	16.74 (6.94)	80.70 (12.14)	62.87 (9.69)
A-4	12.49 (11.75)	16.61 (7.77)	58.87 (12.88)	36.14 (10.90)
O-1	27.14 (15.73)	27.68 (10.82)	44.16 (17.39)	39.78 (15.21)
O-2	2.67 (10.78)	−3.90 (8.17)	73.44 (11.59)	43.94 (11.36)
O-3	24.97 (11.87)	16.83 (8.14)	31.10 (13.15)	17.37 (11.45)
O-5	1.84 (11.06)	7.65 (7.11)	−12.35 (12.24)	−4.56 (10.01)
O-6	5.32 (12.97)	14.94 (7.82)	−29.05 (14.33)	−19.04 (10.97)
1	−54.42 (17.45)	−69.90 (11.06)	61.22 (18.41)	90.46 (14.15)
N	8.59 (2.64)	3.18 (1.78)	21.41 (2.88)	8.87 (2.50)
R-2	1.42 (9.28)	14.67 (5.91)	−26.07 (10.23)	−12.47 (8.31)
R-3	−27.28 (8.22)	−27.92 (5.92)	−36.91 (9.11)	−37.02 (8.34)
L-2	−9.19 (8.41)	1.31 (6.67)	−1.33 (9.31)	6.01 (9.40)
L-3	−4.16 (9.76)	6.79 (6.81)	−20.98 (10.78)	−12.97 (9.58)
Y/1000	36.45 (1.33)	47.97 (0.85)	—	—
H/1000	4.76 (0.76)	28.42 (10.10)	—	—
S_u	237.53	145.73	263.45	205.33
R^2	0.280	0.531	0.114	0.069

performance in the case of A_4 are obscure. Clearly it is not simply because the deep freeze was a "new" product in 1950; the same was true for television. It may be that the purchase and use of a deep freeze requires a quite discontinuous change in habits and routine besides a heavy capital expenditure and that adaptability in this sense is poorly represented among the set of explanatory variables. Many other rationalizations are possible of course; a purely statistical one is that a relatively small proportion of the sample owned a deep freeze. Perhaps there are too few of them to warrant any general conclusion.[1] For T the fault may well be a technical one rather than a basic weakness in the notion that the automobile is a prime symbol of status and hence explainable in terms of education, occupation, etc. The variable T was derived by imputing a value to the end-of-year inventory and deducting auto purchases made during the year. It has become apparent that either the values imputed to the inventory were too small or the purchases were exaggerated because mean values of T for many age × education × occupation classes are very small and some indeed are negative. Although a simple bias which leaves relative magnitudes unaltered should not erase the hypothesized relationships, it is possible that some more complex error has done so.

On the subject of the low R^2's generally for durable goods, it must be remembered that such goods are only durable relative to cottage cheese and shoeshines. They do wear out or become obsolete and require replacement in a fairly regular cycle. Thus, even if it were possible to predict closely the rate and/or quality of consumption of services of durable goods, a large amount of variability would remain simply because consumers stand at different points in their inventory cycle. This phenomenon will obviously be more important for specific items than for aggregates. The same principle can be applied to installment debt if households make time purchases and then generally wait until they are repaid before incurring more debt.

An examination of the coefficients of the education variables makes it clear that, in general, more education implies larger stocks of assets and correspondingly lower debt. The two exceptions are mortgage debt and television. Since mortgage debt is usually directly offset by an asset of greater value and, unlike installment debt, has an "inventory cycle" closely related to the life cycle, the observed result is not really contrary.[2] The case of television is not so easily dismissed. The result is, however, consistent with findings of an intensive study of television ownership by Dernburg. Using 1950 census tract statistics Dernburg found support for the hypothesis that television is an inferior good with respect to education.[3] Total durables (A_f) shows a weak tendency to level off at least for the highest education class; perhaps this is due to the influence of television on the total. The finding that durable inventories are positively related to education is consistent with the notion that education enhances income prospects and that the education coefficients are really coefficients of expected income. This notion is, however, contradicted by the finding that C and minus I are also positively related to education; apparently high education implies higher saving inclusive of durables.

The coefficients of the age dummies seem to follow fairly regular patterns. Values of durable stocks decline with age excepting deep freeze (A_4) and automobile (T). Older households, in other words, have older durable goods on the average. They also have less mortgage debt and installment debt; the former is attributable to the coincidence of the mortgage and life cycles; the latter is consistent with the concomitant additional pattern of increasing cash balances. The pseudo-stock, insurance premiums, appears to level off or even fall for the oldest age class, although the evidence is thin when Y and H are controlled. This may well be a result of the completion of the payment periods on terminal life and endowment policies. The general pattern of age coefficients meshes nicely with a life cycle interpretation. The lower levels of durable consumption of older households can be attributed in part to lower expected incomes. It is very hazardous, however, to generalize about life cycle patterns from cross-section data in an expanding economy.

The pattern of coefficients of occupational variables is not nearly as consistent and regular as is the pattern for the age variables. If the occupations are ranked by mean income level, the order is O-2, O-1, O-3, O-4, O-5, and O-6. In several of the regressions the coefficients follow the order an expected income hypothesis would suggest. Where there is significant divergence from this pattern, as in the cases of automobile and mortgage debt, the status symbol character of automobile and house (or neighborhood) may be involved. Another kind of divergence is the low value of insurance premiums for self-employed – perhaps businessmen seek security from business and other assets instead of from insurance. Within the household furnishings category, professional workers appear to be relatively more interested in furniture than in appliances, compared to self-employed and to the other groups. Skilled workers and self-employed are the biggest TV owners.

The family size coefficients are significant in most regressions. Surprisingly, in the television regressions the effect of N is weak. The results show most emphatically that larger households have less cash and more durables – particularly laundry equipment.

The region coefficients are significant as a group in most of the household durable goods regressions but seem to add little in the T, M, and C regressions. The general tendencies indicate that western home owners hold more durables, and southern and western renters less, than their northern counterparts. In addition there was definitely less television ownership in the South and West; presumably because of the scarcity of stations in those areas in 1950. The renter difference noted above is perhaps partly a difference in custom regarding furnishings in rented dwellings and partly the result of some basic difference in the status value and permanence of rental arrangements between the regions. As for the positive effect in the case of western home owners, it may also be attributable to differences in local custom and styles of living.

The community size variables similarly are of major value only for durables. Non-metropolitan renters appear to supply relatively more of their own durable goods. The small cities class, both owners and renters, have larger stocks of radios and phonographs than the other two classes, but less TV, again the result of differences in station availability.

The preceding variables collectively account for a great deal, but by no means all, of the systematic variation among households in economic status. Even among households alike in age, education, occupation, family size, and location, there remain considerable differences. Two direct measures of economic status are used here: current income and housing level. Both may be regarded as representing imperfectly the series of past and expected incomes that determine the level and structure of a household's present possessions. Probably housing level better reflects the economic status to which the household has in the past adjusted its holdings of durable goods and other assets. Since moving is a major and expensive decision, housing level will remain the same through temporary fluctuations of income and will be adjusted only for lasting changes. But housing level is probably slow to adjust to permanent changes, and thus for some households with steadily growing income it may be an outdated indicator of economic status. Because of short-term fluctuations, to which the household would not adjust its whole pattern of asset holdings, current income is not a reliable indicator of future economic status. However, over a group of households, even when all the other variables including housing level are held constant, there is probably a correlation between current incomes and expected future incomes. The relative strength of Y in determining the demand for insurance suggests that Y contains some permanent elements that H does not. Indeed for some consumers, insurance and home investment may be substitute ways of providing security. For these reasons it would be an overstatement to identify H with variations in "permanent income", and Y for given levels of H as variations in "temporary income". Moreover, both H and Y have relationships of complementarity with certain assets or debts, and these relationships confound their influences as measures of economic status. The strengths of the effects of H on furnishings, and of Y on cash holdings (for transactions purposes, presumably) are probably to be interpreted in this way.

Nevertheless, it is interesting to compute the effects on each stock of a change in income accompanied by the appropriate change in housing level; this represents a long-run income coefficient, which can be compared with the short-run coefficient of Y alone for given H. For this purpose a maximum adjustment of H is taken to be one which maintains the H/Y ratio constant. If the marginal propensity to consume housing is lower than the average propensity, then the long-run income coefficient will be correspondingly closer to the short-run coefficient. The average H/Y ratios used for computing the long-run coefficients were estimated as the ratio of mean H to mean Y for the middle two age classes. For home owners the value was approximately 2.07; for renters it was 0.15. Table 36.21 shows the calculated long- and short-run income coefficients. The housing coefficient is multiplied by 2.07 or 0.15 to obtain "adjusted" housing coefficients which are commensurable with current (short-run) income coefficients. The current income coefficient is then added to the adjusted housing coefficient to obtain long-run income coefficients.

The negative current or short-run income coefficients in the A_f and T regressions seem to call for special comment. So far as T is concerned, it was noted earlier that the method of computing the variable is somewhat

Table 36.21
Computations of long- and short-run income coefficients for stocks

Dependent variables	Housing coefficient	"Adjusted" housing coefficient	Short-run income coefficient*	Long-run income coefficient*
Home owners:				
A_1	$7.98	$16.52	$10.73	$27.25
A_2	−0.89	−1.84	4.33	2.49
A_3	1.74	3.60	2.20	5.80
A_4	0.99	2.05	2.37	4.42
A_5	0.46	0.95	0.72	1.67
A_6	0.52	1.08	2.72	3.80
A_7	2.05	4.24	5.69	9.93
A_f	7.06	14.61	−39.55	−24.94
T	13.10	27.12	−13.91	13.21
M	148.52	307.43	−15.96	291.47
I	0.07	0.14	0.57	0.71
C	31.13	64.44	131.92	196.36
Z	4.76	9.85	36.45	46.30
Renters:				
A_1	131.18	19.68	6.25	25.93
A_2	−18.35	−2.75	0.77	−1.98
A_3	10.47	1.57	0.32	1.89
A_4	0.71	0.11	0.28	0.39
A_5	13.01	1.95	1.09	3.04
A_6	6.55	0.98	1.29	2.27
A_7	25.16	3.77	4.68	8.45
A_f	100.18	15.03	−8.34	6.69
T	170.20	25.53	−0.35	25.18
M	251.65	37.75	−11.17	26.58
I	−3.03	−0.45	1.39	0.94
C	103.52	15.53	102.19	117.72
Z	28.42	4.26	47.97	52.23

* Per $1000 of income.

suspect. Here, if there is a tendency for a positive amount of automobile investment in years of positive transitory income, then households that purchased during the year will be likely to have understated beginning-of-the-year T. A_f was also computed by deducting purchases from year-end stocks, and it is possible that the same kind of bias has distorted its relation to income.

Correlations among sets of stock variables are shown in Tables 36.22 to 36.25. For a given set of n stock variables, the correlations are shown

Table 36.22

Home owners, correlations among stocks (× 1000)

Before regression:

	A_1	A_2	A_3	A_4	A_5	A_6	A_7	T	M	I	C	Z
A_1	349	136	204	079	187	192	078	036*	162	051	074	122
A_2	076	238	150	034*	139	123	-0-	-0-	077	072	-0-	-0-
A_3	130	105	304	095	168	108	069	-0-	139	039	-0-	117
A_4	-0-	-0-	058	192	061	088	-0-	034*	029*	-0-	057	147
A_5	117	091	105	-0-	228	140	048	-0-	121	038*	-0-	058
A_6	140	076	040	057	088	279	-061	-0-	066	071	039	099
A_7	055	-039	041	-0-	031*	-094	197	049	102	035*	-0-	113
T	-0-	-0-	-0-	-0-	-0-	-0-	041	085	048	-0-	-0-	-0-
M	110	034*	081	-0-	069	062	077	039	294	130	-111	105
I	-0-	052	-0-	-0-	-0-	-0-	035*	-0-	109	180	-074	-030*
C	072	-0-	040	-0-	-0-	-0-	-0-	-0-	-126	-063	184	073
Z	061	-0-	069	122	-0-	071	096	-0-	080	-048	062	257

After regression:

	A_1	A_2	A_3	A_4	A_5	A_6	A_7	T	M	I	C	Z
A_1	235	106	130	-0-	134	130	040	-0-	049	041	032*	-0-
A_2	074	180	109	-0-	099	080	-0-	-0-	-0-	033*	-0-	-0-
A_3	103	089	196	051	117	038*	032*	-0-	031*	-0-	-0-	-0-
A_4	-0-	-0-	045	091	034*	046	-0-	-0-	-031*	-0-	-0-	045
A_5	101	072	089	-0-	204	097	031*	-0-	040	052	-0-	-0-
A_6	113	056	-0-	039	076	198	-079*	-0-	-0-	031*	-0-	-0-
A_7	043	-0-	-0-	-0-	031*	-087	126	052	-0-	-0-	-0-	-0-
T	-0-	-0-	-0-	-0-	-0-	-0-	052	063	-0-	-0-	-0-	-0-
M	044	-0-	-0-	-033*	032*	-0-	034*	-0-	202	106	-156	-0-
I	-0-	-0-	-0-	-0-	-0-	051	-0-	-0-	097	135	-049	-0-
C	036*	-0-	-0-	-0-	-0-	-0-	-0-	-0-	-154	-037*	174	-045
Z	-0-	-0-	-0-	042	-0-	-0-	-0-	-0-	-0-	-0-	-048	078

Note: In matrices above -0- has replaced correlations not significant at 0.05, asterisks denote non-significance at 0.01.

Table 36.23

Renters, correlations among stocks ($\times 1000$)

Before regression:

	A_1	A_2	A_3	A_4	A_5	A_6	A_7	T	M	I	C	Z
A_1	406	250	196	100	213	180	173	047	066	097	-0-	136
A_2	199	350	230	043	107	115	-0-	-0-	-0-	149	-0-	-0-
A_3	087	188	329	060	199	107	091	-0-	046	081	-0-	052
A_4	070	-0-	035*	136	-0-	049	048	032*	045	-0-	032*	043
A_5	137	-0-	145	-0-	295	133	093	-0-	061	037*	-0-	101
A_6	127	044	047	032*	086	249	-0-	037*	-0-	103	040*	071
A_7	153	-082	067	-0-	049	-068	246	057	-0-	-0-	-0-	128
T	-0-	-0-	-0-	-0-	-0-	-0-	048	104	-0-	-0-	-0-	060
M	042*	-0-	034*	037*	042	079	-0-	-0-	098	199	-062	-0-
I	045	115	-0-	-042	-0-	-0-	-0-	-0-	-0-	-059	192	174
C	-0-	-0-	-0-	-0-	-0-	-0-	-0-	-0-	-0-	-0-	169	192
Z	087	-0-	-0-	-0-	058	048	097	049	-0-	-0-	-0-	260

After regression:

	A_1	A_2	A_3	A_4	A_5	A_6	A_7	T	M	I	C	Z
A_1	370	272	168	090	169	160	120	-0-	055	103	-0-	032*
A_2	224	346	218	048	101	098	-0-	-0-	-0-	129	-0-	048
A_3	080	172	288	055	161	070	078	-0-	034*	060	-0-	038*
A_4	067	-0-	034*	125	-0-	044	049	-0-	040*	033*	-0-	-0-
A_5	115	-0-	122	-0-	238	100	070	-0-	048	093	-0-	044
A_6	122	037*	062	032*	070	209	052	-0-	-0-	-0-	-0-	-0-
A_7	112	-056	-0-	039*	048	-054	173	052	-0-	-0-	-042	-0-
T	-0-	-0-	-0-	-0-	-0-	-0-	052	083	-0-	-0-	-0-	046
M	037*	-0-	-0-	035*	036*	073	-0-	-0-	092	179	-050	-0-
I	056	098	-050	-038	-0-	-0-	-0-	-042	-0-	-048	076	-0-
C	-0-	-0-	-0-	-0-	-0-	-0-	-0-	-0-	042	-0-	042	088
Z	-0-	036*	-0-	-0-	-0-	-0-	-0-	-0-	-0-	-0-	-0-	088

Note: In matrices above -0- has replaced correlations not significant at 0.05, asterisks denote non-significance at 0.01.

Table 36.24
Home owners, correlations among stocks (× 1000)

Before regression:

	A_f	T	M	I	C
A_f	169	-0-	149	078	-073
T	-0-	057	048	-0-	-0-
M	133	048	216	130	-111
I	057	-0-	115	155	-074
C	-054	-0-	-094	-057	157

After regression:

	A_f	T	M	I	C
A_f	129	-0-	057	130	-035*
T	-0-	030	-0-	-0-	-0-
M	105	-0-	212	106	-156
I	049	-0-	095	122	-049
C	-0-	-0-	-0-	-059	070

Table 36.25
Renters, correlations among stocks (× 1000)

Before regression:

	A_f	T	M	I	C
A_f	146	-0-	057	130	-035*
T	-0-	040	062	-0-	-0-
M	054	-0-	062	-0-	-062
I	127	-0-	-0-	144	-059
C	-0-	-0-	-0-	-059	070

After regression:

	A_f	T	M	I	C
A_f	140	-0-	049	128	-034*
T	-0-	046	053	-0-	-042*
M	046	-0-	053	-0-	-050
I	126	-0-	-0-	137	-046
C	-0-	-041*	-0-	-046	070

Note: In matrices above -0- has replaced correlations not significant at 0.05, asterisks denote non-significance at 0.01.

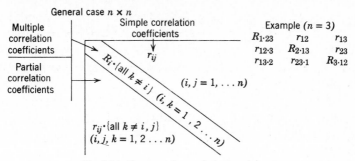

Fig. 36.1. Format of correlation matrices.

in an $n \times n$ matrix. The ith diagonal element of the matrix shows the multiple correlation of the ith variable with the remaining $n - 1$ variables. An above-diagonal element (i, j), $i < j$, is the simple correlation between the ith and the jth variables. The corresponding below-diagonal element (j, i), $j > i$, is the partial correlation between the same two variables, account having been taken of the remaining $n - 2$ variables. The general schema of this correlation matrix is shown in Figure 36.1. For each set of stock variables, two matrices are shown for home owners and two for renters. One matrix of each pair represents the correlations of deviations from the over-all mean, the other represents the correlations of deviations from regressions of Type I as shown in Tables 36.8 to 36.20. The purpose of presenting both matrices is to see in what way the common dependence of the stock variables on the demographic and economic explanatory variables alters their association with each other. The four matrices are presented for the following two sets of variables:

(1) Twelve stocks $(A_1, A_2, A_3, A_4, A_5, A_6, A_7, T, M, I, C, Z)$ in Tables 36.22 and 36.23.

(2) Five stocks (A_f, T, M, I, C) in Tables 36.24 and 36.25.

Two general impressions, confirmatory of the basic hypothesis, emerge from inspection of these correlation matrices:

(1) In general, the correlations are positive between assets and negative between assets and debts. The exceptions have fairly obvious specific explanations; for example, the negative correlation between radio-phonograph and television holdings indicates substitutability between these recreational goods. The general pattern is that those who have more of all assets – households advance on all fronts together, keeping some

balance among accumulations of different assets and reductions of debt. The same impression, with the same type of exceptions, is given by the regressions themselves. As between demographic and socio-economic groups, as well as within groups, those who have more tend to have more quite generally.

(2) Much, but by no means all, of the interdependence among stocks when expressed as deviations from over-all means turns out to be due to the common dependence of stocks on the explanatory variables of the regressions.

4. The Flow Calculations

The analysis of the flow variables is almost parallel to the stock analysis. The same types of calculations have been made except that the flows take the role of the stocks, and five stock variables (A_f, T, M, I, C) are added to the list of independent or explanatory variables. The F-ratios for five analysis of variance tests are shown in Table 36.26. The regression coefficients, standard error S_u, and R^2 for the "pooled" regression of each flow on the whole list of independent variables are shown in Tables 36.27–30.

A cursory glance at Table 36.26 discloses many more non-significant relationships than were found for the stocks. In general the demographic dummy variables are of less importance for flows than for stocks, although there are several notable exceptions. It is worth pointing out that the factors represented by age and education, where those variables are significant, are not at all well represented among the other independent variables. A comparison of tests (3) and (4) shows that the significance of A and E is almost always enhanced by controlling family size, region, community size, income, housing level, and the five stock variables. Furthermore, test (5) shows that even where there is no significant additive effect of A and E, there is evidence of significant interaction with at least some of the other independent variables. The specific nature of such interaction has not yet been explored.

The R^2's for flows in Tables 36.27–36.30 are somewhat higher than those found for stocks. Values below 0.20 are almost the exception instead of the rule; some are as high as 0.70. Apparently flows are easier

Table 36.26
"F"-tests for flow regressions

Variable	(1) Simple effects of occupation		(2) Effects of N, R, L, Y, H, and Σ when added to occupation		(3) Additive effects of age and education when added to occupation		(4) Additive effects of age and education when added to O, N, R, L, Y, H and Σ		(5) Interaction of age and education with O, N, R, L, Y, H, Σ minus the additive age, education effects	
	Owners	Renters	Owners	Renters	Owners	Renters	Owners	Renters	Owners	Renters
Durable goods purchases (E_f)	14.33†	10.65†	479.61†	571.57†	20.58†	11.64†	64.43†	17.93†	2.95†	2.79†
Auto purchase (ΔT)	10.75†	10.60†	1057.30†	598.10†	1.58	8.11†	6.12†	15.83†	1.29*	2.93†
Mortgage debt change (ΔM)	2.81*	1.99	36.10†	850.56†	24.70†	1.18	81.51†	1.39	3.03†	2.60†
Installment debt change (ΔI)	1.04	1.25	126.41†	191.06†	0.51	1.67	0.43	1.98	2.18†	1.69†
Change in cash balances (ΔC)	0.93	0.34	47.66†	291.47†	1.80	1.93	4.34†	6.20†	3.84†	21.57†
Change in assets (ΔA)	8.02†	1.03	41.62†	60.22†	14.46†	1.45	30.23†	1.34	1.56†	9.08†
Change in debts (ΔD)	1.78†	1.34	134.76†	261.20†	17.63†	0.79	43.87†	5.72†	2.66†	15.95†
Saving (S)	11.50†	1.22	151.60†	503.91†	6.14†	2.10	2.71*	5.95†	3.58†	4.71†
Degrees of freedom: used	5	5	12	12	5	5	5	5	185	185
remaining	4567	3822	4555	3810	4562	3817	4550	3805	4365	3620

Note: * denotes significance at 0.05 level; † denotes significance at 0.01 level.

Table 36.27
Flow regression coefficients for E_f and ΔT

Inde-pendent variable	Durable good purchase (E_f)		Auto purchase (ΔT)	
	Home owners	Renters	Home owners	Renters
E-2	14.62 (20.42)	1.05 (13.09)	39.24 (25.74)	40.42 (22.30)
E-3	27.78 (28.95)	10.31 (18.86)	7.52 (36.49)	82.52 (32.12)
A-2	−81.15 (24.34)	−37.70 (13.22)	10.16 (30.69)	−8.47 (22.50)
A-3	−198.18 (26.40)	−79.88 (15.31)	6.34 (33.28)	−31.68 (26.07)
A-4	−272.50 (28.32)	−131.55 (17.16)	−34.70 (35.70)	−101.72 (29.22)
O-1	−35.30 (36.49)	26.02 (23.76)	25.83 (46.00)	27.92 (40.46)
O-2	−1.37 (29.98)	−1.80 (17.98)	8.68 (37.79)	47.50 (30.63)
O-3	−13.41 (27.55)	−9.86 (17.89)	−46.37 (34.72)	0.68 (30.47)
O-5	−17.36 (25.63)	−19.04 (15.61)	−61.73 (32.31)	−41.04 (26.58)
O-6	−38.58 (30.07)	−52.91 (17.22)	−123.95 (37.91)	−84.44 (29.32)
1	680.01 (42.79)	322.28 (25.07)	147.95 (53.94)	159.61 (42.69)
N	1.14 (6.15)	2.99 (3.94)	−25.12 (7.76)	−25.23 (6.72)
R-2	−10.67 (21.54)	−26.55 (13.06)	35.39 (27.15)	0.65 (22.25)
R-3	60.36 (19.08)	−15.83 (13.04)	86.77 (24.06)	90.14 (22.21)
L-2	−7.47 (19.50)	3.16 (14.67)	40.12 (24.58)	64.26 (24.98)
L-3	−19.77 (22.70)	−15.76 (14.95)	40.58 (28.62)	45.57 (25.45)
Y/1000	42.74 (3.16)	20.41 (1.91)	44.72 (3.98)	21.55 (3.26)
H/1000	9.74 (1.84)	82.76 (22.30)	10.50 (2.32)	87.42 (37.98)
A_f	−0.6143 (0.0138)	−0.2143 (0.0111)	0.0662 (0.0174)	0.0783 (0.0189)
T	0.0086 (0.0094)	0.0153 (0.0075)	−0.6591 (0.0118)	−0.6246 (0.0128)
M	−0.0004 (0.0033)	0.0172 (0.0072)	−0.0111 (0.0042)	0.0142 (0.0124)
I	0.1226 (0.0790)	0.1616 (0.0446)	−0.1256 (0.0996)	−0.0796 (0.0760)
C	0.0100 (0.0033)	0.0079 (0.0035)	0.0082 (0.0042)	0.0217 (0.0059)
S_u	550.20	319.76	693.57	544.49
R^2	0.602	0.184	0.740	0.665

Note: All coefficients are in dollars. Estimated errors in parentheses.

to predict than stocks partly because stocks themselves can be used as predictors.

Turning to the regressions and examining the education coefficients, one notes at all age levels a tendency to dissave more by borrowing as education is increased. In the discussion of stocks it was proposed that the generally high levels of observed assets attributed to education was evidence of *higher* past saving by the relatively highly educated. A possible reconciliation is that the saving measure adopted does not include purchases of durables and automobiles while the high asset position noted above included the stocks of such goods. Among renters there was

Table 36.28
Flow regression coefficients for ΔM and ΔI

Inde-pendent variable	Mortgage debt change (ΔM)		Installment debt change (ΔI)	
	Home owners	Renters	Home owners	Renters
E-2	90.61 (72.19)	4.20 (29.71)	5.72 (11.60)	8.23 (12.26)
E-3	223.25 (102.32)	− 39.49 (42.79)	11.70 (16.44)	34.34 (17.66)
A-2	− 649.60 (86.05)	− 13.28 (29.98)	4.01 (13.82)	3.62 (12.37)
A-3	− 1250.19 (93.32)	7.89 (34.74)	− 4.30 (14.99)	7.68 (14.33)
A-4	− 1387.62 (100.11)	8.20 (38.93)	− 6.60 (16.08)	− 13.53 (16.06)
O-1	243.40 (128.98)	38.66 (53.90)	− 14.71 (20.72)	0.98 (22.24)
O-2	− 12.83 (105.97)	0.29 (40.80)	40.09 (17.03)	26.10 (16.84)
O-3	− 58.19 (97.37)	20.31 (40.60)	29.93 (15.64)	22.55 (16.75)
O-5	− 33.00 (90.60)	15.51 (35.42)	22.07 (14.56)	6.12 (14.61)
O-6	− 17.82 (106.31)	− 11.63 (39.06)	0.72 (17.08)	6.80 (16.12)
1	1588.21 (151.26)	44.88 (56.87)	22.53 (24.30)	1.64 (23.47)
N	− 15.61 (21.75)	− 1.00 (8.95)	− 3.16 (3.49)	− 7.45 (3.69)
R-2	− 16.48 (76.13)	− 2.76 (29.64)	16.04 (12.23)	− 8.77 (12.23)
R-3	206.08 (67.45)	− 12.25 (29.59)	9.77 (10.84)	14.84 (12.21)
L-2	− 30.16 (68.91)	25.25 (33.28)	10.82 (11.07)	− 7.70 (13.73)
L-3	− 187.88 (80.25)	− 13.50 (33.91)	− 11.43 (12.89)	19.63 (13.99)
Y/1000	− 61.81 (11.15)	3.30 (4.34)	− 0.25 (1.79)	0.93 (1.79)
H/1000	60.10 (6.51)	− 74.71 (50.59)	1.55 (1.05)	73.59 (20.88)
A_f	− 0.4664 (0.0489)	− 0.0193 (0.0252)	0.0093 (0.0078)	0.0094 (0.0104)
T	0.0443 (0.0332)	− 0.0019 (0.0171)	− 0.1787 (0.0053)	− 0.2661 (0.0071)
M	− 0.2174 (0.0117)	− 0.8569 (0.0165)	0.0025 (0.0019)	0.0052 (0.0068)
I	0.6348 (0.2794)	− 0.0009 (0.1012)	0.0317 (0.0449)	0.0115 (0.0418)
C	0.0500 (0.0117)	− 0.0004 (0.0079)	− 0.0019 (0.0019)	− 0.0035 (0.0032)
S_u	1944.89	725.41	312.47	299.34
R^2	0.153	0.730	0.251	0.378

Note: All coefficients are in dollars. Estimated errors in parentheses.

a further significant tendency for the higher education classes to purchase more autos at the expense of C and I.

The main effect of age on the flows is to diminish the rate of purchase of T and A_f, entirely consistent with the smaller stock of these items noted in the preceding section. Older home owners seem to pay off mortgage debt more rapidly, as well as increase cash balances. No similar behavior is apparent for renters – perhaps their balances are nearer to a stationary equilibrium. The only significant coefficients in the saving equations are the negative ones for the 45–54 age class. The reasons for the unusually high spending in that age class are obscure.

Table 36.29
Flow regression coefficients for ΔC and ΔA

Inde-pendent variable	Change in cash balances (ΔC)		Change in assets (ΔA)	
	Home owners	Renters	Home owners	Renters
E-2	−0.38 (69.45)	−148.06 (75.83)	43.20 (119.92)	16.52 (75.51)
E-3	45.72 (98.45)	−249.68 (109.24)	168.81 (169.98)	174.31 (108.77)
A-2	26.86 (82.79)	−149.39 (76.53)	−754.63 (142.95)	102.11 (76.21)
A-3	271.29 (89.78)	−232.05 (88.68)	−1528.49 (155.02)	69.05 (88.30)
A-4	294.70 (96.32)	11.19 (99.38)	−1492.05 (166.32)	131.56 (98.96)
O-1	2.84 (124.10)	−113.14 (137.60)	410.42 (214.27)	272.75 (137.01)
O-2	−82.69 (101.96)	−290.61 (104.15)	60.95 (176.05)	93.66 (103.71)
O-3	54.51 (93.69)	7.92 (103.63)	−17.74 (161.76)	36.74 (103.19)
O-5	−4.18 (87.17)	103.19 (90.41)	122.61 (150.51)	−12.61 (90.03)
O-6	−38.59 (102.29)	249.94 (99.71)	216.85 (176.61)	81.96 (99.29)
1	−430.24 (145.54)	−966.32 (145.17)	1127.21 (251.29)	347.27 (144.56)
N	−51.51 (20.93)	−75.18 (22.84)	−139.29 (36.14)	−2.88 (22.74)
R-2	86.86 (73.25)	174.94 (75.67)	64.49 (126.47)	−68.37 (75.35)
R-3	−2.01 (64.90)	71.82 (75.53)	279.26 (112.06)	35.61 (75.21)
L-2	−14.38 (66.30)	−29.08 (84.96)	−108.82 (114.48)	−6.69 (84.60)
L-3	6.67 (77.22)	157.10 (86.56)	−194.97 (133.32)	−98.87 (86.19)
Y/1000	117.32 (10.73)	479.15 (11.09)	282.34 (18.53)	−34.45 (11.04)
H/1000	−31.48 (6.27)	−845.45 (129.15)	−0.41 (10.82)	−671.64 (128.60)
A_f	0.2414 (0.0471)	−0.0252 (0.0643)	−0.2983 (0.0813)	0.1578 (0.0640)
T	0.1300 (0.0320)	0.1659 (0.0437)	0.3974 (0.0552)	0.1612 (0.0435)
M	0.0078 (0.0113)	0.1208 (0.0421)	−0.2176 (0.0194)	−1.1485 (0.0419)
I	−0.2105 (0.2688)	−0.4377 (0.2585)	0.4619 (0.4641)	0.4094 (0.2574)
C	−0.2199 (0.0113)	−0.2020 (0.0201)	0.0563 (0.0194)	−0.0280 (0.0200)
S_u	1871.29	1851.83	3231.01	1843.95
R^2	0.116	0.523	0.135	0.227

Note: All coefficients are in dollars. Estimated errors in parentheses.

Among the occupation coefficients there are few significant relationships. Between wage and salary groups (all but O-2) there is some tendency for the blue-collar end of the scale to refrain from purchases of durables and to increase assets of other kinds, including cash, as evidenced by the saving coefficients. Businessmen seem to raise funds by increasing debts and reducing cash. Since there seems to be no offsetting increase in the observed assets, it is possible that the funds were spent on business investment.

Most of the effects of region and community size that were noted in the stock section are substantiated by the flow relations. Where smaller

Table 36.30
Flow regression coefficients for ΔD and S

Independent variable	Change in debts (ΔD)		Savings (S)	
	Home owners	Renters	Home owners	Renters
E-2	138.61 (98.30)	171.15 (92.16)	−95.41 (73.80)	−154.63 (70.99)
E-3	306.59 (139.34)	411.87 (132.76)	−137.78 (104.61)	−237.57 (102.27)
A-2	−686.51 (117.18)	183.80 (93.02)	−68.12 (87.98)	−81.70 (71.65)
A-3	−1358.66 (127.08)	269.20 (107.78)	−169.82 (95.41)	−200.15 (83.02)
A-4	−1534.51 (136.33)	115.09 (120.78)	42.46 (102.36)	16.46 (93.04)
O-1	278.69 (175.64)	267.48 (167.23)	131.73 (131.87)	5.26 (128.82)
O-2	53.32 (144.31)	299.60 (126.58)	7.63 (108.35)	−205.94 (97.50)
O-3	−32.21 (132.60)	118.36 (125.95)	14.47 (99.56)	−81.62 (97.02)
O-5	−32.48 (123.38)	−61.50 (109.88)	155.08 (92.63)	48.89 (84.61)
O-6	−22.37 (144.77)	258.61 (121.18)	239.22 (108.69)	176.65 (93.35)
1	1928.63 (206.00)	1017.39 (176.44)	−801.42 (154.66)	−670.13 (135.91)
N	46.92 (29.62)	76.61 (27.76)	−186.21 (22.24)	−79.48 (21.38)
R-2	−14.13 (103.67)	−153.14 (91.96)	78.61 (77.84)	84.77 (70.84)
R-3	246.04 (91.86)	43.34 (91.80)	33.22 (68.97)	−7.73 (70.71)
L-2	−85.80 (93.85)	71.00 (103.25)	−95.02 (70.46)	−77.70 (79.53)
L-3	−316.20 (109.29)	−211.48 (105.20)	121.23 (82.05)	112.62 (81.03)
Y/1000	−83.89 (15.19)	−505.77 (13.48)	366.23 (11.40)	471.32 (10.38)
H/1000	63.80 (8.87)	942.53 (156.97)	−64.21 (6.66)	−1614.17 (120.91)
A_f	−0.6903 (0.0666)	0.1573 (0.0782)	0.3921 (0.0500)	0.0005 (0.0602)
T	−0.1377 (0.0452)	−0.3701 (0.0531)	0.5351 (0.0340)	0.5313 (0.0409)
M	−0.2203 (0.0159)	−0.8968 (0.0511)	0.0027 (0.0120)	−0.2517 (0.0394)
I	0.2868 (0.3805)	0.1822 (0.3141)	0.1751 (0.2857)	0.2272 (0.2420)
C	0.0576 (0.0159)	0.0724 (0.0244)	−0.0013 (0.0120)	−0.1005 (0.0188)
S_u	2648.55	2250.64	1988.50	1733.62
R^2	0.073	0.485	0.326	0.617

Note: All coefficients are in dollars. Estimated errors in parentheses.

stocks were observed before, smaller flows tend to maintain stocks at a relatively low level. An exception to this appears for T in the case of suburban dwellers. They did not show significantly higher auto stocks than metropolitan households, but they appear to be increasing at a faster rate.

The income and housing level coefficients again are highly significant, accounting in large measure for the relatively high R^2's. The only exception is for change in installment debt – it appears to be as unrelated to Y and H as was the stock of installment debt. The long- and short-run income coefficients have been computed for the flows exactly as they

Table 36.31
Computations of long- and short-run income coefficients for flows

Dependent variables	Housing coefficient	"Adjusted" housing coefficient	Short-run income coefficient*	Long-run income coefficient*
Home owners:				
E_f	$9.74	$20.16	$42.74	$62.90
ΔT	10.50	21.73	44.72	66.45
ΔM	60.10	124.40	−61.80	62.60
ΔI	1.55	3.20	−0.25	2.95
ΔC	−31.48	−65.16	117.32	52.16
ΔA	−0.41	−0.85	282.34	281.49
ΔD	63.80	132.06	−83.89	48.17
S	−64.21	−132.91	366.23	233.32
Renters:				
E_f	82.76	12.41	20.41	32.82
ΔT	87.42	13.11	21.55	34.66
ΔM	−74.71	−11.20	3.30	−7.90
ΔI	73.59	11.03	0.93	11.96
ΔC	−845.45	−126.81	479.15	352.34
ΔA	−671.64	−100.73	−34.45	−135.20
ΔD	942.53	141.37	−505.77	−364.40
S	−1614.17	−242.12	471.32	229.20

* Per $1000 of income.

were for the stocks. The calculations are shown in Table 36.31. It is interesting to note the implication that for home owners short-run increases of income result in debt reduction while long-run changes result in debt expansion. For renters, both kinds of income change reduce debt but the effects of short-run changes are more marked. The negative income effect on asset change for renters may indicate some substitutability between present wealth and future income; in the case of home owners, the same effect may operate but, if so, it is offset by home investment. The differences between short- and long-run coefficients for saving are definitely in the direction, if not in the amount, predicted by the permanent income hypothesis.

Finally there are the five stock variables, A_f, T, M, I, and C, which were introduced in the flow regressions. The hypothesis was that there is a balance among stocks which households tend to maintain; that, in other words, when an asset is above its equilibrium level changes will tend to reduce it and/or increase other assets. Reduction of debt will, of course, imply reduction of assets. This should show up in negative coefficients for an asset when it appears in "its own" flow regression and positive coefficients in other regressions. Making necessary allowances for the negative nature of debts, one can derive a pattern of signs for the five stock coefficients. The estimated coefficients show little statistically significant divergence from this pattern of signs. Indeed, for home owners there is only one exception to the pattern – the positive effect of cash balances on mortgage debt change. For renters, there are three exceptions, but two of them relate to mortgage debt and the hypothesis really is barely applicable in this case. The third exception indicates a positive effect of installment debt on durable purchases.

Correlation matrices were computed as before; Tables 36.32 and 36.33 show a set for variables E_f, ΔT, ΔM, ΔI, ΔC, and S. The lower part of

Table 36.32
Home owners, correlations among flows ($\times$ 1000)

Before regression:

	E_f	ΔT	ΔM	ΔI	ΔC	S
E_f	255	078	222	–0–	– 121	–0–
ΔT	101	528	–0–	513	– 063	– 175
ΔM	206	– 048	300	–0–	– 217	– 103
ΔI	– 058	500	–0–	526	–0–	– 184
ΔC	– 077	– 036*	– 176	052	355	288
S	034*	– 085	– 052	– 119	272	352

After regression:

	E_f	ΔT	ΔM	ΔI	ΔC	S
E_f	261	055	159	–0–	– 122	– 214
ΔT	–0–	308	–0–	238	– 037*	– 216
ΔM	135	– 034*	230	–0–	– 179	– 092
ΔI	– 030*	222	032*	250	–0–	– 105
ΔC	– 044	–0–	– 153	043	320	273
S	– 179	– 189	–0–	– 068	250	389

Note: In matrices above –0– has replaced correlations not significant at 0.05, asterisks denote non-significance at 0.01.

Table 36.33
Renters, correlations among flows (× 1000)

Before regression:

	E_f	ΔT	ΔM	ΔI	ΔC	S
E_f	135	045	–0–	–0–	040*	–045
ΔT	062	624	–0–	611	–064	–224
ΔM	–0–	–0–	236	–0–	–0–	138
ΔI	–075	586	035*	622	–0–	–186
ΔC	102	042	–190	119	732	705
S	–099	–126	232	–132	729	752

After regression:

	E_f	ΔT	ΔM	ΔI	ΔC	S
E_f	370	057	–0–	–0–	–180	–354
ΔT	–084	463	–0–	273	–222	–383
ΔM	–0–	039*	117	–0–	–047	067
ΔI	–038*	249	–0–	296	–0–	–125
ΔC	–050	–109	–077	108	420	392
S	–328	–316	104	–070	313	580

Note: In matrices above –0– has replaced correlations not significant at 0.05, asterisks denote non-significance at 0.01.

each table shows correlations between residuals from regressions listed in Tables 36.27–36.30. In most cases the interrelationships among the flows have been substantially reduced by allowing for their common dependence on a set of independent variables. In the case of saving, however, the exclusion of E_f and ΔT from the saving concept is strongly underlined by the negative correlations between S and both E_f and ΔT. This substitutability between purchases of durable goods and autos and other forms of investment is even more apparent when considering the correlation of residuals. Furthermore, after regression the partial correlation shows that E_f and ΔT themselves are substitutes at least for the renters.

5. Conclusion

The elementary hypotheses expressed at the outset have, on the whole, been sustained by the statistical results. There is evidence that households tend to maintain some sort of balance in their capital accounts both between assets yielding direct services and financial assets, and between liquid funds and liabilities. Furthermore, the precise nature of the preferred portfolio toward which adjustments are made seems to be related to the explanatory variables employed, and presumably therefore, to the more fundamental but unobserved measures of a household's social, economic, biological, and environmental characteristics. The flow regressions have also shown that adjustments in capital account items tend to eliminate rather than perpetuate deviations from a basic or preferred portfolio pattern.

Some of the specific results pertaining to automobile and durable goods stocks have been clouded by inadequacies of the method used for evaluating such stocks. Whether an attempt at direct measurement of the value of, say, a nine-year-old refrigerator would provide more conclusive results is at least problematical. Each of the variables for which dollar values were assigned on the basis of one-digit codes has, no doubt, added to the crudeness of the analysis.

The handicap of working with only a part of the household's balance sheet has lent some inconclusiveness to the findings. There is no way of assuring, for instance, that the separate relationships estimated for the several stocks and flows are consistent with each other in view of the accounting structure within which those relationships must operate. Because of the ambiguities of durable goods accounting in imperfect markets this would be difficult at best. But if complete or almost complete household balance sheets were available, advantageous use could be made of the structure imposed by accounting identities.

Almost by definition a one-period cross-section analysis is drastically limited in its ability to provide generalizations about the dynamics of capital account changes in response to altered external or life-cycle situations. A panel study is much better for this purpose. The results obtained in this study must definitely be viewed as suggestive rather than conclusive in this regard.

To close on a more positive note, despite the obvious reservations the investigation has at least shown that analysis of household capital accounts is a promising source of insights about household economic behavior. It can provide insights relevant to the household sector's impact on the economy's flows via household investment in durable goods as well as to the household's impact on the various financial asset markets.

Notes

[1] This consideration really implies that a more appropriate model for analysis of deep freeze ownership would be the probit regression model. See Tobin: "Estimation of Relationships for Limited Dependent Variables," *Econometrica*, 26, No. 1 (Jan. 1958), 24-36. (Chapter 44 below.)

[2] In the whole sample of home owners the correlation between M and H is equal to 0.294, and probably is much higher within age classes.

[3] Thomas F. Dernburg, "Consumer Response to Innovation," in *Studies in Household Economic Behavior* (New Haven: Yale University Press, 1958), 28-31.

CHAPTER 37

ON THE RELEVANCE OF PSYCHOLOGY TO ECONOMIC THEORY AND RESEARCH

Recent developments in economic theory have emphasized the dependence of economics on assumptions regarding the motivations of economic behavior. Economists naturally turn to psychology in their quest for valid and fruitful assumptions, and they have learned with some disappointment that there are no ready-made answers. The motivations of economic behavior remain a challenge to both disciplines.[1]

Neoclassical economic theory was able to describe a determinate economic system and to infer many of its properties by making very simple assumptions about the behavior of the individual decision-making units of the system. The main assumption was *rationality*, in the sense that each individual chooses, among the range of alternative actions open to him, the one whose consequences he prefers to all the rest.[2] This requires that the individual have a consistent and transitive ordering of the objects of choice, in the following sense: If A and B are such objects, then either A is preferred to B, B to A, or there is indifference between A and B. Moreover, if A is preferred to B, and B is preferred (or indifferent) to C, then A is preferred to C.[3]

The assumption of rationality in this sense is of considerably greater generality than is conveyed by the caricatures of "economic man" that too often represent economic theory in the eyes of other social scientists and, indeed, of some economists themselves. No restriction is placed on the dimensions of objects of choice that are relevant to their ordering. Within the framework of the theory, workers may rank alternative job opportunities according to quite different criteria from wages alone.

By James Tobin and F. Trenery Dolbear Jr. Reprinted from *Psychology: A Study of Science*, Sigmund Koch (Ed.), vol. 6 (New York: McGraw-Hill, 1963).

Businessmen may reckon profits as only one among a number of outcomes on which they decide among alternative courses of action. Rationality does imply that, other things being equal, a larger sum of money will be preferred to a smaller. But if other things are not equal, rationality means nothing more than subjective consistency in the ordering of alternatives. Thus it is a mistake to identify rationality with the motivation of materialistic self-interest.

One assumption that economists make about this preference field is often the basis for misunderstanding. This assumption concerns the phenomenon suggested by the phrase "diminishing marginal utility", although this phrase is an inaccurate description. Diminishing marginal utility suggests that the more an individual has of some object, the less his satisfaction will be increased by giving him an additional unit of the same thing. So stated, the proposition seems to contradict psychological findings concerning the relationship of aspiration to achievement. Basing his position on these findings, as well as on survey evidence regarding levels of aspiration for accumulation of durable goods and savings, Katona criticizes the "saturation" implications of economists' utility theory. Actually, however, the theory is non-committal on the question whether marginal utility diminishes or increases as successive additions of the same goods are made. The theory does assume that it is generally possible to keep an individual at the same utility or satisfaction level when depriving him of a unit of commodity A provided he is compensated by adding an appropriate quantity of commodity B. The theory further assumes that the smaller the amount of A left to the individual – and correspondingly the larger the amount of B – the more compensation in the form of B will be required for loss of another unit of A. This can be interpreted to say that, whatever the absolute marginal utilities may be, the marginal utility of B declines *relative to that of A* as the quantity of B increases relative to the quantity of A. Economists have always been impressed by the boundlessness of human wants and have denied the possibility of universal saturation.[4] They do assume, however, the need for maintaining some kind of balance between objectives. Individuals may aspire to ever higher levels of consumption of all kinds, as well as to ever higher levels of savings and leisure. Since means are limited, these goals conflict; one can be approached only at the expense of another. Although an individual cannot be absolutely saturated with any desirable object, he can become relatively saturated. If he is relatively saturated with liquid assets, for example, he would be glad to have more, but he would prefer to have more durable consumer's goods.

Economics has sought to be neutral with respect to the sources of preferences, but it has purchased this neutrality at the cost of substantive content. Results that are determinate when business decisions are assumed to depend only on maximizing profits, for example, become indeterminate in fact (though still determinate in principle) when less measurable objectives of business policy are admitted (Papandreou 1952; Shackle 1949). In the field of consumer behavior, the formation of preferences from experience, observation, and advertising is at least as important a phenomenon as purchasing based on given preferences.[5] But economics looks to psychology to explain the formation of preferences.

General as they are, the usual formulations of the preference fields of economic units have implicitly involved some questionable propositions. First, a consumer's rankings of alternative "market baskets" of goods and services have traditionally been taken to depend only on the amounts of various commodities *he* consumes, not on the amounts other consumers are simultaneously consuming. This disregard of social interdependence in consumption contradicts everyday observation as well as the presumptions of sociology and social psychology. In recent years, there have been a number of attempts to correct the traditional individualistic bias of economics (Baumol 1952; Duesenberry 1949; Johnson 1954; Leibenstein 1950).

Second, as a legacy of Benthamite utilitarianism, economic theory has tended to formulate work as a source of disutility and thus to assume that it is preferred to leisure solely because of the income it brings. The discovery of "human relations" in industry, a subject on which there has been considerable convergence between psychology and labor economics, has taught economists that the satisfactions of life occur on the job as well as after hours.

Third, the preference field of economic theory is an attribute of a single mind. Yet the basic economic decision-making units are really groups rather than individuals – households, corporations, governments, and trade unions.[6] So far, we lack any satisfactory theory of the manner in which the effective preference fields of groups are formed. Indeed, as a logical matter, it is not possible in general to derive an ordering of alternatives for the group from conflicting rankings by group members (Arrow 1951a).

Rationality requires that the outcomes of alternative courses of action be known with certainty to the decision-maker. Given such certainty, it is clearly irrational to choose any outcome other than the most preferred. But if outcomes are uncertain, there is no obvious definition of rational choice. A number of decision criteria for situations of uncertainty have been suggested (Arrow 1951b; Luce and Raiffa 1957). Among them is the "minimax" strategy: For every possible action, assume the worst outcome, then choose the action whose worst outcome is least bad. This was first suggested as the correct strategy in playing a zero-sum game where your strategy is known to your opponent, who is trying to do his best against you (Von Neumann and Morgenstern 1953). Even in a game situation, it is a highly conservative strategy, and the person who follows it may find himself sacrificing the chance of large gains merely in order to avoid the possibility of small losses (Ellsberg 1956). In situations where the environment is neutral, it is even more clear that it is excessively conservative. Consequently, there is considerable doubt that the minimax criterion should be recommended to decision-makers, and, of course, even greater doubt that it describes actual behavior.

An alternative decision criterion is maximization of expected (in the probability sense) utility. This requires that the decision-maker rank not only outcomes but differences in utilities of outcomes. Not only can he say that he prefers A to B; he can say whether the degree of preference of A over B is greater or less than that of C over D. This implies that values (on a scale unique up to a linear transformation) can be attached to the outcomes themselves. The criterion also assumes that the decision-maker attaches probabilities of occurrence to the various outcomes. Since economic decisions generally occur in non-recurrent situations for which objective probabilities cannot be calculated, these probabilities must be subjective estimates.[7] This decision rule avoids the overconservative implications of the minimax strategy. But in the nature of the case, there can be no proof that it is more nearly optimal than other principles of decision. As to its descriptive realism, economics and psychology have found another area of convergence in experimental measurement of utility and subjective probability. Experiments have been designed to test whether subjects' choices can be regarded as maximization of expected utility (Davidson and Suppes 1957; Edwards 1954, 1961). These experiments involve procedures similar to the scaling of sensations and attitudes, which has a long tradition in psychology (Clark 1954). A major difference, however, is this: Since economists regard utility and subjective probability as personal to each subject, they cannot follow the psychologists' technique of treating the responses of different subjects as replications of observations from the same population of choices. This greatly complicates experimental testing of the expected utility hypothesis; at the moment, we have little idea of the size or characteristics of the population groups whose behavior can be represented as maximization of expected utility.

Even if these groups turn out to be significant in the economy, further questions remain: How are subjective estimates of utility and probability formulated? Is it useful to break the decision process into these components, or is it better looked upon as a unit? Lately economists have learned how difficult and costly it is to be rational – or, in the case of uncertainty, to apply any of the suggested criteria of "quasi-rationality". Indeed the development of management science and operations research since World War II has opened a fertile field for economists, statisticians, and mathematicians, increasing the efficiency of business decisions (Case Institute 1958). If the economic model did not fit the world, one is tempted to wonder whether the world is being made over to fit the model. But in the last analysis, rationality cannot apply to situations of uncertainty. It may be that, instead of seeking a quasi-rationality which can be applied to these situations, we should, as descriptive scientists rather than advisers, look more directly for the manners in which individuals and groups simplify and structure complicated situations in which they must make decisions whose outcomes they cannot control or predict.[8]

Psychologists and economists have barely begun to exploit the possibilities of fruitful collaboration in empirical research on economic behavior. The pioneering work at the Survey Research Center, led by George Katona, has shown that the social sciences have in the sample survey a powerful tool applicable to research on economic behavior as well as on public opinion. Considerable further development of the tool is necessary to utilize its full research potential. Two lines that such development might take may be mentioned.

(1) Surveys of economic behavior can be designed specifically for research on the strategic relationships between variables, rather than for the primary purpose of making estimates of population frequencies and averages. Research-oriented surveys would place less emphasis on representative sampling of the population, and more focus on observations strategic for measuring the relationships under study. Surveys would take on experimental design, in which some variables are deliberately held constant and others made to differ as much as possible. Successive reinterviews of identical respondents would be used to obtain information on reactions to change in circumstances over time.

(2) Psychological characteristics of respondents can be measured in order to seek their relationship to economic behavior. Katona's work has concentrated on measuring a particular category of psychological variables, mainly respondents' optimism or pessimism about the economic future. These attitudes of optimism or pessimism are relevant to the short-term outlook for consumer spending. They cannot help very much in the making of longer-run economic predictions. For that task, it would be valuable to explore the relationship of economic behavior – e.g., spending and saving – to more fundamental and permanent dimensions of personality. Without measurement of such dimensions, there are some unresolvable ambiguities of interpretation of the results of economic surveys. For example, Katona cites findings that people with substantial liquid assets tend to add more, not less, to their total assets than people whose existing stocks are low. It is a matter of some economic importance whether this finding reflects (1) the fact that persons of a thrifty disposition have saved more in the past and continue to save more than persons of a different personality, or (2) a tendency for a given individual to save more in liquid form, the greater his initial holdings of liquid assets. If the finding reflects the former, then it still may be true that for persons of given personality, high liquidity promotes spending rather than saving (Tobin 1957). But if, as Katona believes, it reflects the latter, then it would be foolish to worry about possible inflationary effects of high liquidity. Thus the relationship of economic behavior to personality attributes is not only a subject of interest in itself; it is also essential for correct interpretation of observed relations among economic magnitudes.

References

Angell, J.W., "Uncertainty, likelihoods, and investment decisions," *Quart. J. Econ.*, 74 (1960), 1-28.

Arrow, K.J., "Alternative approaches to the theory of choice in risk-taking situations," *Econometrica*, 19 (1951a), 404-37.

Arrow, K.J., *Social Choice and Individual Values* (New York: Wiley, 1951b).

Baumol, W.J., *Welfare Economics and the Theory of the State* (Cambridge, Mass.: Harvard Univ. Press, 1952).

Block, H.D. and J. Marschak, "Random orderings and stochastic theories of responses," in *Contributions to Probability and Statistics*, I. Olkin *et al.* (Eds.) (Stanford, Calif.: Stanford Univ. Press, 1960).

Case Institute of Technology, Operations Research Group. *A Comprehensive Bibliography on Operations Research through 1956, with Supplement for 1957* (New York: Wiley, 1958).

Clark, L. (Ed.), "The choices consumers make: a panel on the technical problems of measuring preferences," in *Consumer Behavior* (New York: N.Y. Univ. Press, 1954), 88-95.

Davidson, D. and J. Marschak, "Experimental tests of a stochastic decision theory," in *Measurement: Definitions and Theories*, C.W. Churchman and P. Ratoosh (Eds.) (New York: Wiley, 1959).

Davidson, D. and P. Suppes (with S. Siegel), *Decision Making: an Experimental Approach* (Stanford, Calif.: Stanford Univ. Press, 1957).

Debreu, G., "Stochastic choice and cardinal utility," *Econometrica*, 26 (1958), 440-44.

Debreu, G., "Topological methods in cardinal utility theory," in *Mathematical Methods in the Social Sciences, 1959*, K.J. Arrow *et al.* (Eds.) (Stanford, Calif.: Stanford Univ. Press, 1960).

Duesenberry, J.S., *Income, Saving, and the Theory of Consumer Behavior* (Cambridge, Mass.: Harvard Univ. Press, 1949).

Edwards, W., "The theory of decision making," *Psychol. Bull.*, 51 (1954), 380-417.

Edwards, W., "Behavioral decision theory," *Ann. Rev. Psychol.*, 12 (1961), 473-98.

Ellsberg, D., "Theory of the reluctant duelist," *Amer. Econ. Rev.*, 46 (1956), 909-23.

Ferber, R., "Research on household behavior," *Amer. Econ. Rev.*, 52 (1962), 19-63.

Galbraith, J.K., *The Affluent Society* (Cambridge, Mass.: The Riverside Press, 1958).

Haring, J.E. and G.C. Smith, "Utility theory, decision theory, and profit maximization," *Amer. Econ. Rev.*, 49 (1959), 566-83.

Hayes, S.P., "Some psychological problems of economics," *Psychol. Bull.*, 47 (1950), 289-330.

Hicks, J.R., *A Revision of Demand Theory* (New York: Oxford, 1956).

Johnson, H.G., "The macro-economics of income redistribution," in *Income Redistribution and Social Policy*, A.T. Peacock (Ed.) (London: Cape, 1954).

Leibenstein, H.S., "Bandwagon, snob, and Veblen effects in the theory of consumers' demand," *Quart. J. Econ.*, 64 (1950), 183-207.

Luce, R.D., *Individual Choice Behavior* (New York: Wiley, 1959).

Luce, R.D. and H. Raiffa, *Games and Decisions: Introduction and Critical Survey* (New York: Wiley, 1957), Chap. 13.

Mack, Ruth P., "Economics of consumption," in *Survey of Contemporary Economics*, vol. 2, B.F. Haley (Ed.) (Homewood, Ill.: Irwin, 1952).

Marschak, J., "Theory of an efficient several-person firm," *Papers & Proc. Amer. Econ. Rev.*, 50 (2) (1960), 541-48.

Papandreou, A.G., "Some basic problems in the theory of the firm," in *A Survey of Contemporary Economics*, vol. 2, B.F. Haley (Ed.) (Homewood, Ill.: Irwin, 1952).

Samuelson, P.A., *Foundations of Economic Analysis* (Cambridge, Mass.: Harvard Univ. Press, 1947), Chaps. 5, 6, 7.

Savage, L.J., *The Foundations of Statistics* (New York: Wiley, 1954).

Shackle, G.L.S., *Expectations in Economics* (New York: Cambridge, 1949).

Simon, H.A., "Theories of decision-making in economics and behavioral science," *Amer. Econ. Rev.*, 49 (1959), 253-83.

Tobin, J., "Consumer debt and spending: some evidence from analysis of a survey," in *Consumer Installment Credit*, Part II, vol. 1, Board of Governors of the Federal Reserve System (Washington: U.S. Government Printing Office, 1957), 521-45. (Chapter 35 above.)

Von Neumann, J. and O. Morgenstern, *The Theory of Games and Economic Behavior*, 3rd ed. (Princeton, N.J.: Princeton Univ. Press, 1953).

Notes

[1] Simon (1959) and Hayes (1950) provide extended discussion of some of these problems. See also the articles of Katona and Simon in *Psychology: A Study of Science*.

[2] For a careful presentation of the economic theory of choice see Hicks (1956) and Samuelson (1947).

[3] Recently economists have recognized what psychologists have long maintained – individuals do not always make the same choice when faced with the same alternatives. To avoid the neoclassical conclusion that indifference must be assumed to explain inconsistencies, a theory of *probabilistic choice* has evolved. For a definition of rationality assuming probabilistic choice, e.g., if *A* is preferred to *B*, then the probability of choosing *A* rather than *B* is greater than one-half (see Block and Marschak 1960; Davidson and Marschak 1959; Debreu 1958, 1959; Luce 1959).

[4] This is why economists, in general, have been less impressed than the general public with such books as John Kenneth Galbraith's *The Affluent Society* (1958).

[5] A discussion of some factors which appear to influence consumer behavior may be found in Duesenberry (1949), Mack (1952), and Ferber (1962).

[6] A decision procedure for a firm with a team of decision-makers who possess a single objective for the firm is described by Marschak (1960).

[7] Methods for obtaining these subjective probabilities are described in Savage (1954).

[8] Shackle (1949) attempts an approach of this kind (see also Angell 1960; Haring and Smith 1959).

CHAPTER 38

ON THE PREDICTIVE VALUE OF CONSUMER INTENTIONS AND ATTITUDES

The calculations reported in this note are designed to appraise the predictive value of certain consumer intentions and attitudes. The appraisal is made by comparing the intentions and attitudes expressed by individual households at the beginning of a year with their subsequent economic behavior. Are households which express optimistic attitudes and positive intentions more likely to spend and less likely to save than other households? Do the answers to attitudinal and intentions questions provide information of value in predicting the buying behavior of households? If so, does this information supplement or merely repeat the predictive information contained in financial, economic, and demographic data concerning households?

1. Relevance and Necessity of Cross-section Tests

A cross-section test involves a microscopic study of the correlation in a sample of households between attitudes and intentions, on the one hand, and economic action, on the other. The relevance of such a test to the general question of the predictive value of consumer attitudes and intentions seems to me self-evident. Indeed I do not see how the predictive

Reprinted from *The Review of Economic Statistics*, 41 (February 1959), 1-11.

I am indebted to a number of institutions and individuals for making possible the research of which this is a part. The research was begun during my tenure of a Social Science Research Council Faculty Fellowship, during which I enjoyed for a semester the hospitality of the University of Michigan Survey Research Center under a program financed by the Carnegie Foundation for bringing visiting scholars to the Center. The research continued at Yale under a grant from the Ford Foundation. I am much indebted to Harold Watts and to my undergraduate bursary aide at Yale, Donald Hester, for computational assistance. *Statistics*, 41 (February 1959), 1-11.

value of these data can be adequately appraised without confronting the attitudes and intentions of individual households with the record of their subsequent behavior. But it is possible to interpret George Katona, the pioneer student and chief collector of consumer anticipations data, as challenging this point of view.[1] Therefore I must begin by defending it.

First, concerning the *relevance* of a microscopic study of fulfillment of attitudes and intentions, I am indebted to my colleague Arthur Okun for formalizing the argument that lay behind the position of the Smithies Committee.[2]

Suppose that, for a homogeneous population of consumer units, x_t is the proportion who take a certain action (e.g., buy durable goods) during period t. Let p_t be the proportion who express at the beginning of period t an attitude "favorable" to the action (e.g., it's a good time to buy). Let r_t be the proportion of the favorable respondents who take the action, and let s_t be the proportion of the unfavorable respondents who take the action. The following identity holds:

$$x_t = r_t p_t + s_t(1 - p_t) = (r_t - s_t)p_t + s_t.$$

If the attitude is to have predictive value, for the whole population from year to year or quarter to quarter, there must be a positive correlation over time between x_t and p_t.

A microscopic study of fulfillments by individual households is designed to discover for a given time period t whether r_t significantly exceeds s_t (e.g., whether consumers who say it's a good time to buy actually are more likely to buy than other consumers). Can x_t and p_t be positively correlated when there is no significant difference between r_t and s_t?

It is possible to imagine situations in which x_t and p_t are correlated but $r_t - s_t$ is zero or negative. But the models are either so clearly inapplicable to consumer behavior or so artificial and special that they make the point quite eloquently – it is not reasonable to expect correlation between x_t and p_t unless r_t exceeds s_t. If a sample of the U.S. population had been asked in January 1957 whether they expected to get Asian flu during the next six months, very few would have answered yes. Asked the same question in July 1957, many more would have responded affirmatively. Presumably the proportions of pessimistic expectations would be highly and positively correlated with actual incidence of flu in the two periods. But within the July sample, there might well be no difference in incidence between the pessimists who predict they will become ill and the optimists who expect to escape. Here the probability of occurrence (p_t) is in any period roughly uniform throughout the population. If for each individual the probability of a positive expectation depends directly on the probability of occurrence, there will be more positive expectations in the second period than in the first. But there is no reason to believe that probability of occurrence in any one period is associated with the qualities of optimism or pessimism that lead to differences in expectations.

Suppose that each consumer has a constant threshold level of probability $\bar{\pi}$, so that if and only if the probability π of his buying exceeds $\bar{\pi}$ will he express a favorable anticipation. If there is a general increase in π's from one period to the next, there will be an increase in both x_t and p_t. If all individuals have the same threshold $\bar{\pi}$, or if the thresholds are distributed independently of the probabilities π, in a cross-section of individuals in any period r_t would exceed s_t, i.e., there would be more buying by optimists than by pessimists. To avoid this conclusion, it is necessary to imagine that individuals with high probabilities of buying π also have high thresholds $\bar{\pi}$, and individuals with low buying probabilities π have low thresholds $\bar{\pi}$. In this case, differences between attitudinal answers by different consumers would tell more about their differences in thresholds than their differences in action.

Although this special kind of model would make it possible to regard a reinterview test of the difference between r_t and s_t as irrelevant to the predictive value of over-all proportions, it is a highly artificial and implausible construct for the voluntary economic decisions of households. If there is such a strong correlation between action probability and attitude threshold across individuals, the same mechanism may operate for a single individual over time. We could not then have confidence in the predictive value of year-to-year changes in p_t.

Second, the *necessity* of testing at the individual level the predictive value of attitudes and intentions follows inexorably from the inadequacy of any other kind of test. Aggregate statistics from successive surveys form a time series that can be compared with aggregate time series of consumer purchases or saving components. In the paper cited above, Okun gives a thorough review of the evidence provided by comparing these aggregates. He finds the evidence inconclusive, and it could scarcely be otherwise. Only 11–13 observations are available. Since these are roughly quarterly observations, the notorious serial persistence of economic time series makes it doubtful that there are as many as 11–13 *independent* observations. Proper allowance for seasonal effects and for the undeniable influences of other "objective" variables would further reduce the number of degrees of freedom available for testing the influence of attitudes and intentions. If Katona believes he has observed that changes in an attitudinal index lead to changes in expenditures on durable goods,[3] he has not based this belief on any rigorous statistical test.

2. Data and Variables

In the 1953 *Survey of Consumer Finances* (conducted for the Board of Governors of the Federal Reserve System by the Survey Research Center of the University of Michigan), 1036 of the spending units interviewed were spending units who had also been interviewed in the 1952 *Survey*. For the spending units in this reinterview sample, it is possible to compare economic behavior during 1952, as reported in early 1953, with attitudes and intentions expressed in early 1952.[4]

The present report makes such comparisons for a part of the reinterview sample and for three specific kinds of economic behavior. Certain kinds of spending units have been excluded from the complete reinterview sample in order to eliminate some of the biggest sources of heterogeneity. After these exclusions there remain 652 spending units for analysis. The exclusions are as follows: (a) Farm households. (b) Secondary spending units. These are individuals who live in the dwelling unit of another (primary) spending unit but maintain significantly separate finances. This is a heterogeneous group, including aged parents, teenage children, and resident servants. (c) Spending units with 1952 disposable income less than $1000. These spending units were segregated for separate analysis for a technical reason. Many of the variables used in the main analysis are proportions of income. The advantage of using such proportions is that dividing by income tends to standardize the variance of variables which otherwise display a larger variance at high incomes than at low incomes. However, this process also creates extreme values for spending units with incomes near zero. It seems better to analyze such observations separately, rather than to permit them to affect the results of the main analysis. (d) Spending units from whom any of the following items of information was not obtained: income in 1951, and 1952; outstanding personal non-mortgage debt in early 1952, and in early 1953; liquid asset holdings in early 1952, and in early 1953; age of head of household; marital status.

The three kinds of behavior measured and investigated are (1) *expenditures*, E, during 1952 on cars and major household goods, as reported in the 1953 interview; (2) *change in personal non-mortgage debt* outstanding, ΔD, measured by subtracting debt reported in 1952 from the amount reported in 1953; and (3) *change in liquid asset holdings*, ΔL, during 1952, measured by subtracting the holdings reported in 1952 from the amount reported in 1953.

Expenditures, E, are purchases of new or used cars, appliances, and furniture, net of the proceeds of sales or trade-ins. Expenditures may or may not involve equal cash outlays by the spending unit; to the extent that purchases are financed by incurring installment debt, they contribute both to variable (1), expenditures, and to variable (2), increase in debt. The debt involved in variable (2) is meant to include all debt for non-business purposes except home mortgages. It is mainly debt incurred for the purchase of consumer durable goods. Liquid asset holdings, the change in which is the third variable, comprise checking and savings accounts in banks and savings and loan associations and holdings of government savings bonds.

In the analysis each of the variables enters as a proportion of the 1952 disposable income, Y (income less estimated federal income tax liability), of the spending unit. As mentioned above, the variances of such variables as E, ΔL, and ΔD are greater at higher income levels than at lower. Expressing the variables as proportions of income avoids some of the difficulties which this systematic heterogeneity in the variances would present for the application of analysis of variance and regression techniques to these data.

The fact that the analysis concerns proportions of 1952 income is important in interpreting the results of tests of the predictive value of attitudes expressed at the beginning of 1952. What is being tested is not the usefulness of these attitudes as predictors of the absolute levels of

1952 behavior variables. It is rather their usefulness as predictors of the levels of these behavior variables relative to 1952 incomes.

It is relative levels rather than absolute levels which attitudes and intentions data are likely to be asked to predict in short-run forecasting of general economic activity. For the household sector as a whole, income depends to a large extent on occurrences and decisions in other sectors of the economy, governments, and businesses. Household spending and saving during a year will be influenced by changes in household incomes, and these changes will frequently not be anticipated by households at the beginning of the year. So far as absolute levels of expenditures and savings are concerned, the indications of beginning-of-year attitudes and intentions may be canceled by subsequent unanticipated changes in income. This will be true of many individual households even when aggregate household income is stable. And in years of changes in aggregate economic activity, it will be true of the household sector as a whole. Prediction of absolute levels of behavior variables is thus too severe a test.

Prediction of relative levels demands less. The indications of beginning-of-year attitudes and intentions do not need to be translated into action regardless of income developments during the year. The low-income optimist need not turn out to spend more than the high-income pessimist. He need only turn out to spend more than the low-income pessimist.

A complete forecasting model will predict household income with the help of information about government and business activity. The forecaster does not want to know households' prospective spending on the assumptions that households themselves may be making about their incomes. He wants to know households' prospective spending on assumptions regarding household income that are consistent with his information about other economic sectors. Thus the forecaster is more interested in attitudes and intentions as predictors of levels relative to income than as predictors of absolute levels.

Current income is by no means the only variable that will affect households' behavior with respect to durable goods, liquid assets, and debt. There are numerous other relevant economic, financial, and demographic attributes of households. These "objective" variables may be of use in prediction if they are either (a) capable of being known or estimated in advance of the period for which forecast is to be made, or

(b) like current income, endogenous to the complete economy-wide forecasting model being used. In assessing the predictive value of attitudes and intentions data, therefore, it is important to consider these "psychological" variables both as substitutes for and as complements to the objective variables. There are, then, three related but distinct questions:

(1) What is the predictive success of a psychological variable or set of psychological variables taken alone?

(2) To what extent can psychological variables take the place of objective predictors of household behavior? To put the same question another way, do objective variables contain any predictive information that is not contained in answers to questions about attitudes and intentions? The practical importance of this question is that attitudes and intentions data may be easier and cheaper to collect.

(3) To what extent can objective variables take the place of psychological predictors of household behavior? In other words, do attitudes and intentions contain any predictive information that is not contained in economic, financial, and demographic characteristics?

To contribute to answers to these questions, I have computed regressions of the three behavior variables E/Y, $\Delta D/Y$, and $\Delta L/Y$ against a common set of objective variables: Y_{-1}/Y, L/Y, D/Y, A, and M, where

Y_{-1} = 1951 income of the spending unit, after estimated federal tax liability, as reported in the 1952 *Survey*;

L = total holding of liquid assets, January 1, 1952, reported by the spending unit in the 1952 *Survey*, including checking accounts, savings accounts, and savings bonds;

D = outstanding personal debt (debt other than business and real estate indebtedness) as of January 1, 1952, as reported in the 1952 *Survey*;

A = age of the head of the household as reported in the 1953 *Survey*, on the following scale:

Age 18–24 $A = 1$
    25–34 $A = 2$
    35–44 $A = 3$
    45–54 $A = 4$
    55–64 $A = 5$
    65– $A = 6$;

M = marital status of the head of household:
   M = 1 if married and spouse present,
   M = 0 otherwise.

The three regressions are shown in Table 38.1. In each regression, income change from 1951 to 1952 enters in two forms: as a continuous variable, and as a three-way principle of classification. The reason for introducing it in the second form is to allow for interaction effects between income change and the other explanatory variables, as well as for additive effects.

3. Tests of Predictive Value

The psychological variables tested are listed in Table 38.2. For the most part, the "variable" is simply a classification of respondents according to their answers to the question indicated. Except for row 4, all the questions are ones that were asked in early 1952. Row 4 refers to income expectation in early 1953, *after* the end of the year for which the behavior variables were measured. The reason for including this test is as follows: A whole year may be too long to expect attitudes to persist and to continue to exert such influence as they may have on behavior. The Survey Research Center, indeed, conducts attitudinal surveys at intervals of 3–6 months. Presumably many of the income expectations expressed in early 1953 were already formed sometime in 1952 and could have been influencing buying and saving in that year. Such expectations might have been caught in an interim survey during 1952.

Tests of specific buying intentions, as distinguished from more diffuse attitudes, are given in rows 7 and 8. Buying intentions are the result of answers to two questions: "Do you expect to buy a car this year, in 1952?" and "Do you expect to buy any large items such as furniture, a refrigerator, radio, television set, household appliances and so on – during this year, 1952? ... Anything else? ..." In each case, if the answer was affirmative or "it depends", the respondent was asked how much he thought he would spend. For test 7, responses to these two questions were divided into three classes: will buy (including everyone who gave a non-zero dollar amount as expected expenditure); will not buy (negative answers to both questions); and other responses (not ascertained, etc.). For test 8, the dollar amounts given in answer to the two questions were added together to give the variable P, expected expenditure. This was then expressed as a ratio of 1952 disposable income, P/Y. Linear regressions on P/Y were computed for each of the six dependent variables, three original variables, and three residuals from the Table 38.1 regressions.

Rows 9 and 10 refer to an attitudinal index. Katona holds that it is the Gestalt or cluster of attitudes, rather than attitudes taken singly, that matters.[5] Under his direction the Survey Research Center has constructed a time series index of attitudes and intentions.[6] The relation over time between this index and actual expenditures on durable goods in relation to income is the main basis for the claim that attitudinal indicators have predictive value. Okun's calculations show that this claim is not solidly supported by the evidence. To the extent that the index can predict aggregate durable goods expenditure in ratio to disposable income in the one or two quarters following the quarter in which the survey is made, its predictive success is due entirely to its buying-intentions components; the other components, more diffuse attitudinal indicators, make no net contribution. However, recent calculations by Eva Mueller at the Survey Research Center show that different conclusions result from different formulations of the forecasting relationship. In particular, if the two-quarter period to be predicted is taken to include the quarter in which the survey occurred whenever the survey took place in the first month of a quarter, the entire success of the index in predicting the six-months' ratio of durables expenditures to disposable income can be attributed to diffuse attitudes rather than to buying intentions. The main lesson to be drawn is that the observations are too few and too ambiguous to permit conclusive tests.

In order to make the same kind of test on cross-section data, a somewhat analogous index of attitudes, omitting buying intentions, for an individual respondent was constructed from questions 1, 2, 3, and 5, as follows: For each question, the answer of a respondent was valued as optimistic $(+1)$, neutral or no answer (0), or pessimistic (-1). These values were summed over the four questions to give each respondent a score, some integer from -4 to $+4$ inclusive. A test for the significance of differences in the behavior variables for the nine possible scores was

Table 38.1

Regression coefficients (estimated standard errors), primary non-farm spending units with 1952 incomes $1000 or greater

Dependent variable	Income change	M	A	L/Y $Y_{-1}/Y < 0.8$	L/Y $0.8 \leq Y_{-1}/Y < 1.3$	L/Y $1.3 \leq Y_{-1}/Y$	D/Y $Y_{-1}/Y < 0.8$	D/Y $0.8 \leq Y_{-1}/Y < 1.3$	D/Y $1.3 \leq Y_{-1}/Y$
E/Y	Up			−0.003 (0.010)			+0.056 (0.093)		
	Little change	+0.020 (0.014)	−0.020[a] (0.004)		−0.004 (0.001)			+0.010 (0.029)	
	Down					+0.012 (0.010)			+0.006 (0.097)
ΔL/Y	Up			−0.311[a] (0.082)			−2.64[a] (0.058)		
	Little change	−0.213[a] (0.082)	+0.072[a] (0.023)		−0.289[a] (0.031)			−0.075 (0.200)	
	Down					−0.214[a] (0.095)			−0.212 (0.232)
ΔD/Y	Up			−0.027[a] (0.009)			−0.733[a] (0.059)		
	Little change	+0.019 (0.012)	−0.006[a] (0.002)		−0.011 (0.007)			−0.573[a] (0.051)	
	Down					−0.024 (0.020)			0.886[a] (0.104)

Table 38.1 (continued)

Dependent variable	Income change	Y_{-1}/Y			Constants			R^2	Standard error of estimate
		$Y_{-1}/Y < 0.8$	$0.8 \leq Y_{-1}/Y < 1.3$	$1.3 \leq Y_{-1}/Y$	$Y_{-1}/Y < 0.8$	$0.8 \leq Y_{-1}/Y < 1.3$	$1.3 \leq Y_{-1}/Y$		
E/Y	Up	+0.026 (0.077)			+0.113[a] (b)				
	Little change		−0.117[a] (0.052)			+0.240[a] (b)		0.23	0.125
	Down			+0.032[a] (0.008)			+0.070[a] (b)		
$\Delta L/Y$	Up	−0.113 (0.633)			+0.377[a] (b)				
	Little change		−0.097 (0.270)			+0.186[a] (b)		0.38	0.768
	Down			+0.367[a] (0.044)			−0.560[a] (b)		
$\Delta D/Y$	Up	−0.070[a] (0.041)			+0.117 (b)				
	Little change		−0.032 (0.023)			+0.093 (b)		0.35	0.155
	Down			+0.010 (0.011)			+0.104 (b)		

[a] Significant at 10 per cent level.

[b] The significance of the three constants may be considered jointly, by testing the hypothesis that they are, except for sampling variation, equal, i.e., that classification by income change does not really affect the level of the relationship. This hypothesis would be rejected for E/Y (F-ratio of 5.2 with 2 and 638 degrees of freedom) and $\Delta L/Y$ (F-ratio of 7.3, 2, and 638 degrees of freedom). But it cannot be rejected for $\Delta D/Y$ (F-ratio of 0.05).

Table 38.2
Tests of significance of relation of E/Y, $\Delta D/Y$, and $\Delta L/Y$ to selected variables

Variable	Number of classes into which observations were divided (k)	F-ratios					
		Original variables (d.f. $k-1$ and $652-k$)			Residuals from Table 38.1 regressions (d.f. $k-1$ and $638-k$)		
		E/Y	$\Delta D/Y$	$\Delta L/Y$	E/Y	$\Delta D/Y$	$\Delta L/Y$
1. Would you say you folks are better off or worse off financially now than you were a year ago? Asked in 1952.	4	6.6[b]	0.4	1.0	2.4	0.1	2.7[a]
2. Are you folks making as much money now as you were a year ago, or more or less? Asked in early 1952.	4	5.4[b]	1.0	9.8[b]	1.2	0.5	6.5[b]
3. How about a year from now – do you think you people will be making more money or less money than you are now, or what do you expect? Asked in early 1952.	4	1.7	0.1	4.3[b]	0.5	0.5	2.4
4. Same question as 3, but asked in early 1953.	4	10.2[b]	1.4	3.9[b]	6.3[b]	1.0	2.6
5. Do you think this is a good time or a bad time to buy automobiles and large household items? Asked in early 1952.	6	1.9	0.9	0.8	1.6	0.8	0.8
6. Now, speaking of prices in general, I mean the prices of the things you buy, do you think they will generally go up during 1952, or go down, or stay about where they are now? Asked in early 1952.	9	1.1	0.8	0.6	0.7	0.7	0.6
7. Do you plan to buy a car or any large household items in 1952? Asked in early 1952.	3	15.1[b]	1.3	0.1	13.3[b]	1.7	1.0
8. Linear regression on ratio of total anticipated 1952 expenditure on cars and large household items to realized 1952 income.	2 parameters estimated	20.6[b]	5.8[a]	0.0	72.0[b]	9.5[b]	0.7
9. Attitudinal index (see text).	9	2.3	1.9	1.3	0.8	1.1	0.7
10. Linear regression on attitudinal index (see text).	2 parameters estimated	9.8[b]	0.5	0.9	1.1	0.0	2.0

[a] Significant at 5 per cent level.
[b] Significant at 1 per cent level.

Table 38.3

	Number of cases	Mean E/Y	Mean residual E/Y
Better off; slightly better	208	0.114	0.018
No better; no worse	221	0.068	−0.004
Worse off; slightly worse	203	0.058	−0.011
Undecided; don't know	3	0.068	−0.006
Not ascertained	17	0.048	−0.031
All	652	0.079	−0.000

carried out, and reported in row 9 of Table 38.2. In row 10, a test of linear regression on the index score is reported.[7]

The nature of the tests reported in Table 38.2 may be illustrated by considering the first one in detail. The 652 cases were classified according to their answers to the question, "Would you say you folks are better off or worse off financially now than you were a year ago?" asked early in 1952. The numbers falling into each class are shown in the first column of Table 38.3. In the second column the average value of E/Y is shown for each class. In this case, it is noteworthy that the mean for the first class, respondents who are feeling better off, is extraordinarily high. But the question arises whether the differences among the class means represent real differences attributable to the principle of classification, or whether they are differences that could have arisen by chance, from a random division of the 652 cases into five classes of these sizes. This question can be answered, for any arbitrary level of statistical significance, by comparing the differences among class means with the dispersion of values of individual observations. If the differences among means are large relative to the variances of individual observations around the means, then it seems unlikely that the differences among means could arise by chance. But if the differences among class means are small and individual observations scatter widely about the means, it seems likely that the differences among means reflect nothing more than the inherent wide variability of the phenomenon being measured. The F-ratio reported in Table 38.2 is a measure of the size of the differences among class means relative to the variation of the individual observations. In this case its value, 6.6, is significant at the 1 per cent level. That is, there is no more than 1 chance in 100 that differences among means of the magnitude observed (and shown in column 2 of Table 38.3) would have arisen by chance from a population in which there were really no differences in behavior as between respondents who answered this question differently. (In calculating this F-ratio, it was considered that the data were classified into four groups rather than five; a similar reduction of the number of classes was assumed for other attitudinal questions. This was done in order to avoid counting the inevitable residual classes like "Not ascertained" against the performance of the question.)

In interpreting the results shown in Table 38.2, the tests of buying intentions, numbers 7 and 8, should be considered separately from the tests of other attitudinal questions. The higher F-ratios shown in test 8 compared with test 7 indicate that the quantitative information on expected purchases is important; the simple classification into "will buy" or "will not buy" does not explain as much of the variation of the dependent variables E/Y and $\Delta D/Y$ as regression on P/Y. For these variables E/Y and $\Delta D/Y$, both the original variables and the residuals, regression on P/Y has by far the highest F-ratio of all the tests in Table 38.2. It is the only test where a significant relation to debt behavior appeared. For both variables, it is interesting that the regression on P/Y is more significant for the residuals than for the original variables. Intended expenditure is complementary to the "objective" variables included in the regression; it contains more information when used in conjunction with "objective" variables than when used alone. It is the only test in Table 38.2 of which this is true.

Clearly, buying intentions provide predictive information regarding durable goods expenditures and debt behavior that is not contained in the objective characteristics of the household. This is shown by the significance of the relation of residual E/Y and residual $\Delta D/Y$ to the variable P/Y. If the regressions of Table 38.1 are expanded to include P/Y as an additional explanatory variable, the coefficients indicate the best way to use expected expenditure is in combination with the objective variables. The expanded regressions are shown in Table 38.4. According to these regressions, a dollar increase in expected expenditure indicates a 30-cent increase in actual expenditure and a 15-cent increase in debt accumulation.

Buying intentions do not seem to be an adequate substitute for the "objective" variables. By itself the variable P/Y explains only $3\frac{1}{2}$ per cent of the original variance of E/Y. This indicates a significant relationship, but the objective variables of the Table 38.1 regression account for 23 per cent of the original variance and make a highly significant supplement to P/Y. The same conclusion is even stronger for $\Delta D/Y$ and $\Delta L/Y$. One might have hoped that buying intentions themselves would embody all the effects of economic, financial, and demographic circumstances, that the respondents themselves, in expressing intentions, would fully reflect these as well as other less systematic determinants of their own behavior. Were this hope justified, short-term forecasting would be greatly simplified. It would suffice to collect buying intentions from a sample of households; the respondents themselves would do the otherwise laborious jobs of data collection, analysis, and calculation necessary to make predictions from "objective" variables. The evidence shows that this hope is far from realized. Buying intentions contain useful predictive information, but they are complementary to objective variables, not substitutes for them.

The more diffuse attitudinal questions are strikingly less successful as predictors than the buying intentions questions. This is true, as Table 38.2 shows, whether these questions are tested separately (tests 1–6) or combined in an index (tests 9–10). Although several of the F-ratios are significant on the original variables E/Y and $\Delta L/Y$, none of them is strikingly large. Moreover, almost invariably the F-ratio is lower for the residuals than for the original variables, indicating that the predictive information contained in the attitudinal answers duplicates some of the information contained in the "objective" variables. In two cases, tests 1 and 2, a significant effect on residual $\Delta L/Y$ remains. But the direction of this effect is contrary to the direction one would expect on Katona's general hypothesis that optimism and feelings of well-being favor spending, while pessimism and feeling worse off lead to saving. In this case, those who felt "better off" or reported that they were "making more" tended to add more to their liquid assets than those who felt "worse off" or reported "making less". The only other significant F-ratio for the residuals concerns the effect of end-of-year income expectations on durable goods expenditure. I would be more inclined to attach importance to this result if *beginning-of-year* income expectations had shown a similar result.

Buying intentions have predictive value; other attitudinal questions do not. This conclusion is the inescapable testimony of this analysis of

Table 38.4

Regression coefficients, primary non-farm spending units with 1952 incomes $1000 or greater

Dependent variable	Income change	M	A	L/Y			D/Y		
				$Y_{-1}/Y < 0.8$	$0.8 < Y_{-1}/Y < 1.3$	$1.3 < Y_{-1}/Y$	$Y_{-1}/Y < 0.8$	$0.8 < Y_{-1}/Y < 1.3$	$1.3 < Y_{-1}/Y$
E/Y	Up	+0.022	−0.015	−0.001			+0.039		
	Little change				−0.000			+0.014	
	Down					+0.012			+0.016
ΔL/Y	Up	−0.212	+0.075	−0.316			−2.65		
	Little change				−0.289			−0.072	
	Down					−0.214			−0.204
ΔD/Y	Up	+0.019	−0.004	−0.030			−0.746		
	Little change				−0.011			−0.571	
	Down					−0.024			−0.879

Table 38.4 (continued)

Dependent variable	Income change	Y_{-1}/Y			Constants			
		$Y_{-1}/Y < 0.8$	$0.8 < Y_{-1}/Y < 1.3$	$1.3 < Y_{-1}/Y$	$Y_{-1}/Y < 0.8$	$0.8 < Y_{-1}/Y < 1.3$	$1.3 < Y_{-1}/Y$	P/Y
E/Y	Up	+0.021			+0.083			
	Little change		−0.137			+0.231		+0.305
	Down			+0.032			+0.030	
$\Delta L/Y$	Up	−0.136			+0.356			
	Little change		−0.115			+0.179		+0.212
	Down			+0.367			−0.587	
$\Delta D/Y$	Up	−0.072			+0.102			
	Little change		−0.045			+0.089		+0.149
	Down			+0.010			+0.084	

the evidence of this reinterview sample. It was also the conclusion of a previous analysis employing a different approach on the same sample.[8] Other evidence, based on different survey data or different techniques of analysis, may point to different conclusions.[9] But no such evidence has yet been presented.[10]

Katona has reacted strongly to the report of the Smithies Committee for distinguishing, in its conclusions about predictive value, between intentions data and other attitudinal questions in the same manner as this paper has done.[11] The burden of proof seems to be on him to support the statement: "Some available evidence about isolated buying intentions is relatively 'good', some 'not so good'; the same is true of other expectations and attitudes. First of all, however, the two are theoretically and practically so closely related that their separation is not justified."

In view of the negative conclusions about the predictive value of attitudinal data other than buying intentions, "it is time to emphasize", to quote the Smithies Committee, "... that prediction, at least in the fairly direct sense in which we have been discussing it, is by no means the only use of attitudinal data. ... These data have considerable descriptive interest in themselves, as measures of households' assessments of their own well-being, as clues to the sources of popular feeling of anxiety and security. It may well be as important for the social scientist to explain fluctuations in measures of this kind as to try to use such measures to explain spending and saving behavior. Moreover, if spending units are to be interviewed for other purposes anyway, as in the case of the *Surveys of Consumer Finances*, the additional cost of attitudinal data is negligible. Indeed questions of this kind have considerable value just in arousing the cooperative interest of the respondent.[12]"

I would not conclude without stressing the very considerable debt the profession owes George Katona and his colleagues at the Survey Research Center for their imaginative and pioneering work in the collection and interpretation of buying intentions and attitudinal data. Without their leadership, we might still be talking about the importance of consumer psychology for short-term business fluctuations and bemoaning our inability to observe and measure it. Thanks to the experience they are accumulating, we can investigate the questions which attitudes are the most important ones to investigate in periodic surveys and what is the best way to use these data in combination with other economic information.

Notes

[1] George Katona, "Federal Reserve Board Committee Reports on Consumer Expectations and Saving Statistics," this *Review*, 39 (February 1957), 19-44. Katona tells me that he does not regard this article as challenging the relevance of reinterview tests. Evidently he does challenge their necessity. He says: "Reinterviews represent one important way to test. But aggregative tests may contribute to the understanding of consumer behavior and may indicate that expectations and intentions are relevant and useful, even if a reinterview test is not conclusive."

Katona criticizes the concern of the Smithies Committee, of which I was a member, for insisting on confirmation of predictive value at the level of the individual household. It is a travesty of the Smithies Committee report to attribute to it "the assumption ... that the individual 'fulfillment' rate alone matters". Obviously what matters is the aggregate prediction. The question at issue is whether one can have confidence in aggregate predictions based on the overall proportions of favorable attitudes in a sample, if these attitudes turn out to bear no relation to the behavior of the individuals who expressed them.

[2] "... it would surely be very difficult to construct a plausible model of human behavior, even allowing for much purely random and idiosyncratic differences among individuals, on which attitudes could influence subsequent behavior of large groups without influencing the behavior of those who were observed to hold them." *Report of Federal Reserve Consultant Committee on Consumer Survey Statistics* (Smithies Committee) (Washington 1955), p. 61.

Okun's argument is given in his paper, "Value of Anticipations Data for Forecasting National Product," *Cowles Foundation Discussion Paper No. 40*, prepared for the Universities–National Bureau Conference on the Quality and Economic Significance of Anticipations Data.

[3] See "Federal Reserve Board Committee Reports...," *op. cit.*, 43, and *Consumer Expectations 1953-56*, p. 99.

[4] Thanks are due the Center and the Board of Governors for permission to analyze these data.

[5] "Federal Reserve Committee Report," *op. cit.*, 42-43.

[6] See *Consumer Expectations 1953-56*, Chapter 6.

[7] The questions in the 1952 *Survey of Consumer Finances* were not the same as the attitudinal questions in the periodic surveys from which the Survey Research Center has constructed its aggregative index (*Consumer Expectations 1953-56*, pp. 94-95). Consequently, the attitudinal index tested here differs in several respects from the attitudinal component of the Center's index:

(1) My index includes year-ahead income expectation, No. 3 in Table 38.2; the Center's index has instead, "Now looking ahead – do you think that a year from now you people will be better off financially, or worse off, or just about the same as now?" This difference does not appear to be crucial.

(2) My index includes No. 2 in Table 38.2, "... making as much money now as a year ago". The Center's index does not.

(3) The Center's index includes two questions on expected business conditions, one referring to the next year and the other to the next five years. Neither question was asked in the 1952 *Survey of Consumer Finances*.

(4) The Center's index includes price expectations. I deliberately omitted this (No. 6 in Table 2) because of the ambiguity whether to regard expectations of, say, price increases as favorable or unfavorable to spending. The Center's arbitrary treatment (price stability, large increases, and small decreases are favorable expectations; small increases are unfavorable) is surely an example of the kind of manipulation of the data that ought to be avoided.

[8] L.R. Klein and J.B. Lansing, "Decisions to Purchase Consumer Durable Goods," *Journal of Marketing*, 20 (October 1955), 109-32.

[9] "It is always possible, however, that the results would look different if somewhat different procedures were used. In particular, a separation of the dependent purchase variable into cars and other durables, perhaps even dividing other durables into specific items, might yield less impressive results for purchase intentions and more significant results for the more diffuse attitudes. In the analyses we have been summarizing, the pooling of all items, in both actual and intended purchases, means that the intentions variable must be interpreted less as reflecting the execution of definite specific plans than as reflecting a rather diffuse disposition to buy durable goods. It is also quite possible that attitudes are multiplicative rather than additive in their effects, that the 'interactions' of attitudinal variables with each other and with other variables would turn out to be more important than the 'main effects'. Thinking it is a good time to buy durable goods may, for example, do nothing to the purchases of an aged low-income consumer with pessimistic income expectations, but it may make a considerable difference for a young and optimistic high-income consumer." *Report of Consultant Committee on Consumer Survey Statistics*, 65.

[10] In an article which appeared since this paper was prepared, "The Effects of Consumer Attitudes on Purchases," *American Economic Review*, XLVII (December 1957), 946-65, Eva Mueller has analyzed the predictive value of attitudes and intentions in reinterview samples June 1954-December 1954 and June 1955-December 1955. Her regressions (2) and (4) confirm for both periods the conclusions of my analysis of the 1952-53 reinterview sample. In a recent unpublished paper, "Consumer Attitudes: Their Influence and Forecasting Value," she reports similar regressions and similar results for the first half of 1956 and the period December 1955-February 1957. This paper also presents calculations on the aggregative data prompted by initial versions of Okun's paper. As mentioned above, these calculations show that it is possible to formulate the equation and define the variables in ways that attribute predictive value to attitudinal questions rather than to buying intentions.

[11] "Federal Reserve Committee Reports...," *op. cit.*, 43.

[12] *Report of Consultant Committee on Consumer Survey Statistics*, 65-66.

PART VI

RATIONING

CHAPTER 39

A SURVEY OF THE THEORY OF RATIONING

The rationing of consumers' goods raises for economic theory the
question of analyzing economic behavior in a different institutional
environment from the free market which theory has traditionally
assumed. The question becomes the more compelling because in some
countries rationing is evidently more than a temporary wartime measure
and because elsewhere emergencies that may give rise to rationing seem
to be increasingly frequent. This paper seeks to survey the accommoda-
tion of economic theory to rationing.

1. Rationing as a Multiple-currency System

Rationing may be represented as the replacement of a single-currency
system with a multiple-currency system. Each household receives incomes and pays prices not only in money but also in various ration
currencies. However, the analogy cannot be pressed too far without
obscuring some of the essential features of rationing. Compared to
money, ration currencies are limited in the functions which they can
perform. One criticism that can be advanced against the present theory
of consumer behavior under rationing, which will be reviewed below, is
that its usefulness for the study of realistic problems of policy is impaired
by its assumption of complete symmetry between ration currencies and
money.

1.1. The following are important characteristic differences between
ration currency and money:

(1) The size of a household's ration income is independent of the work
supplied by the household. Ration allowances are not really analogous

Reprinted from *Econometrica*, 20 (October 1952), 521-53.

to money income but, at best, only to money *transfer payments*. This difference is, of course, essential to an important social objective of rationing, which is to prevent inequalities in earning power from resulting in inequalities in certain kinds of consumption.

A loose link between labor supply and ration income is provided in some features of rationing schemes in practice and in some proposed plans. Occupational distinctions between consumers in the size of their rations, to the extent that they do more than reflect differences in needs, are an example. The "expenditure ration" proposal in Scitovsky (1942, pp. 121–24), recently elaborated by Scitovsky *et al.* (1951, Chapter 3 and Appendix I), departs from the usual principle of equality and makes ration income a function of money income.

(2) Saving is not possible in ration currency. A household cannot increase its future ration income or even its future consumption of rationed goods by failing to spend its entire current ration income.[1] A given issue of ration currency becomes invalid after a set date, or is subject to invalidation without notice by the rationing authority.[2]

(3) The multiple-currency system introduced by rationing is asymmetrical in the respect that in one of the currencies, money, and in no other currency every commodity has a price. Money is the only currency which traverses the complete circuit from households to households. Even for rationed goods, it is not practicable to dispense with money payments, because the sellers of consumers' goods must obtain a currency which can be used throughout the productive process.[3] Conversely, no ration currency applies to every commodity. The fact that labor – or leisure – and command over future consumption goods have no price in ration currency has already been pointed out. Any actual rationing system would, if only from administrative necessity, have other omissions too.

1.2. Various kinds of rationing may be distinguished. *Points rationing* refers to a ration currency which applies to two or more goods at established *points prices*. A system of points rationing might involve several ration currencies, but generally a given commodity would not require more than one kind of points. A special case, *value rationing*, sets the points prices of the goods covered by a particular ration currency in proportion to their money prices. *Straight rationing*, or specific rationing, means that a ration currency is applicable to only one commodity.

2. The Behavior of the Individual Consumer under Rationing

The principal application of economic theory to the multiple-currency system introduced by rationing is to examine the consequences of imposing multiple budget constraints, instead of a single budget constraint, on the maximization of utility by an individual consumer. As in other areas of the theory of consumer choice, two approaches are used in the literature, one two-dimensional and geometric, the other multidimensional and symbolic. The institution of rationing in Great Britain early in World War II inspired a series of articles in English journals designed to incorporate rationing into the general theory of consumer choice which had, just prior to the war, been expounded by Hicks. These articles followed, for the most part, the example of the text of *Value and Capital* rather than that of its appendices. It was not until after the war that a general multidimensional treatment of the problem was provided by Samuelson (1947) and, independently, by Graaff (1948), although the primary conditions for a maximum under rationing had been mentioned in a footnote by Scitovsky (1942), and no doubt others had worked out the analysis.

2.1. Two-dimensional arguments are essentially inadequate for the treatment of the problem and can easily be misleading. The arguments used are of two types: one attempts to explain the changes wrought by rationing in the individual's choice between two commodities; the other to explain the effects of rationing on the individual's demand for one commodity in terms of all others, or so-called "money".

2.1.1. The following argument, concerning the choice between two commodities, was developed in a series of articles by Worswick (1944), Rothschild (1945), and Makower (1945–46). Between two commodities x_1 and x_2, an indifference map is drawn on the assumption that consumption of every other commodity is constant. The assumption also fixes the amounts of given money and ration incomes which are available for the purchase of x_1 and x_2. Given the price ratios, both in terms of money, p_1/p_2, and in terms of ration currency, p_1'/p_2', the problem is to determine the amounts x_1 and x_2. Three cases are distinguished, corresponding to Figures 39.1, 39.2, and 39.3. In each Figure, LM represents the possibilities open to the consumer with the allotted sum of money, ignoring the existence of rationing, and $L'M'$ the possibilities open with

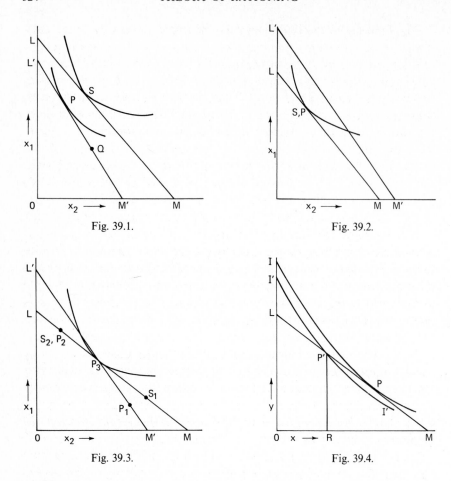

Fig. 39.1.   Fig. 39.2.

Fig. 39.3.   Fig. 39.4.

the allotted sum of ration currency, ignoring the necessity for paying money prices. P in each Figure represents the optimum possible choice of the consumer. Figure 39.1 is supposed to represent a *points standard*, in which the choice is made as if money were not involved because the constraints of rationing are more restrictive. Figure 39.2 is supposed to represent the opposite situation. In Figure 39.3 the effective possibility locus for the consumer is not $L'M'$ as in Figure 39.1, or LM as in Figure 39.2, but the broken line LP_3M'. It is conceived that, depending on the shape of the indifference curves, the choice could be in the LP_3 segment, at a point like P_2, in the P_3M' segment, at a point like P_1, or at P_3 itself.

An equilibrium of the P_3 type exerts a special fascination because, if the search of the consumer for maximum utility is interpreted literally as an attempt to equate his marginal rate of substitution between two commodities with their price ratio, this position seems to imply some frustration. The money–price ratio invites the consumer to leave P_3 by substituting in one direction, but his ration allowance will not permit it; the ration–price ratio invites him to do the opposite, but his money allowance forbids.

The only "equilibrium" in the three diagrams which exhausts the assumed amounts of both kinds of currency allotted to the two commodities in P_3. In every other case the P's leave the consumer with an unspent margin of one of the currencies. Unless the marginal utility of that currency is zero, the consumer will not be indifferent to the size of this margin. In Figure 39.1, for example, position Q leaves the consumer with more excess money than position P, and the diagram gives no grounds for determining which of the two positions will be preferred. Rothschild recognized this indeterminacy but was not led by this recognition to question the whole technique. Actually the assumption that purchases of other commodities are fixed cannot be maintained. In the case depicted in Figure 39.1, there will be a reshuffling of other purchases so that they require more money and, perhaps, less points. This process will move $L'M'$ and LM closer together, and may also alter the indifference map, until an equilibrium like P_3 is achieved. The same remarks apply to Figure 39.2 and to any position like P_1 or P_2 in Figure 39.3. However, if rationing is ineffective and the marginal utility of points zero, the unspent points at P in Figure 39.2 will have no influence on the consumer's behavior. Except for this possibility, the only tenable representation of choice between two commodities under a dual-currency system is P_3 in Figure 39.3. There is, of course, nothing odd or frustrating about this position. Under a two-currency system the consumer's optimum position involves equating the marginal rate of substitution between two commodities not to their price ratio in either currency but to a weighted average of the two price ratios.

The diagrams make more sense if x_1 and x_2 are taken to be the only rationed commodities and if positions S on LM represent the pre-rationing situation. But it remains true that in the case of Figure 39.1 and of S_1 in Figure 39.3, LM must shift downwards; and the optimum position under rationing will be at a point where LM and $L'M'$ intersect, not necessarily at P or P_1.

2.1.2. In the other use of two-dimensional geometric argument, one commodity x is plotted against "money", representing all other commodities. Clearly this technique does not lend itself to the depiction of the results of anything except straight rationing of one commodity. The one "commodity" might, however, be a Hicksian group of rationed goods. (Within such a group both the structure of relative points prices and the structure of relative money prices must remain constant. But the ratio between any given points price and the corresponding money price need not be constant.) In Figure 39.4, the vertical axis measures total expenditure on commodities other than x and the horizontal axis measures total consumption of x. OL is total money income. The size of the ration is R; the effect of rationing is indicated by comparing P' with P, the pre-rationing equilibrium.

The main application of this apparatus is to the evaluation of the decrease in welfare due to rationing. Various devices were suggested by Nicholson (1942–43) and Kaldor (1941) to measure the income equivalent of the movement from indifference curve I to I'. And this analysis, applied to the whole British population as the consumer, was the basis for an attempt by Nicholson to estimate numerically the change in the cost of living occasioned by rationing.

2.2. The more general approach to the analysis of consumer behavior under rationing, worked out by Samuelson and Graaff, conceives of the consumer as maximizing a utility function

$$u(x_1, x_2, \ldots, x_n) \tag{1}$$

subject to the multiple restraints,

$$\sum_{i=1}^{n} p_{ji}x_i = R_j \quad (j = 0, 1, 2, \ldots, m)(m + 1 < n), \tag{2}$$

where x_i is amount consumed of the ith good ($i = 1, 2, \ldots, n$); p_{ji} its price in the jth currency ($j = 0, 1, 2, \ldots, m$), and in particular p_{0i} its price in money; R_j the consumer's income in the jth currency, and in particular R_0 his income in money. The conditions for a maximum are (2) plus a set of equations,

$$u_i - \sum_{j=0}^{m} \lambda_j p_{ji} = 0 \quad (i = 1, 2, \ldots, n), \tag{3}$$

where u_i is the partial derivative of (1) with respect to x_i, and λ_j a Lagrange multiplier identified with the marginal utility of the jth kind of income. Conditions (3) were pointed out by Scitovsky (1942).

In (3), $\lambda_j = 0$ whenever the equality sign does not hold in (2); in that case rationing by currency j is not effective and the marginal utility of that ration income is zero. If saving is one of the n commodities, this cannot happen for money ($j = 0$).

The system of $n + m + 1$ equations formed by (2) and (3) may be differentiated to give partial derivatives of the n x_i's and $m + 1$ λ's with respect to each of the p_{ji} and R_j. Together with the secondary conditions for the maximum, this process gives results quite analogous to the similar procedure in the theory of consumer choice in a single-currency system.

This analysis may be applied to two kinds of problems: (1) the relationships among these partial derivatives of demand functions under a given regime of rationing, and (2) the relationships between the partial derivatives of demand functions under a given rationing regime and the partial derivatives of free-market, single-currency demand functions or of the demand functions in a different rationing regime. (A given *regime* is characterized by a constant list of effective ration incomes R_j for which $\lambda_j \neq 0$. Changes in the parameters R_j and p_{ji} constitute a change in regime if and only if they make some previously effective ration ineffective.) The two kinds of applications will be considered in turn.

2.2.1. Let D be the $m + n + 1$ rowed determinant:

$$\begin{vmatrix} 0 & 0 & \cdots & 0 & p_{01} & p_{02} & \cdots & p_{0n} \\ 0 & 0 & \cdots & 0 & p_{11} & p_{12} & \cdots & p_{1n} \\ \cdots\cdots\cdots\cdots\cdots\cdots\cdots\cdots\cdots\cdots\cdots \\ \cdots\cdots\cdots\cdots\cdots\cdots\cdots\cdots\cdots\cdots\cdots \\ 0 & 0 & \cdots & 0 & p_{m1} & p_{m2} & \cdots & p_{mn} \\ p_{01} & p_{11} & \cdots & p_{m1} & u_{11} & u_{12} & \cdots & u_{1n} \\ p_{02} & p_{12} & \cdots & p_{m2} & u_{21} & u_{22} & \cdots & u_{2n} \\ \cdots\cdots\cdots\cdots\cdots\cdots\cdots\cdots\cdots\cdots\cdots \\ \cdots\cdots\cdots\cdots\cdots\cdots\cdots\cdots\cdots\cdots\cdots \\ p_{0n} & p_{1n} & \cdots & p_{mn} & u_{n1} & u_{n2} & \cdots & u_{nn} \end{vmatrix}$$

Let $D(a)$ be the cofactor of a, where a can be any element of D. The effect on the demand for x_i of a change in p_{jk}, compensated in the usual sense by a change of the income R_j, is given by:

$$\left(\frac{\partial x_1}{\partial p_{jk}}\right)_{\text{comp}} = \frac{\partial x_i}{\partial p_{jk}} + x_k \frac{\partial x_i}{\partial R_j} = \frac{\lambda_j D(u_{ik})}{D}. \tag{4}$$

All the restrictions which hold in regard to the compensated price derivatives in a single-currency system hold also in a regime of rationing for these generalized compensated price derivatives, and it is unnecessary to review them in detail here. The Slutsky equation holds in any currency: the derivative of x_i with respect to a compensated change in p_{jk} is equal to the derivative of x_k with respect to a compensated change in p_{ji}. Demand functions are homogeneous of degree zero in each currency separately, i.e., with respect to each set of variables.

It is worth noting that

$$\frac{\left(\dfrac{\partial x_i}{\partial p_{jk}}\right)_{\text{comp}}}{\left(\dfrac{\partial x_i}{\partial p_{gk}}\right)_{\text{comp}}} = \frac{\lambda_j}{\lambda_g}. \tag{5}$$

This implies that the nature of the relationship between any pair of commodities, x_i and x_k, i.e., substitution, complementarity, or independence, is the same in all currencies. Sugar and tea cannot be complements in money and substitutes in points. (This does not say, of course, that the relationship between two commodities is the same under rationing as it would be in a single-currency regime. Indeed two commodities which are normally complements may be made substitutes by placing them, and only them, in a single ration group.) However, it is possible for the same good to be *inferior* in one currency and *superior* in another. These observations are due to Graaff (1948).

2.2.2. More interesting problems arise in attempting to make comparisons between demand functions under rationing and under a single-currency regime, or comparisons between different rationing regimes. Samuelson (1947, p. 168) has pointed out that the introduction of additional constraints decreases numerically the response of the demand for any commodity to compensated changes in its own price. [$D(u_{ii})/D$, which is necessarily negative as a secondary condition of the maximum, becomes smaller numerically as the number of constraints, $m + 1$, becomes larger.]

For the special case of a system of *straight* rationing, comparisons of demand derivatives between regimes have been presented by Tobin and Houthakker (1951). Suppose that for each of the ration currencies $(j = 1, 2, \ldots, m)$, all prices are zero except p_{jj}, which is one. The constraints (2) then reduce to:

$$x_j = R_j \quad (j = 1, 2, \ldots, m),$$

$$\sum_{i=1}^{n} p_{0i} x_i = R_0. \tag{6}$$

Then, the effect of a change in a ration on the demand for an unrationed good is given by:

$$\frac{\partial x_i}{\partial R_j} = \frac{D(p_{ji})}{D} = \frac{D'(u_{ij})}{D'(u_{jj})}, \tag{7}$$

where D' is D with all the price vectors, except the first row and column $(j = 0)$, deleted, and with the rows and columns corresponding to every rationed good, except the jth, deleted. The meaning of (7) may be made clearer by noting that when only one good x_j is rationed the effect of a change in the size of the ration R_j on the demand for any commodity x_i is equal to the effect in a free market of a compensated change in the price of x_j on the demand of x_i, divided by the effect of the same price change on the demand for x_j itself. This leads to the following relationships, where a barred partial derivative sign refers to a derivative under rationing and an unbarred sign to a derivative of a free-market demand function:

$$\frac{\bar{\partial} x_i}{\bar{\partial} R_0} = \frac{\partial x_i}{\partial R_0} - \sum_{j=1}^{m} \frac{\bar{\partial} x_i}{\bar{\partial} R_j} \frac{\partial x_j}{\partial R_0} \quad (i = 1, 2, \ldots, n), \tag{8}$$

$$\frac{\bar{\partial} x_i}{\bar{\partial} p_{0k}} = \frac{\partial x_i}{\partial p_{0k}} - \sum_{j=1}^{m} \frac{\bar{\partial} x_i}{\bar{\partial} R_j} \frac{\partial x_j}{\partial p_{0k}} \quad (i, k = 1, 2, \ldots, n). \tag{9}$$

These equations have been repeated here because they will be useful in Section 3 of the paper. Similar relationships can be found comparing demand derivatives in two different regimes of rationing.

A serious limitation of these comparisons is that they are strictly valid only at a given point. They compare changes in demand, due to changes in some demand parameter, from a starting-point common to a free-market regime and to a regime of rationing. It is imagined that, under both regimes, the consumer is faced with the same income and same prices and has chosen to make the same set of purchases. The effect of changing his income or some price on his choice is then examined both when he is subject and when he is not subject to the additional constraints of rationing. More interesting comparisons cannot be made without imposing on the consumer's demand functions more restrictions than are implied by the pure theory of choice.

2.2.3. A problem relevant to the estimation of the welfare consequences of rationing is to find the "virtual" system of free-market prices which would induce a consumer of a given money income to take precisely the same amount of each commodity as he consumes under rationing. Rothbarth (1941), who introduced the notion of a *virtual price system*, suggested that it be found in practice by searching free market budget records for a collection of purchases comparable to the collection in a budget under rationing. Graaff (1948) set forth a method which depends instead on observations of demand function derivatives during rationing. Let p_i' be the *virtual* price of commodity x_i, and let λ' be the *virtual* marginal utility of money income. Then

$$u_i = \lambda' p_i' = \lambda_0 p_{0i} + \sum_{j=1}^{m} \lambda_j p_{ji}. \tag{10}$$

Multiplying the second equality by x_i and summing over all i, gives:

$$\lambda' R_0 = \lambda_0 R_0 + \sum_{j=1}^{m} \lambda_j R_j.$$

Solving this for λ' and substituting in (10), Graaff obtains:

$$\left(\lambda_0 + \sum_{j=1}^{m} \lambda_j \frac{R_j}{R_0} \right) p_i' = \lambda_0 p_{0i} + \sum_{j=1}^{m} \lambda_j p_{ji},$$

and

$$p_i' = \frac{p_{0i} + \sum_{j=1}^{m} \lambda_j/\lambda_0 \, p_{ji}}{1 + \sum_{j=1}^{m} \lambda_j/\lambda_0 \, R_j/R_0}. \tag{11}$$

Now the ratios λ_j/λ_0 can be evaluated from (5) provided that for each ration currency a pair of commodities can be found for which non-zero compensated price derivatives can be observed both in money and in the ration currency. Everything else in (11) is easily observable under rationing.

2.3. All of the analysis of this section assumes that rationing establishes a true multiple-currency system, that there is no market mechanism by which one currency can be exchanged for another. If an individual can buy or sell a ration currency at a market exchange rate with money, rationing by that currency imposes no additional constraint upon him. It only changes his money income and the effective money prices of goods and services, and its effects can be handled by the theory of consumer behavior in a single-currency regime. If r_j is the price in money of a unit of ration currency j, the consumer's money income is augmented by $r_j p_j$ and the money price of any commodity, say x_i, is increased by $r_j p_{ji}$.

A well-organized black market for rationed commodities is equivalent to a market for ration currency. It establishes indirectly an exchange rate between money and ration currency. If p'_{0i} is the black market money price of x_i and p_{0i} its official price, then the implicit money price of the ration currency is

$$r_j = \frac{p'_{0i} - p_{0i}}{p_{ji}}. \tag{12}$$

3. Collective Demand under Rationing

The aggregation of individual demand functions under rationing involves, in addition to the usual difficulties of aggregation, the special complication that different individuals are subject to different regimes. Indeed if there are m ration currencies there are $\sum_{j=1}^{m} C_j^m$ conceivable rationing regimes, and in addition the single-currency regime in which no rations are effective. Any change in the parameters of demand, i.e., money incomes, ration incomes, or prices will shift some consumers from one regime to another. One of the factors determining aggregate demand for any set of parameter values is, therefore, the distribution of consumers, at those values, among rationing regimes.

This subject has not received the emphasis given in the literature to the theory of individual demand underrationing, and it will be discussed here for the simplest of cases, i.e., *straight* rationing of only one commodity. The major investigation of the aggregation problem under rationing is by Malmquist (1948, Chapter 2) in his study of the demand for liquor in Sweden, where liquor has long been rationed. Malmquist derives expressions for collective income, price, and ration elasticities of demand for the rationed good in terms of individual demand elasticities. These relationships necessarily depend on certain assumptions regarding the distribution of individuals by income and by a random variable representing "tastes". Incomes and tastes are taken to be the factors determining whether or not rationing is effective for a particular consumer.

I shall not reproduce Malmquist's argument. Instead I shall illustrate what is involved by an example in which individual demand in the absence of rationing is a linear function, and uniform, except for a random term to permit differences in *tastes*, for all individuals. This simplifying assumption will permit investigation of the effects of rationing on the whole collective demand function and not just on its elasticities or derivatives at a point. Moreover, I shall consider also the effects of rationing on the collective demand for an unrationed good; this analysis will employ some of the results cited in 2.2.2. concerning the comparison of the slopes of individual demand functions under two regimes.

3.1. Suppose that the free-market demand of an individual for the rationed good, given the prices of other goods, is given by

$$c = b_0 + b_1 y + b_2 p + e, \tag{13}$$

where y is the individual's money income, p the price of the good, and e a random variable. The expected value of the conditional distribution of e for any y is assumed to be zero. The corresponding collective demand function, relating average consumption to average income and to price is

$$\bar{c} = b_0 + b_1 \bar{y} + b_2 p. \tag{14}$$

Similarly, suppose that the free-market demand of an individual for another good is given by

$$c' = b_0' + b_1' y + b_2' p + e'. \tag{15}$$

The collective counterpart of this is

$$\bar{c}' = b_0' + b_1'\bar{y} + b_2'p. \tag{16}$$

We shall assume that, when the first good is rationed at level R, the individual demand for the unrationed commodity is

$$c'(R) = c' + b_3'(R - c), \tag{17}$$

where c' and c are the free-market levels of consumption from Equations (15) and (13), respectively. Equation (17) says that under rationing, demand for an unrationed good exceeds or falls short of its free market level by an amount which is proportional to the shortage of the rationed good. If the two goods are substitutes, b_3' will be negative; if they are complements, positive.

When (15) and (13) are substituted in (17), $c'(R)$ is a linear function of R, p, and y with the following constants: the constant term is $b_0' - b_3'b_0$; the coefficient of y is $b_1' - b_3'b_1$; the coefficient of p is $b_2' - b_3'b_2$. It will be noted that these coefficients are consistent with (8) and (9) in Section 2.2.2. [However, it is not possible to conform completely with the results of Section 2.2.2. within the framework of uniform linear demand functions. According to (7), b_3' for each individual should be equal to $(b_2' + cb_1')/(b_2 + cb_1)$, where c is the individual's free-market demand for the rationed commodity; consequently this ratio of compensated price derivatives depends on y and p and is different for different individuals.]

If rationing were effective for all individuals, the average consumption of the two goods would be:

$$\bar{c}(R) = R, \tag{18}$$

$$\bar{c}'(R) = \bar{c}' + b_3'(R - \bar{c}); \tag{19}$$

but in general rationing will be effective for only part of the population. Hence consumption of the rationed good will be a kind of weighted average of (14) and (18); and demand for the unrationed good will be a similar weighted average, with the same weights, of (16) and (19). The weights are, of course, themselves variables. The proportion of individuals for whom rationing is effective and the share of total income which they receive vary inversely with R and p. Assuming that the distribution of relative income $(y/\bar{y})$ is invariant with $\bar{y}$, these proportions also vary directly with $\bar{y}$. (These statements assume that the rationed good is not an *inferior* good.) At high price, generous ration, and low average income, collective demand for the two-goods will be close to its free-market values as given by (14) and (16); at low price, low ration, and high average income, demand will approach its values for universally effective rationing, as given by (18) and (19).

Average consumption of the rationed good, under incompletely effective rationing, is given by:

$$\bar{c}^* = \bar{c} + \int\limits_{y} \int\limits_{e = R - b_0 - b_1 y - b_2 p}^{\infty} (R - b_0 - b_1 y - b_2 p - e) f(e, y; \bar{y}) \, de \, dy,$$

$$(20)$$

where $f(e, y; \bar{y})$ is the joint density function for the distribution of individuals by e and y when mean income is $\bar{y}$. The second term is the integral, over all individuals for whom rationing is effective, of *shortages* $(R - c)$ imposed by rationing. Consequently, using (17), we can express the average consumption, under partially effective rationing, of the unrationed good, as follows:

$$\bar{c}'^* = \bar{c}' + b_3'(\bar{c}^* - \bar{c}).$$

$$(21)$$

In the sections which follow, the relationships developed in this section will be illustrated graphically.

3.2. Figure 39.5 summarizes the effects of rationing on individual and collective demand for the rationed good, in relationship to income, with price assumed constant. *ABC* represents the average consumption of individuals with income y in the absence of rationing. It also represents the collective free-market relationship between over-all average consumption and average income. If there were no differences in tastes among individuals, rationing at level R would change the individual function to the broken line *ABD*, and the collective function to curve *AD*. Given differences in tastes, it is possible that rationing will be effective for some individuals even at low incomes. Consequently, the average consumption of individuals with income y will follow a curved path below *ABD*, like *AD*; and collective average consumption at average income $\bar{y}$ will follow a similar but lower curve.

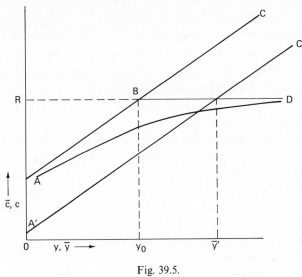

Fig. 39.5.

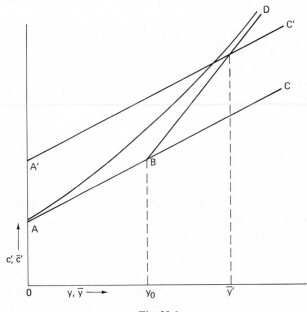

Fig. 39.6.

Figure 39.6 summarizes the effects of rationing on the individual and collective income–consumption relationships for an unrationed substitute. At individual income level y_0 rationing becomes effective for a consumer of average tastes, and the substitute acquires some of the suppressed effects of changes in income on demand for the rationed good. ABC, ABD, and AD are the analogues of the curves with the same labels as in Figure 39.5.

3.3. Before proceeding to diagrams picturing price–consumption and ration–consumption relationships, we will use Figures 39.5 and 39.6 in connection with a digression concerning interpersonal transfers of rations. The analysis which has been presented in Section 3.1 assumes that no such transfers occur. In the opposite case, perfect transfer – i.e., no individual fails to draw his full ration so long as anyone else has unsatisfied demand for the rationed good – collective average consumption would follow the broken line ABD.

A question of interest, in the case of perfect transfer, is the determination of the market price of coupons. A positive price for coupons cannot arise unless the demand for coupons at a zero price exceeds the supply. It cannot arise, therefore, at a level of average income $\bar{y}$ below y_0 in Figure 39.5. The establishment of a positive price for coupons has two effects on the individual, as noted in Section 2.3: an increase in the effective price of the commodity and an increase in income. Establishment of a ration coupon price r will change individual demand and collective average demand alike by $(b_2 + Rb_1)r$. Average consumption must be equal to R; consequently,

$$r = \frac{R - \bar{c}}{b_2 + Rb_1} = \frac{b_1(y_0 - \bar{y})}{b_2 + Rb_1}. \tag{22}$$

Substituting this value for r in the individual demand function, we find that average individual consumption at income y becomes $R + b_1(y - \bar{y})$ when collective average income is greater than y_0. For example, when average income is $\bar{y}_1$ in Figure 39.5, the pattern of individual consumption at various income levels is given by $A'C'$ instead of ABC. Thus the establishment of a market in coupons induces below-average-income individuals, whether or not they would take their full rations in the absence of such a market, to reduce their consumption in order to permit individuals with incomes above average to consume more than the ration.

Similarly labeled curves and points in Figure 39.6 illustrate the effects of a market in coupons on demand for the unrationed commodity. [The establishment of the coupon price r has the same effect on demand for the unrationed substitute as the imposition of rationing without transfer, and therefore Figure 39.6 can describe the results in either case. For an individual at the threshold between effective and ineffective rationing, establishment of the coupon price r is equivalent to a compensated increase in the price of the rationed good. His consumption of the unrationed good will therefore change by $r(b'_2 + Rb'_1)$; the consumption of other individuals will change by the same amount since the demand function is assumed to be linear. The change in collective consumption of the substitute is therefore $r(b'_2 + Rb'_1)$. By (22) $r = (R - \bar{c})/(b_2 + Rb_1)$. Therefore, the change in collective demand for the unrationed good is $[(b'_2 + Rb'_1)/(b_2 + Rb_1)] (R - \bar{c})$. If b'_3 is taken, as it should be, to be the ratio between the compensated price derivatives of the two goods at R, this change in demand is identical with the change due to rationing, $b'_3(R - \bar{c})$, illustrated in Figure 39.6.]

3.4. Figures 39.7 and 39.8 show the relationships between collective average consumption and the size of the ration, R, for the rationed good and for a substitute, respectively. In each diagram, ABC represents the relationship if rationing were completely ineffective; BD the relationship if rationing were completely effective; curve AD the actual relationship under rationing; and broken line ABD the relationship given perfect transfer of coupons.

3.5. Figures 39.9 and 39.10 show the relationships between collective average consumption and the price of the rationed good p, for the rationed good and for a substitute, respectively. The lines and curves in these diagrams have the same interpretations as the lines and curves of the same labels in Figures 39.7 and 39.8. In Figure 39.10 it is assumed that rationing changes the sign of the coefficient of the price of the rationed good in the demand function for the substitute from positive to negative. This is possible because rationing reduces this coefficient, algebraically, but it is, of course, only illustrative; the price coefficient, even for a substitute, need not be positive in the first place and if it is, the effects of rationing may not be strong enough to change its sign.

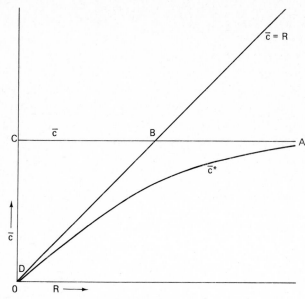

Fig. 39.7.

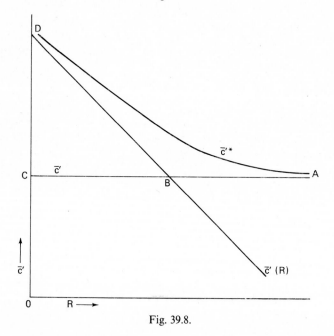

Fig. 39.8.

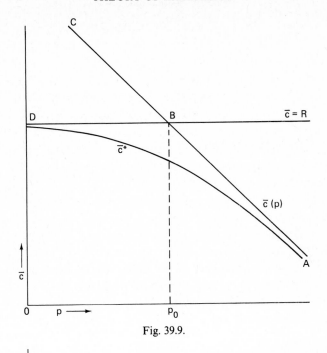

Fig. 39.9.

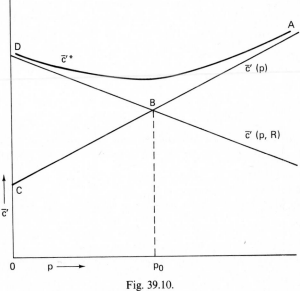

Fig. 39.10.

4. The Incentive to Work under Rationing and Taxation

4.1. The theory reviewed in this paper has rarely been applied to the issues of policy presented by rationing. These issues have been debated on less abstract ground. Is rationing a more efficient method of achieving the social objectives which inspire it than alternative measures? In the circumstances in which rationing is adopted or seriously considered, these objectives are threefold: (1) restriction of total consumption demand to limited available supplies in order to avoid inflation, (2) a more egalitarian distribution of consumption, at least of socially defined "necessities", and (3) maximization of production, largely for purposes other than consumption. Since consumption is the ultimate incentive for work, there may be some conflict between the first two objectives and the third. The case for rationing is that it can accomplish the first two objectives without the damaging effects of heavy taxation on incentives. An important item in the evaluation of rationing as a policy is, therefore, comparison of its effects on incentives with those of taxation.

The tax measures with which rationing should be compared are the income tax and the spendings tax. Either tax could in principle bring consumer demand into line with available supply. But probably, neither can be as effective an instrument of equalization of consumption as rationing. (However, some of the equalization which rationing seems to provide may be illusory. By itself, rationing does nothing to guarantee that every consumer will be able to buy the rations; and it may be very difficult in practice to prevent inequalities due to transfers of rations among individuals.) If rationing is also superior in preserving incentives, the case for it is clear. But if a tax measure is less damaging to incentives, the issue depends on judging whether the additional equalization achieved by rationing is worth more than the relative loss in work and production.

Rationing removes the incentive to work to the extent that this incentive is provided by the opportunity to increase consumption of the rationed commodities. It retains the incentive to work to buy unrationed goods and to save. An income tax retains the incentive to work in order to consume "scarce" commodities; but it generally impairs the incentive by reducing the yield, in terms of all commodities and of saving, of additional effort. A spendings tax also retains the incentive to work in order to buy more of the scarce commodities; it differs from the income tax in reducing the amount of these commodities which additional effort will yield, while maintaining the amount of other commodities and of saving obtainable by additional work. (The case for rationing, and for a spendings tax, as against an income tax, is strongest when the future consumption toward which present saving is directed is not expected to be subject to the restrictions placed on current consumption. A policy which relies heavily on saving to provide incentive to work requires the expectation that some day it will be possible to use the savings.)

Which of the three measures will, while restricting a consumer's purchases of scarce commodities to his proper share, induce him to do the most work? The customary assumption that the consumer's money income is a parameter makes the theory of consumer choice, as reviewed in Section 2, inapplicable to this problem. As suggested in Section 1, the model of rationing used in the theory is too symmetrical a multiple-currency system. It conceals the important institutional fact that at least two "commodities" open to the choice of the consumer, saving and leisure, are unrationed; they have prices in only one currency, money. The theory has been used to evaluate the welfare consequences of rationing in comparison with excise and income taxation (Reder 1942), but it has not been applied to an evaluation of incentive effects.

4.2. In this section a model is presented under very simplifying assumptions, and used to investigate the incentive question. Consider a household with a money income Y from sources other than its own labor, and with a given number of man-hours M at its disposal. These man-hours can be devoted either to leisure, x_3, or to work, $M - x_3$, at wage rate p_3. With its money income, $Y + (M - x_3)p_3$, the household purchases two commodities: x_1 at price p_1 and x_2 at price p_2. The first, x_1, stands for the scarce consumption goods which are candidates for rationing. The second, x_2, stands for other consumption goods and, most important, for future consumption purchased by current saving. The household's demand for x_1 must be limited to a given amount X_1 by one of three alternative techniques: (r) rationing, (s) an increase in p_1 (a proportional spendings tax), (t) a reduction in money income Y and in the money wage rate p_3 (a proportional income tax). It is assumed that each measure is, or at least is believed to be, temporary. Therefore the composition of x_2 is not affected by the introduction of rationing, because in the future savings will be able to be spent without such restriction. Nor is the price of x_2, p_2, affected by the increase in price of x_1; the spendings tax is believed to be temporary. It is assumed that the utility function of the household is quadratic; this makes it possible to investigate finite changes. The problem is of interest only when, as normally would be expected, consumption and leisure are both *superior* goods and are substitutes for each other.

The details are worked out in the Appendix. It is shown there that, on these assumptions, the household will do more work and take less leisure if its consumption is restricted by a spendings tax than if its consumption is restricted by rationing. The income effects of the price increase force the household to work longer hours than under rationing. As between rationing and an income tax, no general statement is possible.

There is, therefore, no clear-cut case for rationing on incentive grounds. Its advantages as an instrument of equalization remain; and the better a tax is as an equalizer, the worse will be its incentive effects. It would be difficult to design a spendings tax that would have the relatively favorable effects of the proportional tax used in this analysis on the incentives of an individual, and at the same time discriminate sufficiently in tax rate as between individuals to achieve substantial equalization of consumption. All that the argument of this section says is that these advantages of rationing are not reinforced by relatively favorable incentive effects but are purchased at some cost in incentives.

5. Rationing and Economic Welfare

5.1. *Trade in Rations among Consumers*

Does trade among consumers in ration currencies and money lead to greater economic welfare than a regime in which transfers of rations are effectively prohibited? In practice, governments attempt to prevent trade and to keep their ration currencies inconvertible; both police power and social opprobrium are mobilized against "black" markets. In contrast, the instincts of economists are to approve opportunities for exchanging ration currencies for each other and for money, on the general principle that increasing the choices available to individuals cannot fail to augment economic welfare. The discussion of this issue will be in terms of a welfare comparison of *convertible rationing*, in which trade in ration currencies and money is permitted, with *inconvertible rationing*, in which it is not permitted.[4]

In part, of course, divergence between economic opinion and government practice on issues of this kind is due to the fact that public policy is not based on the criteria of welfare economics. Those criteria are individualistic: if a consumer chooses freely to trade his milk ration and his family's for chances in a football pool, welfare economics presumes that he is the judge of his own well-being and his family's and is made better off by the trade. A government concerned for the nutrition of its workers and its children may well disagree. Considerations of this kind in favor of inconvertible rations will be ignored in the following discussion, but they should not be forgotten in making judgments about policy.[5]

5.1.1. Assume, to begin with, that: (1) Prices, both in money and in ration currencies, of all consumers' goods are constant. (2) Total supplies of all consumers' goods are fixed. This may be true either (a) because of government controls over supplies or (b) because producers have adjusted the supplies of consumers' goods to their constant relative money prices. (3) The money and ration incomes of each consumer are constant. (4) Rationing is effective for every consumer; there are, even when ration currencies are inconvertible, no unused coupons.

On these assumptions, the establishment of convertibility cannot worsen the position of any consumer and may improve the positions of some consumers. The case for permitting trade between any two consumers is clear. Given the total quantities of consumers' goods available to the two of them, inconvertible rationing forces them off their Edgeworthian contract curve. If they are free to trade, they can strike a bargain which will make neither worse off and at least one party better off.

The establishment of a competitive market in ration currencies, with a uniform money price for each currency, cannot diminish welfare. In such a market, every consumer will be able to buy, if he chooses, the same bill of goods he obtained under inconvertible rationing. The establishment of a money price for a ration increases equally both the money cost of that bill of goods and the consumer's money income (see Sections 2.3 and 3.3). It also permits every consumer to obtain, if he wishes, a different bill of goods, one that was not available to him under inconvertible rationing. If all consumers were identical, the establishment of convertibility would leave every consumer with the same bill of goods as under inconvertible rationing. The money price for a ration currency, which the market would set, would simply be that price at which each consumer would be satisfied to consume his rations and, therefore, neither to buy nor to sell any ration currency.[6] But since consumers differ in tastes and incomes, the price of ration currency established in the market will lead some to buy ration currency and others to sell. Both buyers and sellers will obtain collections of goods which they prefer to the bills of goods they received under inconvertible rationing.

5.1.2. Assumption (4) that rationing is effective for all consumers is crucial to the foregoing argument. If some consumers have unused coupons, convertibility will enable them to sell their surplus to persons who do not have enough. With fixed supplies of consumers' goods [assumption (2)], the use of these previously idle coupons must reduce some consumers' ability to buy the rationed goods. The effective money price of rationed goods must rise by more than the money value of the coupons; since previously unused points will now be presented against an unchanged supply of rationed goods, the points prices of rationed goods will have to rise. Consequently, some consumers – those who were using their full rations and even perhaps some who were not – will not be able to buy the same collection of commodities as before. They will lose the benefit they gained under inconvertible rationing from the inability of other consumers to use their complete rations. Some will be more than compensated for this loss by the possibility of consuming, even on unfavorable terms, increased amounts of the rationed commodities; these consumers indeed constitute the market for unused rations. But others may not be compensated. It is therefore impossible to assert that free exchange of ration currency for money will augment welfare when there are unused rations which are not matched by unsold supplies of rationed goods.[7]

5.1.3. The argument of Section 5.1.1. indicates that, on the same assumptions, the distribution among consumers of given supplies of consumers' goods can be improved by a consolidation of ration currencies. Suppose, for example, that tea and coffee are separately rationed. If consumers generally are taking the coffee ration because they cannot get more tea, a market in the two rations would establish a premium on tea coupons in terms of coffee coupons. Such a market would not prevent anyone from consuming his full tea and coffee rations as before. But it would permit an American in England to indulge his extraordinary preference for coffee by turning his tea coupons over to a native with an abnormally strong preference for tea. The results of this free market can be duplicated administratively by consolidating the two rations into one ration income and establishing points prices that (1) enable any consumer to consume the same combination of tea and coffee as under separate rationing and (2) equate demands for the two commodities to their given total supplies.[8] This does not mean that every consolidation of rations is bound to be an improvement. The points prices established may satisfy the second condition but not the first.[9] Moreover, the reservation of Section 5.1.2. applies here also; if there are unused coupons under separate rationing, it will not be possible to establish a consolidated ration with points prices that permit every consumer to obtain the same collection of goods as under separate rationing.

The fact that it cannot always be asserted that establishing convertibility or consolidating rations will make no consumer worse off is, of course, no reason to stick to inconvertible, multiple rationing. It merely means that the choice between the two situations involves a judgment about distributions of welfare among individuals. An important advantage of convertibility or consolidation, which is not revealed by the static calculations of welfare economics, is greater responsiveness to changes in consumer preferences and in supplies of consumers' goods.

5.1.4. The establishment of a market in ration currencies to replace inconvertible rationing is, of course, not equivalent to the abolition of rationing. Both steps would restore a single-currency regime, but there are important differences, both in distribution of income and in allocation of resources. Even if the pattern of consumer supply is unchanged, the distribution of income is altered, in an egalitarian direction, by the institution of ration incomes. To say that convertibility of rations is superior, in a welfare sense, to inconvertibility is not to say that no rationing is superior to rationing, whether the rationing is convertible or not. Both convertible rationing and no rationing are optimum situations in this sense: they meet the condition that between any pair of goods the marginal rates of substitution for all consumers be equal. The optimum achieved by convertible rationing dominates, on the four assumptions of Section 5.1.1., the non-optimal situation of inconvertible rationing that it replaces. The optimum achieved by a free competitive market in consumers' goods, with no rationing, does not dominate a regime of rationing.

Rationing, whether convertible or inconvertible, also alters the pattern of consumer supply; and to its effects on the allocation of the resources available for producing consumers' goods we turn in the following section.

5.2. *Rationing and the Allocation of Resources*

Assume: (1) that fixed amounts of productive resources are available for the production of consumers' goods, and (2) that these amounts are allocated among the producers of consumers' goods by a single-currency competitive market.

The pattern of consumer supply is then determined so that the marginal rate of substitution in production between any two consumers' goods is equal to the ratio of their money prices. Since the structure of money prices is not changed by shifting from inconvertible rationing to convertible rationing, neither is the pattern of consumer supply changed. But rationing of either variety results in a pattern different from the one that would exist in the absence of rationing.

The change in resource allocation due to rationing is comparable to the change due to a system of excise taxes on rationed goods. This is clear in the case of convertible rationing, where the money cost of obtaining the ration currency needed to buy a unit of a commodity is a pseudo excise tax. These costs differ from real excise taxes in two respects: the rates are established in the market; and consumers are given a "subsidy", the money value of their ration incomes, equal to the "taxes" they pay. But they are like excise taxes in producing a divergence between the structure of prices effective for consumer choices and the structure facing producers.

Under certain assumptions, it is possible to argue that the allocation of resources is changed for the worse by rationing. The necessary assumptions are those which must be made to prove the allocative superiority of income taxation over excise taxation (Friedman 1952).[10] The conclusion that rationing distorts the allocation of resources depends on the absence of other sources of divergence between the relative price structures facing producers and consumers. Conceivably, resource allocation could be improved by rationing: for example, if a system of genuine excise taxes fell heavily on unrationed goods. In practice, however, rationing is not likely to improve resource allocation in this manner. For example, rationing only accentuates the distortion of resource allocation due to the fact that leisure is not taxed.

The argument of this section cannot prove that the situation of no rationing is one of greater economic welfare than the situation of rationing. The distribution of incomes is altered by rationing so that some consumers may be made better off even though rationing entails a departure from the conditions of optimum allocation. What may be argued is that there are alternative measures which would be of equal benefit to those who gain from rationing and would leave some other consumers better satisfied.

5.3. *The Rationing of Scarce Resources and the Setting of Points Prices*

The argument, of Section 5.2, against rationing on allocational grounds breaks down if resources are not competitively allocated among producers of consumers' goods. One particular departure from competition is of special interest, i.e., the rationing to producers of a factor of production. For various reasons which need not be discussed here, governments faced with severe scarcity of a factor of production prefer to allocate it by rationing than by the price system. Shipping space for wartime Britain, hard currencies for postwar Britain, steel and other metals in this country provide well-known examples.

What is the relationship of consumers' goods rationing to factor rationing? There are two related problems to which consumer rationing is relevant. One is to achieve equality among consumers in their indirect use of the scarce factor. The second is to make the rationing of the factor among different uses correspond to consumer preferences.

5.3.1. Assume that a factor of production is abnormally scarce and in inelastic supply. A competitive market would allocate the factor by bidding up its price. The conditions of an optimum allocation would be met, but there might be unwelcome distributional effects of two kinds. First, the owners of the scarce factor would enjoy large rents. Second, the consumption of products using the scarce factor would be confined to persons of high incomes. The first effect could be avoided, without any change in resource allocation, by a tax on the use of the factor. But consumer rationing is necessary to avoid the second effect. Rationing is the more necessary if the social objective is equality in opportunities to consume the goods that use the scarce factor, while inequality in money incomes is preserved. Can a rationing system accomplish this objective and at the same time meet the conditions of optimum allocation? To ask the same question another way, is it possible for a rationing system to have no allocative effects beyond those of an excise tax on the scarce factor?

Evidently, it is not wholly possible. So long as the principle of equality of ration incomes is respected, there must be some divergence between the relative price structure for consumers and the relative price structure for producers. But an integrated scheme of producer and consumer rationing can keep this divergence to a minimum. Such a scheme would have the following institutional features: (a) Consumers are allotted equal ration incomes applicable to goods which require the scarce factor in production. (b) Points prices of the rationed consumers' goods are proportional to their money prices. Money prices are free to be set in the competitive market. (c) Consumers pay for rationed goods in both ration currency and money. Producers are issued a ration currency applicable to the rationed factor in exchange for an equivalent amount of their ration currency receipts from consumers. (d) The money price of the rationed factor is controlled, but its ration price is set in the market. (e) Trade in coupons and money is permitted among consumers and, separately, among producers. But trade of this kind could not be permitted between producers and consumers without undermining the principle of equality of consumers' ration incomes. This principle would be violated if it were possible for producers to augment their ration incomes by using their receipts of ration currency in consumption. For this reason, it is essential that consumers' ration currency be canceled as soon as it has been used to buy consumers' goods and that the producers' ration currency for which it is exchanged be valid only for the purchase of the rationed factor.

This scheme would have the following consequences for the allocation of resources:

(1) The marginal rate of substitution between any two factors of production would be the same for all producers. Between two unrationed factors, it would be equal to their money–price ratio. Between the

rationed factor and unrationed factor, the common price ratio would reflect, in addition to the controlled money price of the rationed factor, the cost of obtaining the ration currency necessary to buy it. This cost is a pseudo excise tax on the rationed factor. These conditions meet the requirements for an optimum allocation of factors among products; no exchange of factors could increase the output of any product without decreasing the ouput of some other product.

The significance of (e), trade in coupons and money among producers, is to make the effective price ratio between rationed and unrationed factors the same for all producers. If producer rations were inconvertible, then, whether the source of producers' ration incomes were consumer purchases or arbitrary allocations, the marginal worth of ration currency would not be same for every producer. Consequently, the effective price of the rationed factor, for decisions concerning its use relative to other factors, would not be the same for all producers. The economy would be operating short of its production possibility locus.

(2) The marginal rate of substitution in production between any two rationed goods would be equal to their money–price ratio. The same is true for any two unrationed goods. Between a rationed good and un-rationed good, the effective price ratio for producers would reflect not only the money price of the rationed good but a pseudo subsidy equal to the value to producers of the ration currency earned by selling the rationed good.

(3) The marginal rate of substitution in consumption between any two rationed goods, or between any two unrationed goods, would be the same for all consumers and equal to their price ratio. For rationed goods, this is true because points prices are proportional to money prices, according to (b), and every consumer's marginal rate of substitution is equated, as shown in Section 2, to a weighted average of the money and points price ratios. The marginal rate of substitution in consumption between a rationed good and an unrationed good would reflect not only the money price of the rationed good but the cost of obtaining the ration currency necessary to buy it. This cost is a pseudo excise tax on rationed goods. Convertibility of consumer ration currency makes it the same for all consumers. Thus, the system meets the requirement that no exchange of goods among consumers could increase the utility of any consumer without decreasing the utility of someone else.

(4) The only departure from the conditions of optimal allocation is the possible divergence between the pseudo excise taxes of (3) and the pseudo subsidies of (2). That is, the money value of consumers' ration currency need not be the same as the money value of the equivalent amount of producers' ration currency. Thus, the marginal rate of substitution between rationed and unrationed goods is not the same in production as in consumption. Ration currency has less value in the producers' realm and, therefore, too few unrationed resources are devoted to the production of rationed goods. This is the price paid for the preservation of consumer equality.

(5) The rationing of the scarce factor works like an excise tax, not only in its effects on the demand for the factor but also in its effects on the incomes of owners of the scarce factor. Their rents are taxed away and distributed to consumers in the form of equal incomes.

5.3.2. The rationing system outlined above is a system of *value rationing* (see Section 1.2). Is this method of establishing points prices important, or would some other method do just as well? Any other method would lead to wider divergences between the relative price structures effective for consumers and producers. The effective price ratio between two rationed goods is of the form $(p_1 + \lambda p'_1)/(p_2 + \lambda p'_2)$, where p_1 and p_2 are the money prices, p'_1 and p'_2 the points prices of the two goods, and λ is the marginal worth of ration currency.[11] λ is, as noted above, not the same for producers and for consumers. Therefore the price ratio is not the same for producers and consumers except under value rationing, which sets $p'_1/p'_2 = p_1/p_2$. (Value rationing has an additional advantage if consumers' ration currency is not convertible. In that case λ would vary among consumers, and only under value rationing would the marginal rate of substitution between two rationed goods be the same for all consumers.)

This objection to other methods of establishing points prices applies to a principle recommended by several writers: Scitovsky (1942), Neisser (1943), and Graaff (1947–48). The principle is to set the points prices of a consumer's good in proportion to the input of the rationed factor required for its production. The motivation of this proposal is evidently to provide consumers with equality of command over the scarce resource, and possibly also to make allocations of the factor to producers responsive to consumers' preferences as expressed in their ration expenditures.

Both objectives can be accomplished, with better consequences for the allocation of resources, by the system of value rationing outlined above.

6. Further Problems

Outside the theory of rationing, as reviewed in this paper, stand certain possible effects of rationing on consumer behavior that, from the standpoint of the pure theory of choice, are either "irrational" or represent dynamic change in tastes. The mere fact that a good is rationed may cause a consumer to buy his full quota even though in a free market he would purchase less. A cartoon in *Punch* showed a housewife regarding a pantry full of margarine and explaining to her husband that she had just now realized she didn't *have* to take her weekly margarine ration. Experience under rationing may alter the consumer's scale of preferences. He may learn to like the pattern of expenditures into which rationing forces him, or to dislike it even more intensely than if it had not been forced upon him.

Finally, the individualistic approach of the theory of consumer choice and of welfare economics may well obscure social effects of rationing of much greater importance than the effects which our atomistic theory discloses. For example, the feeling of sharing equally in an emergency situation may be more important for production and welfare than the individual incentives and choices on which economic analysis has traditionally centered. The modification of the theory of consumer behavior to take account of interdependence among the preferences of different consumers has not been applied to rationing. Since rationing is egalitarian, its effects might look quite different if the arguments in the consumers' utility functions were not absolute physical quantities but, as in Duesenberry's theory (1949), were amounts relative to the consumption of others.

Appendix to Section 4.2

The household maximizes a utility function $u(x_1, x_2, x_3)$ subject to the constraints imposed by prices, wage rate, non-wage income, and rationing. Prior to the imposition of any measure to restrict consumption x_1, the household is subject to the constraint:

$$p_1 x_1 + p_2 x_2 + p_3 x_3 = p_3 M + Y. \tag{A.1}$$

Let x_{10}, x_{20}, x_{30} be the values which maximize u subject to (A.1). The three methods for reducing x_1 from x_{10} to X_1 correspond to the following three alternative new constraints:

$$x_1 = X_1, \qquad\qquad\qquad \text{(rationing)} \quad \text{(A.2r)}$$

$$p_1 x_1 + p_2 x_2 + p_3 x_3 = p_3 M + Y,$$

$$p_{1s} x_1 + p_2 x_2 + p_3 x_3 = p_3 M + Y, \quad \text{(spendings tax)} \quad \text{(A.2s)}$$

$$p_1 x_1 + p_2 x_2 + p_{3t} x_3 = p_{3t}(M + Y/p_3). \text{ (income tax) } \text{(A.2t)}$$

Maximization of u subject to (A.2r) leads to (X_1, x_{2r}, x_{3r}). p_{1s} is chosen so that maximization subject to (A.2s) leads to (X_1, x_{2s}, x_{3s}). p_{3t} is chosen so that maximization subject to (A.2t) leads to (X_1, x_{2t}, x_{3t}). The problem is to compare x_{3r}, x_{3s}, x_{3t}, the amounts of leisure "purchased" by the household when its consumption is restricted to X_1 by the three alternative measures.

It is assumed that the utility function is quadratic, so that maximization subject to (A.1) gives the following linear equations (in which $a_{ij} = a_{ji}$ and λ is a Lagrange multiplier, identified with the negative of the marginal utility of income):

$$(1, 2, 3) \quad a_{i1} x_{10} + a_{i2} x_{20} + a_{i3} x_{30} + p_i \lambda = a_i \quad (i = 1, 2, 3),$$

$$(4) \qquad p_1 x_{10} + p_2 x_{20} + p_3 x_{30} = p_3 M + Y. \tag{A.3}$$

Maximization subject to (4.2r), rationing, gives:

$$(2, 3) \quad a_{i1} X_1 + a_{i2} x_{2r} + a_{i3} x_{3r} + p_i \lambda_r = a_i \quad (i = 2, 3),$$

$$(4) \qquad p_1 X_1 + p_2 x_{2r} + p_3 x_{3r} = p_3 M + Y. \tag{A.4r}$$

Maximization subject to (4.2s), spendings tax, gives:

$$(1) \qquad a_{11} X_1 + a_{12} x_{2s} + a_{13} x_{3s} + p_{1s} \lambda_s = a_1,$$

$$(2, 3) \quad a_{i1} X_1 + a_{i2} x_{2s} + a_{i3} x_{3s} + p_i \lambda_s = a_i \quad (i = 2, 3)$$

$$(4) \qquad p_{1s} X_1 + p_2 x_{2s} + p_3 x_{3s} = p_3 M + Y.$$

$$\tag{A.4s}$$

Maximization subject to (4.2t), income tax, gives

$$(1, 2) \qquad a_{i1}X_1 + a_{i2}x_{2t} + a_{i3}x_{3t} + p_i\lambda_t = a_i \quad (i = 1, 2),$$

$$(3) \qquad a_{31}X_1 + a_{32}x_{2t} + a_{33}x_{3t} + p_{3t}\lambda_t = a_3,$$

$$(4) \qquad p_1X_1 + p_2x_{2t} + p_{3t}x_{3t} = p_{3t}(M + Y/p_3). \qquad \text{(A.4t)}$$

Let A be the determinant of (4.3):

$$\begin{vmatrix} a_{11} & a_{12} & a_{13} & p_1 \\ a_{21} & a_{22} & a_{23} & p_2 \\ a_{31} & a_{32} & a_{33} & p_3 \\ p_1 & p_2 & p_3 & 0 \end{vmatrix}.$$

Let K_{ij} be the cofactor of the element in the ith row and jth column of A, divided by A.

Following are the relationships between the change in purchase of leisure x_3 and the change in purchase of scarce consumption goods x_1, under the three alternatives:

$$\frac{x_{3r} - x_{30}}{X_1 - x_{10}} = K_{13}/K_{11}, \qquad \text{(A.5r)}$$

$$\frac{x_{3s} - x_{30}}{X_1 - x_{10}} = \frac{\lambda_s K_{13} + X_1 K_{43}}{\lambda_s K_{11} + X_1 K_{41}}, \qquad \text{(A.5s)}$$

$$\frac{x_{3t} - x_{30}}{X_1 - x_{10}} = \frac{\lambda_t K_{33} + (x_{3t} - M - Y/p_3)K_{43}}{\lambda_t K_{31} + (x_{3t} - M - Y/p_3)K_{41}}. \qquad \text{(A.5t)}$$

Proof of (A.5r): Subtract each equation in (A.4r) from the correspondingly numbered equation in (A.3). We have

$$a_{i2}(x_{20} - x_{2r}) + a_{i3}(x_{30} - x_{3r}) + p_i(\lambda - \lambda_r) = -a_{i1}(x_{10} - X_1)$$
$$(i = 2, 3),$$

$$p_2(x_{20} - x_{2r}) + p_3(x_{30} - x_{3r}) = -p_1(x_{10} - X_1).$$

Solving these three equations for $(x_{30} - x_{3r})$ gives (4.5r).

Proof of (A.5s): Subtract each equation in (A.4s) from the corresponding equation in (A.3). We have

$$a_{11}(x_{10} - X_1) + a_{12}(x_{20} - x_{2s}) + a_{13}(x_{30} - x_{3s})$$
$$+ p_1(\lambda - \lambda_s) = \lambda_s(p_{1s} - p_1),$$

$$a_{i1}(x_{10} - X_1) + a_{i2}(x_{20} - x_{2s}) + a_{i3}(x_{30} - x_{3s})$$
$$+ p_i(\lambda - \lambda_s) = 0 \quad (i = 2, 3),$$

$$p_1(x_{10} - X_1) + p_2(x_{20} - x_{2s}) + p_3(x_{30} - x_{3s}) = X_1(p_{1s} - p_1).$$

Solving these four equations gives $(x_{30} - x_{3s})/(p_{1s} - p_1)$ equal to the numerator of (A.5s) and $(x_{10} - X_1)/(p_{1s} - p_1)$ equal to the denominator.

Proof of (A.5t): Subtract each equation in (A.4t) from the corresponding equation in (A.3). We have

$$a_{i1}(x_{10} - X_1) + a_{i2}(x_{20} - x_{2t}) + a_{i3}(x_{30} - x_{3t})$$
$$+ p_i(\lambda - \lambda_t) = 0 \quad (i = 1, 2),$$

$$a_{31}(x_{10} - X_1) + a_{32}(x_{20} - x_{2t}) + a_{33}(x_{30} - x_{3t})$$
$$+ p_3(\lambda - \lambda_t) = \lambda_t(p_{3t} - p_3),$$

$$p_1(x_{10} - X_1) + p_2(x_{20} - x_{2t}) + p_3(x_{30} - x_{3t})$$
$$= (x_{3t} - M - Y/p_3)(p_{3t} - p_3).$$

Solving these four equations gives $(x_{30} - x_{3t})/(p_{3t} - p_3)$ equal to the numerator of (A.5t) and $(x_{10} - X_1)/(p_{3t} - p_3)$ equal to the denominator.

From (A.5) we obtain

$$\frac{x_{3r} - x_{30}}{x_{3s} - x_{30}} = \frac{\lambda_s K_{11} K_{13} + X_1 K_{41} K_{13}}{\lambda_s K_{11} K_{13} + X_1 K_{43} K_{11}}, \qquad \text{(A.6rs)}$$

$$\frac{x_{3r} - x_{30}}{x_{3t} - x_{30}} = \frac{\lambda_t K_{13}^2 + (x_{3t} - M - Y/p_3) K_{41} K_{13}}{\lambda_t K_{11} K_{33} + (x_{3t} - M - Y/p_3) K_{43} K_{11}}. \qquad \text{(A.6rt)}$$

If it is possible to determine whether expressions (A.6) are greater or smaller than one, it is possible to determine whether more or less leisure is taken under rationing than under the alternative policies. The following things are known about the components of (A.6), either from the assumptions of the problem or from the secondary conditions for a maximum in the initial situation (A.3): $\lambda_s, \lambda_t < 0$; $K_{11}, K_{33} < 0$; $X_1 > 0$; $(x_{3t} - M - Y/p_3) < 0$; $K_{11} K_{33} > K_{13}^2$. We may assume further that x_1 is not an *inferior* good; consequently a rise, not a fall, in its own price is required to restrict its consumption, and the denominator of (A.5s) is positive. Moreover, the incentive problem to which the argument is directed arises only if leisure and consumption are substitutes, i.e., K_{13} is positive. This means that $(x_{3r} - x_{30})$ is, of course, positive. It also means that the common first term of both numerator and denominator in (A.6rs) is positive. Consequently,

$$x_{3r} \gtreqless x_{3s} \quad \text{as} \quad K_{41}K_{13} \gtreqless K_{43}K_{11}. \tag{A.7}$$

Now on our assumptions $K_{41}K_{13}$ is positive. (K_{41} is the derivative of demand for x_1 with respect to income, and we have assumed that x_1 is not an *inferior* good.) Provided leisure is likewise not an *inferior* good (i.e., provided K_{43} is positive), $K_{43}K_{11}$ is negative and x_{3r} must exceed x_{3s}. Less work is done under rationing than under a spendings tax. (If leisure is an *inferior* good, the opposite result is possible, but not necessary.)

Turning to (A.6rt), the first terms in both numerator and denominator are negative, and the term in the denominator is numerically the larger of the two. The numerator as a whole is negative; by assumption it takes a reduction in the wage rate and in money income, not an increase, to restrict consumption of x_1. The second term in the numerator is, on our assumptions, negative. If leisure is a *superior* good, the second term in the denominator is positive. But since the first term in the denominator is numerically larger than the first term in the numerator, no general conclusion can be drawn. Restriction of demand by income taxation may result in a greater or smaller shift from work to leisure than restriction by rationing. (If leisure is an *inferior* good, either result is still possible, but it becomes more likely that the comparison is favorable to the tax.)

The meaning of "superior" and "inferior" in the present context needs clarification, because money income is not a parameter to the consumer, as it is in the usual analysis of consumer choice. Here a good is *superior* (*inferior*) if, at given prices and wage rate, an increase in that part of money income which is independent of the consumer's choice between work and leisure, would increase (decrease) his consumption of the good.

References

Duesenberry, J.S., *Income, Saving, and the Theory of Consumer Behavior* (Cambridge, Mass.: Harvard University Press, 1949), 128 pp.

Friedman, M., "The 'Welfare' Effects of an Income Tax and an Excise Tax," *Journal of Political Economy*, 60 (February 1952), 25-33.

Graaff, J. de V., "Rothbarth's 'Virtual Price System' and the Slutsky Equation." *Review of Economic Studies*, 15, No. 38 (1947-48), 91-95.

Graaff, J. de V., "Towards an Austerity Theory of Value," *South African Journal of Economics*, 16 (March 1948), 35-50.

Haraldson, W.C., "A Note on Welfare Economics and Rationing," *Quarterly Journal of Economics*, 58 (November 1943), 146-48.

Kaldor, N., "Rationing and the Cost of Living Index," *Review of Economic Studies*, 8, No. 3 (June 1941), 185-87.

Kalecki, M., "General Rationing," Oxford Institute of Statistics: *Studies in War Economics* (Oxford: Blackwell, 1947), 137-41.

Kershaw, J.A. and H. Alpert, "The Invalidation of Ration Currency," *Journal of Social Issues* (Fall 1947), 40-48.

Lerner, A.P., *The Economics of Control* (New York: The Macmillan Co., 1944), xxii + 428 pp., 50-54.

Lloyd, E.M.H., "Some Notes on Point Rationing," *Review of Economic Statistics*, 24 (May 1942), 49-52.

Makower, H., "Rationing and Value Theory," *Review of Economic Studies*, 13, No. 34 (1945-46), 75-80.

Malmquist, S., *A Statistical Analysis of the Demand for Liquor in Sweden* (Uppsala: Apelbergs Boktryckeriaktiebalag, 1948), 135 pp.

Neisser, H.P., "Theoretical Aspects of Rationing," *Quarterly Journal of Economics*, 57 (May 1943), 378-97.

Nicholson, J.L., "Rationing and Index Numbers," *Review of Economic Studies*, 10 (Winter 1942-43), 68-72.

Reder, M.W., "Welfare Economics and Rationing," *Quarterly Journal of Economics*, 57 (November 1942), 153-59.

Rothbarth, E., "The Measurement of Changes in Real Income under Conditions of Rationing," *Review of Economic Studies*, 8 (February 1941), 100-107.

Rothschild, K.W., "Rationing and the Consumer," *Oxford Economic Papers*, No. 7 (March 1945), 67-82.

Samuelson, P.A., *Foundations of Economic Analysis* (Cambridge, Mass.: Harvard University Press, 1947), xii + 447 pp., 163-71.

Scitovsky, T. de, "The Political Economy of Consumers' Rationing," *Review of Economic Statistics*, 24 (August 1942), 114-24.

Scitovsky, T. de, E. Shaw, and L. Tarshis, *Mobilizing Resources for War* (New York: McGraw-Hill, 1951), x + 284 pp.

Tobin, J. and H.S. Houthakker, "The Effects of Rationing on Demand Elasticities," *Review of Economic Studies*, 18, No. 3 (November 1951), 140-153.

Worswick, G.D.N., "Points, Prices, and Consumers' Choice," *Oxford Institute of Statistics Bulletin*, 6 (February 1944), 33-39.

Notes

[1] The Scitovsky proposal mentioned above would not permit future use of unused expenditure rations; but interest on the associated money saving would increase future money incomes and, therefore, future expenditure rations.

[2] During World War II, O.P.A. suddenly invalidated without notice sugar stamps which housewives had been saving. Public opinion, though momentarily indignant, reacted much less violently than if an outstanding issue of Federal Reserve Notes should suddenly be declared worthless (see Kershaw and Alpert 1947).

[3] There have been, however, various proposals for systems in which ration currency not merely supplements but replaces money for certain transactions. Of these, the most drastic was the proposal of Colin Clark, reported by Scitovsky (1942, p. 119), to suspend the use of money in favor of ration currency for the duration of the war. Scitovsky's own proposal envisages a more limited replacement of money, in which consumers buy their ration incomes from the state and sellers of consumers' goods redeem their ration currency receipts. See also the discussion of "over-all rationing" by Neisser (1943).

[4] Trade in rationed commodities is equivalent to trade in ration currencies (see Section 2.3 above), so long as rationed commodities cannot be obtained from producers without ration currency. The discussion will therefore apply to all *black market* transactions among consumers, but not to the blacker market in which goods move from producers to consumers, by-passing the rationing mechanism.

[5] On the functions of rationing in promoting public health and educating consumer tastes, see Scitovsky (1942).

[6] The existence of such a price is assured by the fact that the derivative of demand for a commodity with respect to a compensated change in its own price is necessarily negative. A rise in the price of the ration of a commodity amounts to a compensated change in its price.

[7] Convertibility may be advocated on egalitarian grounds in order to give consumers who are too poor to utilize their rations, the chance to sell part of their surplus coupons for money that will enable them to use the rest of the surplus themselves. [Thus Kalecki (1947) proposed that the rationing authority offer to redeem coupons for money up to a limit for each person of half the ration.] Neisser (1943, pp. 396-97) after making this argument worries about the increase in points prices that would occur if the poor sold to other consumers. He fears that they might lose in this way as much as or more than they gain from selling. This fear seems unfounded. Real income, measured in terms of the cost of buying the bill of goods received under inconvertible rationing, remains the same for the community as a whole and decreases for those who are using their full rations. It must increase for some consumers. The biggest gainers are those – the lowest-income groups in Neisser's argument – who have the most unused coupons to sell. The consumers who will be squeezed are those who, whether by income or by taste, were just about satisfied with the ration. They will be forced to reduce their consumption of rationed goods both by the sellers of coupons, who have increased real incomes, and by the buyers of coupons, who value the rationed goods so highly that they increase their consumption of them in spite of their loss of real income. (Kalecki's proposal would remove the second source of pressure, since coupons would only be sold to the state and canceled.)

[8] The existence of a points price ratio which satisfies both of these conditions is assured by the argument of note 6.

[9] Thus Neisser's fear (1943, p. 391) that consolidation of rations may force a consumer unwillingly to reduce his consumption of a specific good has justification. For this reason,

he prefers a number of ration currencies, convertible into each other, to a single currency for all rationed goods. A similar argument is behind Scitovsky's principle that substitutes should be grouped but complements rationed separately. Graaff (1948) makes an eloquent plea for consolidation of rations into a single points currency. In claiming that multiplicity of ration currencies "must result in a less favoured pattern of expenditure for each consumer" (p. 46), he apparently ignores the reservations mentioned in the text and in this note.

[10] Reder (1942) argues that, of three possible methods of reducing a single consumer's purchase of a particular commodity to a given amount – rationing, excise tax, and income tax – rationing would leave the consumer on the highest indifference curve and income tax on the lowest. This argument depends on the assumption that the consumer's money income before taxes and the prices of all consumers' goods are the same in all three situations. Rationing then permits the consumer to purchase unrationed goods with money which he would otherwise have to pay in taxes. As Friedman has shown, it is dangerous to draw welfare conclusions for the whole economy from arguments of this kind. The choices open to the economy are exaggerated by the assumption of constant money income and prices. If the consumption of a good must be restricted, it is because productive resources are being withdrawn from production for consumers; these resources are not available to expand the output of unrationed consumers' goods. A true comparison of the three methods must assume that the same quantities of resources are available in all three cases. It then appears, as indicated in the text, that rationing is equivalent to excise taxation and that both are inferior, so far as allocation is concerned, to income taxation (see also Haraldson, 1943).

[11] For a producer, λ is the addition to profit which an increment of ration income would make possible. When trade among producers in ration currency and money is permitted, λ becomes equal to the price of ration currency for all producers. For consumers, λ is the ratio of the marginal utility of ration income to the marginal utility of money income.

CHAPTER 40

THE EFFECTS OF RATIONING ON DEMAND ELASTICITIES

1. What are the effects of rationing on the elasticities of demand for unrationed goods? How should elasticities observed under a régime of partial rationing be expected to differ from those observed in a free market? This question is of practical interest to the econometrician who would like to use in building his statistical demand functions the well-documented experience under rationing during and since the war. Unfortunately we cannot provide here a practical method for assimilating such data to free market records. We shall, however, present some theorems, derived from the pure theory of consumer behaviour, on the relationships between demand elasticities under rationing and those in a free market. These relationships are expressed entirely in terms of quantities which can in principle be observed and measured, either during rationing or in a free market. In this respect they are on the same plane as similar theorems – e.g. the Slutsky equation – from the theory of consumer choice in a free market and are neither more nor less helpful to the econometric investigation of demand.

2. Specifically, we shall investigate the relationships between the effects on demand during rationing [1] of changes in prices, incomes, and rations and the effects on demand in a free market of changes in prices and incomes. We shall rely on the mathematical theory of consumer choice but the essential key to the relationships we shall develop is intuitively obvious. A housewife may obtain less sugar either because it is rationed and the ration is curtailed or because, in a free market, its price goes up. In either case she will tend to make up for this deprivation by buying more jam and sweets, assuming these are unrationed – partly

By James Tobin and H.S. Houthakker. Reprinted from *Review of Economic Studies*, 18 (1951), 1-14.

at the expense of goods which are complementary to sugar, say, margarine and lard. The same basic relations of substitution and complementarity between goods are displayed in either case. The two events – a ration change and a price change in a free market – do have different income effects, but these are not difficult to sort out. The key to the problem is the basic similarity of the substitution effects.

3. Let us attempt to make more precise the relationship between (a) the effect, in a régime of partial rationing, on the demand for a given unrationed commodity, say, jam, of a change in the ration of another good, say, sugar, and (b) the effect, in a free market, on the demand for jam of a change in the price of sugar. Both of these effects are in principle observable and measurable; the practical statistical difficulties of measuring either of them from time series are, of course, formidable, but these do not concern us here. Assume that sugar is the only rationed commodity; the theory does not differ essentially in the more complicated case where several commodities are rationed, and this case is discussed in the Appendix. Suppose that the sugar ration q_n is changed by a small amount dq_n. Denote the consumer's income by M and the price of sugar by p_n. The income $(M - p_n q_n)$ available for the purchase of unrationed goods is changed by the amount $-p_n\,dq_n$. Imagine now the change dp_n in the sugar price and the change dM in the consumer's income which in a free market would (1) induce the consumer to change his sugar consumption x_n by exactly the same amount as the change dq_n in the ration, and (2) change the amount which the consumer would spend on goods other than sugar by exactly the same amount, $-p_n\,dq_n$, as in the case of rationing. These imagined, or virtual, changes in price and income, which together are the free market equivalent of a change in the ration, depend on two characteristics of the consumer's free market demand function for sugar: its derivatives with respect to sugar price and income, $\partial x_n/\partial p_n$ and $\partial x_n/\partial M$. We have:

$$dx_n = dq_n. \tag{1}$$

The imagined change in free market sugar consumption is to be equal to the change in the ration.

$$dx_n = \frac{\partial x_n}{\partial p_n}\,dp_n + \frac{\partial x_n}{\partial M}\,dM. \tag{2}$$

This change in the free market demand could be accomplished by changes in sugar price and in income, in amounts which depend on the price and income derivatives of the demand function for sugar.

$$d(M - p_n x_n) = - p_n \, dq_n. \tag{3}$$

The imagined free market change in expenditure on other commodities due to these changes in sugar price and in income is to be the same as the one caused by the change in the sugar ration.

From (3) we see that the change in income which we must imagine to accompany our virtual change in price is an old friend to students of *Value and Capital*. It is simply the change in income which would permit the consumer to buy, if he chose to, the same bundle of sugar and other commodities after the price change as before. For, from (3) we have:

$$dM - x_n \, dp_n - p_n \, dx_n = - p_n \, dx_n$$

or

$$dM - x_n \, dp_n = 0. \tag{4}$$

A price change accompanied by such a change in income is called a "compensated price change".

Consequently, we can find from (2) the amount of the virtual price change required to alter sugar consumption by the same amount as the change in the ration. Substituting (1) and (4) in (3), we have:

$$dq_n = \frac{\partial x_n}{\partial p_n} dp_n + x_n \frac{\partial x_n}{\partial M} dp_n,$$

or

$$dp_n = \frac{1}{\partial x_n/\partial p_n + x_n(\partial x_n/\partial M)} dq_n. \tag{5}$$

The expression in the denominator of (5) is a characteristic of the consumer's free market demand function for sugar: the measure of the effect on sugar demand of a compensated change in sugar price.

What we are seeking is a way of measuring, in terms of characteristics of the consumer's free market demand functions, the effect of a change in the sugar ration on the demand x_i for an unrationed commodity, jam. We have now found, in (5), the free market equivalent of a change in the sugar ration: a compensated change in sugar price which has the same effect as the ration change both on sugar consumption and on other expenditure. The only remaining step, therefore, is to evaluate the effect on jam demand of this free market equivalent, the compensated change in sugar price. This depends on two characteristics of free market demand function for jam: its derivatives with respect to the price of sugar and with respect to income:

$$dx_i = \frac{\partial x_i}{\partial p_n} dp_n + \frac{\partial x_i}{\partial M} dM \qquad (6)$$

or, by (4),

$$dx_i = \frac{\partial x_i}{\partial p_n} dp_n + x_n \frac{\partial x_i}{\partial M} dp_n. \qquad (7)$$

Combining (5) and (7), we obtain:

$$\frac{dx_i}{dq_n} = \frac{\partial x_i/\partial p_n + x_n(\partial x_i/\partial M)}{\partial x_n/\partial p_n + x_n(\partial x_n/\partial M)}, \qquad (8)$$

or, in words,

$$\frac{\text{effect on demand for jam}}{\text{of change in sugar ration}} = \frac{\text{effect on demand for jam of compensated change in sugar price}}{\text{effect on demand for sugar of compensated change in sugar price}}.$$

The expression in the numerator of (8) is a measure of the substitutability of jam for sugar. It is negative if the two commodities are substitutes, positive if they are complements. The expression in the denominator is never positive.[2]

It follows, therefore, that a reduction in the sugar ration – prices and income remaining unchanged – will increase the consumption of unrationed substitutes and diminish the demand for unrationed complements. But the main significance of the result is not this intuitively obvious proposition but the demonstration that the effect of a ration change may be described in terms of the conventional characteristics of free market demand functions.

4. We must now consider certain other characteristics of a consumer's demand function for jam, an unrationed commodity, under a régime of sugar rationing. Specifically, what are the effects of changes in the prices

of sugar, jam, and other unrationed goods and of changes in income? How are these effects related to the corresponding characteristics of the jam demand function in the free market? In answering these questions, our success in Section 3 in finding an expression for the one characteristic of the demand function under rationing which has no free market counterpart will be of considerable help. Let us call the expression we have denoted by dx_i/dq_n in (8) $\boldsymbol{dx_i/dq_n}$ from now on, using bold type d's in the expression which measures the effect of a change in the ration when other determinants of demand, prices and income, are held constant, to indicate that this is a characteristic of a demand function modified by rationing and not of a free market demand function.

First let us consider the effect, during sugar rationing, of a change in the consumer's income on his demand for jam. The effect will not be the same as in a free market, where the consumer would be free to respond to a rise in income by increasing his sugar consumption. This increase in sugar expenditure, which rationing prohibits, will be diverted to other commodities, especially to commodities like jam, which are good substitutes for sugar. The income-elasticity of the demand for jam will, accordingly, be larger during sugar rationing than in a free market. It is also true, but less obvious, that the income-elasticity of demand for a complement of sugar, say butter, is diminished by sugar rationing.

A precise determination of the effect of rationing on income-elasticity may be achieved by means of the same device of imagination employed in Section 3. Suppose that, under sugar rationing, there is a small increase $\boldsymbol{dM}$ in the consumer's income. He cannot, of course, increase his consumption of sugar. The amount of his income available for expenditure on other commodities is increased by the full $\boldsymbol{dM}$. In a free market, what changes dp_n in the price of sugar and dM in his income would have the equivalent effects: (1) of inducing no change in sugar consumption, and (2) of providing him with an increase equal to $\boldsymbol{dM}$ in expenditure on other commodities? Finally, what change in the consumption of jam would be induced in a free market by these imagined equivalent changes in sugar price and in income? This will be what we are seeking – the change in the consumption of jam due to an increase in income during sugar rationing. We have, then:

$$dx_n = dq_n = 0. \tag{9}$$

Sugar consumption cannot be changed, as the ration is constant.

$$dx_n = \frac{\partial x_n}{\partial p_n} dp_n + \frac{\partial x_n}{\partial M} dM. \tag{10}$$

Same as (2),

$$d(M - x_n p_n) = \boldsymbol{dM}. \tag{11}$$

The virtual free market change in expenditure on other commodities is to be equal to the assumed increase in income under rationing.

$$\boldsymbol{dx_i} = \frac{\partial x_i}{\partial p_n} dp_n + \frac{\partial x_i}{\partial M} dM. \tag{12}$$

Same as (6).

From (11), using (9), we have:

$$dM = \boldsymbol{dM} + x_n \, dp_n. \tag{13}$$

Substituting (9) and (13) in (10) we obtain:

$$\frac{\partial x_n}{\partial p_n} dp_n + \frac{\partial x_n}{\partial M} \boldsymbol{dM} + x_n \frac{\partial x_n}{\partial M} dp_n = 0,$$

or,

$$dp_n = \frac{-\partial x_n/\partial M}{\partial x_n/\partial p_n + x_n(\partial x_n/\partial M)} \boldsymbol{dM} \tag{14}$$

and, substituting (14) in (13), we obtain:

$$dM = \frac{\partial x_n/\partial p_n}{\partial x_n/\partial p_n + x_n(\partial x_n/\partial M)} \boldsymbol{dM}. \tag{15}$$

(14) and (15) are the virtual equivalent price and income changes which we are seeking. We can assess their effects on jam demand by making use of (12):

$$\frac{\boldsymbol{dx_i}}{\boldsymbol{dM}} = \frac{-\partial x_i/\partial p_n \, \partial x_n/\partial M + \partial x_i/\partial M \, \partial x_n/\partial p_n}{\partial x_n/\partial p_n + x_n(\partial x_n/\partial M)}. \tag{16}$$

(16) gives the effect of a change in income on the demand for jam during sugar rationing, in terms of characteristics of the free market demand functions for sugar and jam. Since we are interested in comparing this constrained effect of a change in income with the unconstrained response to income change in a free market, let us subtract from both sides of (16) the free market income-derivative of the jam demand function $\partial x_i / \partial M$. This gives us:

$$\frac{dx_i}{dM} - \frac{\partial x_i}{\partial M} = -\frac{\partial x_i/\partial p_n + x_n(\partial x_i/\partial M)}{\partial x_n/\partial p_n + x_n(\partial x_n/\partial M)} \frac{\partial x_n}{\partial M}. \tag{17}$$

The fraction in this expression is already familiar to us from Section 3. Using (8), we arrive at:

$$\frac{dx_i}{dM} - \frac{\partial x_i}{\partial M} = -\frac{dx_i}{dq_n} \frac{\partial x_n}{\partial M}. \tag{18}$$

Unless the rationed good is in the free market an inferior good (so that $\partial x_n/\partial M$ is negative), we know from Section 3 that (18) will be positive for a pair of substitutes and negative for a pair of complements. This confirms the statement made at the beginning of this section concerning the effects of rationing on income-elasticities.

5. By the same method employed in Sections 3 and 4 – the method of imagining, for any given change in the determinants of demand during rationing, those changes in the price of the rationed good and in income which would in a free market have equivalent effects both on the consumption of the rationed good and on total expenditure on other commodities – it is possible to derive expressions for the other characteristics of demand functions during rationing. It would be both tedious and superfluous to give the details of these derivations. The theorems are in any case proved in the Appendix with greater mathematical rigour and for the general case where more than one commodity is rationed. The results are of the same form as the comparison (18) between the income-derivative in the free market and during rationing. They are summarized by:

$$\frac{dx_i}{dp_j} - \frac{\partial x_i}{\partial p_j} = -\frac{dx_i}{dq_n} \frac{\partial x_n}{\partial p_j}. \tag{19}$$

For example:

effect on demand for jam of change in price of but- ter when sugar is rationed	effect on demand for jam of change in price of but- ter in a free market =

$-$ effect on demand for jam of change in sugar ration $\times$ effect on demand for sugar of change in price of butter in a free market.

Relationship (19) is quite general. It holds:

   (a) when $i = j$; i.e., for own-price derivatives;

   (b) when $i \neq j$; i.e., for cross-price derivatives;

   (c) when $j = n$; i.e., when the commodity whose price changes is the rationed good itself;

   (d) when $i = n$; in this case the equation is true, since $dx_n/dq_n = 1$, but trivial.

(19) refers to *ceteris paribus* price-derivatives, which measure the effect on demand of a change in some price when all other prices and income remain constant. From (19) and (18) a similar relationship may be derived for compensated price-derivatives, which measure the effect of a change in some price accompanied by a compensating change in income, as explained in Section 3:

$$\left(\frac{dx_i}{dp_j} + x_j\frac{dx_i}{dM}\right) - \left(\frac{\partial x_i}{\partial p_j} + x_j\frac{\partial x_i}{\partial M}\right) = -\frac{dx_i}{dq_n}\left(\frac{\partial x_n}{\partial p_j} + x_j\frac{\partial x_n}{\partial M}\right)$$

$$(20)$$

(20) has the same general applicability as (19).

   Particular interest attaches to the special case $(i = j)$ of compensated own-price derivatives. Here it is possible, as is proved in the Appendix, to make a general statement: rationing will always increase algebraically (reduce numerically) the effect on x_j of a compensated change in its own price. This is true whether the rationed good x_n is an "inferior" or "superior" good and whatever the relationship – substitutability or complementarity – between x_j and x_n. It is also shown in the Appendix that the compensated own-price derivative will always be smaller (numerically) the greater the number of rationed goods. No such general rule applies to the *ceteris paribus* own-price derivative. Rationing, as we have just seen, reduces the "substitution effect", but we learned in Section 4 that it normally increases the "income effect".

6. The preceding discussion has assumed that only one commodity is rationed. If rationing is more general, the relationships are more complicated. In particular, the effect of a change in a ration on the demand for an unrationed commodity does not have the simple interpretation of Section 3. It depends not only on the characteristics of the free market demand functions involving the two commodities directly concerned – in our example, sugar and jam – but also on characteristics of demand functions involving the remaining rationed commodities. But once this ration-derivative is known, the other relationships are straightforward extensions of those given for the single-ration case in Sections 4 and 5: the extensions of (18), (19) and (20), respectively, are given below; the proofs are reserved for the Appendix. It is assumed that goods $m + 1$, $m + 2, \ldots, n$ are rationed, and goods $1, 2, \ldots, m$ are unrationed.

$$\frac{dx_i}{dM} - \frac{\partial x_i}{\partial M} = - \sum_{k=m+1}^{n} \frac{dx_i}{dq_k} \frac{\partial x_k}{\partial M}, \tag{21}$$

$$\frac{dx_i}{dp_j} - \frac{\partial x_i}{\partial p_j} = - \sum_{k=m+1}^{n} \frac{dx_i}{dq_k} \frac{\partial x_k}{\partial p_j}, \tag{22}$$

$$\left(\frac{dx_i}{dp_j} + x_j \frac{dx_i}{dM}\right) - \left(\frac{\partial x_i}{\partial p_j} + x_j \frac{\partial x_i}{\partial M}\right) = - \sum_{k=m+1}^{n} \frac{dx_i}{dq_k}\left(\frac{\partial x_k}{\partial p_j} + x_j \frac{\partial x_k}{\partial M}\right). \tag{23}$$

All these results can be easily expressed in terms of elasticities instead of derivatives. For this purpose, we adopt the following notation:

$\eta_{i0} = \partial x_i/\partial M \; M/x_i =$ income elasticity of demand for the ith good, in a free market.

$\eta'_{i0} = dx_i/dM \; M/x_i =$ the corresponding elasticity under rationing.

$\eta_{ij} = \partial x_i/\partial p_j \; p_j/x_i =$ elasticity of demand for the ith good with respect to the price of the jth good, in a free market.

$\eta'_{ij} = dx_i/dp_j \; p_j/x_i =$ the corresponding elasticity under rationing.

$\eta'_{iq_k} = dx_i/dq_k \; q_k/x_i =$ the elasticity of demand for the ith good with respect to the ration of the kth good.

$w_i = p_i x_i/M =$ the proportion of total income devoted to expenditure on the ith good.

Then the counterparts of (21), (22) and (23) are

$$\eta'_{io} - \eta_{io} = - \sum_{k=m+1}^{n} \eta'_{iq_k} \eta_{ko}. \tag{21a}$$

$$\eta'_{ij} - \eta_{ij} = - \sum_{k=m+1}^{n} \eta'_{iq_k} \eta_{kj}. \tag{22a}$$

$$\left(\frac{\eta'_{ij}}{w_j} + \eta'_{io} \right) - \left(\frac{\eta_{ij}}{w_j} + \eta_{io} \right) = - \sum_{k=m+1}^{n} \eta'_{iq_k} \left(\frac{\eta_{kj}}{w_j} + \eta_{ko} \right). \tag{23a}$$

7. The theory makes possible comparison of demand elasticities not only as between a régime of rationing and a free market, but also as between one régime of rationing and another. As an example, suppose that in one régime x_n is rationed but x_k is not and in another both x_n and x_k are rationed. What is the effect of rationing x_k on the response of the demand for an unrationed good, x_j, to a change in the ration of x_n? The answer is given by the following equation:

$$\left(\frac{dx_j}{dq_n} \right)_{k,n} - \left(\frac{dx_j}{dq_n} \right)_n = - \left(\frac{dx_j}{dq_k} \right)_{k,n} \left(\frac{dx_k}{dq_n} \right)_n; \tag{24}$$

where, for example, $(dx_j/dq_n)_{k,n}$ refers to the régime in which both x_k and x_n are rationed. This equation holds for the addition of one good x_k to the ration list no matter how many other goods are rationed along with x_n. This relationship is the key to finding the effects on income and price derivatives or elasticities of changes in the list of rationed goods.

8. A serious limitation of the theory developed in this paper is the mathematically necessary assumption that the starting point [3] from which we measure changes in a consumer's demand is the same under rationing as in a free market. This assumption is necessitated by the fact that the derivatives and elasticities which we wish to compare are themselves functions of quantities, prices, and income. Their values in two situations cannot be compared unless they refer to a common point. The assumption means that, in our theory, the restraints imposed by rationing have the odd implication that rationing may not only deny desired goods to consumers but force unwanted goods upon them.

Consequently, our results strictly correspond to the usual meaning of "rationing" only for those changes in the determinants of demand which would cause the free demand for every rationed good to exceed the ration.

To make statements relevant to the more interesting situation, where rationing places the consumer at quite a different point from that which he would choose in a free market, it seems necessary to place restrictions on the consumer's utility function or, what amounts to the same thing, to place restrictions, additional to those implied by the theory of consumer's choice, on his demand functions. Actually in usual econometric work on consumer demand such restrictions are inevitably assumed. For example, some or all of the derivatives or elasticities of demand functions are taken to be constants. If the econometrician dealing with rationing experience as well as free market data is willing to permit himself similar latitude, he may be able to apply the comparative relationships which will be developed below, even though the commodity points at which consumers find themselves under rationing are rarely duplicated in a free market.

9. This paper has attempted to show how the characteristics of demand functions which interest the economist and econometrician – derivatives and elasticities with respect to prices and income – are altered by partial rationing. The derivatives and elasticities in a free market situation can be compared with those in a régime of rationing; and in Section 7 it is shown that similar comparisons can be made between two different rationing situations. These relationships are meaningful implications of the theory of consumer behaviour; they can, at least in principle, be refuted by observations which can be made either during rationing or in a free market. It is this important fact which may make them of some value to statistical estimation of demand functions. For better or for worse, controls such as rationing can no longer be regarded as unusual and temporary. If we regard experience under controls as distorted and discard it as irrelevant to our science, we cut ourselves off from a major source of modern empirical material. It is hoped that this paper goes a small way towards showing how that material may be used.

Appendix

A1. We make the customary assumption that in a free market a consumer maximizes a utility function $u(x_1, \ldots, x_n)$, where x_i is his consumption of the ith good, subject to the condition $\sum_{i=1}^{n} p_i x_i = M$, where p_i is the price of the ith good and M is the consumer's income. We define U as the $n + 1$-rowed determinant:

$$
\begin{vmatrix}
0 & u_1 & u_2 & \cdots & u_n \\
u_1 & u_{11} & u_{12} & \cdots & u_{1n} \\
u_2 & u_{21} & u_{22} & \cdots & u_{2n} \\
\vdots & \vdots & \vdots & & \vdots \\
u_n & u_{n1} & u_{n2} & \cdots & u_{nn}
\end{vmatrix}
$$

and $U_{ij}(i, j = 0, 1, 2, \ldots, n)$ as the co-factor of the element of U in the ith row and jth column. Further, we define $U_{i_1 j_1 i_2 j_2 \cdots i_m j_m}$ as the co-factor resulting from deleting from U rows $i_1, i_2, \ldots, i_m$ and columns $j_1, j_2, \ldots, j_m$. Clearly this symbol has meaning only if $i_1 \neq i_2 \neq \cdots \neq i_m$ and $j_1 \neq j_2 \neq \cdots \neq j_m$ and $m \leq n$.

A2. In the case of a free market the following relationships are familiar deductions from the assumption made above:[4]

$$
\frac{\partial x_i}{\partial M} = \frac{\mu U_{0i}}{U} \quad (i = 1, 2, \ldots, n) \tag{A.1}
$$

$$
\frac{\partial x_i}{\partial p_j} = -x_j \frac{\mu U_{0i}}{U} + \frac{\mu U_{ij}}{U} \quad (i, j = 1, 2, \ldots, n). \tag{A.2}
$$

Here μ is the Lagrange multiplier in the conditional maximization described in Section A1 and is identified with the marginal utility of income:

$$
u_i = \mu p_i \quad (i = 1, 2, \ldots, n).
$$

From (A.2), because U is symmetrical, is derived the Slutsky equation

$$
\frac{\partial x_i}{\partial p_j} + x_j \frac{\partial x_i}{\partial M} = \frac{\partial x_j}{\partial p_i} + x_i \frac{\partial x_j}{\partial M}. \tag{A.3}
$$

(A.1), (A.2) and (A.3) can be expressed in terms of partial elasticities instead of partial derivatives. For this purpose it is convenient to make the following definition in addition to those of Section 6:

$$\sigma_{ij} = \sigma_{ji} = \mu \frac{U_{ij}}{U} \frac{M}{x_i x_j} \quad (i, j = 1, 2, \ldots, n). \tag{A.1a}$$

Then:

$$\eta_{ij} = -w_j \eta_{i0} = w_j \sigma_{ij} \quad (i, j = 1, 2, \ldots, n) \tag{A.2a}$$

$$\frac{\eta_{ij}}{w_j} + \eta_{i0} = \frac{\eta_{ji}}{w_i} + \eta_{j0} \quad (i, j = 1, 2, \ldots, n). \tag{A.3a}$$

A3. Suppose now that the situation of the consumer is in every respect the same as in Sections A1 and A2, except that we add to the budget restriction of Section A1 the following "rationing" restrictions on his behaviour:

$$x_k = q_k \quad (k = m + 1, m + 2, \ldots, n). \tag{A.4}$$

These restrictions represent straight rationing of $n - m$ of the n commodities, and the unrationed goods can be designated, without loss of generality as goods $1, 2, \ldots, m$. We now examine, as in Section A2, the changes in quantities x_i due to changes in the parameters confronting the consumer, which now include the rations q as well as prices p and money income M. The derivatives, and elasticities, of the x_i with respect to these parameters can then be compared with the "free market" derivatives and elasticities of Section A2.

Maximization of the utility function subject to the budget restriction and the constraints (A.4) results in the following set of equations:

$$x_h = q_h \quad (h = m + 1, m + 2, \ldots, n)$$

$$\sum_{i=1}^{n} p_i x_i = M$$

$$u_i = \mu p_i \quad (i = 1, 2, \ldots, m). \tag{A.5}$$

Since, according to our assumption, the set of x_i is identical with that of the free market situation, the $u_i(x_1, x_2, \ldots, x_n)$ are also the same.

Prices p_i have also been assumed unchanged. Consequently μ in (A.5) is the same μ as in Section A2.

Differentiating (A.5) partially with respect to M, we have:[5]

$$\frac{dx_h}{dM} = 0 \quad (h = m+1, m+2, \ldots, n)$$

$$\sum_{j=1}^{m} p_j \frac{dx_j}{dM} = 1 \tag{A.6}$$

$$-p_i \frac{d\mu}{dM} + \sum_{j=1}^{m} u_{ij} \frac{dx_j}{dM} = 0 \quad (i = 1, 2, \ldots, m)$$

and

$$\frac{dx_j}{dM} = \begin{vmatrix} 0 & p_1 & \cdots & 1 & \cdots & p_m \\ p_1 & u_{11} & \cdots & 0 & \cdots & u_{1m} \\ \vdots & \vdots & & \vdots & & \vdots \\ p_m & u_{m1} & \cdots & 0 & \cdots & u_{mm} \\ 0 & p_1 & \cdots & p_j & \cdots & p_m \\ p_1 & u_{11} & \cdots & u_{1j} & \cdots & u_{1m} \\ \vdots & \vdots & & \vdots & & \vdots \\ p_m & u_{m1} & \cdots & u_{mj} & \cdots & u_{mm} \end{vmatrix}$$

$$= (-1)^j \mu \frac{\begin{vmatrix} u_1 & u_{11} & \cdots & u_{ij-1} & u_{ij+1} & \cdots & u_{1m} \\ u_2 & u_{21} & \cdots & u_{2j-1} & u_{2j+1} & \cdots & u_{2m} \\ \vdots & \vdots & & \vdots & \vdots & & \vdots \\ u_m & u_{m1} & \cdots & u_{mj-1} & u_{mj+1} & \cdots & u_{mm} \end{vmatrix}}{\begin{vmatrix} 0 & u_1 & & \cdots & & u_m \\ u_1 & u_{11} & & \cdots & & u_{1m} \\ \vdots & \vdots & & & & \vdots \\ u_m & u_{m1} & & \cdots & & u_{mm} \end{vmatrix}}$$

$$(j = 1, 2, \ldots, m).$$

Hence

$$\frac{dx_j}{dM} = \frac{\mu U_{0j;\, m+1, m+1;\, m+2, m+2;\, \ldots;\, nn}}{U_{m+1, m+1;\, m+2, m+2;\, \ldots;\, nn}} \quad (j = 1, 2, \ldots, m). \tag{A.7}$$

Similarly differentiating (A.5) partially with respect to p_k ($k \leq m$) (the price of an unrationed good), we have:

$$\frac{dx_h}{dp_h} = 0 \quad (h = m + 1, m + 2, \ldots, n)$$

$$\sum_{j=1}^{m} p_j \frac{dx_j}{dp_k} = -x_k \tag{A.8}$$

$$-p_i \frac{d\mu}{dp_k} + \sum_{j=1}^{m} u_{ij} \frac{dx_j}{dp_k} = \begin{cases} 0 & (i \neq k) \\ \mu & (i = k) \end{cases} \quad (i = 1, 2, \ldots, m)$$

$$\frac{dx_j}{dp_k} = \frac{\begin{vmatrix} 0 & p_1 & \cdots & -x_k & \cdots & p_m \\ p_1 & u_{11} & \cdots & 0 & \cdots & u_{1m} \\ \vdots & \vdots & & \vdots & & \vdots \\ p_k & u_{k1} & \cdots & \mu & \cdots & u_{km} \\ \vdots & \vdots & & \vdots & & \vdots \\ p_m & u_{m1} & \cdots & 0 & \cdots & u_{mm} \end{vmatrix}}{\begin{vmatrix} 0 & p_1 & \cdots & p_j & \cdots & p_m \\ p_1 & u_{11} & \cdots & u_{1j} & \cdots & u_{1m} \\ \vdots & \vdots & & \vdots & & \vdots \\ p_k & u_{k1} & \cdots & u_{kj} & \cdots & u_{km} \\ \vdots & \vdots & & \vdots & & \vdots \\ p_n & u_{m1} & \cdots & u_{mj} & \cdots & u_{mm} \end{vmatrix}} .$$

Hence (changing the price subscript from k to i for convenience in what follows):

$$\frac{dx_j}{dp_i} = -x_i \frac{dx_j}{dM} + \frac{\mu U_{ij;\, m+1,\, m+1;\, \ldots\, nn}}{U_{m+1,\, m+1;\, \ldots;\, nn}} \quad (i, j = 1, 2, \ldots, m) \tag{A.9}$$

Differentiating (A.5) partially with respect to p_k ($k > m$), (the price of a rationed good), we have:

$$\frac{dx_h}{dp_k} = 0 \quad (h = m + 1, m + 2, \ldots, n)$$

$$\sum_{j=1}^{m} p_j \frac{dx_j}{dp_k} = -q_k \tag{A.10}$$

$$-p_i \frac{d\mu}{dp_k} + \sum_{j=1}^{m} u_{ij} \frac{dx_j}{dp_k} = 0 \quad (i = 1, 2, \ldots, m).$$

Hence:

$$\frac{dx_j}{dp_k} = -q_k \frac{dx_j}{dM} \quad \begin{array}{l} (j = 1, 2, \ldots, n) \\ (k > m). \end{array} \tag{A.11}$$

Finally, differentiating (A.5) partially with respect to q_k $(k > m)$, (the size of a ration), we have:

$$\frac{dx_h}{dq_k} = \begin{cases} 0 \ (h \neq k) \\ 1 \ (h = k) \end{cases} \quad (h = m + 1, m + 2, \ldots, n)$$

$$\sum_{j=1}^{m} p_j \frac{dx_j}{dq_k} = -p_k$$

$$-p_i \frac{d\mu}{dq_k} + \sum_{j=1}^{m} u_{ij} \frac{dx_j}{dq_k} = -u_{ik} \quad (i = 1, 2, \ldots, m) \tag{A.12}$$

and:

$$\frac{dx_j}{dq_k} = \frac{\begin{vmatrix} 0 & p_1 & \cdots & p_k & \cdots & p_m \\ p_1 & u_{11} & \cdots & u_{1k} & \cdots & u_{1m} \\ \vdots & \vdots & & \vdots & & \vdots \\ p_m & u_{m1} & \cdots & u_{mk} & \cdots & u_{mm} \\ 0 & p_1 & \cdots & p_j & \cdots & p_m \\ p_1 & u_{11} & \cdots & u_{1j} & \cdots & u_{1m} \\ \vdots & \vdots & & \vdots & & \vdots \\ p_m & u_{m1} & \cdots & u_{mj} & \cdots & u_{mm} \end{vmatrix}}{} \quad (j = 1, 2, \ldots, m).$$

Hence:

$$\frac{dx_j}{dq_k} = \frac{U_{kj;m+1,m+1;\ldots)kk(\ldots;nn}}{U_{m+1,m+1;\ldots,nn}} \quad \begin{array}{l} (j = 1, 2, \ldots, m) \\ (k > m). \end{array} \tag{A.13}$$

[The notation $)kk($ means that the subscripts kk are omitted from the sequence.]

A4. In what follows we rely heavily on the following application of Jacobi's theorem concerning reciprocal matrices:[6]

$$\frac{U_{ij,m+1,m+1;\ldots nn}}{U_{m+1,m+1;\ldots nn}} 1 = -\sum_{k=m+1}^{m} \frac{U_{ik}U_{kj;m+1,m+1;\ldots)kk(\ldots nn}}{U U_{m+1,m+1;\ldots;nn}} + \frac{U_{ij}}{U}. \tag{A.14}$$

For by Jacobi's theorem:

$$U^{n-m+1}U_{ij;m+1,m+1;\ldots;nn} = \begin{vmatrix} U_{ij} & U_{i,m+1} & \cdots & U_{in} \\ U_{m+1,j} & U_{m+1,m+1} & \cdots & U_{m+1,m} \\ \vdots & \vdots & & \vdots \\ U_{nj} & U_{n,m+1} & \cdots & U_{nn} \end{vmatrix}$$

$$= U_{ij}U^{n-m}U_{m+1,m+1\ldots nn} - U^{n-m}\sum_{k=m+1}^{n}$$

$$\times U_{ik}U_{kj,m+1,m+1,\ldots)kk(\ldots nn}.$$

Applying (A.14) (with $i = 0$) to (A.7), and using (A.13), we obtain

$$\frac{dx_j}{dM} = \frac{\mu U_{0j}}{U} - \sum_{k=m+1}^{n}\frac{dx_j}{dq_k}\mu\frac{U_{0k}}{U}$$

and, using (A.1), we arrive at the following comparison of the income derivative under rationing with its counterpart in a free market:

$$\frac{dx_j}{dM} - \frac{\partial x_j}{\partial M} = \sum_{k=m+1}^{n}\frac{dx_j}{dq_k}\frac{\partial x_k}{\partial M} \qquad (j = 1, 2, \ldots, n). \ [7] \qquad \text{(A.15)}$$

Applying (A.14)–(A.9), again using (A.13), we obtain

$$\frac{dx_j}{dp_i} = -x_i\frac{dx_j}{dM} + \frac{\mu U_{ij}}{U} - \sum_{k=m+1}^{n}\frac{dx_j}{dq_k}\frac{\mu U_{ik}}{U}$$

and using (A.2),

$$\frac{dx_j}{dp_i} = -x_i\frac{dx_j}{dM} + \frac{\partial x_j}{\partial p_i} + x_i\frac{\partial x_j}{\partial M} - \sum_{k=m+1}^{n}\frac{dx_j}{dq_k}\left(\frac{\partial x_k}{\partial p_i} + x_i\frac{\partial x_k}{\partial M}\right).$$

From (A.15) it then follows that, for $(i \leqq m)$,

$$\frac{dx_j}{dp_i} - \frac{\partial x_j}{\partial p_i} = -\sum_{k=m+1}^{n}\frac{dx_j}{dq_k}\frac{\partial x_k}{\partial p_i} \qquad (j = 1, 2, \ldots, n). \ [8] \qquad \text{(A.16)}$$

Applying (A.15)–(A.10), we have for $i > m$,

$$\frac{dx_j}{dp_i} = -x_i\frac{\partial x_j}{\partial M} + \sum_{k=m+1}^{n}\frac{dx_j}{dq_k}x_i\frac{\partial x_k}{\partial M}$$

and using (A.2):

$$\frac{dx_j}{dp_i} - \frac{\partial x_j}{\partial p_i} = -\mu \frac{U_{ji}}{U} - \sum_{k=m+1}^{n} \frac{dx_j}{dq_k} \frac{\partial x_k}{\partial p_i} + \sum_{k=m+1}^{n} \frac{dx_j}{dq_k} \mu \frac{U_{ki}}{U}$$

$$= -\sum_{k=m+1}^{n} \frac{dx_j}{dq_k} \frac{\partial x_k}{\partial p_i} - \frac{\mu}{U U_{m+1,m+1;\ldots;nn}} \times$$

$$\left[U_{ij} U_{m+1,m+1;\ldots nn} - \sum_{k=m+1}^{n} U_{ik} U_{kj;m+1\ldots)kk(\ldots nn} \right]$$

The expression in brackets vanishes because in the summation k takes, among other values, the value i. The expression involves the expansion of a determinant with two identical rows; it is:

$$\frac{1}{U^{n-m}} \begin{vmatrix} U_{ij} & U_{im+1} & \cdots & U_{in} \\ U_{m+1j} & U_{m+1,m+1} & \cdots & U_{m+1n} \\ \vdots & \vdots & & \vdots \\ U_{ij} & U_{im+1} & \cdots & U_{in} \\ \vdots & \vdots & & \vdots \\ U_{nj} & U_{nm+1} & \cdots & U_{nn} \end{vmatrix}.$$

Consequently (A.16) applies for all i, whether smaller or larger than m. (A.16) refers to *ceteris paribus* changes in prices; a similar relationship can be derived from (A.15) and (A.16) for compensated changes in prices.

$$\left(\frac{dx_j}{dp_i} + x_i \frac{dx_j}{dM} \right) - \left(\frac{\partial x_j}{\partial p_i} + x_i \frac{\partial x_j}{\partial M} \right) = -\sum_{k=m+1}^{n} \frac{dx_j}{dq_k} \left(\frac{\partial p_k}{\partial p_i} + x_i \frac{\partial x_k}{\partial M} \right). \tag{A.17}$$

A5. In the simplest case, where only one good, say x_n, is rationed we have by (A.13).

$$\frac{dx_j}{dq_n} = \frac{U_{nj}/U}{U_{nn}/U}. \tag{A.18}$$

From the secondary conditions for the maximum which is described in Section A2, it can be deduced that U_{nn}/U is negative.[9]

Therefore, dx_j/dq_n is positive if x_j and x_n are "substitutes", negative if they are "complements", on Hicks' definitions of these terms. Equations (A.15), (A.16) and (A.17) now reduce to (18), (19) and (20) respectively.

We can now prove the statement at the end of Section 5, viz., that rationing will always increase algebraically (reduce numerically) the effect on x_j of a *compensated* change in its own price p_j.[10]

For, using (A.2) and (A.18), we have

$$\left(\frac{dx_j}{dp_j} + x_j \frac{dx_j}{dM}\right) - \left(\frac{\partial x_j}{\partial p_i} + x_j \frac{\partial x_j}{\partial M}\right) = \frac{-\mu(U_{jn}/U)^2}{U_{nn}/U} > 0.$$

$$(A.19)$$

Moreover, from the same mathematical argument [11] it follows that the rationing of x_{n-1}, in addition to x_n, will further reduce (numerically) the compensated own-price derivative. This derivative will be smaller (numerically) the greater the number of rationed goods.

Notes

1 We shall be dealing only with "straight rationing". For points rationing cf. J. de V. Graaff, "Rothbarth's 'Virtual Price System' and the Slutsky Equation," this *Review* (1948-49), 91 and the literature quoted there.

[2] See J.R. Hicks, *Value and Capital*, 1st ed. (Oxford 1939), 32, 309-11.

[3] This point is $(x_1, x_2, ..., x_n, p_1, p_2, ..., p_n, M)$, a set of quantities, prices, and income. Because of the homogeneity of demand functions in the p_i and M a proportional change in prices and income between the two situations – rationing and free market – would be admissible, but this would be only a trivial gain in generality.

[4] See Hicks, *op. cit.*, 307-9.

[5] To avoid confusion with similar expressions for the free market situation of Section A2, derivatives appropriate to rationing will be in bold type, thus dx_j/dM.

[6] A.C. Aitken, *Determinants and Matrices* (Edinburgh 1949), p. 98.

[7] (A.15) holds trivially for rationed goods because for $n < m$:

$$\frac{dx_n}{dM} = 0, \qquad \frac{dx_n}{dq_k} = \begin{cases} 0 \ (h \neq k) \\ 1 \ (h = k) \end{cases}.$$

[8] (A.16) also holds trivially for rationed goods.

[9] Hicks, *op. cit.*, p. 310.

[10] This is pointed out by P.A. Samuelson, *Foundations of Economic Analysis* (Cambridge, Mass.: 1947), p. 168. It is an application of his "generalised Le Chatelier principle", pp. 36-38. (Cf. also *Economica*, 1949, p. 160, No. 1.)

[11] Samuelson, *op. cit.*, 36-38.

CHAPTER 41

ESTIMATES OF THE FREE DEMAND FOR RATIONED FOODSTUFFS

Few people would like to regard food rationing as a permanent feature of the British economy, although it has had to be continued for a much longer period than could have been foreseen when it was introduced. The prospect of a partial or complete abolition of the rationing system will therefore always be borne in mind, and it is then imperative to know what quantities of the commodities concerned would be demanded in a free market after derationing.

The question which we shall try to answer here is: how large a supply would be required to satisfy the unrationed demand of United Kingdom consumers at the prices obtaining in the middle of 1951? In order to arrive at such estimates we shall naturally have to make a number of simplifying assumptions and use incomplete or approximate statistical data, so that the results are necessarily uncertain. We shall indicate the principal sources of inaccuracy; at the same time we wish to state our conviction that the following estimates, if properly interpreted, will be of real usefulness in the consideration of economic policy.

The method employed consists essentially in the extrapolation of pre-war experience to the circumstances of 1951, making allowance for such changes as can be ascertained and expressed quantitatively. The basis for comparison will be the year 1938, both because it was the last year in which there was a free market to register the unconstrained preferences of consumers and because the statistics for that year are relatively complete and comparable to post-war figures.

The main determinants of consumer demand for any good are:

By H.S. Houthakker and James Tobin. Reprinted from *Economic Journal*, 62 (March 1952), 103-18.

(1) tastes;
(2) the level and distribution of real disposable income;
(3) the prices of the good itself and of its substitutes and complements;
(4) related rations.

We shall discuss these factors in turn, and then indicate how their effect was measured, if at all.

(1) *Tastes* have no doubt been influenced by the course of events since 1938, but this may have affected basic foods to a smaller extent than, say, cigarettes or coffee. In any case there is no information on these changes in preferences, and we have perforce ignored them. Demand analyses for the inter-war period showed that although the demand for some of the commodities here considered appeared to move steadily upwards or downwards independently of the economic variables, these long-term trends were very small and in no case statistically significant. We have therefore ignored these movements also.

(2) The level of *real disposable income* (consumer income after direct taxes on income in £ of 1938 purchasing power) has not changed much between 1938 and 1951. Although for some time in 1949 and 1950 income per head had been rather higher than in 1938, the increase in direct taxation and in prices after the Korean crisis reduced the increase of 1951 over 1938 to only $1\frac{1}{2}$ per cent. As the income elasticities for rationed foods are nearly all less then unity, this means a rise of less than $1\frac{1}{2}$ per cent in the free demand for them. In the case of "inferior" goods demand will fall.

The distribution of disposable income is well known to be less unequal now than it was in 1938. Income has been shifted from households with high incomes to households with low and moderate incomes. It depends on the shape of the Engel curves (which represent the relation between income and the consumption of a particular item) how this will affect demand. The Engel curves used here are, apart from some complications to be discussed below, of the constant-elasticity or logarithmic type:

$$y_i = a_i M^{b_i}, \tag{1}$$

where y_i is the quantity of the ith good and M disposable income; b_i is the income elasticity and a_i is a scale constant. If the income elasticity lies between 0 and 1 a redistribution of income as described will increase the free demand for the good concerned, for the potential consumption of those with high incomes will fall by less than the increase in demand from those benefiting. We have in fact

$$dy_i = a_i b_i M^{b_i - 1} dM, \tag{2}$$

from which we can see that if $b_i - 1 < 0$ the absolute value of dy_i will be lower as the M which experiences the change of dM is higher. The opposite situation will arise if $b_i > 1$, i.e., if the good is a luxury in the technical sense, or if it is inferior ($b_i < 0$), although the reasons for the fall in demand are different in the two cases. If $b_i = 0$ or $b_i = 1$ redistribution of income has no effect on consumption.

There is abundant evidence for preferring curvilinear Engel functions such as (1) to straight lines;[1] if the latter type held empirically the distribution of income could be left out of account.[2]

In practice it was found necessary to introduce two additional variables into (1). Family size has been taken into account by dividing both consumption and income by the number of persons per family.[3] Furthermore, comparisons between the 1937–38 working-class and the 1938–39 middle-class budget studies brought to light differences in consumption which could not be explained by differences in income and family size alone, and which were therefore ascribed to social factors. On the other hand, the assumption that the income elasticities (or more precisely the elasticities with respect to total expenditure) were the same for the two groups appeared to be acceptable. It was therefore considered sufficient to adjust the constant a_i in Equation (1) by a "social class coefficient".[4] The equation can then be rewritten

$$\frac{y_i}{n} = a_i c_i \left(\frac{M}{n}\right)^{b_i}, \tag{3}$$

where n is the number of persons and c_i the social class coefficient, which equals 1 for working-class families and is to be estimated for other households. It is usually found to be smaller than one for basic foods (see Appendix B).

These refinements imply that we have to look separately at income in working-class and in other families and that it is no longer total household income, but income per person which is relevant.

The actual extent of the redistribution of income since 1938 is difficult to evaluate owing to the notorious inadequacy of the data. Income-tax statistics are not directly applicable because of the differences between "tax units" and households: many households consist of more than one tax unit. Details of the calculations are given in Appendix A.

(3) *Own and related prices* have been deflated by the general price level of consumer goods. Strictly speaking, the latter should have been corrected because of the shortages in some important non-food markets, such as houses and motor cars, which deprive prices in those markets of their economic significance. Unfortunately there is no satisfactory method of making this allowance. The fact that we use an index with current weights in itself lessens the significance of these disturbing factors.

Statistically it is not possible to measure more than a few of the cross-elasticities (elasticities with respect to prices of substitute or complementary goods); only those that improved the regression equations have been taken into account. In several cases the influence of other prices is found to be at least as important as that of the commodity's own price.

(4) *Related rations* have to be considered if some goods are rationed while others are not, as this may affect the demand for the unrationed commodities. Thus if margarine were free while butter were still restricted this would have a somewhat similar effect on margarine demand as a high butter price: in both cases there would be a substitution of margarine for butter. This analogy has been worked out theoretically elsewhere [5] and has been applied here in one case, although this implies a generalization of the theory to finite changes and to aggregate demand which in principle requires separate justification.

We now come to the estimation of the demand functions, which has proceeded along well-known lines,[6] combining family budgets and time series. The principal innovation consists in allowing for quality variations with income: if income goes up, the quantity bought does not go up as rapidly as the money expenditure on an item of consumption because the average price per unit goes up as well.[7]

The family budgets utilized are the two pre-war surveys already referred to.[8] The time series are for the period 1920–38, except in the case of butter and sugar which were still rationed in 1920; the basic figures are due to Stone.[9]

We have to make it clear that our results do not bear on all the consequences of the problem of derationing, especially when the related problem of subsidies is taken into account. If demand were brought into line with the present level of supplies by increasing prices according to our calculations this would have important repercussions on wages and other incomes, as well as on taxation, since subsidies would disappear. On the other hand, a rise in prices might lead to increased supplies from abroad or from home producers; in fact, from a policy point of view there is no reason to attach special significance to current levels of supplies. Our calculations bear only on demand,[10] however, and we cannot enter into these wider questions. Our object is to estimate the present gap between supply and free demand; although we have taken into account a considerable variety of determinants of consumption our technique is still essentially a partial equilibrium method.

We shall now discuss the calculations for individual commodities, set out in Appendix B. These have been made for all rationed foods with the exception of cheese and sweets, for which no satisfactory demand analyses could be undertaken. Some minor varieties of the meat and cooking fats rations have also been omitted.

It will be seen that the most important changes in free demand since 1938 would result from price variations; the effect of income never amounts to more than a few per cent. We have, nevertheless, thought it worth while to study income redistribution in some detail, as this seems to be the only way to assess its importance and because great significance is sometimes attached to it.

Turning to the individual foods, we see that universal derationing in the circumstances of mid-1951 without other accompanying measures would reveal large shortages in tea, butter and most varieties of meat, a small shortage of sugar, a small surplus of bacon and larger surpluses of eggs, cooking fats and margarine. These surpluses, needless to say, would be the result of people's trying to buy more of other commodities that have been freed. The position can be most conveniently surveyed if we look at the foodstuffs in groups.

Let us first consider tea, of which current levels of supply (corresponding to a basic ration of 2 ounces per week) would have to be increased by 46 per cent to meet free demand. On the basis of a price elasticity of -0.39 equilibrium could also be attained by a price rise of about 160 per cent, which is, of course, beyond all possibilities and far more than the current rate of subsidy. Without a considerable increase in imports the derationing of tea is therefore a remote prospect.

Sugar is a more interesting case, as the shortage is estimated at only 16 per cent (with a basic ration of 10 ounces and various extra allowances). This was before the recent price increase, which reduced the calculated shortage substantially. It should be pointed out, however, that the take-up of the sugar ration at the moment shows no sign of saturation, so that our conclusions must be regarded with some caution, as indeed they must be in all cases. We would, nevertheless, venture to predict that a small increase in supplies, or a small rise in prices (e.g., a removal of the subsidy, which would add 17 per cent to the retail price) might change the situation drastically. Alternatively, when a decrease in some rations is contemplated sugar would seem to be one of the places where least harm would be done.[11]

For the rest we can distinguish two groups of rationed foods, viz., fats and meat. In the fats group the crucial commodity is butter, for which the free demand would correspond to a basic ration of 7.1 ounces instead of 4 ounces. If this quantity were in fact available margarine demand would drop to 41 per cent of present supply and the demand for cooking fats to 64 per cent of present supply. In absolute figures this means a fall of 2.4 ounces of margarine and 0.8 ounce of cooking fats, so that the total weight of fat consumption would remain unchanged. Fats rationing is therefore necessary because the composition of supplies, rather than their physical quantity, does not agree with consumers' preferences. This is also reflected in the well-known fact that the margarine and cooking fats rations are not fully taken up.[12] No practicable price adjustments could remedy this situation.

Especially in the case of margarine, the demand elasticities are somewhat uncertain owing to statistical difficulties, resulting apparently from improvements in the quality of margarine. This factor may well have continued to operate during and after the war, and may have been accompanied by a fall in the quality of butter, thus upsetting our assumption of unchanged tastes, but it is difficult to take it into account. If we use the elasticities calculated to estimate the effect of butter rationing on margarine demand [13] we find an elasticity of the latter with respect to the former of -0.56, i.e., an increase in the butter ration of 1 per cent reduces free margarine demand by 0.56 per cent. Applied to a butter ration of about 57 per cent of free demand, and combined with the changes in income and the price of margarine given in the commodity table, we would get a surplus of margarine of 41 per cent of present supplies, instead of the 59 per cent we get when butter is assumed to be free. Consequently, there would still be a substantial surplus; too much should not be made of this calculation, however, which is based on very uncertain premises and given merely as an example.

The last group we have to consider consists of meat and its substitutes bacon and eggs.[14] Taking the five varieties of carcass meat together, we find that free demand would exceed present supplies by approximately 100 per cent; there is a shortage of all types of meat, which is most marked in the case of pork and home-produced mutton. Only in the case of imported mutton would demand in a completely free market be anywhere near current supplies, which does not, of course, mean that the derationing of this item could be contemplated without large increases in the supplies of other commodities.

The small surpluses of bacon and eggs, of 6 per cent and 18 per cent respectively, can be entirely explained by the shortage of meat. It will be noticed that these surpluses would be considerably larger but for the low current price of meat, which on the other hand helps to keep free meat demand at a high level. It would not be true to say that an increase in the price of meat would go far towards relieving the meat shortage, but it would nevertheless be a useful preliminary to derationing as some of the increased meat supplies then required would no longer serve merely to replace available supplies of bacon and eggs: under rationing the prices of rationed goods only influence the demand for unrationed commodities through income effects; their level is therefore only of monetary and budgetary importance and its discussion outside the scope of this paper.[15]

In concluding we wish to acknowledge the help of the Statistics and Intelligence Division of the Ministry of Food at many stages of the work; the Ministry is not responsible for any opinions or calculations here presented. Mr. J.R.N. Stone, Director of the Department of Applied Economics, has given us the benefit of his advice. We are also greatly indebted to Mr. S.J. Prais, who has assisted in the preparation of this paper. The computations were carried out at the Department and at the National Institute of Economic and Social Research. Considerable use was also made of the electronic computer of the University Mathematical Laboratory in Cambridge.

Appendix A

To allow for redistribution of income it was necessary to divide the population into two classes, to one of which the coefficients c_i should be applied. In accordance with the two budget surveys just referred to, the dividing line has been taken at an income of the head of the household before tax of £250 in 1938. It has been assumed that disposable household incomes of families with a given size in the top group are distributed according to the Pareto curve

$$N(M) = AM^{-\alpha} = Aa \int_{M}^{\infty} x^{-\alpha-1}\, dx, \tag{A.1}$$

where $N(M)$ is the number of incomes greater than M and A and a are constants. There is little or no information in the distribution of low incomes, particularly before the war, and as redistribution within that group can have only a very small effect on demand, all households belonging to it were supposed to have the same disposable income. These hypotheses, crude though they are, do not seriously distort the crucial fact of a large-scale transfer of income from the higher to the lower group.

The next step is to work with income per person rather than household income. The paucity of information on this subject again calls for additional assumptions. The most remarkable change is the considerable increase in the number of households from about 12.5 millions in 1938 to nearly 15 millions in 1951,[16] leading to a decrease in average family size. For the lower income group we have again assumed that all households are of average size; for the top group (4) has been applied to each family size n separately, viz.,

$$N_n(M) = A_n M^{-\alpha_n}, \tag{A.2}$$

where the coefficients α_n may differ to allow for the larger number of supplementary earners in larger families. The distribution of income per head for each family size is then

$$N_n\left(\frac{M}{n}\right) = A_n\left(\frac{M}{n}\right)^{-\alpha_n}. \tag{A.3}$$

Combining (3) and (A.3) and using (A.2), we get the following expression for the total consumption of the ith good by families of size n:

$$na_i c_i A_n \alpha_n \int_{M/n}^{\infty} x^{b_i - \alpha_n - 1} dx = na_i c_i A_n \frac{\alpha_n}{\alpha_n - b_i}\left(\frac{M}{n}\right)^{b_i - \alpha_n}. \quad \text{(A.4)}$$

The total number of persons in this size group being given by (A.3) multiplied by n, we find for their average consumption per head:

$$a_i c_i \frac{\alpha_n}{\alpha_n - b_i}\left(\frac{M}{n}\right)^{b_i}. \quad \text{(A.5)}$$

If we take M to be the dividing line required by the social class coefficient (say M_c), and write $M_c/n = x_n$, we get for the average consumption per head of all families taken together:

$$y_i = w_0 a_i x_0^{b_i} + \sum_{n-1}^{\infty} w_n a_i c_i \frac{\alpha_n}{\alpha_n - b_i} x_c^{b_i}, \quad \text{(A.6)}$$

where the w's indicate the relative frequency of each type of family in the population (so that $\Sigma w = 1$; w_0 is the frequency of families in the lower income group) and x_0 is the average income per head below the dividing line.

The numerical work on income distribution is based principally on Inland Revenue data, on the National Income White Paper (forecasts for 1951 were obtained) and on a sample survey carried out by the Ministry of Food in September 1950. These sources of information are not completely consistent, and various adjustments had to be made. The White Paper figures were used to compare real disposable income per head in 1938 and 1951, showing the $1\frac{1}{2}$ per cent increase already mentioned in the text. Inland Revenue data for 1937–38 [17] had to be reconverted into household income per head, for which purpose the distribution of families by size [18] was assumed to be independent of income. The treatment of incomes below the line has been explained in the text; their income per head was found to be £63. For the other households of each size class (families with nine or more persons were ignored) the number of supplementary earners was taken to be proportional to the number of persons other than the head of the household (the chance of such a person being an earner was 23.3 per cent). The average income of supplementary earners was £191, consequently the average contribution of persons other than the head to household income was £45 (23.3 per cent of £191); this figure has been used both for 1938 and for 1951 (in 1938 prices). The lower limit M_c for each household size n was therefore taken to be £$\{250 + 45(n - 1)\}$, so that for that size

$$x_n = £\,\frac{250 + 45(n - 1)}{n},\tag{A.7}$$

with some allowance for taxation in the smaller size classes. Similar calculations for 1951 were made on the basis of the Ministry of Food income survey (x_0 was equal to £70). The w_n in (A.6) were taken from the distribution of families by size ($w_0 = 0.81$ in both years) and the a_n were in fact taken to be independent of n. By applying (A.6) to income per head (i.e., by putting $a_i = b_i = c_i = 1$) we can then estimate a by the well-known "mean law",[19] obtaining $a = 2.34$ for 1938 and $a = 3.09$ for 1951. These values are very different from those between 1.5 and 2 one usually finds quoted, but these refer to the distribution of incomes before tax rather than to incomes per head after tax.

Finally, (A.6) can be computed for 1938 and 1951, and their ratio represents the proportionate effect on demand of the combined change in the level and distribution of income between these two dates. It will be seen that these effects are relatively small, but this does not appear to be due to the methods of calculation used, for rather different methods used in earlier stages of this inquiry gave much the same results.

Appendix B

Table 41.1 gives for each of twelve commodities the effects of the various changes in the factors determining demand, together with the relevant elasticities which are set out in more detail in Appendix C. The changes are expressed as ratios, so that an entry 1.052 means an increase of 5.2 per cent. The change due to income has been calculated by the method of Appendix A, using the income elasticity and the social-class coefficient c as stated in the table. The product of the changes due to each factor (last column) is the total change in demand again expressed as a ratio with the 1938 figure equal to unity. When this is also done for current supply (i.e., supply at the annual rate for the middle of 1951) the "shortage" follows, expressed as a fraction of current supply. Thus a shortage of 0.34 means that current supply would have to be increased by 34 per cent to be equal to demand in a completely free market at current prices and income. A negative shortage of say −0.16 means that 16 per cent of present supply would be surplus in a free market at current prices.

Table 41.1

Commodity No. 1: Tea

Demand factor	Change since 1938	Elasticity	Change in demand (%)
1. Income	—	0.39	1.033
$c = 0.398$			
2. Own price	0.74	−0.39	1.123
3. Related price:			
Coffee	1.812	0.21	1.036
Cumulative effect of changes on demand			1.202
Change in supply since 1938			0.822
Current shortage			0.462

Commodity No. 2: Sugar

Demand factor	Change since 1938	Elasticity	Change in demand (%)
1. Income	—	0.26	1.020
$c = 0.631$			
2. Own price	0.967	−0.43	1.015
Cumulative effect of changes on demand			1.035
Change in supply since 1938			0.891
Current shortage			0.162

Table 41.1 (*continued*)

Commodity No. 3: Butter

Demand factor	Change since 1938	Elasticity	Change in demand (%)
1. Income	—	0.39	1.025
$c = 0.848$			
2. Own price	0.812	−0.48	1.105
Cumulative effect of changes on demand			1.133
Change in supply since 1938			0.640
Current shortage			0.770

Commodity No. 4: Margarine

Demand factor	Change since 1938	Elasticity	Change in demand (%)
1. Income	—	−0.24	0.980
$c = 0.842$			
2. Own price	0.818	−0.75	1.163
3. Related price:			
Butter	0.812	0.27	0.945
Cumulative effect of changes on demand			1.077
Change in supply since 1938			2.639
Current shortage			−0.592

Commodity No. 5: Cooking fats

Demand factor	Change since 1938	Elasticity	Change in demand (%)
1. Income	—	0.21	1.017
$c = 0.576$			
2. Own price	0.83	−0.56	1.107
Cumulative effect of changes on demand			1.126
Change in supply since 1938			1.713
Current shortage			−0.343

Table 41.1 (*continued*)

Commodity No. 6: Eggs

Demand factor	Change since 1938	Elasticity	Change in demand (%)
1. Income	—	0.47	1.029
$c = 0.847$			
2. Own price	1.215	−0.35	0.934
3. Related price:			
Total meat	0.732	0.70	0.804
Cumulative effect of changes on demand			−0.772
Change in supply since 1938			0.948
Current shortage			−0.185

Commodity No. 7: Bacon

Demand factor	Change since 1938	Elasticity	Change in demand (%)
1. Income	—	0.46	1.039
$c = 0.363$			
2. Own price	0.848	−0.86	1.152
3. Related price:			
Total meat	0.732	1.59	0.609
Cumulative effect of changes on demand			0.729
Change in supply since 1938			0.777
Current shortage			−0.062

Commodity No. 8: Pork

Demand factor	Change since 1938	Elasticity	Change in demand (%)
1. Income	—	0.51	1.046
$c = 0.257$			
2. Own price	0.986	−0.66	1.009
3. Related price:			
Mutton	0.650	0.82	0.702
Cumulative effect of changes on demand			0.741
Change in supply since 1938			0.099
Current shortage			6.488

Table 41.1 (*continued*)

Commodity No. 9: Home-produced beef and veal

Demand factor	Change since 1938	Elasticity	Change in demand (%)
1. Income	—	0.34	1.023
c = 0.832			
2. Own price	0.606	−0.41	1.228
3. Related price:			
Imported mutton	0.706	0.50	0.840
Cumulative effect of changes on demand			1.056
Change in supply since 1938			0.510
Current shortage			1.070

Commodity No. 10: Imported beef

Demand factor	Change since 1938	Elasticity	Change in demand (%)
1. Income	—	−0.27	0.977
c = 0.648			
2. Own price	0.861	−0.32	1.049
3. Related price:			
Home-produced beef	0.606	1.02	0.600
Cumulative effect of changes on demand			0.615
Change in supply since 1938			0.256
Current shortage			1.401

Commodity No. 11: Home-produced mutton

Demand factor	Change since 1938	Elasticity	Change in demand (%)
1. Income		0.74	1.025
c = 1.082			
2. Own price	0.591	−1.67	2.407
3. Related price:	0.591	−1.67	2.407
Home-produced beef and veal	0.606	1.68	0.431
Cumulative effect of changes on demand			1.064
Change in supply since 1938			0.364
Current shortage			1.922

Table 41.1 (*continued*)

Commodity No. 12: Imported mutton and lamb

Demand factor	Change since 1938	Elasticity	Change in demand (%)
1. Income		0.05	1.003
$c = 0.971$			
2. Own price	0.706	−0.58	1.224
3. Related price:			
Imported beef	0.861	1.12	0.846
Home-produced mutton	0.591	0.95	0.607
Cumulative effect of changes on demand			0.630
Change in supply since 1938			0.592
Current shortage			0.064

Appendix C

Table 41.2 gives the estimates of the various coefficients on which the calculations are based. The first four columns of coefficients (each followed by its standard error) are derived from the 1937–38 Ministry of Labour and the 1938–39 Civil Service Statistical and Research Bureau family budget surveys; the last two from time series for the period 1920–38, using first differences without trend. The social-class factors are not the same as shown in the commodity tables; they are given as estimated from the equation

$$\log y_i = a + b_{1i} \log E/n + b_{2i}s,[20]$$

where y_i is the expenditure on the ith commodity, b_{1i} is the total expenditure elasticity, E is total expenditure, n is the number of persons, b_{2i} is the social-class factor given below and s is a dummy variable which equals 0 for working-class and 1 for middle-class families. The coefficient in the commodity table is the anti-logarithm of b_{2i}.

The quality coefficient is b_{3i} in the equation

$$p_i = a' + b_{3i} \log E/n,$$

Table 41.2

Estimation source	Family budgets				Time series	
Commodity	Total expendi-ture elasticity	Social-class factor	Quality coefficient	Quality elasticity	Own-price elasticity	Related price elasticity
1. Tea	0.49 (±0.03)	−0.40 (±0.04)	4.42 (±0.46)	0.068	−0.39 (±0.14)	0.21 (±0.13) (coffee)
2. Sugar	0.33 (±0.02)	−0.20 (±0.03)	0.26 (±0.04)	0.042	−0.43 (±0.15)	—
3. Butter	0.45 (±0.03)	−0.07 (±0.02)	0.57 (±0.21)	0.016	−0.48 (±0.17)	—
4. Margarine	−0.20 (±0.07)	−0.07 (±0.04)	1.32 (±0.21)	0.076	−0.75 (±0.33)	0.27 [3]
5. Cooking fats	0.26 (±0.02)	−0.24 (±0.04)	0.48 (±0.15)	0.025	−0.56 (±0.08)	—
6. Eggs	0.59 (±0.04)	−0.07 (±0.02)	0.28 (±0.04)	0.073	−0.46 (±0.15)	0.56 (±0.44) (total meat)
7. Bacon	0.64 (±0.04)	−0.44 (±0.05)	5.36 (±0.56)	0.126	−0.86 (±0.11)	1.59 (±0.44) (total meat)
8. Pork	0.54 (±0.05)	−0.39 (±0.11)	5.54 (±1.19)	0.137	−0.66 (±0.17)	0.82 (±0.47) [11 + 12]
9. Home-produced beef and veal	0.70 (±0.09)	−0.08 (±0.06)	5.95 (±0.91)	0.179	−0.41 (±0.16)	0.50 (±0.15) [12]
10. Imported beef and veal	−0.12 (±0.13)	−0.19 (±0.07)	5.52 (±0.88)	0.179	−0.32 (±0.52)	1.02 (±0.45) [9]
11. Home-produced mutton	1.03 (±0.10)	0.03 (±0.06)	3.34 (±1.25)	0.205	−1.67 (±0.42)	1.68 (±0.42) [9]
12. Imported mutton	0.24 (±0.15)	−0.01 (±0.09)	6.38 (±1.01)	0.186	−0.58 (±0.44)	{ 1.13 (±0.42) [10] / 0.96 (±0.52) [11]

where p_i is the average unit price (in pence per lb.) of the ith commodity and E/n is in £ per year. The quality elasticity is taken at $E/n = 100$, which is close to the average total expenditure per head of the population. The actual income elasticities used in the commodity tables are the difference of b_{1j} and b_{3j} multiplied by 0.9 so that they refer to quantities rather than expenditures and to disposable income rather than total expenditure, the factor 0.9 being the estimated elasticity of total expenditure with respect to income.[21]

The own-price elasticities do not require any explanation; they have been included even when they were not statistically significant. The cross-price elasticities have been taken into account in all cases where their introduction reduced the residual variance of the regression variables; the commodity to which they refer is indicated in brackets, usually by its number in the table. In fact, a much larger number of possible substitutes and complements was considered in the regression analyses. The demand equation for margarine was found by analysing the regression of the quantity ratio between butter and margarine on their price ratio; hence the absence of one of the standard errors.

Notes

[1] Cf. H.S. Houthakker, "The Econometrics of Family Budgets," *Journal of the Royal Statistical Society*, Series A (1952) and the literature quoted there. This paper will be referred to as "Family Budgets".

[2] Cf. P. de Wolff, "Income Elasticity of Demand: a Micro-economic and a Macro-economic Interpretation," *Economic Journal* (1941), 140.

[3] In principle one would have to give different weights to persons of different age and sex according to the commodity concerned, but this is not yet possible statistically.

[4] Cf. "Family Budgets", especially Section 7.

[5] J. Tobin and H.S. Houthakker, "The Effects of Rationing on Demand Elasticities," *Review of Economic Studies* (1950-51), 140.

[6] Cf. J. Tobin, "A Statistical Demand Function for Food in the U.S.A.," *Journal of the Royal Statistical Society*, Series A (1950), 113; Richard Stone, "The Demand for Food in the United Kingdom before the War," *Metroeconomica* (1951), 8.

[7] Cf. "Family Budgets", Section 4; more extensively H.S. Houthakker and S.J. Prais, "Les Variations de Qualité dans les Budgets de Famille," *Economie Appliquée* (1952), 65-78.

[8] Further details of the analysis in "Family Budgets".

[9] *Op. cit.*

[10] This is not strictly true, as we have used "single equation methods", which may not be completely accurate in separating demand and supply factors. In other words, our demand elasticity may in fact include a certain element of supply response, but this is not necessarily

a drawback for the present purpose. The information for undertaking a "simultaneous equations" approach is unfortunately not available.

[11] The situation is somewhat complicated by an important trade consumption of unsubsidized sugar, so that it would not be practicable to deration while retaining the subsidy.

[12] We have found no evidence of a significant complementarity between sugar and margarine or cooking fats. If this existed the low take-up of these commodities might be due to the shortage of sugar, which would prevent people from making cakes, so that fats consumption would rise if sugar were freed; this is in fact sometimes advanced as an argument for maintaining margarine rationing. In any case, according to our calculations the free demand for sugar does not exceed present supplies very seriously.

[13] Cf. Tobin and Houthakker, "The Effects of Rationing on Demand Elasticities," loc. cit., especially, p. 142, formula (3.8).

[14] Cheese also appears to belong to this group, but the heterogeneity of this commodity has made it impossible to arrive at statistically and theoretically acceptable demand elasticities.

[15] We have not been able to calculate the shortage of bacon and eggs when meat rationing is taken into account, as we did for margarine. The reason is a theoretical defect of the estimates of the various price elasticities; although the own-price and cross-price elasticities of the different kinds of meat have the correct signs, their magnitudes are such that the own-price elasticity of total meat is positive.

[16] Estimates for 1937 and 1949 are given in F. Harrison and F.C. Mitchell, *The Home Market*, 1950 ed. (revised by Mark Abrams).

[17] As dealt with by T. Barna, *Redistribution of Income through Public Finance in 1937* (Oxford 1945) and H.S. Houthakker, "Some Calculations on Electricity Consumption in Great Britain," *Journal of the Royal Statistical Society*, Series A (1951), 359, especially Table I.

[18] Given in *The Home Market*, p. 43.

[19] Cf., for instance, Barna, loc. cit., p. 258, formula (3).

[20] Cf. "Family Budgets", Section 7.

[21] *Ibid.*, 8.

PART VII

ECONOMETRICS

CHAPTER 42

A STATISTICAL DEMAND FUNCTION FOR FOOD IN THE U.S.A.

Quantitative data relating to the demand for consumers' goods and services are, for the most part, of two very different kinds, time series and family budget surveys. Time series are generally aggregate data: observations in successive periods of the total national consumption of a commodity and of possible explanatory variables, principally national income and prices. A family budget survey is a set of observations, for a single time period, of the expenditures on the goods by families who differ in income, size, and other characteristics. The premise of this paper is that a statistical demand function should be consistent with both kinds of observations.

Most statistical analysis of consumer behaviour has relied exclusively on one or the other of the two types of data.[1] The relationship of national consumption to other national aggregates has been found from time series, without investigation of the consistency of this aggregate demand function with the evidence concerning family behaviour. Or budget data have been analysed to determine the effects of family income and other variables on family expenditures, without considering the consistency of the estimates of these effects with time series of aggregate variables.

There are both economic and statistical reasons for basing quantitative demand analysis on a combination of time series and budget data. The economic reason is the obvious fact that aggregate consumption and income are the sums of the consumptions and incomes of families.[2] Any relationship among these and other aggregates is the reflection of a multitude of family consumption decisions. A hypothesis concerning the

Reprinted from *Journal of the Royal Statistical Society*, 113, Series A, Part II (1950), 113-41. The author wishes to express his gratitude for the hospitality of the Department of Applied Economics of the University of Cambridge in making their facilities available to him for the completion of this work.

determination of aggregate demand should be derived from a hypothesis about family expenditure. The connection between the family demand function and its aggregate counterpart will, in general, involve the joint distribution of families by income and by the other variables in the family demand function.[3]

Statistically, widening the scope of the observations on which statistical demand analysis is based increases the possibility of rejecting hypotheses and improves the estimates of the parameters of demand functions (Marschak 1939b, p. 487; 1943, p. 42). The increase in statistical power is due not merely to the addition of new information, but to the addition of information of a different nature. Economic time series are notoriously poor material for choosing among hypotheses; and simply extending the length of their span does not eliminate the difficulty. The estimation of parameters from time series encounters many statistical pitfalls, which need not be rehearsed here (Stone 1948). These difficulties are mitigated if it is possible on the basis of other information to restrict the field of acceptable hypotheses and the range of possible parameter values.

Budget studies provide observations in which the persistent correlations of some explanatory variables over time are broken; indeed, they constitute an experiment in which certain relevant variables, such as prices, are constant while others, chiefly income, vary. Moreover, microeconomic data escape some of the difficulties of identification to which aggregate time series are subject. For example, an observation of aggregate demand is also an observation of total supply, and the observed relationship of total consumption to other macroeconomic variables may reflect the operation of a supply function as well as a demand function. But the observed consumption of a family is unambiguously a point on its demand function, since a single family could have bought more or less of the commodity without affecting its price. For these reasons, the use of budget data may help to rescue statistical demand analysis from the traps encountered in relying exclusively on time series. But for the same reasons, budget statistics are by themselves insufficient to test a complete hypothesis concerning demand or to estimate all the parameters of a demand function, at least until surveys made at different times are much more numerous than at present. Some of the relevant variables change only with time, and their effects cannot be evaluated without appeal to time series of aggregates.

This paper is an attempt to derive two related statistical demand functions for food for the U.S.A., one the family demand function and the other the aggregate demand function, by combining information from budget surveys and from time series. "Food" is treated as a single commodity, and variations over time in the quantity and price of this commodity are measured by index numbers. The variables determining family food demand are assumed to be disposable family income in the current and preceding years, family size, the food price index and the index of prices of other consumers' goods. The form of the function assumed implies that the elasticity of demand with respect to each of these variables is constant. In Section 1 the elasticities of family food expenditure with respect to family income and size, with prices constant, are estimated from budget data. The estimate of income-elasticity is interpreted as the sum of the elasticity with respect to current income and the elasticity with respect to income of the previous year. This interpretation is justified by the evidence for a lag in adjustment of food expenditure to changes in income and by the high correlation of family incomes in two successive years. In Section 2 the aggregate demand function is derived from the family function. Under certain realistic assumptions concerning the distribution of families by income and size, it is shown that the aggregate function has the same form and the same elasticities as the family function. Given the estimate of the sum of the two income-elasticities obtained in Section 1, the parameters of the two demand functions are estimated in Section 3 by multiple correlation of time series of aggregates. Section 4 examines the relationships between food expenditure and family income in budget surveys made at different times to see if the differences among these relationships can, with the parameter estimates obtained in Section 3, be attributed to differences in prices and lagged income.

1. The Family Food Demand Function

1.1. *The Form of the Function*
The family food demand function is assumed to be:

$$c_t = k y_t^{\alpha_1} y_{t-1}^{\alpha_2} P_t^\beta Q_t^\gamma n_t^\delta, \tag{1}$$

where

c_t = quantity of food consumed by a family in year t, whether purchased, received in kind, or home-produced.

y_t = disposable family income for year t: money income plus income in kind, including gifts in money or in kind from other families, less direct taxes and gifts to other families.

P_t = index of food prices, average for year t.

Q_t = index of prices of other consumers' goods, average for year t.

n_t = number of persons in the family in year t, counting a person in the family for a fraction of the year as the same fraction of a full person.

α_1 = elasticity of food demand with respect to current income.

α_2 = elasticity of food demand with respect to previous year's income.

β = elasticity of food demand with respect to food price index.

γ = elasticity of food demand with respect to non-food price index.

δ = elasticity of food demand with respect to family size.

k is a constant which depends on the units in which the variables are measured. (In general, lower-case letters indicate microeconomic variables, and capital letters macroeconomic variables. Greek letters are used for the elasticities.)

Function (1) is chosen in preference to a linear relationship for a combination of reasons: (a) The relationship between family income and food expenditure in budget data is obviously not linear; as would be expected on *a priori* grounds, the marginal propensity to consume food decreases with income. A linear relationship between the logarithms gives a good fit to the data without requiring additional parameters. (b) This form of the family demand function implies, under certain simple and plausible aggregation assumptions, an aggregate relationship of the same functional form with the same elasticities. (See Section 2.) (c) Consistency of consumer behaviour requires that the sum of the elasticities of demand with respect to variables of a monetary dimension be identically zero. This theoretical proposition is, of course, not a licence to impose the zero-sum restriction on statistical estimates of elasticities. But it is a reason for adopting a form for statistical demand functions which permits but does not enforce results conforming with the "homogeneity postulate". Function (1) has this property: if y_t, y_{t-1}, P_t and Q_t

exhaust the variables of monetary dimension relevant to food demand, then the "homogeneity postulate" implies:

$$\alpha_1 + \alpha_2 + \beta + \gamma = 0. \tag{2}$$

A linear function in the same variables does not have this property unless it goes through the origin. It is true that the use of functions of the form of (1) for more than one commodity is inconsistent with another requirement of the theory of consumer choice, namely the Slutsky condition on cross-elasticities. Moreover, such a function could not be used for every consumer's good, including saving, without violating the identity of the sum of expenditures and income. But the present investigation concerns only one commodity (Stone 1945, pp. 293–294).

1.2. *The Effect of Previous Year's Income*

Information from budget surveys can provide only two of the five equations required to evaluate all the exponents in (1). The remaining equations must be determined by time series correlation of aggregate data. Budget data can yield, under certain assumptions to be set forth in this section, an estimate of the sum $\alpha_1 + \alpha_2$, which will be called α, and of δ.

Since the observations reported in a budget study refer to a common time period, P_t and Q_t are constant over all families. Consequently (1) becomes

$$c_t = k_t' y_t^{\alpha_1} y_{t-1}^{\alpha_2} n^{\delta}, \tag{3}$$

where $k_t' = k P_t^{\beta} Q_t^{\gamma}$ is constant over all families in year t.

If a budget study classified families according to their previous year's income, current income and size, the three elasticities α_1, α_2 and δ could be estimated directly from budget data. In the absence of data concerning lagged income, none of the three exponents can be estimated without assuming either an equation involving the parameters or a relationship between y_t and y_{t-1}.

The usual procedure is to assume $\alpha_2 = 0$, i.e. that there is no lag in the adjustment of consumption to income. Then α_1 can be evaluated from budget data by regression of consumption on current income, taking account of family size.

However, the adjustment of consumption, even food consumption, to family income is in fact not instantaneous. The hypothesis of a lag in the relationship of food demand to income is supported not only by common sense but by the evidence of budget data. The 1941–42 survey for the U.S.A. shows food expenditures in the first quarter of 1942 separately for two classes of urban families, those whose annual rates of income were lower than in 1941 by 5 per cent or more, and those whose incomes were higher than in 1941 by 5 per cent or more. Fig. 42.1 shows the average food expenditure at eight 1942 income levels for these two groups of families, and for the sample as a whole (including families who experienced less than 5 per cent change in income).[4] The comparison is strong evidence of a lag in adjustment of food expenditure to income level. For each of the eight current income-classes of families, average expenditure is higher for those who suffered a fall in income than for those who experienced a rise. These data do not permit the evaluation of α_2, but they indicate that it is significantly bigger than zero.[5] Moreover, current family income is certainly highly correlated with previous year's income. Table 42.1 shows the distribution of families of six 1941 income classes by 1942 income. Average income in the first quarter of 1941 was at an annual rate 7 per cent higher than 1941 average income, and Table 42.1 therefore shows that more families moved to higher brackets than to lower. The correlation between the two years' incomes means that the regression coefficient of family consumption on current income

Table 42.1

Percentage distribution of 1942 money incomes for city families of six 1941 income-classes

1941 Money income (dollars)	1942 Money income (Dollars, annual rate based on first quarter)					
	0-500	500-1,000	1,000-1,500	1,500-2,000	2,000-3,000	Over 3,000
0-500	78	16	5	..	1	..
500-1,000	9	66	18	5	2	..
1,000-1,500	2	10	52	27	8	1
1,500-2,000	1	1	11	50	35	2
2,000-3,000	..	1	2	7	63	27
Over 3,000	..	..	..	..	13	85

Source: B.L.S. (1942), Table 4, p. 423, and Table 6, p. 424.

reflects the effect of past income as well. Neglect of the lag results in an over-estimate of α_1 as well as an under-estimate of α_2. The customary assumption that $\alpha_2 = 0$ must be replaced by an alternative assumption which recognizes the importance of past income and its correlation with current income.

Assume, therefore, that the geometric average previous year's income $\bar{y}_{t-1}$ of an income class of families of given size with current income $\bar{y}_t$ is given by

$$\bar{y}_{t-1} = \frac{Y_{t-1}}{Y_t} \bar{y}_t, \tag{4}$$

where Y_t is average disposable income per family in year t.[6] Every group of families, classified by current income, is assumed to have undergone the same relative change in income; it is not required that each individual family experience the same change. From (3) it follows that the geometric average consumption $\bar{c}_t$ of a group of families of size n with geometric average incomes $\bar{y}_t$ and $\bar{y}_{t-1}$ is given by

$$\bar{c}_t = k_t' \bar{y}_t^{\alpha_1} \bar{y}_{t-1}^{\alpha_2} n^\delta. \tag{5}$$

Substituting (4) in (5),

$$\bar{c}_t = k_t'' \bar{y}_t^\alpha n^\delta, \tag{6}$$

where $\alpha = \alpha_1 + \alpha_2$, and

$$k_t'' = \left(\frac{Y_{t-1}}{Y_t}\right)^{\alpha_2}, \qquad k_t' = k\left(\frac{Y_{t-1}}{Y_t}\right)^{\alpha_2} P_t^\beta Q_i^\gamma$$

is constant over all income-size groups of families.

This method of allowing for the influence of lagged income is compelled by the inadequacy of data concerning the quantitative effect of past income on food consumption and concerning the joint distribution of families by incomes in two successive years. Table 42.1 indicates that assumption (4) is not far wide of the mark. There is some evidence (Mack 1948) that assumption (4) errs by attributing too low a lagged income to families of low current income and too high a lagged income to families of high current income.[7] If this is true, the use of assumption (4) will give too low an estimate of α; more of the observed consumption of low-income families and less of that of high-income families will be due

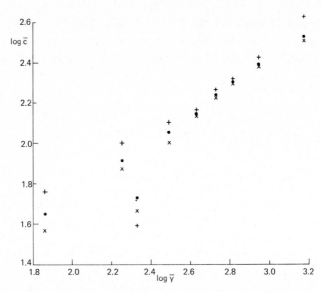

Fig. 42.1. Money expenditure for food and disposable income, all urban families, first quarter 1942. ● All families. × Families with incomes 5 per cent or more higher than 1941. + Families with incomes 5 per cent or more lower than 1941.

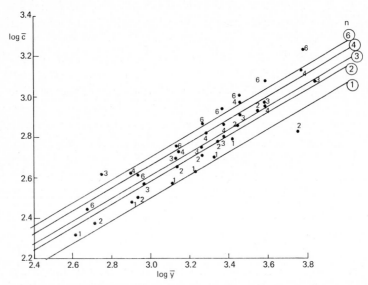

Fig. 42.2. Family income and food expenditure for various sizes of family, 1941. Budget study observations ● n. Regression $\log \bar{c} = 0.82 + 0.56 \log \bar{y} + 0.25 \log n$.

to past income than assumed in (6). In Fig. 42.1 this bias should be revealed in a flatter slope for the whole sample than for the two groups classified by direction of income change. Fig. 42.1 does not show serious bias of this kind.

1.3. *The Family Demand Function Estimated from 1941 Budget Data*

The parameters of function (6) can now be estimated from budget data. In terms of the logarithms of the variables (6) becomes

$$\log \bar{c}_t = \log k''_t + \alpha \log \bar{y}_t + \delta \log n. \tag{7}$$

In fitting (7) to budget data, a difficulty arises because of the manner in which the basic observations are summarized for publication. Observations of $(\bar{c}, \bar{y}, n)$ are not presented. The reported observations are arithmetic rather than geometric means for consumption and income. The arithmetic means will not be far from function (6) except for income-classes within which the function diverges markedly from a straight line. Clearly the reported averages for the open-ended upper income-classes in budget studies should not be used in fitting non-linear demand functions. In the present case inclusion of these observations would seriously over-estimate income-elasticity. For other income-classes, the reported arithmetic means have been treated as observations of $(\bar{c}, \bar{y}, n)$.

With this qualification, the 1941 urban budget study (B.L.S. 1945) provides observations of $(\bar{c}, \bar{y}, n)$ for $n = 1, 2, 3, 4$. Observations for $n \geq 5$ are also reported, and it is possible to compute for each income-class the average size of families of five or more. It is assumed that the variances of n about these averages are so small that no significant error is introduced by assuming that all the large $(n \geq 5)$ families in each income-class are of the average size of large families in that class. With this assumption, there are 37 observations $(\bar{c}, \bar{y}, n)$. These are shown in Table 42.2.

These data yield the following regression of $\log \bar{c}$ on $\log \bar{y}$ and $\log n$:

$$\log \bar{c} = 0.82 + 0.56(\pm 0.03) \log \bar{y} + 0.25(\pm 0.07) \log n,$$
$$R^2 = 0.93. \tag{8}$$

In Figure 42.2 function (6) with constants based on regression (8) is plotted on income and consumption axes, separately for $n = 1, 2, 3, 4, 6$. The observations on which the regression is based are also shown, each

Table 42.2

Observations of average food consumption, $\bar{c}$, average disposable income, $\bar{y}$, and family
size, n, for 37 groups of urban families classified by income and size, 1941.

$\bar{y}$ (dollars)	$\bar{c}$ (dollars)	n (number)	$\bar{y}$ (dollars)	$\bar{c}$ (dollars)	n (number)
421	210	1	2,872	770	3
824	301	1	3,864	934	3
1,287	369	1	6,925	1,198	3
1,703	433	1	799	419	4
2,150	506	1	1,401	531	4
2,655	621	1	1,939	658	4
520	239	2	2,414	725	4
869	319	2	2,878	935	4
1,379	454	2	3,895	907	4
1,846	517	2	5,983	1,349	4
2,262	600	2	484	279	6.4
2,855	723	2	873	409	6.4
3,611	849	2	1,364	569	6.2
5,593	673	2	1,849	732	6.1
456	417	3	2,345	866	5.8
936	368	3	2,891	1,020	5.8
1,357	499	3	3,936	1,197	6.3
1,837	562	3	6,056	1,708	6.3
2,408	629	3			

Source (B.L.S. 1945):

Disposable income, $\bar{y}$: for each size category.

"Average amount of income: Total" (Table 18, pp. 96-100).

   − "Personal tax payments" (Table 19, pp. 102-105).

   − $\frac{1}{2}$ "Gifts and contributions" (Table 19, pp. 102-105).

The last item is subtracted in order to avoid counting twice those transfers in money or
in kind which are included in the income of the recipient. Not all of the amount reported
under the heading "gifts and contributions" is of this nature. Support of religious and
educational institutions and community enterprises are properly consumption expenditures which create income rather than transfers. Not all gifts in kind from other families
were reported in the income and consumption of the recipient; only gifts in the major
categories of consumption were so treated (p. 17). Accordingly not all gifts in kind should
be excluded from the income and consumption of the donors. Averages for seven kinds of
"gifts and contributions" are presented only for large groups of families, not for the income-
size-classes considered here. The fraction $\frac{1}{2}$ is a guess of the proper amount to subtract,
based on a rough division of the average amount of "gifts and contributions" for all urban
families (Table 12, p. 87) between transfers and consumption.

Food consumption $\bar{c}$: for each size category.

"Food: Total" (Table 20, pp. 111-19).

Family size n: The last eight entries in this column are estimates of the average size of
families of 5 or more. Table 1a, p. 69, gives for each of six income-classes the number of
families of each size from 1 to 6, and the number of size 7 or larger. Table 1, p. 68, gives

the total number of urban families of all sizes in each income-class, and Table 2, p. 70, gives the average size of families in each income-class. The total number of persons in families of 5 or more and the total number of such families can therefore be computed for each income-class.

tagged with the value of n for the observation. (The points labelled "6" refer to families of five or more persons.)

The values computed for α and δ confirm a fact noted in previous analyses of budget data and known to every housewife, the economies of large family food consumption. Since the sum of α and δ is less than one, a doubling of both income and family size would not double food consumption. At the same *per capita* income, *per capita* food expenditure is smaller the larger the size of the family. This is, of course, partly due to lower consumption by children. But it may also be explained partly by indivisibilities in kitchen inputs and partly by external economies. Recipes which require one egg and serve four persons are not available to the woman who is cooking for two. The bargains obtained by purchasing large quantities do not help the small family which cannot use up a large can before it either spoils or crowds the refrigerator.

1.4. *The Evidence of Other Budget Studies*

The 1941 urban budget study has been used, in preference to other surveys of national scope, to derive the income-elasticity of family food demand for two reasons. The concepts of income and food consumption used in the 1941 urban sample are the most inclusive, and this study permits the most satisfactory allowance for family size, which on *a priori* grounds would be expected to be the most important variable other than income.

The estimate of income-elasticity derived from 1941 urban data will be applied in Section 3 to time series observations for the whole economy. Is the estimate applicable to the rural part of the population? Is the estimate applicable to years other than 1941? The present section endeavours both to check the estimate against the evidence of urban budget surveys made in other years and to see whether rural families have the same income-elasticity of demand as urban families.

Unfortunately, for the same reasons that the 1941 urban study is superior to others, it is impossible to duplicate the calculation of income-elasticity in (8) for other years. Comparisons can usually be made only by limiting the 1941 data to the concepts of income and food consumption used in the other studies. Also, a less precise adjustment for the effects of family size must be made. It is then possible to examine the consistency of the income–consumption relationships in various budget studies, but not to check the exact magnitude of the income-elasticity obtained in (8).

1.4.1. The other urban budget studies of national scope with which the 1941 results should be compared are the 1918 survey of urban workers with families of 4 or more (B.L.S. 1924) and the all-inclusive survey of 1935–36 (U.S. National Resources Committee 1939, 1941). Two less extensive studies made in 1927–28 provide material for another inter-temporal comparison of income–food consumption relationships.[8] One of these concerns federal employees in five cities; the other covers railroad maintenance-of-way employees in ten states. The samples are considerably smaller than those of the three national surveys, and they are samples of two special groups. Moreover, it is necessary to splice the two studies together in order to cover a wide income range. For these reasons, the relationship between income and food consumption obtained from 1927–28 data is less reliable than those derived from the other studies. Finally, the only post-war budget data available refer to families in three cities, Richmond, Va., Washington, D.C., and Manchester, N.H., for the year 1947 (B.L.S. 1949). Since prediction is the ultimate objective of quantitative economics, comparison of pre-war and post-war budget data has a special interest which justifies using these limited data. In addition, samples of two kinds of rural families, farm and non-farm, are available for 1941 (U.S. Department of Agriculture 1943) and for 1935–36 (U.S. National Resources Committee 1941). These studies permit an examination of the difference between rural and urban consumption behaviour as well as additional checks of the consistency of income-elasticity over time.

1.4.1.1. These other studies do not present data classified according to family size. Instead of observations of $(\bar{c}, \bar{y}, n)$, like those of the 1941 urban study, they report only observations of $[\bar{c}, \bar{y}, \bar{n}(\bar{y})]$, where $\bar{n}(\bar{y})$ is the average size of families in a given income-class, with mean income $\bar{y}$.[9] To eliminate the effects of differences in family size on the comparison of one budget sample with another, observations of this kind must be adjusted to a common value of $\bar{n}$. The adjustment must not require information on the distribution of family sizes about the means $\bar{n}(\bar{y})$.

The approximate adjustment here employed assumes that the 1941 urban relationship between family size and food consumption applies to the other samples. The term n^δ in (6) is replaced by a linear expression in n:

$$\bar{c} = k_t''\bar{y}^\alpha(a + bn). \tag{9}$$

Therefore the average consumption of families of all sizes in a given income-class is given by

$$\bar{c} = k_t''\bar{y}^\alpha[a + b\bar{n}(\bar{y})]. \tag{10}$$

An actual observation $[\bar{c}, \bar{y}, \bar{n}(\bar{y})]$ is adjusted to a hypothetical observation $(\bar{c}', \bar{y}, \bar{n}')$ for the same income but for a standard size n' by

$$\bar{c}' = \bar{c}\left(\frac{a + b\bar{n}'}{a + b\bar{n}}\right). \tag{11}$$

This adjustment assumes nothing concerning the value of α.

In practice the comparisons between budget studies concern only families of two or more persons. For $2 \leqq n \leqq 7$, n can be approximated linearly by $1.032 + 0.092n$.[9]

1.4.1.2. The differences among the budget studies with respect to definitions of income and food consumption are set forth in Table 42.3. Three types of information are distinguished; to each type correspond two definitions, one of income and the other of food expenditure. The

Table 42.3
Definitions of disposable income and food consumption in various budget data

Type	Definition of disposable income	Definition of food consumption	Budget data available for comparison
I	Disposable money income + Rent imputed to owner-occupiers + Other income in kind, including food	Money expenditure + Value received in kind (compensation, gifts, relief, home-grown)	Rural non-farm families, 1935-36 and 1941 Farm families, 1935-36 and 1941
II	Disposable money income + Imputed rent	Money expenditure	Urban families, 1927-28, 1935-36 and 1941
III	Disposable money income	Money expenditure	Urban families, 1918, 1941 and 1947

table lists budget surveys which can be compared on the basis of information of each type.

1.4.1.3. The observations reported in all the studies were adjusted to an average family size of 3.5 by the method outlined in Section 1.4.1.1. For each sample a line was then fitted by least squares to the logarithms of the observations of disposable income and food consumption. The slope of this line is an estimate of the income-elasticity of food demand. The estimates from those samples which use the same type of information can then be compared to check the consistency of the family income-elasticity over time. Only for information of Type I is there any reason to expect the estimates of income-elasticity to agree with the estimate of 0.56 obtained in regression (8). The other types of information exclude food received in kind; since this is most important, relative to money expenditures, for low-income families, its omission should result in a higher estimate of income-elasticity.

Table 42.4 reports the regressions between the logarithms of food consumption and family income for each of the samples listed in Table

Table 42.4

Relationships of food consumption, adjusted to family size 3.5, to disposable income in various budget data for families of two or more persons

	Type of information	Budget sample	Regression $\log \bar{c} =$
1.	I	Rural non-farm, 1935-36	$0.92 + 0.55 \log \bar{y}$
2.	I	Rural non-farm, 1941	$1.02 + 0.53 \log \bar{y}$
3.	I	Farm, 1935-36	$1.16 + 0.37 \log \bar{y}$
4.	I	Farm, 1941	$1.15 + 0.35 \log \bar{y}$
5.	II	Urban, 1927-28	$0.57 + 0.68 \log \bar{y}$
6.	II	Urban, 1935-36	$0.76 + 0.61 \log \bar{y}$
7.	II	Urban, 1941	$0.64 + 0.65 \log \bar{y}$
8.	III	Urban, 1918	$0.89 + 0.57 \log \bar{y}$
9.	III	Urban, 1941	$0.68 + 0.64 \log \bar{y}$
10.	III	Richmond, Va., 1947	$0.81 + 0.64 \log \bar{y}$
11.	III	Washington, D.C., 1947	$0.96 + 0.59 \log \bar{y}$
12.	III	Manchester, N.H., 1947	$1.00 + 0.59 \log \bar{y}$

Sources of data on which the regressions were calculated:

(1) U.S. National Resources Committee (hereafter, N.R.C.) (1941), Table 161, p. 56.

(2) and (4) U.S. Department of Agriculture (hereafter, U.S.D.A.) (1943), Table 49, pp. 156-57, and Table 50, pp. 159-60.

(3) N.R.C. (1941), Table 144, p. 51.

(5) Leven *et al.* (1934), Appendix B, Table 1, pp. 246-49, lines D and E.

(6) N.R.C. (1941), Table 178, p. 61.

(7) and (9) B.L.S. (1945), Table 19, p. 102, and Table 20, p. 109.

(8) B.L.S. (1924), Table 1, p. 4. This study does not report tax payments. However, in 1918, families of the large size to which the sample was confined had such small direct tax liabilities that it is safe to take money income before taxes as a measure of disposable money income.

(10), (11) and (12) B.L.S. (1949).

In regressions 6 and 7, the observations for the lowest-income class of each sample were omitted. If they are included the slopes are, respectively, 0.57 and 0.69; the erratic nature of the lowest-income observations in the two years can be seen in Figure 42.5. The explanation, and the justification for their omission, is that the exclusion of food received in kind affects the 1935-36 and 1941 samples unequally. The 1935-36 sample does not include recipients of relief; the 1941 sample does. Relief recipients rely much more on food received in kind than non-relief families of the same income. Consequently the 1935-36 low-income group shows higher money expenditures for food than the 1941 sample, and in both years the low-income point is out of line with the other observations.

42.3. The regressions, together with the adjusted observations on which they are based, are shown in Figures 42.3–42.6.

The significance of the difference between two estimates of the coefficient of log $\bar{y}$ can be tested for each pair of regressions based on the same type of information (Fisher 1946, pp. 140–42). With only one exception, a difference as large as observed would occur in over 10 per cent of samples from a population in which the coefficients were equal.

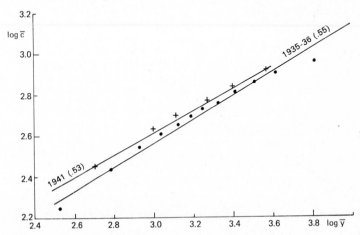

Fig. 42.3. Rural non-farm families' income and food consumption. ● 1935-36. + 1941.

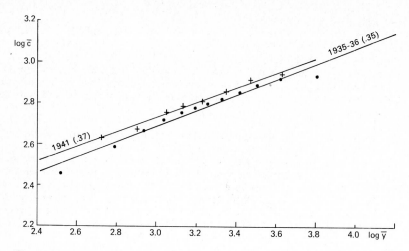

Fig. 42.4. Rural farm families' income and food consumption. ● 1935-36. + 1941.

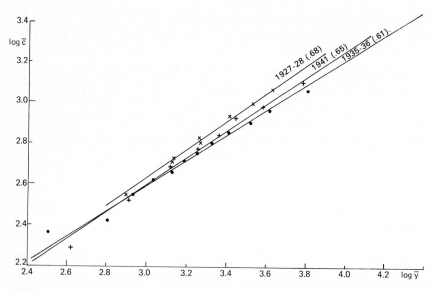

Fig. 42.5. Urban families' income and food consumption. × 1927-28. ● 1935-36. + 1941.

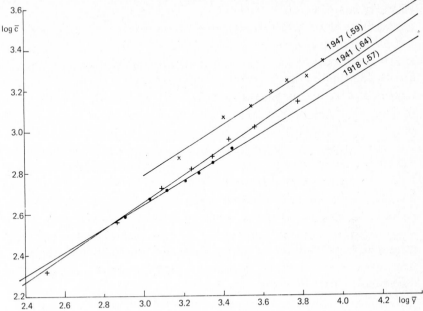

Fig. 42.6. Urban families' income and food consumption. ● 1918. + 1941. × 1947 (Washington, D.C.).

The exception is the pair of regressions 8 and 9; in this case the difference is not significant at the 1 per cent level.

All the regressions reported in Table 42.4 are based on grouped data. None of these studies report budgets of individual families, nor do they estimate the variance of the basic observations about the means for the income-classes. Consequently a better statistical test of the significance of the differences among various sample estimates of the coefficient of log $\bar{y}$ is not possible. These differences must be judged chiefly by the grosser criterion of the degree of accuracy to which the econometrician can aspire.

By this standard the agreement in income-elasticity over time is remarkable. The table contains no evidence to prevent the application of the 1941 estimate to previous or, indeed, post-war years. The error in attributing to rural non-farm families the urban estimate of income-elasticity appears to be negligible. But the behaviour of farm families is significantly different from that of non-farm families. The lower income-elasticity characteristic of farm families, and their higher mean level of food consumption relatĩve to income, are probably associated with the greater importance of home-produced food in farm diets. The increase in urban expenditure for food as income rises represents a shift to higher-quality foods more than an increase in total intake. This shift is perhaps neither as easy nor as necessary for farmers who produce a large part of their own food.

1.5. *The Omission of Variables Other than Income and Family Size*

Family size is the only variable other than family income appearing in (6), the food demand function applicable to budget data. Failure to include family size as a variable would result in a biased estimate of income-elasticity, because family size is correlated with income.

The omission of other variables may be a source of similar bias. Sub-groups of the population may not be homogeneous in food consumption behaviour; there may be significant geographical or occupational differences. These differences may be of two kinds:

(1) Sub-groups may have significantly different income elasticities. In this case the relationship of food consumption to family income could not properly be described by a single coefficient for the whole population.

(2) Sub-groups may show differences in income-elasticity no larger than can be attributed to sampling errors, but may differ significantly in their levels of food consumption. If, in addition, the sub-groups are represented in systematically differing proportions at various income levels, the estimate of income-elasticity based on the whole population will not correspond to the true income-elasticity common to the sub-groups. For example, suppose, as some evidence in the 1935–36 study (N.R.C. 1941) suggests, that food expenditures are highest for given incomes and sizes of family in Eastern metropolises. The high-income portion of the population contains relatively more families from these communities than the low-income groups. This will be reflected in a budget study whose sampling method gives every family in the population an equal chance to be selected. Income-elasticity computed from the whole sample will be an over-estimate, since it will reflect variation in food consumption due not solely to income but also to geography.

The 1941 budget study permits consideration of only one possible determinant of food consumption other than income and family size, namely type of community: urban, rural non-farm, or farm. The discrepancy between farm and non-farm behaviour presents a difficulty in passing from the family demand function to the national demand function. In Section 2 the family function is to be summed over all families in the nation. For purposes of aggregation the simplicity of function (6) is of course a convenience. If the function involved characteristics of families other than income and family size the process of aggregation would be more complicated. If a separate function, with a different income-elasticity, were attributed to the farm population, it would be necessary also to estimate two separate aggregate functions with differing price-elasticities. The required time series are not available. The error of attributing urban behaviour to farm families must be accepted. It is desirable, therefore, to have some indication of its size. In 1941 use of the urban function to estimate farm consumption at all levels of family income yields an estimated average 5 per cent below the actual average consumption of farm families. Since farm consumption was less than one-sixth of national food consumption the error from this source in estimating the average for all families is less than 1 per cent.

Within the urban population there may be divergences of behaviour which are concealed in the 1941 budget data and bias the estimate of income-elasticity. Occupation, size of city, and region may be determinants of food consumption, and the impossibility of allowing for them in the 1941 study may lead to errors.[10] These errors are the price paid for the advantages of the 1941 study, pointed out above, and for a family demand function which can be aggregated without involving in the national function a collection of variables which would place an impossible burden on available time series.

2. Aggregation of the Family Food Demand Function

The problem of aggregation is to derive from the relationship between family income and family consumption a relationship between aggregate income and aggregate consumption. In general aggregate consumption, given the family demand function, depends on the distribution of income, and not simply on the mean of the distribution. Moreover, if family consumption depends on variables other than income – such as family size, in the case of food – aggregate consumption depends on the joint distribution of families by income and these other variables. Whenever this joint distribution is known, an estimate of aggregate consumption can be made by weighting the family demand function according to the joint distribution. The problem of aggregation arises because estimates are required when mean income is the only available information concerning the distribution. Consequently any aggregate relationship requires some assumption concerning the manner in which the joint distribution changes when aggregate income changes. In the nature of the case the assumption cannot be checked every time it is used; otherwise it would not be needed.

2.1. *Aggregation under the Assumption of a "Constant" Income Distribution*

In the particular case of food demand, summing (6) over all families gives mean consumption:

$$C(Y) = k_t'' \sum_{n=1}^{m} \int_0^\infty y^\alpha n^\delta f(y, n; Y) \, dy, \tag{12}$$

where m is the largest size of family and $f(y, n; Y)$ is the density function of the distribution of families by y and n when mean income is Y. The following assumption is made concerning this density function:

$$\lambda f(\lambda y, n, \lambda Y) = f(y, n, Y) \qquad \lambda > 0. \tag{13}$$

A sufficient but not necessary condition for (13) to be satisfied is that every family share a change in aggregate income in proportion to its income and remain of the same size.[11]

From assumption (13) it follows that aggregate food consumption (12) becomes:

$$C(Y) = M k_t'' Y^\alpha, \tag{14}$$

where M is a constant depending on the distribution of families by income and size.[12]

The same result can be reached from an assumption somewhat weaker than (13) if approximation (9) is used for the family demand function. In this case, knowledge of the entire joint distribution of y and n is not required; since the demand function is linear in n, it is sufficient to know the average family size corresponding to each income level. Let

$$g(y; Y) = \sum_{n=1}^{m} f(y, n; Y)$$

$$\bar{n}(y; Y) = \frac{\sum_{n=1}^{m} nf(y, n; Y)}{g(y; Y)}.$$

Then (13) can be replaced by the weaker conditions:

$$\lambda g(\lambda y; \lambda Y) = g(y; Y) \qquad \lambda > 0 \qquad\qquad (15)^{13}$$

$$\bar{n}(\lambda y; \lambda Y) = \bar{n}(y; Y) \qquad \lambda > 0. \qquad\qquad (16)$$

Summing (9) over all families,

$$C(Y) = \int_{0}^{\infty} k_t'' y^{\alpha}[a + b\bar{n}(y; Y)]g(y; Y)\, dy. \qquad (17)$$

From assumptions (15) and (16) it follows that (17) becomes:

$$C(Y) = M' k_t'' Y^{\alpha}, \qquad\qquad (18)$$

where M' is a constant.[14]

Under the assumptions made in this section, then, the demand function of Section 1 is preserved under aggregation. That is, the relationship between aggregate consumption and aggregate income is of the same form as the relationship between family consumption and family income, and the aggregate income-elasticity is equal to the family income-elasticity α.

2.2. *Evidence Concerning the "Constancy" of the Income Distribution*

The reason for introducing the weaker assumptions concerning the income–family size distribution is that some data bearing on (15) are available. Figure 42.7 presents the cumulative distributions of families of two or more persons by income for 1935–36 and 1941, based on the budget surveys for those years (N.R.C. 1939, Table 24a, p. 86; B.L.S. 1945, Table 1, p. 68). In Figure 42.7 the horizontal axis measures y/Y, the ratio of family income to mean income. The ordinate of each point gives the percentage of families whose incomes, relative to mean income, were lower than the abscissa. If assumption (15) is correct, plotting the distributions in this way should make the 1935–36 and 1941 points fall along the same curve. Figure 42.8 is a similar comparison of the 1941 and 1947

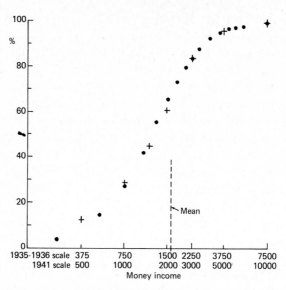

Fig. 42.7. Cumulative income distribution of families of two or more persons, 1935-36 and 1941. ● 1935-36. + 1941.

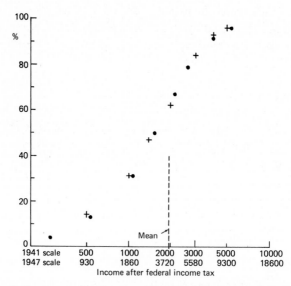

Fig. 42.8. Cumulative income distribution of families, including single individuals, 1941 and 1947. + 1941. ● 1947.

cumulative distributions of families of all sizes by income after federal income tax (*Economic Report* 1949, Table B–3, p. 93, and Table 2, p. 14).

The coincidence of the income distribution observations in different years, when plotted as in Figures 42.7 and 42.8, is of course not conclusive confirmation of the invariance of the distribution either over time or with respect to changes in aggregate income.[15] It does indicate that, in the absence of time series of measures of income inequality,[16] the assumption of a constant degree of inequality will not lead to serious errors in statistical demand analysis.

Assumption (15) does not, of course, imply either (13) or (17). But if (15) – constancy of the Lorenz curve – is correct, errors of aggregation will be due to failure of the assumptions regarding the distribution of families by size. These errors are not likely to be large. For one thing, over-all average family size is nearly constant over the period 1913–41, varying in the narrow range 3.20–3.36.[17] With a constant average family size, it would be difficult to have a reshuffling of the joint distribution of families by income and size which would change aggregate food consumption appreciably. Suppose, to take an extreme and unlikely example, that in the 1941 distribution the average size of families below the median income of $1500 were cut in half and the average size of families with higher incomes increased by 35 per cent. This would leave average family size unchanged. It would increase aggregate food consumption, computed by (12), only 1 per cent.

2.3. *The Aggregate Per Capita Demand Function*

The aggregate demand function (14) or (18) expresses food consumption per family in terms of disposable income per family. For the purposes of Section 3 it is more convenient to measure consumption and income *per capita*. In accordance with assumption (13) or (16), the average size of family N is taken to be constant; in fact, as pointed out above, it varied only slightly over the period under consideration.

Consequently (14) implies

$$C' = \frac{M k_t''}{N^{1-\alpha}} Y'^\alpha, \tag{19}$$

where $C' = C/N$, *per capita* food consumption, and $Y' = Y/N$, *per capita* disposable income.

Substituting the value of k_t'' from (6) gives the complete aggregate demand function

$$C_t' = K Y_t'^{\alpha_1} Y_{t-1}'^{\alpha_2} P_t^\beta Q_t^\gamma, \tag{20}$$

where $K = Mk/N^{1-\alpha}$ is a constant.

3. Estimation of Parameters from Time Series

In accordance with Sections 1 and 2, the sum of the two income-elasticities of food demand is taken to be 0.56, both for the family demand function and for the aggregate demand function. This sum must be split into an estimate of current-income-elasticity α_1, and an estimate of past-income-elasticity α_2. The two price elasticities β and γ must also be evaluated. The purpose of the present section is to obtain these estimates by multiple regression of time series of aggregate data. The parameters, however, apply to the family demand function (1) as well as to the aggregate demand function (20). In Section 4, therefore, the estimates obtained in this section are tested by applying them to family budget observations made in different years.

3.1. A Simple Model of the Retail Food Market
The procedure used in the time series regression assumes the following simple model of the retail food market:

$$S_t = C_t' = K Y_t'^{\alpha_1} Y_{t-1}'^{\alpha_2} P_t^\beta Q_t^\gamma, \tag{21}$$

where S_t is *per capita* food supply for domestic consumption. Y_t', Q_t and S_t are assumed to be exogenous in the sense that none of them depends on the simultaneous values of the other variables in the system. Thus the supply of food, for example, may depend on the price of food in the preceding year, and still be a datum in the year in which it comes on the market.

Over the time period under consideration, 1913–41, both the *per capita* production of food and the *per capita* supply for domestic consumption were nearly constant. Total food production was insensitive in the short run to current economic conditions and was determined instead by weather, government policy, and the state of agricultural technique. The possibility remains that, even though food production may be considered exogenous to our model, the supply for domestic consumption may be influenced by the current price level of food. Changes in stocks of food-stuffs and sales abroad may depend on current prices. A significant relationship of this kind between supply and price would mean that use of the simple model would yield biased estimates of the parameters in the demand equation (Stone 1948, p. 4; Leontief 1948). The possibility of bias from this source will be considered in Section 3.4 below.

The assumptions that income and non-food prices are exogenous to the food market have less theoretical justification. But a model which would explain these variables would cover the whole economy, and the statistical estimation of the parameters in an all-inclusive model is much beyond the scope of this paper.

3.2. The Multiple Regression

The "reduced form" of the simple system (21) is an equation expressing P as a function of the three exogenous variables. In terms of the logarithms of the variables, the equation is:

$$\log P_t = -(1/\beta)\log K + (1/\beta)\log S_t - \left(\frac{\alpha_1}{\beta}\right)\log Y_t'$$
$$- \left(\frac{\alpha_2}{\beta}\right)\log Y_{t-1}' - (\gamma/\beta)\log Q_t. \tag{22}$$

This equation can be written:

$$\log P_t = b_0 + b_1(\log S_t - \alpha \log Y_t')$$
$$+ b_2(\log Y_t' - \log Y_{t-1}') + b_3 \log Q_t. \tag{23}$$

Since the value of α is taken as known, the constants b_0, b_1, b_2, b_3 can be estimated by multiple regression of $\log P_t$ against three variables $(\log S_t - \alpha \log Y_t')$, $(\log Y_t' - \log Y_{t-1}')$ and $\log Q_t$. The parameters of the demand function (20) can then be found as follows:

$$\beta = \frac{1}{b_1}, \quad -\gamma = \frac{b_3}{b_1}, \quad \alpha_2 = \frac{b_2}{b_1}, \quad \alpha_1 = \alpha - \frac{b_2}{b_1}. \tag{24}$$

This multiple regression has been computed from annual data for the 29 years 1913–41. The statistical series used to represent the variables are shown in Table 42.5 and described in the notes to that table.

Table 42.5
Time series of food consumption per capita, disposable income per capita, food price index, non-food price index, and food production per capita

Year t	Food consumption S_t (Index 1935-39 = 100)	Disposable income Y_t' (Dollars)	Food price P_t (Index 1935-39 = 100)	Non-food price Q_t (Index 1935-39 = 100)	Food production Z_t (Index)
1912	..	332	..	..	..
1913	96	343	79.9	65.9	80
1914	97	335	81.8	66.7	82
1915	96	352	80.9	68.3	83
1916	96	408	90.8	71.2	79
1917	96	483	116.9	78.6	79
1918	95	534	134.4	93.7	86
1919	98	603	149.8	105.3	86
1920	97	627	168.8	130.5	82
1921	94	486	128.3	127	78
1922	99	517	119.9	119.5	83
1923	101	589	124	120.9	85
1924	102	584	122.8	121.9	85
1925	101	610	132.9	121.5	80
1926	102	623	137.4	120.7	83
1927	101	618	132.3	119.8	81
1928	102	625	130.8	118.4	83
1929	102	653	132.5	117.4	80
1930	100	574	126	116.1	80
1931	100	480	103.9	111	81
1932	98	365	86.5	103.4	77
1933	97	354	84.1	96.6	77
1934	99	403	93.7	96.7	79
1935	96	442	100.4	97	73
1936	99	509	101.3	97.8	76
1937	100	537	105.3	101.1	78
1938	100	485	97.8	102.3	79
1939	104	517	95.2	101.7	81
1940	105	552	96.6	102.3	84
1941	108	666	105.5	105.1	86
1945	114	1,070	139.1	122.9	..
1946	118	1,127	159.6	129	..
1947	117	1,205	193.8	141	..
1948	113	1,299	210.7	..	..

Sources and explanation of the series:
S_t: Cohen (1948), Table 1, p. 13. The 1948 figure is from *Economic Report* (1949), p. 54. The series is a price-weighted index of quantities computed by the U.S. Bureau of Agricultural Economics. It measures the disappearance of physical quantities of food to domestic

civilian consumption. It does not measure changes in the amount of servicing of food in restaurants or retail outlets, nor does it measure in all cases changes in the amount of processing. For these reasons the series is not strictly comparable to the measure of food consumption in budget data, and it probably understates the amount of variation over time in the supply of "finished" foodstuffs.

Y_t': Computed by dividing figures for national disposable income (Dewhurst *et al.* 1947, Appendix 4, p. 696) by annual estimates of population (U.S. Department of Commerce 1945, p. 8). The figures for 1945-48 are from *Economic Report* (1949), Table C-6, p. 104.

P_t and Q_t: U.S. Department of Commerce (1945), p. 423. The figures for 1945-48 are from *Economic Report* (1949), Table C-20, p. 119. Both series are based on the Bureau of Labor Statistics Consumers' Price Index for moderate-income families in large cities. The series P_t is the Bureau's food price index. The series Q_t is computed from the equation $wP_t + (1 - w)Q_t = I_t$, where I_t is the index for all items and w is the weight given food in the computation of I_t (B.L.S. 1943, p. 13a).

Z_t: Bureau of Agricultural Economics weighted index of physical production of foodstuffs (U.S. Department of Agriculture 1948), adjusted for changes in population.

The results of the regression are as follows:

Regression coefficients:	Demand function parameters:
$b_1 = -1.97 (\pm 0.27)$	$\alpha_1 = 0.44$
$b_2 = -0.24 (\pm 0.16)$	$\alpha_2 = 0.12$
$b_3 = -0.06 (\pm 0.14)$	$\beta = -0.51$
	$\gamma = -0.03$
$(R^2 = 0.87)$	$\alpha + \beta + \gamma = 0.02.$ (25)

In this regression, the coefficient of $\log Q_t$ differs insignificantly from zero, and the significance of the correlation is increased by omitting this variable. The results are then as follows:

Regression coefficients:	Demand function parameters:
$b_0 = 2.95$	$\log K = 1.57$
$b_1 = -1.88 (\pm 0.14)$	$\alpha_1 = 0.45$
$b_2 = -0.2 (\pm 0.12)$	$\alpha_2 = 0.11$
$(b_3 = 0)$	$\beta = -0.53$
	$(\gamma = 0)$
$(R^2 = 0.87)$	$\alpha + \beta + \gamma = +0.03.$ (26)

Figure 42.9 shows the actual time series of the food price index (P_t, not $\log P_t$) and the values of P_t estimated from regression (26). The correlation between the original and calculated series is 0.93.

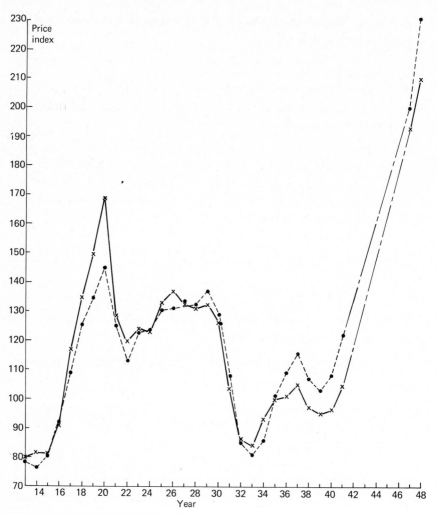

Fig. 42.9. Food Price Index, 1913-41, 1947-48. + ——————— Actual. ● – – – – – Calculated from regression (26).

Confidence limits, with 95 per cent probability, have been computed
for β and α_2.[18] They are:

$$-0.63 < \beta < -0.46$$

$$-0.03 < \alpha_2 < 0.24.$$

Taking α as known from budget data, confidence limits for α_1 can be derived from those for α_2:

$$0.32 < \alpha_1 < 0.59.$$

The sum of the estimates of elasticities in either (25) or (26) does not differ significantly from zero.[19] The results do not contradict the "homogeneity postulate" of economic theory.

3.3. *Estimates Obtained with No Restriction on the Parameters*

In the correlation just described, the sum of the two income-elasticities is taken as known from budget data. How do the estimates of the parameters obtained subject to that restriction compare with estimates based on time series alone? A multiple regression, using the same variables, has been computed to estimate the constants in the following equation:

$$\log P_t = b_0 + b_1 \log S_t - b_2 \log Y'_{t-1} + b_3 \log Q_t + b_4 \log Y'_t. \quad (27)$$

The coefficient b_2 is not significant. With $\log Y'_{t-1}$ omitted from the regression, the results are as follows:

Regression coefficients:	Demand function parameters:
$b_1 = -3.56\,(\pm 0.42)$	$\alpha_1 = -b_4/b_1 = 0.27$
$(b_2 = 0)$	$(\alpha_2 = b_2/b_1 = 0)$
$b_3 = 0.22\,(\pm 0.09)$	$\beta = 1/b_1 = -0.28$
$b_4 = 0.97\,(\pm 0.09)$	$\gamma = -b_3/b_1 = 0.06.$ (28)
$(R^2 = 0.93)$	

The 95 per cent probability confidence limits for the parameters of the demand function, computed in the same manner as those for regression (26), are as follows:

$$0.22 < \alpha_1 < 0.35$$

$$-0.38 < \beta < -0.23$$

$$0.01 < \gamma < 0.12.$$

The unrestricted correlation thus gives significantly lower numerical values for the income- and price-elasticities than the regression restricted by the budget-study estimate. But the regression in which the budget-study estimate is assumed fits the time series almost as well as the unrestricted regression. The reverse is not true. The estimate of income-elasticity in (28) is not consistent with budget data. Moreover, the rejection in (28) of previous year's income as a significant variable is contradicted by the evidence of a lag in the 1941–42 budget study.

The unrestricted correlation is more likely than the restricted regression to give unreliable estimates because of collinearity (Stone 1948, p. 3). The vulnerability of Equation (27) to this danger is due to high correlations among the explanatory variables. A bunch map analysis (Stone 1945, pp. 306–10) is given in Figure 42.10.[20] It shows that log Y'_{t-1} and log Q_t are not useful variables. Their addition to the multiple regression does not improve the bunch maps of the three regressions involving log P_t, log Y'_t, and log S_t. (See the first three columns of diagrams in Figure 42.10.) Moreover, the bunch maps for the regressions of log P_t on log Y'_{t-1} and of log P_t on log Q_t are exploded by the introduction of log Y'_t and log S_t. (See the fourth and fifth columns of diagrams.) Similarly, the bunch maps for the regressions of log S_t on log Y'_{t-1} and log S_t on log Q_t are exploded by adding the other variables. (See the last two columns of diagrams.) The correlations of log Y'_{t-1} and $log\,Q_t$ with log Y'_t and log S_t are too high to enable α_2 and γ to be estimated from times series alone. But if these other variables influence food consumption – and budget data indicate that lagged income, at least, does – the estimates of α_1 and β will reflect their influence.

The restricted correlation is less vulnerable to this kind of error. The independent variables in regression (23) are not the highly correlated variables which appear in (27). The introduction of an outside estimate of α permits a transformation of the variables which eliminates most of the correlation. Between the two explanatory variables used in (26) the correlation is -0.20.

3.4. *The Possibility of Bias due to a Relationship between Supply and Prices*

The danger that a relationship between food supply and price might bias the estimates of the parameters in the demand equation has already been mentioned. The present section fulfils the promise to investigate the possibility by fitting supply and demand equations simultaneously. The two equations of the model are:

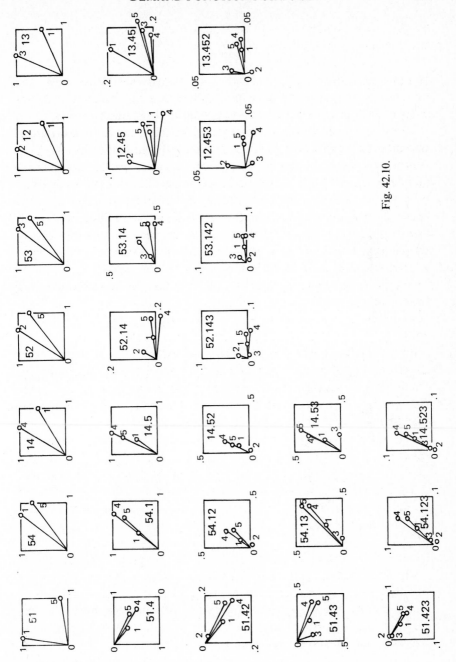

Fig. 42.10.

$$S_t = K Y_t'^\alpha P_t^\beta Q_t^\gamma \quad \text{Demand,}$$

$$S_t/Z_t = A P_t^{\beta'} Q_t^{\gamma'} \quad \text{Supply.} \tag{29}$$

In this model *per capita* domestic food supply is no longer assumed to be exogenous. Instead, *per capita* food production, Z_t, is taken as a predetermined variable. The supply equation states that the share of production going into the domestic retail market depends on food prices and on other prices. A serious study of the determinants of food supply would involve other variables and a more complicated scheme (Girschick and Haavelmo 1947). The purpose of model (29) is only to discover whether the influence of current prices on supply is strong enough to bias the single-equation estimates of the demand parameters. In the demand equation of (29), α is assumed to be known. For the sake of simplicity, past income Y_{t-1}' is omitted from the demand function and α is entirely assigned to current income.

Expressed in terms of logarithms measured from their means, the system is:

$$\log S_t - \alpha \log Y_t' - \beta \log P_t - \gamma \log Q_t = u_{1t} \text{ Demand,}$$

$$\log S_t \qquad\quad - \beta' \log P_t - \gamma' \log Q_t - \log Z_t = u_{2t}$$
$$\text{Supply.} \tag{30}$$

Here u_{1t} and u_{2t} are stochastic variables assumed to be distributed normally with zero means. System (30) can be reduced to two equations, one expressing $\log P_t$ and the other $\log S_t$ in terms of the independent variables:

$$\log P_t - \frac{\alpha}{\beta' - \beta} \log Y_t' - \frac{\gamma - \gamma'}{\beta' - \beta} \log Q_t + \frac{1}{\beta' - \beta} \log Z_t = v_{1t}$$

$$\log S_t - \frac{\beta'\alpha}{\beta' - \beta} \log Y_t' - \frac{\beta'\gamma - \beta\gamma'}{\beta' - \beta} \log Q_t + \frac{\beta}{\beta' - \beta} \log Z_t = v_{2t},$$
$$\tag{31}$$

where:

$$v_{1t} = \frac{u_{1t} - u_{2t}}{\beta' - \beta} \quad \text{and} \quad v_2 = \frac{\beta'u_{1t} - \beta u_{2t}}{\beta' - \beta}$$

are distributed normally with means zero.

Since α is known, and since $\beta/(\beta' - \beta) = \beta'/(\beta' - \beta) - 1$, these two equations may be rewritten:

$$\log P_t - b_{11}(\log Z_t - \alpha \log Y_t') - b_{12} \log Q_t = v_{1t}$$

$$(\log S_t - \log Z_t) - b_{21}(\log Z_t - \alpha \log Y_t') - b_{22} \log Q_t = v_{2t}. \tag{32}$$

Maximum likelihood estimates of b_{11} and b_{12} can be obtained by least squares regression of $\log P_t$ on $(\log Z_t - \alpha \log Y_t)$ and $\log Q_t$, and maximum likelihood estimates of b_{21} and b_{22} can be obtained by regression of $(\log S_t - \log Z_t)$ on the same two variables. From these four coefficients maximum likelihood estimates of the four unknown structural parameters can be derived:

$$\beta = \frac{b_{21} + 1}{b_{11}} \qquad \gamma = b_{22} - \beta b_{12}$$

$$\beta' = \frac{b_{21}}{b_{11}} \qquad \gamma' = b_{22} - \beta' b_{12}. \tag{33}$$

The estimates of the regression coefficients are as follows:

$$
\begin{array}{llll}
b_{11} = -1.06 & b_{12} = 0.29 & (R^2 = 0.65) \\
\quad (\pm 0.35) & \quad (\pm 0.19) \\
b_{21} = -0.15 & b_{22} = -0.02 & (R^2 = 0.1). & (34) \\
\quad (\pm 0.11) & \quad (\pm 0.06)
\end{array}
$$

These estimates give the following values for the structural parameters:

$$
\begin{array}{ll}
\beta = -0.80 & \gamma = 0.21 \\
\beta' = 0.14 & \gamma' = -0.06. \qquad (35)
\end{array}
$$

However, the fit of the second reduced form equation is extremely poor. The multiple correlation coefficient is not significant at the 5 per cent level (Snedecor 1946, Table 13.6, p. 351). The hypothesis that both b_{21} and b_{22} are zero cannot be rejected. Even if $\log Q_t$ is omitted, the regression is not significant; a correlation between $\log S_t/Z_t$ and $(\log Z_t - \alpha \log Y_t')$ numerically as large as observed could occur in over 10 per cent of samples from a population in which the correlation is zero. If b_{21}

and b_{22} are zero, so are the supply equation parameters β' and γ'. Consequently, the hypothesis that β' and γ' are zero cannot be rejected. But if β' and γ' are zero, the supply relation is reduced to

$$\log S_t = \log Z_t + u_{2t}. \tag{36}$$

Provided that u_{2t} is not correlated with u_{1t}, the error term in the demand equation, the maximum likelihood estimates of the demand parameters are the single-equation estimates. The fact that $\log S_t$ appears in both the demand and supply equations is now irrelevant. The only danger in ignoring (36) is that u_{1t} and u_{2t} are correlated. The error terms u_{2t} are a known observed series ($\log S_t - \log Z_t$). Fitting the demand equation so as to maximize the probability that its errors and the known errors u_{2t} come from a joint normal distribution makes no more sense than considering the possibility that the errors u_{1t} are correlated with any other observed series. (Compare Leontief 1948, p. 400.) In any case (36) is not a convincing hypothesis; the correlation (0.38) between $\log S_t$ and $\log Z_t$ is barely significant.

The investigation of this section gives no reason for rejecting the hypothesis of the initial single-equation model that food supply is an exogenous variable. There is no evidence of a significant relationship between supply and prices. Whatever bias may be introduced by ignoring a possible supply relation is surely preferable to the wide bands of error attached to estimates based on the two-equation model.

3.5. *The Problem of Serial Correlation*

One more statistical difficulty must be considered (Stone 1948, p. 12). The parameter estimates of (26) were obtained under the assumption that Equation (23) is satisfied every year subject to an error which is distributed independently of the errors in previous years. This assumption is contradicted by the time series of the estimated residuals. The differences between actual food price and food price calculated from the regression show a cyclical pattern (see Figure 42.9). They also show an over-all downward trend: actual price tends to fall relative to calculated price. The ratio (δ^2/s^2) of the mean square successive difference of the residuals to the variance of the residuals is 0.68. So low a value would occur in less than 0.1 per cent of samples of this size from a population in which the errors in different years are independently distributed (Hart 1942).

The addition of a time trend to the multiple regression does not eliminate serial correlation. The cyclical pattern of the residuals remains. The ratio δ^2/s^2 is increased to 1.08, but this is still significant at the 1 per cent probability level.

A regression has been computed using the first differences of the variables involved in regression (26). The results are as follows:

Regression coefficients: Demand parameters:

$b_1 = -1.74\,(\pm 0.18)$ $\beta = -0.57$

$b_2 = -0.08\,(\pm 0.08)$ $\alpha_2 = 0.05.$ (37)

$(R^2 = 0.82)$

These estimates of the demand parameters are well within the confidence limits for the estimates based on regression (26). Correlation of first differences does not yield significantly different estimates from correlation of the original variables. But the residuals of the regression of first differences do not show the auto-correlation evident in the residuals of the other regression. The ratio δ^2/s^2 is 1.99 – not significant; indeed, the expected value of this ratio for samples of 28 from a population where the errors are not auto-correlated is 2.07.

3.6. *Application to Post-war Experience*

Post-war data offer a considerable challenge to any formula for food demand based on pre-war experience. The wartime expansion of agricultural production has raised the *per capita* supply of food some 15 per cent above the level which persisted with only slight variation over the period 1913–41. Consumer income, in real or money terms, has far exceeded any previous peacetime levels. The price variables too have been carried by inflation beyond the range of experience from which a statistical formula must be derived. The war may have distorted the operation of any time trend detected in peacetime. Abnormal influences on consumer demand – the backlog of demand for durable goods, the extraordinary accumulation of savings during the war, the continuation of rent control – may have indirect repercussions on food expenditure. Finally, years within which prices and other variables change markedly are not a promising period for application of a function in which each variable covers an entire year.

In extrapolating a demand function to new ranges of aggregate income, the use of budget data to estimate income-elasticity has, in theory at least, an advantage over exclusive reliance on time series. Aggregate income may be unprecedentedly high without taking the bulk of families beyond the range of family incomes observed in budget data. An estimate of income-elasticity derived from budget data, applied to a record level of aggregate income, is not necessarily being employed beyond the range of the observations on which it is based.

Judged by food demand functions based solely on pre-war time series, the inflation of food prices after the expiration of price control and the increasing share of consumer income devoted to food expenditure were a mystery. The Department of Commerce found food expenditure in 1948 eight billion dollars more than expected from its pre-war regression of aggregate income and food expenditure (Gilbert 1948; Cohen 1948). The food demand function of Girschick and Haavelmo (1947), obtained by estimating the parameters of this function simultaneously with those of other equations embracing the entire economy, fails to indicate an inflationary gap in food at the end of price control in 1946, or during the inflation of 1947.[21]

Thanks to the use of budget data, the statistical food demand function obtained in this study contains a higher estimate of income elasticity than functions based on time series alone (0.56 compared to 0.3 in the Girschick–Haavelmo study).[22] The function estimated in (26) correctly shows excess demand in 1946. Table 42.6 compares the actual averages of the food price index for three post-war years with values of the index "predicted" by (26); the comparison is also shown in Figure 42.9.

Table 42.6
Average of food price index

	Average of food price index	
Year	Actual	"Predicted"
1946	160	185
1947	194	201
1948	211	232

4. The Family Food Demand Function Over Time

The estimates of elasticities obtained in Section 3 are intended to apply to the family demand function as well as to the aggregate demand function. In Section 1.4 it was shown that budget observations for different years agree fairly well in regard to the slope of the line relating the logarithms of food expenditure and income. They differ, as inspection of Figures 42.3–6 readily reveals, in the level of this line. These differences in level should, according to the family demand function assumed in Section 1, be explained by differences in variables other than current income. The purpose of this section is to see to what extent this explanation is possible.

The family food demand function (1) gives food consumption in physical units or in constant food dollars. For expenditure x_t in current dollars the function becomes

$$x_t = c_t P_t = k y_t \alpha_1 y_{t-1} \alpha_2 P_t^{\beta+1} Q_t^\gamma n^\delta. \tag{38}$$

By assumption (4) concerning the relation of current to past income, the expenditure function is:

$$x_t = k y_t^\alpha \left(\frac{Y_{t-1}}{Y_t}\right)^{\alpha_2} P_t^{\beta+1} Q_t^\gamma n^\delta. \tag{39}$$

For a given year t, P_t, Q_t, and Y_{t-1}/Y_t are constant over all families. If the observations in a budget study for that year are adjusted to a standard family size $\hat{n}$, the relationship between current income and food consumption which the budget data should obey is

$$x_t = m_t y_t^\alpha,$$

where

$$m_t = k \left(\frac{Y_{t-1}}{Y_t}\right)^{\alpha_2} P_t^{\beta+1} Q_t^\gamma \hat{n}^\delta. \tag{40}$$

For two years i and j:

$$\frac{m_i}{m_j} = \left(\frac{P_i}{P_j}\right)^{\beta+1} \left(\frac{Q_i}{Q_j}\right)^\gamma \left(\frac{Y_{i-1}}{Y_i}\right)^{\alpha_2} \left(\frac{Y_{j-1}}{Y_j}\right)^{-\alpha_2}. \tag{41}$$

Table 42.7
Calculated values of m_i/m_j

$i =$	$(j = 1941)$
1918	1.13
1927-28	1.16
1935-36	0.99
1941	1
1947	1.35

If this ratio exceeds one, the logarithmic income–expenditure line should be higher for year i than for year j. Given the estimates of β, γ and α_2 obtained in (26) and the values of P_t, Q_t, Y_{t-1} and Y_t in the two years, the ratio can be computed. Table 42.7 shows its value for five years, with $j = 1941$ in each case.

The levels of the logarithmic income–food expenditure lines based on budget observations in those five years should correspond in rank to the numbers in Table 42.7. Except for 1918, the ranks of the budget study lines with respect to level are consistent with the hypothesis (Figures 42.3–6).

The amount as well as the direction of the shift in the income–consumption lines can be measured and compared with the calculated shift ratios. Lines were fitted by least squares to the observations shown on Figures 42.3–6. Comparison of the levels of these lines is unambiguous only if they are of the same slope. Actually the slopes computed by regression differ slightly (Table 42.4). Therefore, in each comparison of two budget studies the mean of the two least squares slopes is taken as the slope for both lines. The level constant is then chosen so as to obtain the line of best fit with the given slope. For two years i and j we have two lines:

$$\log x_i = a_i + b \log y_i$$
$$\log x_j = a_j + b \log y_j.$$

This pair of lines provides the material for an independent estimate of the shift ratios already calculated, namely anti-log $(a_i - a_j)$. If families behaved over time exactly according to the statistical demand function, this would be equal to m_i/m_j. The two estimates of shift ratios are compared in Table 42.8.

Table 42.8
Shifts in urban income – food consumption relationship

Budget studies compared		Observed shift [anti-log $(a_i - a_j)$]	Calculated shift (m_i/m_j)
i	j		
1935-36	1941	0.95	0.99
1918	1941	0.94	1.13
1927-28	1941	1.09	1.16
1927-28	1935-36	1.14	1.15
1947 Washington	1941	1.3	1.35
1947 Manchester	1941	1.39	1.35
1947 Richmond	1941	1.24	1.35

5. Summary and Conclusion

This investigation of food demand in the U.S.A. has been an experiment in the combination of time series and budget data in statistical demand analysis. The aggregate food demand function has been derived from a family food demand function, and the parameters of both functions have been estimated. Some estimates, applicable to both functions, have been obtained from budget data, and the remaining parameters have been evaluated from time series. Finally, the estimates have been checked by reference to budget observations made in different years.

Refinement of the method is certainly necessary. In particular, estimates from budget data should not be introduced into time series correlation as known with certainty. A maximum likelihood estimate of income-elasticity, for example, would utilize the two kinds of data simultaneously. The practical obstacle to this improvement is the absence of individual family observations in most published budget surveys; the use of grouped data, with no knowledge of the variation of families about the group means, gives a deceptive appearance of precision to budget study estimates. The discrepancy between budget study and unrestricted time series estimates of the same parameter should be eliminated by the use of additional variables to a greater extent than was possible in this study. But this experiment indicates, it is hoped, that further use and development of the method will be fruitful in statistical demand analysis.

References

Cochrane, W.W., "Farm family budgets – a moving picture," *Review of Economic Statistics*, 29 (1947), 189.

Cohen, M., "Food consumption, expenditures, and prices," *Survey of Current Business* (January 1948), 12.

Dewhurst, F. and Associates, *America's Needs and Resources* (New York: Twentieth Century Fund, 1947).

de Wolff, P., "Income-elasticity of demand; a micro-economic and a macro-economic interpretation," *Econ. J.*, 51 (1941), 140.

Fisher, R.A., *Statistical Methods for Research Workers*, 10th ed. (Edinburgh: Oliver & Boyd, 1946).

Gilbert, M., Speech to American Marketing Association, quoted in *New York Times*, June 15, 1948.

Girschick, M.A. and T. Haavelmo, "Statistical analysis of the demand for food," *Econometrica*, 15 (1947), 79.

Haavelmo, T., "Family expenditures and the marginal propensity to consume," *ibid.*, 15 (1947), 335.

Hart, B.I., "Significance levels for the ratio of the mean square successive difference to the variance," *Ann. Math. Stat.*, 13 (1942), 446.

Leontief, W., "Econometrics," in *Survey of Contemporary Economics*, H. Ellis (Ed.) (Philadelphia: Blakiston, 1948), 388.

Leven, M., H.G. Moulton and C. Warburton, *America's Capacity to Consume* (Washington: Brookings Institution, 1934).

Mack, R.P., "The direction of change in income and the consumption function," *Review of Economic Statistics*, 30 (1948), 239.

Marschak, J., "Personal and collective budget functions," *ibid.*, 21 (1939a), 161.

Marschak, J., "Review of Schultz, *Theory and Measurement of Demand*," *Econ. J.*, 49 (1939b), 486.

Marschak, J., "Money illusion and demand analysis," *Review of Economic Statistics*, 25 (1943), 40.

Mendershausen, H., *Changes in Income Distribution during the Great Depression* (New York: National Bureau of Economic Research, 1946).

National Industrial Conference Board, *Economic Almanac* (New York: 1948).

Snedecor, G.W., *Statistical Methods*, 4th ed. (Ames, Iowa: Iowa State College Press, 1946).

Staehle, H., "Short period variations in the distribution of incomes," *Review of Economic Statistics*, 19 (1937), 133.

Staehle, H., "Relative prices and post-war markets for animal food products," *Quarterly Journal of Economics*, 59 (1945), 237.

Stone, R., "The analysis of market demand," *J. R. Statist. Soc.*, 108 (1945), 286.

Stone, R., "The analysis of market demand: an outline of methods and results," *Review of the International Statistical Institute*, 16 (1948), 1.

U.S. Bureau of Labor Statistics, *Bulletin no. 357: Cost of Living in the United States* (Washington: Government Printing Office, 1924).

U.S. Bureau of Labor Statistics, "Income and spending and saving of city families in wartime," *Monthly Labor Review*, 55 (1942), 419.

U.S. Bureau of Labor Statistics, *Description of the Cost-of-Living Index of the Bureau of Labor Statistics* (Washington: Government Printing Office, 1943).

U.S. Bureau of Labor Statistics, *Bulletin no. 822: Family Spending and Saving in Wartime* (Washington: Government Printing Office, 1945).

U.S. Bureau of Labor Statistics, "Family income and expenditures in 1947," *Monthly Labor Review*, 68 (1949), 389.

U.S. Department of Agriculture, *Miscellaneous Publication no. 520: Rural Family Spending and Saving in Wartime* (Washington: Government Printing Office, 1943).

U.S. Department of Agriculture, *Agricultural Statistics* (Washington: Government Printing Office, 1948).

U.S. Department of Commerce, *Statistical Abstract of the United States, 1944-45* (Washington: Government Printing Office, 1945).

U.S. National Resources Committee, *Consumer Expenditures in the United States* (Washington: Government Printing Office, 1939).

U.S. National Resources Committee, *Family Expenditures in the United States* (Washington: Government Printing Office, 1941).

Excerpt from Discussion on Dr. Tobin's Paper by J.R.N. Stone

In the budget data used, total food expenditure is measured, and so a full allowance is made for the cost of processing food and for the various services connected with food whether in retailing or in the catering trade. The time series for food consumption on the other hand is a retail price-weighted index of the quantity of foodstuffs, prepared by the Bureau of Agricultural Economics (for a brief description see "Food Consumption, Expenditures and Prices", by Morris Cohen, in the *Survey of Current Business*, January 1948). As Dr. Tobin points out, it does not measure changes in the amount of services rendered by caterers or in retail outlets, nor in all cases does it measure the amount of processing involved. As can be seen from Table 5, it is remarkably stable over the period 1913–41, and the main justifications for using it are that it is the only uniform series available over the whole period and that it is the series used in an elaborate study by Girschick and Haavelmo (see "Statistical Analysis of the Demand for Food: Examples of Simultaneous Estimation of Structural Equations", in *Econometrica*, April 1947). From 1929 onwards the Department of Commerce has prepared (National Income Supplement to *S.C.B.*, July 1947) as part of its study of aggregate consumers' expenditure a series of total food expenditure which conceptually is more nearly related to the budget data than the series used by Dr. Tobin. This series can be deflated by means of the food component of the cost of living index, but the trouble with it is that it cannot easily be taken back to 1913. Some information for the earlier years is given in the pioneer study of W.H. Lough (*High-level Consumption*, 1935) and a very rough attempt may be made to interpolate this series for non-census years by means of a series given by W.H. Shaw (*Value of Commodity Output since 1869*, 1947). This pieced-together series shows, even when alcoholic drinks are removed from it following the repeal of prohibition, a movement different from and much more variable than that shown by the Bureau of Agricultural Economics index. Inasmuch as this series, while statistically lacking in uniformity, is conceptually more appropriate, I have included analyses based on it in the comparative table given below. For want of a better label I have referred to these analyses as Tobin–Stone without in any way wishing to implicate Dr. Tobin in the use of such a dubious statistical series.

Comparison of Demand Analyses for Food in the U.S.A.

	Period	α_1	α_2	β	γ	Σ
Tobin:						
(1)	1913–41	0.44	0.12	−0.51	−0.03	0.02
(2)	1913–41	0.45	0.11	−0.53	—	0.03
(3)	1913–41	0.27	—	−0.28	0.06	0.05
Girschick and Haavelmo:						
(4)	1922–41	0.25	0.05	−0.25	0	0.05
Stone:						
(5)	1929–41	0.59	—	−0.58	−0.01	0
(6)	1929–41	0.53	—	−0.62	0.55	0.46
(7)	1929–41	0.83	—	−0.90	0.07	—
Tobin–Stone:						
(8)	1913–41	0.61	−0.05	−0.43	−0.11	0.02
(9)	1913–41	0.62	0.12	−0.39	−0.31	0.04
(10)	1913–41	0.69	0.12	−0.51	−0.29	0.01

Analyses (1)–(4) are based on the Bureau of Agricultural Economics series of food consumption, while analyses (5)–(10) are based on the

Department of Commerce series continued backwards in the case of the last three by the method outlined above. In analyses (4), (6) and (7) allowance was made for a residual trend but this was not done in any of the others. Analysis (4) used a linear equation while in all the others the expression used was linear in the logarithms of the variables. In analyses (1), (2), and (8), but not in the others, a restriction was placed on the sum $\alpha_1 + \alpha_2$. A zero indicates the estimated value of a parameter whereas a "—" indicates that the parameter in question was assumed to be zero or, in the final column [analysis (7)], that the sum $\alpha_1 + \beta + \gamma$ was restricted *a priori* to zero.

The first point to notice is that apart from (6) (and (7), which does not count in this connection) the sums of the elasticities shown in the final column are close to zero. This indicates that the proportionality condition is approximately satisfied in each case, which is in accordance with theoretical expectations. Second, the mean values of the parameters in (4) are similar to those in (3) so that the objection to (3) that they do not square with what is known from budget studies can equally be raised against the results of Girschick and Haavelmo as it can against Dr. Tobin's unrestricted equation. Third, (5), apart from the fact that no allowance is made for last year's income, gives results very close to (1). It was not, however, given in my original article ("The Analysis of Market Demand", this *Journal*, pts. III–IV, 1945) because, while it showed a closed bunch map and a high coefficient of multiple correlation, it also showed a highly systematic residual which could be removed by the introduction of a residual trend with the effect on the parameters here listed shown in (6). Thus, of the two equations which I did give, (6) was unsatisfactory since the proportionality condition was so far from being satisfied, while (7) was unsatisfactory since it involved such a large negative residual trend.

Finally, the last analyses make use of the extended Department of Commerce series. In all cases the value of α_1 is substantially higher than in (1) and (2). In (8), where a restriction is placed on the sum $\alpha_1 + \alpha_2$, a negative (though not significant) value is found for α_2 which is not consistent with budget data. In (9) and (10) the income elasticities are determined without restriction. In (9) food consumption is treated as the dependent variable as in (5)–(7), whereas in (10) the food price index is treated as the dependent variable as in (1)–(3). These two analyses do not revert to the values of α_1 given by (3); on the contrary the values obtained are consistently above, not below, those derived from (1) and (2). In addition the value of α_2 is in each case the same as in (1) so that the unrestricted income effect exceeds the value obtained from budget data. This increased effect of income is largely offset by substantial negative values of γ. Thus the use of this alternative series which, for all its short-comings, seems more appropriate than the one used by Dr. Tobin, for combination with the budget data he has used leads to results which still stand in need of reconciliation. There is clearly a need for a more satis-factory time series of food expenditure at constant prices for the years before 1929 than anything available at present.

Reply

Mr. Stone has quite correctly emphasized the conceptual difference between food consumption measured in dollars in budget data and food consumption measured over time by the B.A.E. price-weighted index of physical quantities. This difference has much more serious effects on estimates of income elasticity than I had anticipated. The discrepancy between analyses (3) and (10) in Mr. Stone's table shows the effects on estimates derived without restriction from time series. Evidently a similar discrepancy arises in estimates from budget data. I have recently received, unfortunately only after the preparation and reading of my paper, Miscellaneous Publication 691 of the U.S. Department of Agriculture, *Consumption of Food in the United States, 1909–48* (Washington 1949). (This publication provides for the first time a complete explanation of the B.A.E. index.) Table 50 (p. 143) of this report is an attempt to measure food consumption of families at various income levels, not in dollars but by the same weighted index of physical quantities used to measure national *per capita* food consumption over time. These estimates are extremely rough (see p. 141 of the report), and they leave out of account the most elastic component of food demand, consumption away from home. But they indicate a much lower income-elasticity – in the neighbourhood of 0.2 – than is obtained from budget data when consumption is measured in dollars. In the light of this information I have, of course, to withdraw my objections to the results of analyses (3) and (4) of Mr. Stone's compilation. The values of α in those regressions are not inconsistent with budget data when the same measure of food consumption is used. The time series used in the "Tobin–Stone" analyses, however imperfect, is conceptually the appropriate one to use in conjunction with my analysis of budget data.

Notes

[1] Two exceptions, to which the approach of the present paper owes much, should be noted: Marschak (1943) and Staehle (1945).

[2] For convenience, a single individual will be considered a "family" of one person.

[3] The theoretical connection between the family demand function and the aggregate demand function, via the distribution of families by income, has been considered by Marschak (1939a), Staehle (1937) and de Wolff (1941). A more general treatment is given by Haavelmo (1947).

[4] U.S. Bureau of Labor Statistics (hereafter referred to as B.L.S.), 1945. The sources of the data on which Fig. 42.1 is based are as follows: Table 11, p. 38, gives food consumption by 1942 income-classes for families with changed incomes. Table 20, p. 107, gives this information for the whole sample. Only money income and money expense for food are considered. Families of all sizes are included; the data of Table 11 do not permit elimination of the effects of family size. Since Table 11 does not give average incomes for the various income-classes, the average disposable incomes for the whole sample have been used in plotting all three sets of observations in Fig. 1. These are computed from Table 19, p. 103, by subtracting "Personal tax payments" from "Money income".

[5] Convincing evidence that income change is an important variable not only for food but for other consumption categories and for saving is given by Mack (1948). This evidence is based not only on the 1941-42 budget survey, but on continuing samples of farm families, whose behaviour under rising incomes is summarized in Cochrane (1947).

[6] Since $\bar{y}_{t-1}$, $\bar{y}_t$ are geometric means and Y_{t-1}, Y_t are arithmetic means the question arises whether $\bar{y}_{t-1} = K\bar{y}_t$, summed over all groups of families, implies $Y_{t-1} = KY_t$. This is not in general true, but it is true under the assumption (13) concerning the joint distribution of families by income and size which will be introduced in Section 2 below.

Let $\bar{Y}_{t-1}$ and $\bar{Y}_t$ be the geometric means in the two years. Clearly $\bar{y}_{t-1} = K\bar{y}_t$ implies $\bar{Y}_{t-1} = K\bar{Y}_t$. Assumption (13) is that for all $\lambda > 0$, $\lambda f(\lambda y, n; \lambda Y) = f(y, n; Y)$, where $f(y,n;Y)$ is the density function of the joint distribution when mean income is Y.

$$\log \bar{Y}_{t-1} = \int_0^\infty \log yf(y,n;Y_{t-1})\,dy = \log K + \int_0^\infty \log yf(y,n;Y_t)\,dy$$

$$= \log K\bar{Y}_t.$$

Let $Y_{t-1} = K'Y_t$. Then, using assumption (13),

$$\log \bar{Y}_{t-1} = \int_0^\infty \log K'yf(K'y,n;K'Y)\,K'\,dy = \int_0^\infty \log K'yf(y,n;Y_t)\,dy$$

$$= \log K' \int_0^\infty f(y, n; Y_t) \, dy + \int_0^\infty \log y f(y, n; Y_t) \, dy$$

$$= \log K' \bar{Y}_t.$$

Therefore $K = K'$.

[7] Mrs. Mack's contention is based on the distributions of income change by income level in the 1941-42 budget survey and in the Wisconsin sample of identical taxpayers, 1929-35. However, her 1941-42 data give only direction of income change, not magnitude. The Wisconsin figures cited by Mrs. Mack detect a change in income only when a taxpayer moves from one $500-wide bracket to another, and are confined to incomes below $3,000. No quantitative relationship between income and income change can be formulated from these sources. Moreover, Mrs. Mack also cites a study of Delaware taxpayers for two years, 1937 and 1938, which evidently conforms more closely to assumption (4) than to the pattern of the other two samples.

[8] The data for the 1927-28 studies are given in Leven et al. (1934), Appendix B, Table 1, pp. 246-49, designations D and E. The original sources and the coverage and concepts of the two studies are described on p. 241.

[9] The 1935-36 study does classify data by family size, but not in a manner useful for the purposes of this paper. Families are classified by seven "types", which depend on age composition as well as size. Only in the cases of one- and two-person families is there one-to-one correspondence between "type" and size. Moreover, detailed breakdown of the observations by "type" appears only in publications dealing with specific localities or regions. On the treatment of family size in the 1935-36 survey, see Staehle (1945), pp. 249-51.

[10] Some evidence of the influence of region and size of city may be found in N.R.C. (1941), where urban families are classified, first, by four sizes of cities and, second, by five regions. Unfortunately they are not cross-classified. Regressions for each of the four sizes of city will yield slopes of 0.51, 0.51, 0.53 and 0.46. Regressions for each of the five regions yield slopes of 0.48, 0.50, 0.60, 0.49 and 0.46. Only in the case of the region with slope 0.60 is it necessary to reject the hypothesis that these sub-groups are samples from a population with a common slope. Once again the absence of individual family observations or of estimates of the variances of these observations about the income-class means makes a more satisfactory statistical test of the significance of these differences impossible. Since the slope for the whole sample (0.57) is greater than for all but one of the sub-groups, it is probable that it reflects differences in level of food consumption, due not solely to income but also to size of city or to region. But the errors due to ignoring these determinants of food demand do not appear to be large.

An interesting analysis of the heterogeneity of the family food demand function over various occupational and geographical groups, based on Dutch data for individual families, has been made by G. Stuvel and S.F. James at the Department of Applied Economics, Cambridge, *J. R. Statist. Soc.*, 113, 59.

[11] This is the condition assumed by Marschak (1939a, p. 164, and 1943). It is stronger than necessary.

[12] The proof of (14) is as follows: Let

$$M(Y) = \sum_{n=1}^m \int_0^\infty \left(\frac{y}{Y} \right)^\alpha n^\delta f(y, n; Y) \, dy.$$

Then

$$M(\lambda Y) = \sum_{n=1}^{m} \int_0^\infty \left(\frac{y}{\lambda Y}\right)^\alpha n^\delta f(y, n; \lambda Y) \ dy \quad \lambda > 0$$

$$= \sum_{n=1}^{m} \int_0^\infty \left(\frac{\lambda y}{\lambda Y}\right)^\alpha n^\delta f(\lambda y, n; \lambda Y)\lambda \ dy$$

$$= \sum_{n=1}^{m} \int_0^\infty \left(\frac{y}{Y}\right)^\alpha n^\delta f(y, n; Y) \ dy \text{ by (13)}$$

$$= M(Y) \quad \text{for all } \lambda > 0.$$

[13] It can be shown that (15) is a necessary and sufficient condition for the invariance of the Lorenz curve under changes in mean income.

[14] (17) can be written:

$$C(Y) = (aM_1(Y) + bM_2(Y)) k_t'' Y^\alpha,$$

where

$$M_1(Y) = \int_0^\infty \left(\frac{y}{Y}\right)^\alpha g(y; Y) \ dy$$

and

$$M_2(Y) = \int_0^\infty \left(\frac{y}{Y}\right)^\alpha \bar{n}(y; Y)g(y; Y) \ dy.$$

The proof that $M_1(Y)$ and $M_2(Y)$ are constants is analogous to the proof in the preceding footnote that $M(Y)$ is a constant. Strictly, (9) is an approximation of the family demand function for families of two or more persons. Assumptions (17) and (18) should apply only to $n \geq 2$ and (13) should be retained for $n = (1)$. Then if the proportion of single individuals to larger families is constant, the aggregate function $C(Y)$ will be of the form (14) or (18).

[15] Mendershausen (1946) has shown that inequality was greater in the depression year of 1933 than in the boom year of 1929, and has presented a convincing explanation of this phenomenon.

[16] The only time series on this subject are based on income tax statistics, and concern only the top of the income distribution. Consequently they are useless for the purposes of this paper.

[17] Computed by dividing annual U.S. population estimates (U.S. Department of Commerce 1945, p. 8) by annual estimates of the number of consumer units in the U.S. (National Industrial Conference Board 1948, p. 334).

[18] The following method for computing these confidence limits was kindly pointed out to me by Mr. J. Durbin and Mr. G. Watson, Department of Applied Economics, University of Cambridge. In the case of α_2, consider $(b_2 - \alpha_2 b_1)/S(\alpha_2)$. Here b_2 and b_1 are the regression coefficients in (26) and $S(\alpha_2)^2 = \text{var } b_2 + \alpha_2^2 \text{ var } b_1 - 2\alpha_2 \text{ covar } b_2 b_1$

$$= s^2 \left[\frac{\sum x_1^2 + \alpha_2^2 \sum x_2^2 + 2\alpha \sum x_1 x_2}{\sum x_1^2 \sum x_2^2 - (\sum x_1 x_2)^2}\right], \text{ where } s^2 = \frac{N(1 - R^2) \text{ var log } P}{N - 3}, \ x_1 = \log S_t - \alpha \log Y_t',$$

and $x_2 = \log Y_t' - \log Y_{t-1}'$. Given any α_2, $\left(\dfrac{b_2 - \alpha_2 b_1}{S(\alpha_2)}\right)$ is distributed according to Student's t distribution with $N - 3$ degrees of freedom. Consequently, the probability that $\left(\dfrac{b_2 - \alpha_2 b_1}{S(\alpha_2)}\right)^2 < t_{0.025}^2 = 0.95$, where $t_{0.025}$ is the value of t exceeded with probability 0.025, or exceeded in absolute value with probability 0.05. Therefore $P[(b_2 - \alpha_2 b_1)^2 < t_{0.025}^2 [S(\alpha_2)]^2] = 0.95$

$$P[b_2^2 + \alpha_2^2 b_1^2 - 2\alpha_2 b_1 b_2 - t_{0.025}^2 [S(\alpha_2)]^2 < 0] = 0.95$$

$(b_2^2 + \alpha_2^2 b_1^2 - 2\alpha_2 b_1 b_2 - t_{0.025}^2 [S(\alpha_2)^2]$ is quadratic in α_2 and can be represented by $(\alpha_2 - c_1)(\alpha_2 - c_2)$. Take $c_1 < c_2$. Then

$$P[(\alpha_2 - c_1)(\alpha_2 - c_2) < 0] = 0.95.$$

But $(\alpha - c_1)(\alpha - c_2) < 0$ implies, since $c_1 < c_2, \alpha_2 - c_1 > 0$ and $\alpha_2 - c_2 < 0$, and therefore $c_1 < \alpha_2 < c_2$.

$$P[(c_1 < \alpha_2 < c_2)] = 0.95.$$

A similar procedure applies to the case of β. Here $\left(\dfrac{1 - \beta b_1}{\beta \sigma b_1}\right)$ is distributed by the t distribution with $N - 3$ degrees of freedom. Compare Fisher (1946), pp. 142-45.

[19] This conclusion follows for (26) from testing the significance of the deviation of the estimate of $\beta(= 1/b_1 = -0.53)$ from the assumed true value of $\beta(\beta = -\alpha = -0.56)$ according to the "homogeneity postulate". $\left(\dfrac{1 - \beta b_1}{\beta \sigma_{b_1}}\right)$ is distributed by Student's t distribution with $N - 3 = 26$ degrees of freedom (see preceding note). With the estimates of (26) $t = -0.66$. A deviation of β from $\bar\beta$ as large as or larger than that observed in (26) and in the same direction would be obtained in over 25 per cent of samples. A deviation at least as large in absolute value would occur in over 50 per cent of samples. A similar test, with similar results, can be made for the sum of the elasticities estimated in (25).

[20] In Figure 42.10 the numbers 1, 2, 3, 4, 5 refer, respectively, to $\log S_t$, $\log Y_{t-1}'$, $\log Q_t$, $\log Y_t'$, $\log P_t$. The label on each diagram indicates both the partial regression to which it refers and the set of variables in the complete regression. Thus diagram 51.42 shows the regression coefficients of 5 on 1 in the four regressions involving 5, 1, 4 and 2. The slope of a beam indicates the value of the normalized regression coefficient, and the number at the end of beam indicates the direction of minimization of the regression. Fig. 42.10 is not a complete bunch map analysis for the five variables, because it is clear on economic as well as statistical grounds that 1, 4, 5 must be included in the regression.

[21] For the year 1946 their food demand function yields a *per capita* demand 114 per cent of average consumption for 1935-39, and for 1947, 110 per cent. Actual food supply for domestic consumption was 118 per cent in 1946 and 117 per cent in 1947.

[22] Stone (1945), pp. 325-26, obtains from time series 1929-41 estimates of α and β which agree closely with the estimates of this paper. However, his estimate of γ (approximately 0.55) is radically different.

CHAPTER 43

MULTIPLE PROBIT REGRESSION OF DICHOTOMOUS ECONOMIC VARIABLES

Analysis of economic surveys of samples of households often has the objective of estimating the relationship of a dependent variable to a set of independent variables and of testing hypotheses about that relationship. Typically the dependent variable is a measure reflecting some kind of household behavior or decision, while the independent variables represent characteristics over which the household has less control, at least in the short run. For example, explanation of the variation among households in annual food expenditure may be sought in such independent variables as family income, family size, occupation of head of household, age of head of household, and location. In this example and in many other cases, the dependent variable can take on a large number of possible values along a natural scale. Thus food expenditure, if households report to the nearest dollar, can in principle be any non-negative integer, though its realistic range is doubtless limited. For dependent variables of this kind, the theory of multiple regression – including analysis of variance and covariance – provides an appropriate statistical model.

Sometimes, however, the dependent variable of interest is dichotomous. It can take on only two values, which can for convenience be designated as 1 and 0. The household either owns a house or does not own one; the household either bought a new car last year or did not buy one; or, to cite a variable from a neighboring social science, the head of the household either likes Ike or does not. As in the food expenditure example, a variety of independent variables may be associated with the differences between home-owners and non-home-owners, or car-buyers

Reprinted from Cowles Foundation Discussion Paper No. 1, 1955. Unpublished.

and non-buyers, or supporters and opponents of a Presidential candidate. But the association is necessarily of a different kind. An increase in income may be expected to result in an increase in the food expenditure of a given household. An increase in income may also turn a household from a non-owner into a home-owner. But it cannot make a home-owning household into any more of a home-owner than the household already is.

In the case of food expenditure, it is important to know the exact level of the household's income. In the case of ownership, the important thing is whether or not this income exceeds some critical value.

Linear multiple regression is accordingly not an appropriate model for a dichotomous dependent variable. By the definition of such a variable, its expected value must always be in the interval $(0,1)$, whatever the value of the independent variables. This condition cannot be maintained if the expected value is assumed, as in multiple regression, to be a linear combination of the independent variables. Moreover, the multiple regression model assumes, inappropriately for this case, that the distribution of the dependent variable around its expected value is independent of the level of that expected value. For a dichotomous variable, an expected value of 0.8 means a probability of 0.8 that the value will deviate from expectation by $+0.2$ and a probability of 0.2 that the deviation will be -0.8, while an expected value of 0.4 means deviations of $+0.6$ with probability 0.4 and deviations of -0.4 with probability 0.6.

Probit analysis (see Finney 1952) provides an appropriate model. In biological assay, probit analysis is used to determine the relationship between the probability that organisms will be killed to the strength of the dose of poison administered to them. The dependent variable, for each organism in the sample, is dichotomous: killed or not killed. Each organism is assumed to have a dosage threshold, such that a stronger dose will kill that organism and a weaker dose will not. Over the population of organisms of a given kind, the logarithms of these dosage thresholds are assumed to be normally distributed, with mean and standard deviation estimated from the data by maximum likelihood. The analogous use of probit analysis in economic surveys is illustrated by its application by Farrell (1954) to the relationship between ownership of automobiles and income. In Farrell's application, the dependent variable is defined by whether or not the household owned a car of a given age or younger. Each household is assumed to have an income threshold, such that if its income is bigger than the critical value it owns, while if its income is below the threshold it does not. The logarithms of the income thresholds are assumed to be normally distributed. The parameters of the distribution are estimated by maximum likelihood from data giving the number of sample households observed to own and not to own at various income levels.[1]

In Farrell's application there is only one independent variable, income, to which the probability of car ownership is related. But he and other econometricians are keenly aware that observed differences among households in sample surveys are attributable to a multiplicity of factors. It is not possible to duplicate the experimental control that is feasible in biological assay. Consequently, multiple probit regression is, like multiple linear regression, an essential tool for the analyst of economic surveys. Finney (1952, Chapter 7) explains and illustrates the extension of the Bliss–Fisher maximum likelihood solution to cases with two or more independent variables. The exposition of multiple probit regression which follows in the present paper is not fundamentally different from Finney's treatment. It is, however, oriented to the problems of economic surveys rather than those of dosage-mortality experiments. It differs also in using the exact maximum likelihood equations of Garwood (1941) rather than the approximations of the Bliss–Fisher procedure used by Finney. Fewer iterations are required to compute the solutions of the Garwood equations, and the publication of new tables by Cornfield and Mantel (1950) has removed the practical obstacles to the use of these equations.

1. The Model

Suppose that there is an index I, which is a linear combination of the various independent variables $X_1, X_2, \ldots, X_m$ that determine whether the dependent variable W has the value 0 or 1 for a household:

$$I = \delta_0 + \delta_1 X_1 + \delta_2 X_2 + \cdots + \delta_m X_m. \tag{1}$$

The assumption that I is a linear combination of the X's is neither more nor less restrictive than the similar assumption in conventional multiple regression. There are various devices by which a linear combination of $(X_1, X_2, \ldots, X_m)$ can represent a non-linear function of the observed variables. An X in the index may be the logarithm or the square, or some other function of one of the original observed variables. Or an X in the index may be the product, or some other function, of two or more of the other X's, in order to test and to estimate interactions as well as main effects.

Let I_i be the actual value of the index for the ith household, determined by evaluating (1) for the values of the independent variables that obtain for the ith household. Let $\bar{I}_i$ be the critical value of the index for the ith household: If the actual value of the index I_i equals or exceeds the critical value $\bar{I}_i$, then W_i will be 1; if I_i is less than $\bar{I}_i$, then W_i will be 0.

$$W_i = 1 \quad \text{for} \quad I_i \geqq \bar{I}_i$$

$$W_i = 0 \quad \text{for} \quad I_i < \bar{I}_i. \tag{2}$$

Over the population of households the critical values $\bar{I}_i$ are assumed to be normally distributed with mean 5 [2] and standard deviation 1. This distribution reflects random differences among households, for example differences in personality and taste, that are not represented by any of the variables in the index. Some households would not own a new car unless their income was very high, while others require only a bare margin above subsistence levels to put them over the new-car threshold.

For a given value of the index, I, W will be equal to 1 for those individuals for whom $\bar{I}_i \leq I$, and W will be equal to 0 for those whose $I_i > I$. The probability that, given I, W_i will be equal to 1 is therefore:

$$\Pr(W = 1|I) = \Pr(\bar{I}_i \leq I) = P(I) = \frac{1}{\sqrt{2\pi}} \int_{-\infty}^{I-5} e^{-u^2/2}\, du. \tag{3}$$

Similarly, the probability that, given I, W will be equal to 0 is:

$$\Pr(W = 0|I) = \Pr(\bar{I}_i > I) = [1 - P(I)] = Q(I)$$

$$= \frac{1}{\sqrt{2\pi}} \int_{I-5}^{\infty} e^{-u^2/2}\, du. \tag{4}$$

2. The Maximum Likelihood Solution[3]

A sample of observations at s distinct points $(X_{1j}, X_{2j}, \ldots, X_{mj})$, where $(j = 1, 2, \ldots, s)$ may be summarized as follows: Let n_j be the total number of observations at the jth point. Let r_j be the number of those observations for which W was observed to be 1, and $n_j - r_j$ the number for which W was observed to be 0. The likelihood of the sample is a function of the values $(b_0, b_1, \ldots, b_m)$ assumed for the population parameters $(\delta_0, \delta_1, \ldots, \delta_m)$:

$$L(b_0, b_1, \ldots, b_m) = \prod_{j=1}^{s} [P(b_0 + b_1 X_{1j} + \cdots + b_m X_{mj})]^{r_j}$$

$$\times [Q(b_0 + b_1 X_{1j} + \cdots + b_m X_{mj})]^{n_j - r_j}. \tag{5}$$

Here, as in (3) and (4),

$$P(x) = \frac{1}{\sqrt{2\pi}} \int_{-\infty}^{x-5} e^{-u^2/2}\, du, \quad \text{and} \quad Q(x) = 1 - P(x).$$

Let $Y_j = b_0 + b_1 X_{1j} + \cdots + b_m X_{mj}$; $P_j = P(Y_j)$; $Q_j = Q(Y_j)$. To find the maximum likelihood estimates of the population parameters, it is convenient to find values of the b's to maximize $\log L$ rather than L.

$$L^*(b_0, b_1, \ldots, b_m) = \log L(b_0, b_1, \ldots b_m)$$

$$+ \sum_{j=1}^{s} [r_j \log P_j + (n_j - r_j) \log Q_j]. \tag{6}$$

The conditions for the maximum are the $m + 1$ equations determined by setting the partial derivatives of L^* equal to zero. Let

$$L_i^*(b_0, b_1, \ldots, b_m) = \frac{\partial L^*}{\partial b_i}.$$

Let

$$Z(x) = \frac{dP(x)}{dx} = \frac{-dQ(x)}{dx} = \frac{1}{\sqrt{2\pi}} e^{-x^2/2},$$

and let

$$Z_j = Z(Y_j).$$

Note that $dZ_j/dY_j = -Y_j Z_j$. Let X_0 be identically 1. The equations are:

$$L_i^*(b_0, b_1, \ldots, b_m) = \sum_{j=1}^{s} \left[r_j \frac{X_{ij} Z_j}{P_j} - (n_j - r_j) \frac{X_{ij} Z_j}{Q_j} \right] = 0$$

$$(i = 0, 1, 2, \ldots, m). \tag{7}$$

These non-linear equations can be solved by an iterative process. Let $(b_{00}, b_{10}, \ldots, b_{m0})$ be trial solutions. New estimates $(b_{00} + \Delta b_0, b_{10} + \Delta b_1, \ldots, b_{m0} + \Delta b_m)$ can be found by solving the following set of $m + 1$ linear equations, in which all the L_i^* are assumed to be linear between the trial solution and the real solution.

$$L_i^*(b_{00} + \Delta b_0, b_{10} + \Delta b_1, \ldots, b_{m0} + \Delta b_m)$$

$$= L_i^*(b_{00}, b_{10}, \ldots, b_{m0}) + \sum_{k=0}^{m} \Delta b_k L_{ik}^*(b_{00}, \dot{b}_{10}, \ldots, b_{m0}) = 0$$

$$(i = 0, 1, 2, \ldots, m). \tag{8}$$

The second-order derivatives L_{ik}^* are given by differentiating (7):

$$L_{ik}^*(b_0, b_1, \ldots, b_m) =$$

$$\sum_{j=1}^{s} \left[\frac{r_j X_{ij} X_{kj}(-P_j Y_j Z_j - Z_j^2)}{P_j^2} - \frac{(n_j - r_j) X_{ij} X_{kj}(-Q_j Y_j Z_j + Z_j^2)}{Q_j^2} \right]$$

$$(i, k = 0, 1, 2, \ldots, m). \tag{9}$$

Following the notation of Cornfield and Mantel (1950), let

$$w'_{j\max} = \frac{Y_j Z_j}{P_j} + \frac{Z_j^2}{P_j^2}, \qquad w'_{j\min} = -\frac{Y_j Z_j}{Q_j} + \frac{Z_j^2}{Q_j^2},$$

$$n_j w'_j = r_j w'_{j\max} + (n_j - r_j) w'_{j\min}. \tag{10}$$

Also, let

$$\Delta_{j\max} = \frac{Z_j}{P_j}, \qquad \Delta_{j\min} = \frac{Z_j}{Q_j},$$

$$n_j \Delta_j = r_j \Delta_{j\max} - (n_j - r_j) \Delta_{j\min}. \tag{11}$$

Equation (7) can then be rewritten

$$L_i^*(b_0, b_1, \ldots, b_m) = \sum_{j=1}^{s} X_{ij} n_j \Delta_j = 0 \quad (i = 0, 1, 2, \ldots, m). \tag{12}$$

If w'_j and Δ_j are evaluated for the trial-solution values of the b's, Equations (8) can be rewritten:

$$\Delta b_0 \sum_{j=1}^{s} n_j w'_j + \Delta b_1 \sum_{j=1}^{s} X_{1j} n_j w'_j + \cdots + \Delta b_m \sum_{j=1}^{s} X_{mj} n_j w'_j$$

$$= \sum_{j=1}^{s} n_j \Delta_j$$

$$\Delta b_0 \sum_{j=1}^{s} X_{1j} n_j w'_j + \Delta b_1 \sum_{j=1}^{s} X_{1j}^2 n_j w'_j + \cdots$$

$$+ \Delta b_m \sum_{j=1}^{s} X_{1j} X_{mj} n_j w'_j = \sum_{j=1}^{s} X_{1j} n_j \Delta_j$$

$$\cdots\cdots\cdots\cdots\cdots\cdots\cdots\cdots\cdots\cdots\cdots\cdots\cdots\cdots\cdots\cdots$$

$$\cdots\cdots\cdots\cdots\cdots\cdots\cdots\cdots\cdots\cdots\cdots\cdots\cdots\cdots\cdots\cdots$$

$$\Delta b_0 \sum_{j=1}^{s} X_{mj} n_j w'_j + \Delta b_1 \sum_{j=1}^{s} X_{mj} X_{1j} n_j w'_j + \cdots$$

$$+ \Delta b_m \sum_{j=1}^{s} X_{mj}^2 n_j w'_j = \sum_{j=1}^{s} X_{mj} n_j \Delta_j. \quad (13)$$

Tables of w'_{max}, w'_{min}, Δ_{max}, and Δ_{min} are given in Cornfield and Mantel (1950, pp. 185–88). These tables, entered with the arguments

$$Y_{j0} = b_{00} + b_{10} X_{1j} + b_{20} X_{2j} + \cdots + b_{m0} X_{mj},$$

enable computation of $n_j w'_j$ and $n_j \Delta_j$, and therefore of the coefficients of the Δb's and the constants in (13). Equations (13) have a symmetrical matrix of coefficients and may be solved by methods used for similar simultaneous linear equation systems in multiple linear regressions. The process may be repeated with new provisional estimates

$$(b_{00} + \Delta b_0, b_{10} + \Delta b_1, \ldots, b_{m0} + \Delta b_m),$$

until the Δb's are negligible.

If the final estimates of the δ's are used to evaluate the matrix of coefficients in (13), i.e., to evaluate the second derivatives of L^* at the point of maximum likelihood, the inverse of that matrix gives estimates of the variances and covariances of the estimates of the δ's: $\|\delta_{ik}^2\|$, the matrix of variances and covariances of b_i and b_k, is estimated by $\| -L_{ik}^* \|^{-1}$.

3. Testing of Hypotheses

The likelihood ratio method may be used to test hypotheses about the δ's, singly and jointly. Consider, for one example, the hypothesis that the probability that $W = 1$ is independent of the values of the X's. This common probability would, in accordance with (3), be given by:

$$\Pr(W = 1) = \Pr(\bar{I}_i \leq \delta_0) = P(\delta_0) = \frac{1}{\sqrt{2\pi}} \int_{-\infty}^{\delta_0 - 5} e^{-u^2/2} \, du. \tag{14}$$

Consequently, if the hypothesis is true, the maximum likelihood estimate of δ_0 would be the value of b_0 that maximizes the following expression:

$$L(b_0, 0, 0, \ldots, 0) = [P(b_0)]^r [Q(b_0)]^{n-r}, \tag{15}$$

where $\qquad r = \sum_{j=1}^{s} r_j \quad \text{and} \quad n = \sum_{j=1}^{s} n_j.$

The value b'_0 which maximizes (15) is easily found to be such that:

$$P(b'_0) = r/n. \tag{16}$$

Consequently, the value of the logarithm of the likelihood function evaluated for the maximum likelihood estimate of δ_0 is:

$$L^*(b'_0, 0, 0, \ldots, 0) = r \log \frac{r}{n} + (n - r) \log \frac{n - r}{n}. \tag{17}$$

If the restriction of the hypothesis is removed, the maximum likelihood L^* is obtained from (6), using values of P_j and Q_j corresponding to the maximum likelihood b's. If

$$\log \lambda = L^*(b'_0, 0, 0, \ldots, 0) - L^*(b_0, b_1, \ldots, b_m),$$

then $-2 \log \lambda$ is approximately distributed like chi-square with m degrees of freedom for large samples when the hypothesis is true.[4]

Other hypotheses regarding the values of δ's – for example, that $\delta_k = 0$, or that $\delta_i = \delta_k$ – can also be tested by the likelihood-ratio method. Each test requires that the maximum likelihood estimates of the coefficients be found, and the likelihood function evaluated for these estimates, twice: both with and without the constraints implied by the hypothesis being tested. For a single hypothesis assigning definite values to all the coefficients, it may be convenient to use the hypothesized values as the initial trial values in the iterative process of finding maximum likelihood estimates. Otherwise it may be preferable to avoid the computational burden of the likelihood-ratio test by using a test based on the approximate normality of the distribution of maximum likelihood estimates from large samples: The b_k are approximately distributed by the $(m + 1)$-variate joint normal distribution with means δ_k and a variance-covariance matrix estimated by $\| - L_{ik}^* \|^{-1}$.

4. An Example

For purposes of illustration, an example has been worked out using data from the reinterview portion of the 1952 and 1953 *Surveys of Consumer Finances* conducted by the Survey Research Center of the University of Michigan for the Board of Governors of the Federal Reserve System.[5] These data were obtained from 1036 spending units who were interviewed twice, first in early 1952 and then in early 1953. The variables are as follows:

W: Equal to 1 if the spending unit reported, in the 1953 interview, purchase of an automobile or any large household good (e.g., TV, washing machine, refrigerator) during 1952. Equal to 0 if the spending unit reported that it made no purchase of this kind during 1952. Spending units from whom this information was not ascertained have been omitted from the analysis.

X_1: Disposable income of the spending unit in 1952: the total income of the spending unit, as reported in the 1953 interview, less estimated income tax liability. Spending units with disposable income greater than $10,000 have been omitted from the analysis. The remainder have been classified into ten $1000-wide brackets. X_1 is taken to be the midpoint of the bracket.

X_2: Liquid asset holdings – i.e., total of bank deposits and savings bonds – at the beginning of 1952, as reported by the spending unit in the 1952 interview. Spending units with holdings greater than $10,000 have been omitted from the analysis. The remainder have been classified into seven categories of unequal width, as indicated in Table 43.1. X_2 is taken to be the midpoint of the interval.

Table 43.1

Purchase of durable goods in relation to income and liquid asset holdings: 874 spending units from 1952-53 *Surveys of Consumer Finances*, liquid asset holdings, early 1952

1952 Disposable income	X_1	quantity	X_2: 0 (0)	1-199 (100)	200-499 (350)	500-999 (750)	1000-1999 (1500)	2000-4999 (3500)	5000-9999 (7500)	Total
0-999	500	cell j	1	2	3	4	5	6	7	
		n_j	49	6	5	7	10	7	5	89
		r_j	6	4	0	1	0	0	2	13
		$n_j - r_j$	43	2	5	6	10	7	3	76
1000-1999	1500	cell j	8	9	10	11	12	13	14	
		n_j	40	17	12	3	14	17	5	108
		r_j	13	6	3	1	4	3	0	30
		$n_j - r_j$	27	11	9	2	10	14	5	78
2000-2999	2500	cell j	15	16	17	18	19	20	21	
		n_j	42	34	22	23	21	25	11	178
		r_j	15	13	9	11	9	7	2	66
		$n_j - r_j$	27	21	13	12	12	18	9	112
3000-3999	3500	cell j	22	23	24	25	26	27	28	
		n_j	36	34	34	23	24	30	9	190
		r_j	25	23	18	10	16	11	3	106
		$n_j - r_j$	11	11	16	13	8	19	6	84

Table 43.1 (continued)

		29	30	31	32	33	34	35	
4000-4999	4500	23 / 15 / 8	22 / 15 / 7	21 / 18 / 3	26 / 10 / 16	12 / 6 / 6	39 / 21 / 18	5 / 1 / 4	148 / 86 / 62
		36	37	38	39	40	41	42	
5000-5999	5500	7 / 4 / 3	7 / 2 / 5	14 / 12 / 2	9 / 5 / 4	10 / 5 / 5	11 / 4 / 7	8 / 4 / 4	66 / 36 / 30
		43	44	45	46	47	48	49	
6000-6999	6500	3 / 2 / 1	3 / 0 / 3	6 / 4 / 2	7 / 7 / 0	5 / 1 / 4	7 / 2 / 5	5 / 3 / 2	36 / 19 / 17
		50	51	52	53	54	55	56	
7000-7999	7500	1 / 1 / 0	4 / 3 / 1	0 / 0 / 0	4 / 3 / 1	3 / 1 / 2	4 / 2 / 2	3 / 1 / 2	19 / 11 / 8
		57	58	59	60	61	62	63	
8000-8999	8500	0 / 0 / 0	2 / 2 / 0	2 / 1 / 1	3 / 3 / 0	6 / 4 / 2	6 / 4 / 2	2 / 0 / 2	21 / 14 / 7
		64	65	66	67	68	69	70	
9000-9999	9500	0 / 0 / 0	0 / 0 / 0	2 / 1 / 1	5 / 0 / 5	1 / 0 / 1	6 / 3 / 3	5 / 3 / 2	19 / 7 / 12

The number of each cell, j, is given in the upper left-hand corner of the cell of the other three numbers; the top number is n_j, the total number of spending units; the middle number is r_j, the number who made some expenditure on durable goods; the bottom number is $n_j - r_j$, the number who made no expenditure on durable goods.

Table 43.1 presents, for each pair of values (X_1, X_2), the total number of spending units included in the analysis, n_j; the number for whom $W = 1$, r_j, and for whom $W = 0$, $n_j - r_j$. The frequencies in Table 43.1 should not be taken as representative of the population of the U.S.A. The *Surveys of Consumer Finances* do collect data on distributions of income, liquid assets, and durable goods purchases that are representative of that population; tables on these distributions may be found in *Survey of Consumer Finances* (1952, 1953). But the reinterview sample, on which Table 43.1 is based, fails to be representative insofar as it omits spending units who moved between the two surveys. Moreover, Table 43.1 is based on simple counts of sampled spending units, without allowance for the fact that the sampling design gave some spending units greater probabilities of being included in the sample than others. The purpose of Table 43.1 is not to estimate population frequency distributions, but only to examine the relationship of durable goods expenditure to income and liquid asset holdings within this sample. It is not necessary to consider here how the relationship exhibited in this sample differs from the one that would be exhibited in a complete enumeration. But it may well be that the sample gives unbiased estimates of the parameters of the relationship, even though it gives biased estimates of the separate frequency distributions of the variables.

Tables 43.2–43.8 give the details of the calculations. Table 43.2 shows the values of the coefficients b_0, b_1, and b_2 and of the corrections Δb_0, Δb_1, and Δb_2 in the successive iterations. The final estimate of b_1 is positive and of b_2 negative. The probability of purchasing durable goods increases with income, but decreases with liquid asset holdings. Evidently, large holders of assets are thriftier or older people, who have less inclination or need to buy durable goods. Table 43.3 shows for each point (X_1, X_2) the values of the index $Y(= b_0 + b_1 X_1 + b_2 X_2)$ for the initial assumed values of the b's and for the final estimates of the b's (final iteration). Table 43.4 shows the matrix of coefficients and constants in the simultaneous equations (13) for the various iterations. The manner of calculation of the entries in this matrix may be illustrated, as follows. For cell 1, on iteration 1, the value of Y, X_1, is 3.90 (see Table 43.3). According to Table 43.1, $r_1 = 6$ and $n_1 - r_1 = 4.3$. Entering the table in Cornfield and Mantel (1950, p. 185), with the value of Y_{10}, 3.90, we find: $w'_{1\,min} = 0.34078$, $w'_{1\,max} = 0.81221$, $\Delta_{1\,min} = 0.25205$, $\Delta_{1\,max} = 1.06580$. With

Table 43.2

Iteration	b_0	Δb_1	b_1	Δb_1	b_2	Δb_2
1	3.73333	0.74629	0.033333	−0.018877	0.00	−0.0093209
2	4.47962	−0.07974	0.014456	0.002662	−0.0093209	−0.0029938
3	4.39988	0.009638	0.017118	−0.0010202	0.0123147	0.0038120
4	4.409518	0.027442	0.0160978	−0.0006906	−0.0085027	−0.0008202
5	4.436960	−0.01431	0.0154072	0.0006050	−0.0093229	−0.0002388
Final	4.42265		0.0160122		−0.0095617	

　MULTIPLE PROBIT REGRESSION

Table 43.3

$$Y = b_0 + b_1X_1 + b_2X_2$$

X_1 \ X_2	0	100	350	750	1500	3500	7500
		−0.0095617	0.03346595	0.07171275	0.143415	0.3346595	0.7171275
500	1 3.90 4.50	2 3.90 4.49	3 3.90 4.47	4 3.90 4.43	5 3.90 4.36	6 3.90 4.17	7 3.90 3.79
1500	8 4.23 4.66	9 4.23 4.65	10 4.23 4.63	11 4.23 4.59	12 4.23 4.52	13 4.23 4.33	14 4.23 3.95
2500	15 4.57 4.82	16 4.57 4.81	17 4.57 4.79	18 4.57 4.75	19 4.57 4.68	20 4.57 4.49	21 4.57 4.11
3500	22 4.90 4.98	23 4.90 4.97	24 4.90 4.95	25 4.90 4.91	26 4.90 4.84	27 4.90 4.65	28 4.90 4.27

Table 43.3 (continued)

	29	30	31	32	33	34	35
4500	29 5.23 5.14	30 5.23 5.13	31 5.23 5.11	32 5.23 5.07	33 5.23 5.00	34 5.23 4.81	35 5.23 4.43
5500	36 5.57 5.30	37 5.57 5.29	38 5.57 5.27	39 5.57 5.23	40 5.57 5.16	41 5.57 4.97	42 5.57 4.59
6500	43 5.90 5.46	44 5.90 5.45	45 5.90 5.43	46 5.90 5.39	47 5.90 5.32	48 5.90 5.13	49 5.90 4.75
7500	50 6.23 5.62	51 6.23 5.61	52 6.23 5.59	53 6.23 5.55	54 6.23 5.48	55 6.23 5.29	56 6.23 4.91
8500	57 6.57 5.78	58 6.57 5.77	59 6.57 5.75	60 6.57 5.71	61 6.57 5.64	62 6.57 5.45	63 6.57 5.07
9500	64 6.90 5.94	65 6.90 5.93	66 6.90 5.91	67 6.90 5.87	68 6.90 5.80	69 6.90 5.61	70 6.90 5.23

In each cell the upper number is the value of Y for the initially assumed values of b_0, b_1, and b_2 (iteration 1, Table 43.2), and the lower number is the value of Y for the final estimates of b_0, b_1, and b_2 (last row, Table 43.2).

Table 43.4

$$\sum_{j=1}^{s} n_j w'_j$$
$$\sum_{j=1}^{s} X_{1j} n_j w'_j \quad \sum_{j=1}^{s} X^2_{1j} n_j w'_j$$
$$\sum_{j=1}^{s} X_{2j} n_j w'_j \quad \sum_{j=1}^{s} X_{2j} X_{1j} n_j w'_j \quad \sum_{j=1}^{s} X^2_{2j} n_j w'_j$$

$$\sum_{j=1}^{s} n_j \Delta_j$$
$$\sum_{j=1}^{s} X_{1j} n_j \Delta_j$$
$$\sum_{j=1}^{s} X_{2j} n_j \Delta_j$$

Iteration 1:

b_0	b_1	b_2	=	
506.26226			=	− 36.18095
18,297.96880	850,885.5965			−5273.56185
7358.683175	307,558.8742	316,137.4833		−3261.31942

Iteration 2:

b_0	b_1	b_2	=	
531.68769			=	− 8.64421
19,078.17335	903,006.3782			155.60315
7409.98837	316,237.7764	310,961.1571		−463.98057

Iteration 3:

b_0	b_1	b_2	
525.44381			13.23685
18,917.35435	895,898.72925		435.18985
7206.56012	306,093.18985	298,937.514995	896.75023

Iteration 4:

b_0	b_1	b_2	=	
529.88552			=	− 4.69292
19,044.34130	900,917.4600			−366.59100
7415.665625	325,587.2889	312,111.16541		−277.34406

Iteration 5:

b_0	b_1	b_2	
533.15147			2.29643
19,335.50135	928,779.8088		208.89305
7431.27326	320,036.8671	310,559.7028	13.16229

Table 43.5

Estimates of variances and covariances of coefficients. (Negative of inverse of matrix of second derivatives of logarithm of likelihood function, evaluated at point of maximum likelihood)

+0.007832610900		
−0.0001527020365	+0.00000464654363	
−0.00003006182432	−0.000001134386407	+0.00000510833533

these values, we compute $n_1 w'_1 = r_1 w'_{max} + (n_1 - r_1)w'_{min} = 19.52680$ and $n_1 \Delta_1 = r_1 w'_{max} - (n_1 - r_1)w'_{min} = 1.20335$.

The matrix of coefficients in the last iteration (the first three columns of iteration 5, Table 43.4 is the negative of the matrix of second derivatives of the logarithm of the likelihood function at its maximum. The inverse of this matrix gives the estimates of the variances and covariances of the b's shown in Table 43.5. The estimated coefficient of income X_1, b_1, is 7.4 times its estimated standard error, and the estimated coefficient of liquid asset holdings X_2, b_2, is 4.2 times its estimated standard error.

The hypothesis that the probability of being a buyer of durable goods is independent of both income and liquid asset holdings can be tested by the method outlined above. The total number of spending units in the sample is 874, and of these 388 were buyers while 486 were non-buyers. On the hypothesis that $\delta_1 = \delta_2 = 0$, the maximum likelihood estimate of the probability of buying is 388/874 or 0.444. The corresponding value of the logarithm of the likelihood function (17) is −260.70858. In comparison, the logarithm of the likelihood function, (5), has at its unrestricted maximum, the value −243.622. Thus the statistic λ is 819.3×10^{-20}, and $-2 \log_e \lambda$ is 76.68661. By the chi-square distribution with 2 degrees of freedom, this is significant at the 0.95 level, and the hypothesis must be rejected.

The high value of b_2 relative to its estimated standard error indicates that the hypothesis that $\delta_2 = 0$ can be rejected. This hypothesis can also be tested by the likelihood-ratio method. Table 43.6 reports the results of a series of iterations to obtain maximum likelihood estimates of b_0 and b_1, on the assumption that $b_2 = 0$. Table 43.7 shows the values of Y for the first and last of these iterations. The third column of Table 43.7 shows the observed values of n_j, r_j/n_j, and $(n_j - r_j)/n_j$ for each of the ten levels of income. The fourth column shows, for each level of income, the

Table 43.6

Iteration	δ_0	$\Delta\delta_0$	δ_1	$\Delta\delta_1$
1a	3.73333	0.68260	0.033333	-0.020918
2a	4.41593	-0.05506	0.012415	$+0.001537$
3a	4.36087	0.00137	0.013952	-0.000066
4a	4.36224	-0.00159	0.013886	$+0.000047$
5a	4.36065	-0.00036	0.013933	-0.000005
6a	4.36029	-0.00089	0.013928	0.000015
7a	4.35940	-0.00036	0.013943	-0.000005
8a	4.35904	-0.00089	0.013938	0.000015
Final	4.35815		0.013953	

"predicted" probability of buying P_j and of not buying, Q_j. P_j is the value of the cumulative unit-normal distribution function corresponding to the final iteration Y_j shown in the second column. Q_j is $1 - P_j$. From these values, the logarithm of the likelihood function, (5), can be evaluated at its maximum for $\delta_2 = 0$. Comparing this with the unrestrained maximum gives a likelihood ratio λ of $253.4 \times 10^{-10} \cdot -2 \log \lambda$ is equal to 34.99, which is significant at 0.95 level according to the table of chi-square for 1 degree of freedom.

The example has been presented for illustration of a method rather than for substantive results. Still more variables would be needed for a better explanation of durable goods purchasing behavior. Moreover, it is wasteful of information to disregard amounts spent by those who purchased. Some combination of probit analysis and regression is indicated, to handle a variable with a large probability of having zero value and the remaining probability spread over a positive interval.

Table 43.7

Income X_1	$Y = b_0 + b_1 X_1$ Iteration 1 Final Iteration	n_j r_j/n_j $(n_j - r_j)/n_j$	P_j Q_j
500	1 3.90 4.43	1 89 0.1461 0.8539	0.2843 0.7157
1500	2 4.23 4.57	2 108 0.2778 0.7222	0.3336 0.6664
2500	3 4.57 4.71	3 178 0.3708 0.6292	0.3859 0.6141
3500	4 4.90 4.85	4 190 0.5579 0.4421	0.4404 0.5596
4500	5 5.23 4.99	5 148 0.5811 0.4189	0.4960 0.5040
5500	6 5.57 5.13	6 66 0.5455 0.4545	0.5517 0.4483
6500	7 5.90 5.27	7 36 0.5278 0.4722	0.6064 0.3936
7500	8 6.23 5.40	8 19 0.5789 0.4211	0.6554 0.3446
8500	9 6.57 5.54	9 21 0.6667 0.3333	0.7054 0.2946
9500	10 6.90 5.68	10 19 0.3684 0.6316	0.7517 0.2483

References

Aitchison, J. and J.A.C. Brown, "An Estimation Problem in Quantitative Assay," *Biometrika*, 41 (1954), 338-43.

Aitchison, J. and J.A.C. Brown, "A Synthesis of Engel Curve Theory," *Review of Economic Studies*, 22 (1955), 35-46.

Board of Governors of the Federal Reserve System, "Methods of the Survey of Consumer Finances," *Federal Reserve Bulletin* (July 1950).

Board of Governors of the Federal Reserve System, *1953 Survey of Consumer Finances*, reprinted with supplementary tables from *Federal Reserve Bulletin* (March, June, July, August, and September 1953).

Board of Governors of the Federal Reserve System, *1952 Survey of Consumer Finances*, reprinted with supplementary tables from *Federal Reserve Bulletin* (April, July, August, and September 1952).

Cornfield, J. and N. Mantel, "Some New Aspects of the Application of Maximum Likelihood to the Calculation of the Dosage Response Curve," *Journal of the American Statistical Association*, 45 (1950), 181-210.

Farrell, M.J., "The Demand for Motor Cars in the United States," *Journal of the Royal Statistical Society*, Series A, 117, Part 2 (1954), 171-93.

Finney, D.J., *Probit Analysis*, 2nd ed. (Cambridge: University Press, 1952).

Garwood, F., "The Application of Maximum Likelihood to Dosage Mortality Curves," *Biometrika*, 32 (1941), 46-58.

Klein, L.R. (Ed.), *Contributions of Survey Methods to Economics* (New York: Columbia University Press, 1954).

Mood, A.M., *Introduction to the Theory of Statistics* (New York: McGraw-Hill, 1950).

Notes

[1] A different economic application of probit analysis, to a case where the dependent variable is multi-valued and naturally scaled, has been made by Aitchison and Brown (1954, 1955).

[2] This convention is usual in probit analysis, and the tables are set up accordingly.

[3] The exposition of the maximum likelihood solution that follows is a mathematically simple extension of the Garwood solution (1941 and summary in Cornfield and Mantel 1950) to $m + 1$ dimensions.

[4] Mood (1950), p. 259.

[5] A brief general description of the concepts and methods of the annual *Surveys of Consumer Finances* is given in Board of Governors (1950). For a more complete treatment, see also Klein (1954). Reports of the 1952 and 1953 *Surveys* are given in Board of Governors (1952, 1953). I am grateful to the Survey Research Center and to the Board of Governors of the Federal Reserve System for the unpublished data used below. The paper, as well as the illustration, owes its inspiration to a semester I was enabled to spend at the Survey Research Center in 1953-54 by the hospitality of the Center and its program of post-doctoral fellowships financed by the Carnegie Foundation.

CHAPTER 44

ESTIMATION OF RELATIONSHIPS FOR LIMITED DEPENDENT VARIABLES

"What do you mean, *less* than nothing?" replied Wilbur. "I don't think there is any such thing as *less* than nothing. Nothing is absolutely the limit of nothingness. It's the lowest you can go. It's the end of the line. How can something be less then nothing? If there were something that was less than nothing then nothing would not be nothing, it would be something – even though it's just a very little bit of something. But if nothing is *nothing*, then nothing has nothing that is less than *it* is."

E.B. White, *Charlotte's Web*
(New York, Harper, 1952), p. 28.

1. Introduction

In economic surveys of households, many variables have the following characteristics: The variable has a lower, or upper, limit and takes on the

Reprinted from *Econometrica*, 26 (January 1958), 24-36. I am grateful to colleagues at the Cowles Foundation for Research in Economics at Yale University, in particular Tjalling Koopmans and Richard Rosett, for helpful advice and comments, and to Donald Hester for computational assistance. I am glad to acknowledge that the work represented in the paper was begun during tenure of a Social Science Research Council Faculty Fellowship and finished in the course of a research program supported by the Ford Foundation. I wish to thank also the Survey Research Center of the University of Michigan and the Board of Governors of the Federal Reserve System for the data from the *Surveys of Consumer Finances* used in the illustration. My interest in methods of analysis of survey data derives in large part from a semester I was enabled to spend at the Survey Research Center in 1953-54 by the hospitality of the Center under a program financed by the Carnegie Foundation.

It may be of interest that Mr. Rosett has programmed the iterative estimation procedure of this paper for the IBM Type 650 Data-processing Machine and has applied the technique to a problem involving 14 independent variables.

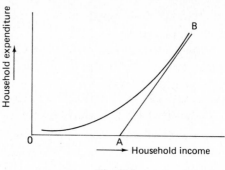

Fig. 44.1.

limiting value for a substantial number of respondents. For the remaining respondents, the variable takes on a wide range of values above, or below, the limit.

The phenomenon is quite familiar to students of Engel curve relationships showing how household expenditures on various categories of goods vary with household income. For many categories – "luxuries" – zero expenditures are the rule at low income levels. A single straight line cannot, therefore, represent the Engel curve for both low and high incomes. If individual households were identical, except for income level, the Engel curve would be a broken line like OAB in Figure 44.1. But if the critical income level OA were not the same for all households, the average Engel curve for groups of households would look like the curve OB. A similar kind of effect occurs under rationing of a consumers' good. The ration is an upper limit; many consumers choose to take their full ration, but some prefer to buy less.[1]

As a specific example, many – indeed, most – households would report zero expenditures on automobiles or major household durable goods during any given year. Among those households who made any such expenditure, there would be wide variability in amount.[2]

In other cases, the lower limit is not necessarily zero, nor is it the same for all households. Consider the net change in a household's holding of liquid assets during a year. This variable can be either positive or negative. But it cannot be smaller than the negative of the household's holdings of liquid assets at the beginning of the year; one cannot liquidate more assets than one owns.

Account should be taken of the concentration of observations at the limiting value when estimating statistically the relationship of a limited variable to other variables and in testing hypotheses about the relationship. An explanatory variable in such a relationship may be expected to influence both the probability of limit responses and the size of non-limit responses. If only the probability of limit and non-limit responses, without regard for the value of non-limit responses were to be explained, *probit analysis* provides a suitable statistical model. (See Cornfield and Mantel 1950.) But it is inefficient to throw away information on the value of the dependent variable when it is available. If only the value of the variable were to be explained, if there were no concentration of observations at a limit, *multiple regression* would be an appropriate statistical technique. But when there is such concentration, the assumptions of the multiple regression model are not realized. According to that model, it should be possible to have values of the explanatory variables for which the expected value of the dependent variable is its limiting value; and from this expected value, as from other expected values, it should be possible to have negative as well as positive deviations.

A hybrid of probit analysis and multiple regression seems to be called for, and it is the purpose of this paper to present such a model.

2. The Model

Let W be a limited dependent variable, with a lower limit of L. The limit may not be the same for all households in the population. Let Y be a linear combination of the independent variables $(X_1, X_2, \ldots, X_m)$, to which W is by hypothesis related.

$$Y = \beta_0 + \beta_1 X_1 + \beta_2 X_2 + \cdots \beta_m X_m. \qquad (1)$$

Households differ from each other in their behavior regarding W for which differences in the independent variables X and the lower limit L do not fully account. Those other differences are taken to be random and to be reflected in ε, a random variable with mean zero and standard deviation σ, distributed normally over the population of households. Household behavior is then assumed to be as follows:

$$W = L \qquad (Y - \varepsilon < L),$$

$$W = Y - \varepsilon. \quad (Y - \varepsilon \leqq L). \tag{2}$$

Let $P(x)$ represent the value of the cumulative unit-normal distribution function at x; let $Q(x) = 1 - P(x)$; let $Z(x)$ be the value of the unit-normal probability density function at x. The distribution of $W - L$ may be derived from the distribution of ε as follows:

For given values of the linear combination Y and the limit L,

$$\Pr(W = L | Y, L) = \Pr(\varepsilon > Y - L) = Q\{(Y - L)/\sigma\}. \tag{3}$$

$$\Pr(W > x \geqq L | Y) = \Pr(Y - \varepsilon > x) = \Pr(\varepsilon < Y - x)$$

$$= P\{(Y - x)/\sigma\}. \tag{4}$$

Consequently, the cumulative distribution function for W, for given Y and L, is:

$$F(x; Y, L) = 0 \quad (x < L),$$

$$F(L; Y, L) = Q\{(Y - L)/\sigma\}, \tag{5}$$

$$F(x; Y, L) = Q\{(Y - x)/\sigma\} \quad (x > L).$$

The corresponding probability density function is:

$$f(x; Y, L) = \frac{1}{\sigma} Z\{(Y - x)/\sigma\} \quad (x > L). \tag{6}$$

The expected value of W for given values of Y and L is:

$$E(W; Y, L) = LQ\{(Y - L)/\sigma\} + \int_{L}^{\infty} \frac{x}{\sigma} Z\{(Y - x)/\sigma\} \, dx$$

$$= LQ\{(Y - L)/\sigma\} + Y \int_{-\infty}^{(Y-L)/\sigma} Z(x) \, dx + \sigma \int_{-\infty}^{(Y-L)/\sigma}$$

$$- xZ(x) \, dx.$$

Since $- xZ(x) = Z'(x) = dZ(x)/dx$, we have:

$$E(W; Y, L) = LQ\{(Y - L)/\sigma\} + YP\{(Y - L)/\sigma\}$$

$$+ \sigma Z\{(Y - L)/\sigma\}. \tag{7}$$

A sample includes q observations where W is at the limit L. Each observation consists of a limit L'_i, to which the dependent variable W'_i is equal, and a set of values of the independent variables $(X'_{1i}, X'_{2i}, \ldots, X'_{mi})$, where i is a subscript to denote the observation and runs from 1 to q. A sample also includes r observations for which W is above the limit L;[3] each one may be described as $(W_j, L_j, X_{1j}, X_{2j}, \ldots, X_{mj})$, where j runs from 1 to r.

Let $(a_0, a_1, a_2, \ldots, a_m, a)$ be estimates of $(\beta_0/\sigma, \beta_1/\sigma, \beta_2/\sigma, \ldots, \beta_m/\sigma, 1/\sigma)$. Let $I'_i = Y'_i a = a_0 + a_1 X'_{1i} + a_2 X'_{2i} + \cdots a_m X'_{mi}$ and let $I_j = Y_j a = a_0 + a_1 X_{1j} + a_2 X_{2j} + \cdots a_m X_{mj}$.

$$\phi(a_0, a_1, \ldots, a_m, a) = \prod_{i=1}^{q} F(L'_i; Y'_i, L'_i) \cdot \prod_{j=1}^{r} f(W_j; Y_j, L_j)$$

$$= \prod_{i=1}^{q} Q\left(\frac{Y'_i - L'_i}{1/a}\right) \cdot \prod_{j=1}^{r} aZ\left(\frac{Y_j - W_j}{1/a}\right)$$

$$= \prod_{i=1}^{q} Q(I'_i - aW'_i) \cdot \prod_{j=1}^{r} aZ(I_j - aW_j). \quad (8)$$

The natural logarithm of ϕ,

$$\ln \phi = \phi^*(a_0, a_1, \ldots, a_m, a)$$

$$\sum_{i=1}^{q} \ln Q(I'_i - aW'_i) + r \ln a - \frac{r}{2} \ln 2\pi$$

$$- \frac{1}{2} \sum_{j=1}^{r} (I_j - aW_j)^2. \quad (9)$$

Let X_0 and X'_0 be identically 1 for all i and j. Then setting the derivatives of ϕ^* equal to zero gives the following system of $m + 2$ equations.

$$\phi^*_k = \frac{\partial \phi^*}{\partial a_k} = \sum_{i=1}^{q} \frac{-Z(I'_i - aW'_i)X'_{ki}}{Q(I'_i - aW'_i)} - \sum_{j=1}^{r} (I_j - aW_j)X_{kj} = 0$$

$$(k = 0, 1, 2, \ldots, m),$$

$$\phi^*_{m+1} = \frac{\partial \phi^*}{\partial a} = \sum_{i=1}^{q} \frac{Z(I'_i - aW'_i)W'_i}{Q(I'_i - aW'_i)} + \frac{r}{a} + \sum_{j=1}^{r} (I_j - aW_j)W_j = 0. \quad (10)$$

These equations are non-linear. The quantity $-Z(x)/Q(x)$ is tabulated as $\Delta_{\min}$ in Cornfield and Mantel (1950, pp. 185–88), where the argument for the table is $x + 5$.

The matrix of second derivatives, obtained by differentiating (10) is given by (11). Here $w'_{\min}(x)$ is the derivative of $-\Delta_{\min}(x)$, and may, like $\Delta_{\min}$, be found by entering the tables of Cornfield and Mantel (1950, pp. 185–88) with the argument $x + 5$.

$$\phi^*_{kt} = \frac{\partial^2 \phi^*}{\partial a_k \, \partial a_t} = -\sum_{i=1}^{q} X'_{ki} X'_{ti} w'_{\min}(I'_i - aW'_i) - \sum_{j=1}^{r} X_{kj} X_{tj}$$

$$(k, t, = 0, 1, \ldots, m),$$

$$\phi^*_{k,m+1} = \frac{\partial^2 \phi^*}{\partial a_k \, \partial a} = \sum_{i=1}^{q} W'_i X'_{ki} w'_{\min}(I'_i - aW'_i) + \sum_{j=1}^{r} X_{kj} W_j$$

$$(k = 0, 1, \ldots, m),$$

$$\phi^*_{m+1,m+1} = \frac{\partial^2 \phi^*}{\partial a^2} = -\sum_{i=1}^{q} W'^2_i w'_{\min}(I'_i - aW'_i) - \frac{r}{a^2}$$

$$-\sum_{j=1}^{r} W_j^2. \tag{11}$$

Newton's method (see Crockett and Chernoff 1955) for iterative solution of (10), also known as the "method of scoring" (see Rao 1952), may be applied as follows: Let

$$(a_0^{(0)}, a_1^{(0)}, \ldots, a_m^{(0)}, \ldots, a_{m+1}^{(0)})$$

be a trial solution, where, for notational convenience, a_{m+1} represents what has previously been written as simply a. (The choice of an initial trial solution will be discussed below.) New estimates

$$(a_0^{(0)} + \Delta a_0, a_1^{(0)} + \Delta a_1, \ldots, a_m^{(0)} + \Delta a_m, a_{m+1}^{(0)} + \Delta a_{m+1})$$

can be found by solving the set of $m + 1$ linear equations (12) for the Δa, where all the ϕ^*_k are assumed to be linear between the trial solution and the real solution.

$$\phi^*_k(a_0^{(0)} + \Delta a_0, \ldots, a_m^{(0)} + \Delta a_m, a_{m+1}^{(0)} + \Delta a_{m+1})$$

$$= \phi^*_k(a_0^{(0)}, a_1^{(0)}, \ldots, a_m^{(0)}, a_{m+1}^{(0)}) + \sum_{t=0}^{m+1} \Delta a_t \phi^*_{kt}(a_0^{(0)}, a_1^{(0)}, \ldots,$$

$$\ldots, a_m^{(0)}, a_{m+1}^{(0)}) = 0 \quad (k = 0, 1, 2, \ldots, m + 1).$$

$$\sum_{t=0}^{m+1} \Delta a_t \phi_{kt}^*(a_0^{(0)}, a_1^{(0)}, \ldots, a_m^{(0)}, a_{m+1}^{(0)})$$

$$= -\phi_k^*(a_0^{(0)}, a_1^{(0)}, \ldots, a_m^{(0)}, a_{m+1}^{(0)}). \tag{12}$$

The process may be repeated with the new estimates as provisional estimates until the Δa are negligible.

If the final estimates a_k are used to evaluate the matrix of second derivatives (11) at the point of maximum likelihood, the negative inverse of that matrix gives large-sample estimates of the variances and co-variances of the estimates a_k around the corresponding population parameters.

3. Tests of Hypotheses

Hypotheses about the relationship of W to one or more of the independent variables X may be tested by the likelihood-ratio method. Consider for example, the hypothesis that $\beta_1 = \beta_2 = \cdots = \beta_m = 0$. This is the hypothesis that neither the probability nor the size of non-zero responses depends on the X's. According to the hypothesis, there remain only two parameters, β_0 and σ, to be estimated so as to maximize (9), which now becomes:

$$\phi^*(a_0, 0, 0, \ldots, 0, a) = \sum_{i=1}^{q} \ln Q(a_0 - aW_i') - \frac{r}{2} \ln 2\pi$$

$$+ r \ln a - \frac{1}{2} \sum_{j=1}^{r} (a_0 - aW_j)^2. \tag{13}$$

The maximizing values of a_0 and a may be found by solving equations (10) similarly simplified by putting all other α_k equal to zero. If (13) is evaluated with these solutions, then the logarithm of the likelihood ratio λ is the difference between (13) and the value of (9) when it is maximized without the constraint of the hypothesis. The statistic $-2 \ln \lambda$ is for large samples approximately distributed by chi-square with m degrees of freedom. In similar fashion other hypotheses about subsets of the β's may be tested.

4. Initial Trial Estimates

The speed of convergence of iteration by Newton's method depends, of course, on the choice of the initial trial estimates. The following procedure for finding initial estimates relies on a linear approximation of the function $-Z(x)/Q(x)$ or, in other words, on a quadratic approximation of $\ln Q(x)$. This approximation converts the first $m + 1$ equations of (10) into linear equations in the a_k for given a. These equations may be solved to give the a_k as linear functions of a. When these solutions are substituted in the $m + 2$nd equation, it becomes a quadratic equation in a.

The function $\Delta_{\min}(x) = -Z(x)/Q(x)$ is graphed in Figure 44.2. Clearly it is not possible to approximate it linearly at all closely throughout its range. The important thing is to have a good approximation in the range where the sample observations are concentrated. There is no point in approximating well at $x = 4$ or $x = 5$ if the sample did not include constellations of the independent variables that made the probability

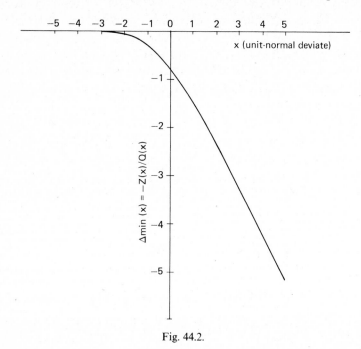

Fig. 44.2.

of limit observations virtually nil. An easily computed estimate of the middle of the relevant range is x_0, the unit-normal deviate such that $Q(x_0) = q/(q + r)$, the proportion of cases in the sample for which the variable W takes on its limit-value. The tangent at x_0 is one possible approximation, but not the best one, since it uniformly over-estimates $\Delta_{\min}$ except at x_0 itself.

Suppose that a linear approximation is fitted graphically:

$$\Delta_{\min}(x) = A + Bx. \tag{14}$$

Substituting (14) in the first $m + 1$ equations of (10) gives

$$\sum_{i=1}^{q} (AX'_{ki} + Ba_0 X'_{0i}X'_{ki} + Ba_1 X'_{1i}X'_{ki} + \cdots Ba_m X'_{mi}X'_{ki}$$

$$- BaW'_i X'_{ki}) - \sum_{j=1}^{r} (a_0 X_{0j}X_{kj} + a_1 X_{1j}X_{kj} + a_m X_{mj}X_{kj}$$

$$- aW_j X_{kj}) = 0,$$

$$a_0 \left[\sum_{j=1}^{r} X_{0j}X_{kj} - B \sum_{i=1}^{q} X'_{0i}X'_{ki} \right] + a_1 \left[\sum_{j=1}^{r} X_{1j}X_{kj} - B \sum_{i=1}^{q} X'_{1i}X'_{ki} \right]$$

$$+ \cdots + a_m \left[\sum_{j=1}^{r} X_{mj}X_{kj} - B \sum_{i=1}^{r} X'_{mi}X'_{ki} \right]$$

$$= a \left[\sum_{j=1}^{r} W_j X_{kj} - B \sum_{j=1}^{q} W'_i X'_{ki} \right] + A \sum_{i=1}^{q} X'_{ki}$$

$$(k = 0, 1, 2, \ldots, m). \tag{15}$$

Solving (15) gives numbers g_k and h_k such that:

$$a_k = g_k + h_k a \qquad (k = 0, 1, 2, \ldots, m). \tag{16}$$

The final equation of (10) is, after using the approximation of (14):

$$\frac{r}{a} + a_0 \left[\sum_{j=1}^{r} X_{0j}W - B \sum_{i=1}^{q} X'_{0i}W'_i \right]$$

$$+ \cdots + a_m \left[\sum_{j=1}^{r} X_{mj}W_j - B \sum_{j=1}^{q} X'_{mi}W'_i \right]$$

$$- a \left[\sum_{j=1}^{r} W_j^2 - B \sum_{i=1}^{q} W'^2_i \right] - A \sum_{i=1}^{q} W'_i = 0. \tag{17}$$

When (16) is substituted in (17), it becomes a quadratic equation in a. The solution of (17) may then be used in (16) to obtain initial trial estimates of all the coefficients.

5. An Example

For purposes of illustration, an example has been worked out using data from the reinterview portion of the 1952 and 1953 *Surveys of Consumer Finances* conducted by the Survey Research Center of the University of Michigan for the Board of Governors of the Federal Reserve System.[4]

The data refer to 735 primary non-farm spending units [5] who were interviewed twice, once in early 1952 and once in early 1953. The frequencies, averages, and other statistics for the reinterview sample should not be taken as representative of the population of the U.S.A. The *Surveys of Consumer Finances* do collect data on distributions of income, liquid assets, and durable goods purchases that are representative of that population; tables on these distributions may be found in *Survey* (1953). But the reinterview sample, on which the calculations of this paper are based, fails to be representative insofar as it omits spending units who moved between the two surveys. Moreover, these calculations are based on simple counts of sampled spending units, without allowance for the fact that the sampling design gave some spending units greater probabilities of being included in the sample than others. The purpose of this example is not to estimate population frequency distributions, but only to examine the relationship of durable goods expenditure to age and liquid asset holdings within this sample. It is not necessary to consider here how the relationship exhibited in this sample differs from the one that would be exhibited in a complete enumeration. But it may well be that the sample gives unbiased estimates of the parameters of the relationship, even though it gives biased estimates of the separate frequency distribution of the variables.

The variables are as follows:

W, the ratio of 1951–52 total durable goods expenditure to 1951–52 total disposable income. Durable goods expenditure is the two-year sum of outlays, net of trade-ins or sales, for cars and major household appliances and furniture. Two-year disposable income is the sum of the two annual incomes reported by the spending unit less estimated federal income tax liabilities. Both expenditure and income were reported for 1951 in the interview in early 1952, and for 1952 in the second interview, in early 1953. Since expenditure is necessarily zero or positive, and since zero and negative incomes have been excluded, the ratio is necessarily zero or positive.

X_1, *the age of the head of the spending unit*, as reported in 1953, on the following scale:

$$
\begin{aligned}
&18\text{--}24 \text{ yrs.} \ldots\ldots\ldots\ldots\ldots\ldots\ldots\ldots\ldots\ldots 1 \\
&25\text{--}34 \text{ yrs.} \ldots\ldots\ldots\ldots\ldots\ldots\ldots\ldots\ldots\ldots 2 \\
&35\text{--}44 \text{ yrs.} \ldots\ldots\ldots\ldots\ldots\ldots\ldots\ldots\ldots\ldots 3 \\
&45\text{--}54 \text{ yrs.} \ldots\ldots\ldots\ldots\ldots\ldots\ldots\ldots\ldots\ldots 4 \\
&55\text{--}64 \text{ yrs.} \ldots\ldots\ldots\ldots\ldots\ldots\ldots\ldots\ldots\ldots 5 \\
&65 \text{ or more yrs.} \ldots\ldots\ldots\ldots\ldots\ldots\ldots\ldots\ldots 6
\end{aligned}
$$

X_2, *the ratio of liquid asset holdings at the beginning of 1951 to 1951–52 total disposable income.* Liquid asset holdings include bank deposits, savings and loan association shares, postal savings, and government saving bonds.

In this example, the lower limit L is zero for all cases. Table 44.1 shows the basic data.

Table 44.2 presents the estimates of the parameters obtained by the initial approximation and reports the successive iterations leading to the maximum likelihood estimates. Estimates are shown also in Table 44.3, on the assumption that there is no relation between W and liquid asset holdings X_2.

Table 44.1
Sums of squares and cross products

	183 limit observations					552 non-limit observations			
	$X_0' = 1$	X_1'	X_2'	W'		$X_0 = 1$	X_1	X_2	W
$X_0' \equiv 1$	183				$X_0 \equiv 1$	552			
X_1'	824	4056			X_1	1976	8060		
X_2'	102.15	552.03	402.3333		X_2	168.06	751.54	255.6740	
W'	0	0	0	0	W	61.449	207.598	20.559	13.113087

Table 44.2
Iterative estimation of parameters

	a_0	a_1	a_2	a
Initial trial values	1.326	−0.2200	0.0330	7.984
First derivatives	−4.398	−21.759	−1.812	0.898
Second derivatives a_0	−680.557			
a_1	−2542.416	−10,805.486		
a_2	−238.41	−1128.653	−535.223	
a	61.449	207.598	20.559	−21.772
Indicated changes	0.0152	−0.00507	0.00199	0.0376
Second trial values	1.3407	−0.2251	0.0350	8.022
First derivatives	−0.047	0.292	0.064	0.002
Second derivatives a_0	−680.260			
a_1	−2540.666	−10,795.522		
a_2	−238.26	−1,127.900	−535.893	
a	61.449	207.598	20.559	−21.688
Indicated changes	−0.0015	0.00037	0.00001	−0.00064
Final estimates	1.3392	−0.2247	0.0350	8.022
Standard errors	(0.118)	(0.0295)	(0.0495)	(0.252)

Table 44.3
Iterative estimation of parameters assuming that $\beta_2 = 0$

	a_0	a_1	a
Initial trial values	1.337	−0.219	8.040
First derivatives	−2.841	−16.124	−0.001
Second derivatives a_0	−680.419		
a_1	−2541.428	10,799.12	
a	61.449	207.598	−21.652
Indicated changes	0.010	−0.004	−0.010
Second trial values	1.347	−0.223	8.030
First derivatives	−0.456	−2.017	+0.116
Second derivatives a_0	−680.179		
a_1	−2539.988	−10,790.472	
a	61.449	207.598	−21.674
Indicated changes	0.001	0.0003	−0.005
Final estimates	1.347	−0.223	8.030
Standard errors	(0.117)	(0.028)	(0.252)

Table 44.4
Estimated variances and covariances of parameter estimates

	a_0	a_1	a_2	a
a_0	+0.0139			
a_1	−0.00318	+0.000867		
a_2	+0.000880	−0.000454	+0.00245	
a	+0.00987	−0.00115	+0.000470	+0.0635

On assumption that $\beta_2 = 0$

	a_0	a_1	a	
a_0	+0.0136			
a_1	−0.00302	+0.000784		
a	+0.00970	−0.00106	+0.0635	

In the approximation used to obtain initial trial values, the function $-Z(x)/Q(x)$ was approximated by the tangent at the point $x_0 = 0.67$, so that $Q(x_0) = 0.25$, the proportion of non-zero cases in the sample. Thus the constants A and B in (15) and (17) were equal to -0.76003 and -0.75771 respectively.

Estimates of the variances and covariances of the parameter estimates can be obtained from the negative of the inverse of the final matrix of second derivatives. These are shown in Table 44.4. The corresponding standard errors of the coefficients are given in the final rows of Tables 44.2 and 44.3.

The size of the standard error of a_2 indicates that the hypothesis that $\beta_2 = 0$, that there is no net relationship between expenditure and liquid asset holding, cannot be rejected. This hypothesis can also be tested, with the same conclusion, by the likelihood-ratio method. At the point of maximum likelihood, unrestricted by this hypothesis, ϕ^* in (9) has the value $722.5 - (552/2) \ln 2\pi$. The final estimates in Table 44.3 correspond to the point of maximum likelihood restricted by the hypothesis that $\beta_2 = 0$. At this point ϕ^* has the value $721.8 - (552/2) \ln 2\pi$. The statistic $-2 \ln \lambda$ is thus equal to 1.4, which is not a significant value of chi-square with one degree of freedom.

A test of the hypothesis that neither age nor liquid asset holding has any effect on expenditure on durable goods may also be made by the likelihood-ratio method. Assume, in accordance with the hypothesis, that $\beta_1 = \beta_2 = 0$. The values of a_0 and a that maximize (13) are found to be 0.4839 and 7.720. For these values, $\phi^* + 552/2 \ln 2\pi$ is equal to 692.7. Hence $-2 \ln \lambda$ is equal to 59.6, a significant chi-square for two degrees of freedom. The hypothesis must be rejected. Thus this test, as well as the size of the estimated standard error of a_1, indicates a significant relationship of durable goods expenditure to age.

The relationship of W to X_1 and X_2, as estimated in Table 44.2, is shown in Figures 44.3 and 44.4, as the broken line ABC. The expected value of W implied by this relationship may be computed from (7) in the manner illustrated in Table 44.5. These points are also shown in Figures

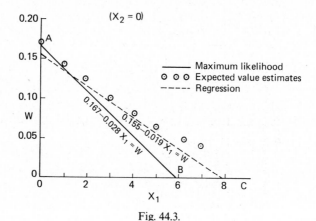

Fig. 44.3.

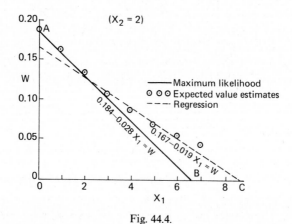

Fig. 44.4.

Table 44.5
Calculation of expected values

X_1	$X_2 = 0$				$X_2 = 2$			
	$I = 1.3392$ $-0.2247X_1$	Calculated probability of buying $P(I)$	$Z(I)$	Calculated expected value $E(W) = (IP + Z)/$ 8.022	$I = 1.4092$ $-0.2247X_1$	Calculated probability of buying $P(I)$	$Z(I)$	Calculated expected value $E(W) = (IP + Z)/$ 8.022
0	1.3392	0.910	0.163	0.172	1.4092	0.921	0.148	0.180
1	1.1145	0.867	0.214	0.147	1.1845	0.882	0.197	0.155
2	0.8898	0.813	0.267	0.123	0.9598	0.832	0.252	0.131
3	0.6651	0.747	0.319	0.102	0.7351	0.768	0.304	0.108
4	0.4404	0.670	0.362	0.082	0.5104	0.695	0.350	0.088
5	0.2157	0.585	0.390	0.064	0.2857	0.612	0.383	0.070
6	-0.0090	0.497	0.399	0.049	0.0610	0.524	0.398	0.054
7	-0.2337	0.408	0.388	0.037	-0.1637	0.435	0.393	0.040
8	-0.4584	0.323	0.359	0.026	-0.3884	0.350	0.370	0.029

Table 44.6
Observed values (all values of X_2)

X_1	Proportion buying	Observed average value of W
1	0.812	0.124
2	0.884	0.118
3	0.862	0.098
4	0.751	0.083
5	0.664	0.145
6	0.516	0.047

44.3 and 44.4. For comparison, the least squares multiple regression of W on X_1 and X_2 has also been plotted. The estimated effect of liquid asset holding X_2 has been illustrated by drawing two graphs relating W to X_1, the first (Figure 44.3) on the assumption that $X_2 = 0$ and the second (Figure 44.4) on the assumption that $X_2 = 2$. Observed proportions buying and average values of W at various levels of X_1, without regard to X_2, are shown in Table 44.6.

The expected value locus, estimated by the method of this paper, is non-linear. It is always above the broken line ABC, asymptotic to AB at the left where the probability of not buying ($W = 0$) approaches zero, and asymptotic to BC at the right where the probability of buying ($W > 0$) approaches zero. Multiple regression approximates this non-linear locus with a linear relationship. As Figures 44.3 and 44.4 show, the approximation is fairly close for the central range of values of the sample. But outside the central range there can be large discrepancies. There are indeed conceivable values of the independent variables for which multiple regression would give negative estimates of the expected value of W. It is true that the absence of negative observations in the sample tends to keep the regression above the axis until extreme values of the independent variables are reached. But this protection is purchased at the cost of making the regression line so flat that expenditure is under-estimated at the opposite end. These discrepancies could be important in predicting expenditure for extreme cases or for aggregates which include extreme cases.

References

Board of Governors of the Federal Reserve System, *1953 Survey of Consumer Finances*, reprinted with supplementary tables from *Federal Reserve Bulletin* (March, June, July, August, and September, 1953).

Cornfield, J. and N. Mantel, "Some New Aspects of the Application of Maximum Likelihood to the Calculation of the Dosage Response Curve," *Journal of the American Statistical Association*, 45 (1950), 181-210.

Crockett, J.B. and H. Chernoff, "Gradient Methods of Maximization," *Pacific Journal of Mathematics*, 5 (1955), 33-50. (Reprinted as Cowles Commission New Series Paper No. 92).

Farrell, M.J., "Some Aggregation Problems in Demand Analysis," *Review of Economic Studies*, 21 (1954), 193-204.

Rao, C.R., *Advanced Statistical Methods in Biometric Research* (New York: John Wiley & Sons, 1952), 165-72.

Tobin, J., "A Survey of the Theory of Rationing," *Econometrica*, 20 (1952), 521-53.

Notes

[1] For a theoretical exposition of the effects on aggregate demand functions of lower or upper limits on individual expenditure in combination with differences in tastes among households, see Farrell (1954) and Tobin (1952), and the literature there cited.

[2] For figures on frequency of purchases and on the distribution of amounts spent among purchasers, see Board of Governors (1953, Part II, Supplementary Tables 1, 5, and 10).

[3] The value of L is assumed to be observable for the whole sample. I have made no investigation of the problems that would be presented by taking it as an unknown to be estimated.

[4] A brief general description of the concepts and methods of the annual *Surveys of Consumer Finances* is given in Board of Governors of the Federal Reserve System, "Methods of the Survey of Consumer Finances," *Federal Reserve Bulletin* (July 1950). For a more complete treatment, see also L.R. Klein (Ed.), *Contributions of Survey Methods to Economics* (New York: Columbia University Press, 1954). Reports of the 1952 and 1953 *Surveys* are given in Board of Governors of the Federal Reserve System, *1952 Survey of Consumer Finances*, reprinted with supplementary tables from *Federal Reserve Bulletin* (April, July, August, and September, 1952), and Board of Governors of the Federal Reserve System, *1953 Survey of Consumer Finances*, reprinted with supplementary tables from *Federal Reserve Bulletin* (March, June, July, August, and September, 1952).

[5] Of the 1036 spending units in the reinterview sample, these 735 have been the subject for calculations for other purposes and are therefore a convenient group to use in this analysis. Excluded are all spending units who had one or more of the following characteristics: (a) farm; (b) secondary, i.e., not the owner or principal tenant of the dwelling; (c) total income for the two years 1951-52 zero or negative; (d) not ascertained as to age of head of spending unit, amount of expenditure on durable goods during 1951-52, or amount of liquid asset holdings in early 1951. In addition, one extreme observation was excluded, where the spending unit has such a low positive two-year income that the ratio of durable goods expenditure and, especially, liquid asset holdings to income were very high.

INDEX